HISTORY OF
NEW ZEALAND
AND ITS INHABITANTS

DOM FELICE VAGGIOLI

Translated by
John Crockett

University of Otago Press

Published by University of Otago Press
PO Box 56/56 Union Street, Dunedin, New Zealand
Fax: 64 3 479 8385; Email: university.press@otago.ac.nz

First published 1896
First English translation 2000
Reprinted 2000, 2001
English translation and 'Introduction' © John Crockett 2000
'Visitors to Nineteenth-Century Aotearoa/New Zealand'
© Tom Brooking 2000

ISBN 1 877133 52 3

The publisher is grateful for the assistance of the
Historical Publications Branch,
Department of Internal Affairs, New Zealand

Printed through Condor Production Ltd, Hong Kong

Contents

Acknowledgements *v*

Introduction *vii*
John Crockett

Visitors to Nineteenth-Century Aotearoa/New Zealand *xix*
Tom Brooking

History of New Zealand and Its Inhabitants *1*
Dom Felice Vaggioli

Notes *313*

Index *331*

Vaggioli found himself in a quandary:

> Should I abandon the idea of writing the *History* after spending so much effort in gathering the material? No. I had promised Cardinal Simeoni, Prefect of Propaganda, to write it. Should I put it off till later? That was no solution. I might die in the meantime.[26]

He pondered his dilemma for a few days before making his decision. He decided to work at his official duties during the day and at night he would work on the *History*. More precisely, in the winter he would work from 7 p.m. until 11.30 p.m., and in summer from 8 until 11.30 p.m. He could work undisturbed as the other monks would be reposing. He wondered, though, whether his health could stand up to such a punishing regime. With pious pragmatism he decided to try out the timetable and trust to Providence.[27] His achievement is even more considerable since he virtually concentrated his writing into the months from November till May, because in the other months he was away from his home monastery in Genoa on official visits and business.

In 1891 his first volume, a natural history of New Zealand, including a study of Maori life and customs, was published with sixty illustrations. Vaggioli put himself under considerable pressure to have the 711-page work written and published within three years:

> I needed all my iron will not to be crushed under the weight of this enormous task which so much affected my sleep and rest.[28]

He worked at a gentler pace on the second volume which, curiously, he considered less important.[29]

There is an intriguing postscript to the publication of the *History*. It could be assumed that there would be no shortage of the work in Italy. But when I visited there in 1996 I came across only a handful of copies in the Benedictine Cassinese Congregation monasteries in northern Italy. Only three other institutions appear to have copies of the *History:* the Vatican Library, the Auckland Catholic diocesan archive and the Auckland Public Library. Vaggioli himself may have sent courtesy copies to Auckland. When I expressed my surprise at this dearth to Dom Callisto Carpenese, Praglia monastery's head archivist, he told me that because of the work's severe criticism of British colonial policy in New Zealand, the British Government, probably early this century, requested the Italian Government to have the *History* suppressed and destroyed.[30] Carpenese alleges that extant copies were collected and deposited in the library of the monastery of San Giovanni Evangelista in Parma. Shortly afterwards, I visited there and spoke to the elderly archivist, Dom Anselmo Bussoni, who confirmed the story, mentioning that as a young monk he had witnessed their destruction.[31] I was unable to find documentary evidence to prove the allegation, but oral confirmation within the Benedictine Order is adamant and unequivocal.

HE TAONGA TENEI? ... AN EVALUATION

Vaggioli's *History* is virtually unknown in New Zealand, probably because it was never translated and copies of the original work are scarce. Few New Zealand historians have referred to it. Simmons (1982) provides the most detailed, albeit superficial, evaluation. He highlights Vaggioli's strong anti-British bias, while acknowledging his scholarship:

> His history of New Zealand, which was the general history of the country and not merely the Catholic history, has a rather anti-British tone which did not endear itself to earlier generations of New Zealanders, and it is inaccurate in places, but it is one of the better histories of New Zealand of that period.[32]

Simmons also suggests that Vaggioli's *History* appeared not to have been translated into English because of its strong pro-Maori stance.[33]

Besides criticisms of factual inaccuracy and anti-British bias, the *History* is criticised by another historian, Riseborough (1983), for being superficial and derivative. She describes the contents of the second volume as 'simply a re-run of the well-known Catholic-Protestant controversy'[34] and comments that the first volume is drawn almost entirely from the works of cited natural scientists and Government statistics.[35] Plainly she views the whole work as having a strongly derivative character. Her overall impression, however, like Simmons, appears to be favourable, and in her opinion the *History* deserves to be better known:

> [Compared to Barsanti] he wrote with more judgement and less bias ... He has a wider knowledge of the country and deeper understanding and compassion for the Maori people, and though he was dependent on English language sources for much of his information, his view and judgement differed from theirs.[36]

It appears Vaggioli's wish to present an independent account of New Zealand history to an Italian audience was as important to him as his Superior's request for information on the Maori, or the Papal directive mentioned earlier. His eagerness to present the truth as he saw it is a frequent theme in his autobiography and correspondence. Writing from Gisborne, he comments:

> I tried to the best of my ability to keep to the truth! English writers, on the other hand, who have written about New Zealand, are more biased towards the Government than the Maori ...[37]

Appeal to the truth was a common charactertistic of earnest nineteenth-century authors and, accordingly, Vaggioli's sense of surety should be regarded with caution. In fact, he often colourfully expresses the prejudices and chauvinism of his era. Vaggioli's unpublished writings, more forcefully and frequently than his *History,* reveal virulent anti-Protestant prejudice and anti-British sentiment. He is seen to be anti-Semitic, bitterly opposed to the Masonic movement and its secularism, and he had no sympathy for the nationalist spirit of the newly founded Italian State. The *History* might thus be adjudged a flawed product of its times and ultimately of minor significance.

In my opinion, however, Vaggioli's *History* transcends his personal prejudices. While the first volume is undoubtedly derivative, the second volume does not deserve the same criticism. It is essentially a bicultural history, describing British colonialism's corrosive penetration into, and undermining effect on, an indigenous culture. Vaggioli offers an original, generally scholarly critique, using resource material intelligently to support his controversial and, for the times, unpopular views. The social history's unique value is to present an independent, non-British account of New Zealand's foundation and development as a British colony, particularly explored as an interplay between the increasingly threatened and disempowered Maori and swelling numbers of land-seeking settlers whose presence was legitimised and supported by Great Britain, then the world's most formidable imperial power.

Vaggioli's sympathy for the Maori was influenced not only by his antipathy towards Britain's perceived exploitative role, but by a philosophical and theological view which saw indigenous peoples as 'noble savages', fellow members of the human race, needing only the benefit of *true* civilisation and the Catholic religion to aid their moral development. Maori were not regarded by Vaggioli as genetically inferior to Europeans, and thus his is not an inherently racist view. His frequent use of the words 'natives' and 'savages' should not be seen as perjorative, but rather as an anachronistic, paternalistic expression of a moral missionary imperative, conveying no inherent sense of racial superiority.

In his autobiography Vaggioli describes positively his first encounter with Maori:

> At Tauranga I saw Maori natives for the first time. They were olive-skinned, tattooed, intelligent, handsome, strong, robust and of average height.[38]

His natural history volume contains a fuller elaboration of his positive, if paternalistic, racial views. Vaggioli argues:

> Savages have an intellect like us. They are our brothers and they only need our assistance to have the same great intellectual awareness and acuteness as us.[39]

In the same volume, he describes Australian Aboriginals with a similar sympathy:

> The Australian (aboriginal) is not a dumb brute, but a rational, intelligent member of the human race.[40]

Vaggioli revisited the plight of Aboriginals with a paper he published in 1899 entitled 'British Australasia'. He exposed the racist theory prevalent in colonial Australia which saw Aboriginals as the 'lowest rung of humanity',[41] genetically inferior to Europeans. Vaggioli described Britain's policy of virtual genocide, citing Aboriginals' decline from an estimated one million in the pre-

Vaggioli (centre, front) in 1911, on the fiftieth anniversary of his profession as a monk.

colonial period to not more than 100,000 by 1897, asserting that the colonists' intention was ultimately to exterminate them.[42]

His prescient observations appear to be supported by events described in Robert Hughes'[43] history of colonial Australia, written nearly a century later, and in the Australian Human Rights Commission's report on the fate of Aboriginal children (1997).

Vaggioli saw Maori as similarly threatened. He was relentlessly critical of British colonial hegemony, Protestant missionaries' self-interest, settlers' greed and Parliamentarians' pursuit of power and wealth; a toxic combination which, in his view, would eventually annihilate the Maori race.

While his sectarianism and chauvinism reflect Vaggioli's nineteenth-century cultural inheritance, his representation and assessment of such events as the signing of the Treaty of Waitangi, the New Zealand Wars and Te Whiti's pacifist movement at Parihaka have a curiously modern ring, anticipating by more than a century the evaluations of Claudia Orange, James Belich and Dick Scott.

I believe that it is mainly because of his perceptive analysis of colonialism as an exploitative process and his non-racist appreciation of indigenous cultures that Vaggioli achieves a level of insight and objectivity unusual for the times, and not represented by contemporaneous British historians writing about New Zealand.

A chilling metaphor elaborated in the final chapter of the social history conveys Vaggioli's understanding of the dangerous effects of British colonialism on the Maori, as well as his grim sense of pessimism regarding their future:

> The unfortunate Maori certainly have to use their wits to save themselves from the grip of the devouring serpent. However, they will never succeed in freeing themselves from its tenacious coils, and will eventually perish forever, overcome by its brutal force.[44]

The Maori have proved to be more durable than Vaggioli imagined, but the legacy of colonialism has clearly remained.

A Comment on the Translation

Vaggioli's prose style is generally direct, vigorous and plain, posing few problems for the translator, apart from the odd archaism or dialectical expression. He occasionally uses the literary convention of addressing the reader. Here I have endeavoured to mirror a sometimes prim, sometimes patronising tone which is more fulsomely expressed when Vaggioli vents his spleen in sallies against Protestantism, British colonialism, settlers' greed, masonic secularism, and irreligion.

Vaggioli's intention was to present a true, objective history of New Zealand. His bias, nonetheless, as I have mentioned elsewhere, is evident. To support his purpose, he rigorously and painstakingly cites and includes quotations from the sources he has consulted. Initially I translated Vaggioli's *History* 'in toto', translating the complete text from Italian to English. I later reviewed this decision when I discovered that the vast majority of the English sources he referred to were available in the Auckland Public Library's New Zealand collection. I decided to restore the original English texts to my translation to obtain the greatest degree of authenticity.

My overall intention has been to translate Vaggioli's *History* as accurately and sympathetically as possible. I have, therefore, replicated his occasional misspellings of Maori and English words, especially regarding place and personal names, craving, like Vaggioli, the gentle reader's understanding and indulgence. However, the index includes modern spellings as well as the spellings used in the text.

I have also attempted in my translation to portray Vaggioli's sense of sureness, zeal and unassailability, values shared by his contemporaries, whether Roman Catholic or Protestant, Italian or British, by using expressions in English which appear racist, patronising and chauvinistic to modern readers, but which would scarce have raised an eyebrow a hundred years ago.

John Crockett
Auckland, February 2000

Visitors to Nineteenth-Century Aotearoa/New Zealand

Isolated New Zealand attracted numerous curious visitors in the nineteenth century in search of the exotic and unusual. Nearly all made some comment on Maori and race relations. Many left behind written reminiscences, especially if they were such famous writers as Anthony Trollope (1872)[1] and Mark Twain (1895),[2] painters (George Angas, Augustus Earle),[3] or such scientists as Charles Darwin (1835),[4] Ernst Dieffenbach (1839)[5] and Andreas Reischek (1877-1889).[6] Radicals, such as the Californian Henry Demarest Lloyd (1899), also dropped in to observe New Zealand as an exemplar of reform, to the extent that the colony earned a reputation as a 'social laboratory' (Lord Asquith's term) by the end of that busy century.[7] Inquisitive, left-leaning political scientists such the Frenchmen André Siegfried and Albert Métin and the English Fabian socialists Sidney and Beatrice Webb also visited fin-de-siècle New Zealand: the French in 1899 and the Webbs in 1898. Numerous politicians, ranging from the English Liberal Sir Charles Dilke to the Irish land radical Michael Davitt (1895), left carefully written accounts.[8] Then there were the children of the wealthy intent on a very 'grand tour' (Constance Astley in 1897),[9] more humble tourists,[10] and, of course, church men and women and missionaries.

Missionaries and church leaders generally viewed Maori as 'hard primitive'/'ignoble savages' (Samuel Marsden, Henry Williams, most of the remaining Anglicans, Methodists and Catholics),[11] but a few inclined towards an alternative 'soft primitive'/'noble savage' type of depiction (Bishop Selwyn and Archdeacon Octavius Hadfield). Most, including Selwyn, also viewed Maori as children requiring education and guidance to reach the status of full, mature and civilised humans. The German missionary Johannes Wohlers assumed an even tougher stance, condemning the Kai Tahu of Ruapuke Island as 'lazy' and 'dirty' 'savages', even though their 'athletic form and graceful bearing looked as stately as the ancient greeks in robes'. He believed that unless help came from outside, this miserable group were destined for 'unavoidable extinction'.[12]

As the century progressed, and especially after the wars of the 1860s, missionary and church attitudes towards Maori hardened, particularly against ideologies of resistance which seemed anti-Christian. Hauhauism headed this list but Papahurihia in the Bay of Islands, Te Kooti's Ringatu faith, and Te Whiti o Rongomai and Tohu Kakahi's alternative religious vision in Taranaki also received little sympathy.[13] Only Hadfield and Mother Mary Aubert, from Toulouse in France, showed much sensitivity as to why Maori retreated from Christianity.[14] Aubert's criticism was much more subtle and less rhetorical than that of the Italian prelate Dom Felice Vaggioli, however.

Churchmen and missionaries, like most of the polyglot group of visiting commentators on New Zealand, basically approved of the whole business of European imperial domination of indigenous peoples and the 'development' of apparently empty lands and 'wilderness'. Darwin found Maori frightening and intimidating. He considered Maori to be 'of a much lower order' than the Tahitians and concluded 'one is a savage the other a civilised man'.[15] Ernst Dieffenbach, the German scientist employed by the New Zealand Company to report on the country's resources, made rather more favourable judgements. He considered Maori to be 'genuinely handsome' but 'half-civilised' and needing much help both to better utilise the country's abundant resources and to resist the deleterious effects of European disease, tobacco and the potato.[16]

A handful of philo-Maori administrators also took a more positive line. The most enthusiastic was Edward Shortland, private secretary to the Governor, who toured the South Island in 1843 to investigate Maori land tenure and title. He admired the formerly poorly regarded Ngai Tahu for their intelligence, artistic ability, technological capacity and powers of memory. Overall he rated them a higher form of being than European whalers.[17] Charles Dilke was almost as flattering, describing Maori in a turn-of-the-century essay as 'one of the finest of aboriginal populations.'[18] On an earlier visit, however, he failed to advance beyond the notion of 'natural selection' and feared that, despite learning how to farm, Maori were doomed to extinction 'Like the Moa'.[19] He also believed that Maori Christianity reverted to barbarism and savagery during the 1860s despite the 'chivalric' quality of the Maori warriors.[20] Interestingly, he judged that despite the respect which European settlers held for Maori, Wiremu Tamihana had been badly mistreated because he acted only as a 'true patriot'.[21]

Both Augustus Earle and George Angas were fascinated by the exotic appearance and customs of Maori. They found them physically attractive but condemned outright the practice of cannibalism, in which they seemed to take a rather prurient and vicarious interest. The two artists rated Maori as superior to American Indians and Australian Aboriginals and liked their sense of 'fun' and hospitality.[22] Earle concluded that if Maori amalgamated with the British a 'powerful and distinguished nation' would emerge, while Angas looked to 'a regular system of government' as holding the key to Maori survival.[23]

Both the French intellectuals Siegfried and Métin went on to become important figures in France and made some telling criticisms of the Liberal Government's policies, but they did not question the view that Maori were dying out despite reasonable treatment at the hands of the British colonisers. Siegfried described Maori as the major 'obstacle' to colonisation and praised them as 'powerful, brave and warlike', but considered them to be in 'fatal' decline and destined to become a 'memory'.[24] Lloyd reversed Darwin's judgement by rating Maori as superior to any other Polynesians, applauded the fact that 'cannibals' had become 'citizens' and lauded the transformation of 'squaws' into 'voters'. But he also concluded that Maori were too few in number to 'colour the strain' and declared New Zealand to be 'a white man's country'.[25] The Webbs seemed little interested, failing to see Maori anywhere, but did make the intriguing comment that there was 'just the suspicion of the Polynesian' in the New Zealand character.[26] Reischek and Trollope, on the other hand, found Maori enticingly exotic and sensually pleasing, in a kind of pre-Edenic way. Trollope also concluded that Maori were the 'most civilised of savages', superior to Aboriginal, American Indian and black African. He also argued that New Zealand had been the most 'justly' colonised country anywhere, even though he disputed the use of labels such as 'rebel' and condemned confiscation of land as unfair. Despite showing some sympathy, Trollope still believed that Maori would soon die out, thereby allowing the advancement of 'civilisation' unimpeded by Maori resistance.[27]

Davitt and Twain were, therefore, unusual in expressing support for Maori resistance to British intrusion. Davitt congratulated Maori on their 'determined stand against extermination' and enthused 'I question whether greater courage or more noble examples of heroism can be found in the annals of modern war than were associated with Rewi's defence of Orakau against General Cameron and Carey's overwhelming forces.' The Irish patriot summed up the history of the colonisation of New Zealand as 'the contest between British settlers and Maori for possession of the land'.[28]

Twain condemned as outrageous the statue in Moutoa Gardens (Pakaitore) celebrating the triumph of civilisation over 'fanaticism and barbarism' because it demeaned the 'Patriotism' of the brave Maori who defended their 'homes' and 'country'. He found the statue to the kupapa, or loyalists, who fought with the British even more demeaning because it encouraged 'treachery, disloyalty, unpatriotism'. In his opinion this monument should be 'dynamited'.[29] But even these two more critical commentators basically accepted notions of British (as opposed to mere English) superiority. French, Austrian, and other European visitors and Americans, including Twain, also accepted basic social Darwinist notions of European superiority and their mission to civilise less fortunate races. Twain, indeed, referred to Maori as 'a superior breed of savages'.[30] His defence was not very different from that of the critical New Zealand historian G.W. Rusden – who ended up in court for his defence of Te Whiti and condemnation of John Bryce.[31]

What makes Dom Felice Vaggioli's memoirs so unusual, therefore, is that he rejects outright the whole project of British and Protestant imperialism. The only other commentator, religious or secular, to make such trenchant criticism of British policy towards the Maori during and after the wars was the Polish nationalist Sygurd Wisniowski, who wrote a novel portraying British settlement in very unflattering terms after a two-year visit in the early 1870s. Published in Warsaw in 1877 and entitled *Tikera or Children of the Queen of Oceania*, it condemned British settlers as a bunch of ruthless and hypocritical land-grabbers. His anonymous hero and narrator complains early in the novel that 'England claims as her mission the world-wide distribution of the Bible. She gives the Bible with one hand and a bottle of fourth-class rum with the other.'[32] The novel concludes with a sharper condemnation of English colonialism when the narrator comments on 'the considerable talent of the Anglo-Saxon and Teutonic settlers for destroying and dissipating all they find.' He becomes even more bitter when he goes on to say:

> At first they have to plunder, exterminate, uproot, to make a desert out of a living country, and then they implant a new life there. They don't want to use what is already in existence. The idea of amalgamating with the natives and appreciating their nobler characteristics never crosses their minds irrespective of their origin, beauty or complexion.

He concludes sardonically 'And yet they seem to be the only successful colonisers'.[33] Yet even Wisniowski is ambiguous about the Maori, whom he portrays as sometimes treacherous and two-faced.

Vaggioli accepts no such qualification and produces a completely fresh interpretation. He may have relied heavily upon the writings of Arthur Thomson and a few others for his factual data, but he inverted the message of progress promulgated by writers like Thomson. Vaggioli debunks British colonisation as an unmitigated disaster and portrays Maori as undeserving victims. He dismisses scientific, cum pseudo-scientific, explanations such as Social Darwinism as mere excuses and sees the world in terms of moral absolutes. As far as he is concerned, the British are in the wrong and the Maori are in the right. Vaggioli saw New Zealand as Maori country, which the British had no moral right to take from them. Consequently, no other commentator is so pro-Maori, and certainly none is as ardently anti-British and anti-Protestant and radically anti-Imperial. His work stands apart from the massive effort at legitimation during the late nineteenth century which produced what P.J. Gibbons has called 'the literature of occupation'.[34] Even that great French champion of Maori rights, Mother Mary (Suzanne) Aubert, behaved diplomatically to win concessions for her flock.[35] Not so Vaggioli.

The other very useful feature of the Italian cleric's tirade is that it was written in the 1880s, a time of depression when relatively few bothered to visit the debt-ridden and struggling colony. For all these reasons this is a most valuable account – biased, slanted, prejudiced and one-sided as it is. Little wonder that the British government kept its publication suppressed for so long, or that the Italians held it as a well-kept secret. If this tome had fallen into the hands of certain propagandists a 'Black Legend' equivalent to that promoted by the Dominican critic of Spain's conquest of Mexico, Fra Bartholomew de las Casas, could have been developed. Such an 'anti-myth' would have challenged the much cosier notion that race relations have been relatively good in New Zealand because the colony was settled by the most enlightened and tolerant of colonisers. Painters such as Theodore De Bry reinforced the critique of de las Casas with grotesque, overblown images of repression, torture, rape and pillage.[36] Imagine if the overwrought imagination of some painter had been affected by Vaggioli's tales of horror! One wonders how such pieces of state propaganda as the school history text *Our Nation's Story* would have coped with this level of lurid verbal and visual condemnation?

This is all counter-factual, of course, because the work was never published in English and languished in Italian libraries far from the self-satisfied world of British colonial administrators and New Zealand politicians and bureaucrats intent upon legitimising Pakeha dominance. And so, at last, the most stinging challenge to the cosy notion that British colonial rule was somehow the kindest variant of European imperialism is made available to all New Zealanders. This is the perfect antidote to what James Belich calls 'the historical amnesia' of New Zealanders.[37]

TOM BROOKING
Dunedin, February 2000

History Of
New Zealand
And Its Inhabitants

By
Dom Felice Vaggioli
Visiting Abbot of the Cassinese Congregation
Reformed Rule

Volume Two
Including 14 Illustrations

Parma
Fiaccadori Press
1896

RITRATTO DELL' AUTORE
Rmo P. D. FELICE VAGGIOLI
ABATE VISITATORE

Portrait of the Author
Most Rev. Father Dom. Felice Vaggioli
Visiting Abbot

Contents

Preface   *9*

Chapter 1   The First Navigators of New Zealand. From 1600 to 1799. *11*
SUMMARY. – 1. Search for new lands in the sixteenth century. – 2. A sunken ship. – 3. Captain Tasman. – 4. Massacre of explorers. – 5. Captain Cook. – 6. Captain De Surville. – 7. Captain Marion du Fresne. – 8. Further visits by Captain Cook. – 9. Europe and the Maori. – 10. Norfolk Island's penal colony. – 11. Description of the Maori towards the end of the eighteenth century.

Chapter 2   Origins of New Zealand Colonisation. From 1800 to 1820. *23*
SUMMARY. – 1. Australia's penal colony. – 2. Sealers. – 3. Pakeha-Maori. – 4. First Maori visits to England. – 5. Description of natives, 1808. – 6. Massacre of crew and passengers of the *Boyd*. – 7. Mainly British bloody reprisals. – 8. Anglican mission's establishment. – 9. Main aim of Protestantism and its founders. – 10. Exploits of first superintendent of New Zealand Anglican mission.

Chapter 3   New Zealand in the Grips of Mayhem and Carnage. From 1821 to 1830. *35*
SUMMARY. – 1. Chief Hongi in England. – 2. His atrocities. – 3. His final campaign and death. – 4. Arms and ammunition trade. – 5. Trade in Maori heads. – 6. Attempted New Zealand colonisation. – 7. European theft and exploitation of Maori tribes. – 8. French scientific expeditions.

Chapter 4   Inter-tribal Warfare, Unrest and Uneasy Peace. From 1830 to 1835. *51*
SUMMARY. – 1. Causes of native fighting. – 2. Rauparaha's violent campaigns. – 3. European collusion in Rauparaha's cannibal atrocities. – 4. Fighting engulfs the country. – 5. Whalers. – 6. Pakeha-Maori. – 7. Rumours of French occupation. – 8. The British Resident and his achievements; A Maori flag. – 9. British troops' atrocities against the Maori. – 10. Anglican missionaries' proposal to be trustees of Maori land.

Chapter 5   Political Unrest; the Catholic Mission. From 1836 to 1840. *71*
SUMMARY. – 1. Baron de Thierry's aspirations and proclamations. – 2. Proposal for a Maori constitution. – 3. The Baron's achievements and

death. – 4. European and Maori skulduggery at Kororareka and elsewhere. – 5. The Kororareka Association. – 6. British government's concerns about New Zealand. – 7. Catholic missionaries; Vicar Apostolic of Western Oceania. – 8. Undermining of Catholic missionaries. – 9. Catholic missionaries' arrival; obstacles and achievements. – 10. Their early successes. – 11. New missionaries and missions. – 12. Catholic and Protesant religion statistics. – 13. The New Zealand Company. – 14. New Zealand Company's devious dealings. – 15. Larceny. – 16. Harmful effects on the Maori.

Chapter 6   New Zealand, a British Colony, Migrants' Arrival. From 1840 to 1844. *93*
SUMMARY. – 1. Governor Hobson's arrival in New Zealand, Sovereign's decrees. – 2. Treaty of Waitangi. – 3. Discussion of its validity. – 4. New colony's militia. – 5. Migrants' arrival in Wellington. – 6. Colony's new capital. – 7. French migrants in Akaroa. – 8. Migrants' arrival in Wanganui, Taranaki, Manukau and Nelson. – 9. Hobson's death; Shortland's administration. – 10. The Wairau massacre. – 11. Governor Fitzroy's peace-making attempts. – 12. Land purchase claims and concessions made by the government commission. – 13. Protestant missionary claims and concessions made to them. – 14. Country's situation by end of 1844.

Chapter 7   Unrest Throughout the Country. From 1845 to 1850. *115*
SUMMARY. – 1. Chief Heke. – 2. Heke destroys Kororareka.– 3. Government declares war on Heke. – 4. A new governor. – 5. Fighting against Heke continues. – 6. Fighting in Wellington. – 7. Uprisings in Wanganui. – 8. The 'Fencibles'. – 9. New migrants in Otago. – 10. 1848 earthquake. – 11. Proposal for an autonomous New Zealand government. – 12. Colonial statistics, 1850-1851.

Chapter 8   Protestant and Catholic Missions. From 1840 to 1860. *137*
SUMMARY. – 1. Governor Grey and Anglican missionaries. – 2. Protestant preaching activity in New Zealand. – 3. Maori Protestant converts and their practice. – 4. Catholic mission in New Zealand. – 5. Differences between Protestant and Catholic missionary education. – 6. Catholic missionary life and activities in New Zealand. – 7. Colonial Catholic education. – 8. Auckland mission's severe trials.

Chapter 9   Colony's Material Development. From 1851 to 1860. *149*
SUMMARY.– 1. New colonists for Canterbury.– 2. Hawkes Bay colony. – 3. New Zealand Company's bankruptcy. – 4. Goldmining in California, Australia and New Zealand. – 5. Colonial constitutional government. – 6. Sir George Grey leaves the colony; Acting-Governor and Parliament's first sessions; a new governor. – 7. Maori love of the land. Formation of Native League to prevent land sales. – 8. The Land League causes inter-tribal fighting. – 9. Earthquake. – 10. Maori arms. – 11. Colonial

legislature and laws; Provincial Councils. – 12. Colony's material development; education, emigration, agriculture, goldmining. – 13. Colonial statistics, 1859.

Chapter 10 Savage Fighting Between the Two Races. From 1860 to 1864. *175*
SUMMARY: 1. Origin of conflict and outbreak of war. – 2. Fighting between the two races in Taranaki. – 3. Governor Browne's departure and Sir George Grey's return as colonial governor. – 4. The Maori king and colonial government. – 5. Grey's Maori policy. – 6. Signs of war. – 7. Merciless fighting in the Waikato and Taranaki. – 8. Maritime disasters. – 9. Fighting in Taranaki. – 10. Fighting in Tauranga. – 11. Prisoners' flight. – 12. New Zealand goldmining; gold prospectors.

Chapter 11 Continuation and End of the War. From 1865 to 1870. *201*
SUMMARY. – 1. Origins of a new Maori religion. – 2. Pai marire or Hauhau. – 3. Their political-religious beliefs. – 4. Wellington, the new capital. – 5. Maori supply and manufacture of weapons. – 6. Fighting in Wanganui. – 7. Opotiki and Wakatane massacres. – 8. Culprits' arrest; a new Hauhau prophet-leader. – 9. Prisoners' escape from Wellington. – 10. Fighting and massacres at Gisborne and Napier. – 11. Fighting in Wanganui and Taranaki. – 12. Colonial parliament's activities. – 13. Sir George Grey's recall. – 14. Wanganui and Taranaki fighting and slaughter. – 15. Prisoners' escape from the Chathams. – 16. Fighting the fugitives. – 17. No quarter given. – 18. Continuation and end of fighting. – 19. War's effects on the two races. – 20. 1869 legislation. – 21. Colonial statistics.

Chapter 12 Colonial Religion. From 1861 to 1879. *235*
SUMMARY. – 1. Evaluation of Protestant sects and Anglicanism in New Zealand. – 2. Mass Maori renunciation of Christianity. – 3. Franciscan missionaries in Auckland diocese. – 4. Missionary Aletag's death; accusations against Catholic missionaries, especially Rev. Garavel. – 5. Maori Catholics' indifference and apostasy. – 6. Monsignor Pompallier's resignation from Auckland diocese; his death. – 7. Dunedin diocese's establishment. – 8. Auckland's new bishop. – 9. Franciscan fathers quit Auckland. – 10. Monsignor Viard's death. – 11. State of Wellington diocese, 1875. – 12. Comparison of Maori and European church membership, 1879.

Chapter 13 Migration, Public Works and Debts. From 1871 to 1880. *259*
SUMMARY. – 1. Colonial legislation. – 2. Julius Vogel's achievements. – 3. Post and telegraph. – 4. Free passage. – 5. Continuous damaging effects of migration. – 6. A more suitable plan for Catholic migration. – 7. Parliament buildings. Colonial railways. – 8. New governors. – 9. National defence. – 10. Abolition of provinces and creation of counties.

– 11. Acquisition of Maori lands. – 12. Slave trading in the Pacific. – 13. Masonic or secular state education. – 14. Effects of anti-Christian education in New Zealand and Europe. – 15. Colonial statistics.

Chapter 14   Exploitation of Natives. From 1881 to 1893. *285*
Summary. – 1. Injustices against Maori. – 2. Prophet Te Whiti. – 3. Prophet's and followers' capture. – 4. Te Whiti's triumph; Government's humiliation. – 5. Peace negotiations between government and King Tawhiao. – 6. Monsignor Steins, Bishop of Auckland. The Benedictine Fathers in New Zealand. – 7. New governors; governors and the people. – 8. Unsuccessful Maori appeal to Queen of England. – 9. Monsignor Luck, Bishop of Auckland. Destruction of St Benedict's church. Monsignor Fines' death. – 10. Te Kooti's fate; Te Whiti's re-imprisonment. – 11. Australasian ecclesiastic congress. Christchurch diocese. – 12. Colonial statistics. – 13. Catholic Maori mission. – 14. Evaluation of European religious practice. – 15. Catholic diocesan statistics. – 16. Evaluation of Maori religion and morality. – 17. Material progress and seeds of moral decline; fears for the future.

List of Illustrations
Volume Two

1	Portrait of the author	*2*
2	Chief Hongi and his wife, 1845	*117*
3	Christchurch, 1860	*151*
4	Napier settlement, 1873	*153*
5	Catholic church and Missionary's house, Coromandel, 1886	*157*
6	Catholic school, Coromandel, 1886	*157*
7	Dunedin, 1870	*173*
8	View of Auckland, 1870	*207*
9	Wellington, colonial capital, 1872	*253*
10	Catholic cathedral, Wellington, 1875	*254*
11	Parliament buildings, built entirely of wood, Wellington	*270*
12	Te Whiti, prophet, Parihaka, 1880	*289*
13	St Benedicts Catholic church, Newton, burnt down in 1886	*296*
14	Catholic cathedral, Auckland, 1885	*301*

Note

Throughout the text, Vaggioli has converted pound sterling values into francs. The conversion rate he used was £1 = 25 francs.

With ecclesiastical and the order's approval.

Preface

In the first volume of this history I described to you as best I could, gentle reader, the natural features of New Zealand; its beauty, its mineral resources, flora and fauna. I then recounted in detail the origins and migration of its native people, as well as their customs, language, ethics, beliefs, traditions, social structure, arts and knowledge; everything that could be revealed about a people entirely unknown to Italians.

In the second volume, paying attention to truth and clarity, I have made available a detailed history of the inhabitants and colonists who emigrated to New Zealand at the end of the last century up to the present day. To help clarify the period's history, I have made every effort to place events in chronological order, and I have referred to Catholic and Protestant writers alike to show my impartiality in dealing with historical events.

It is my hope, dear reader, that when you have read this account, you will not feel that your time has been wasted. I trust that you will thank Providence for now having in your possession important new information. I ask only one thing of you, that you remember me in your prayers. Together we will then draw near to the heavenly kingdom, the source of all knowledge and happiness and the true purpose of our existence in this unhappy world.

Chapter One

The First Navigators of New Zealand From 1600 to 1799

Summary. – 1. Search for new lands in the sixteenth century. – 2. A sunken ship. – 3. Captain Tasman. – 4. Massacre of explorers. – 5. Captain Cook. – 6. Captain De Surville. – 7. Captain Marion du Fresne. – 8. Further visits by Captain Cook. – 9. Europe and the Maori. – 10. Norfolk Island's penal colony. – 11. Description of the Maori towards the end of the eighteenth century.

1. After Christopher Columbus's epic discovery of America in 1492, intrepid explorers of the age were tremendously keen to discover new lands and peoples. This enthusiasm was widespread in the sixteenth century. A fifth of the world's area was discovered, namely Oceania or the Terra Australis. Governments and individuals competed in expeditions which were expected eventually to increase trade opportunities and to expose new lands and peoples to the preaching of Christ's gospel. Discoveries of new lands in the southern region occurred throughout the sixteenth century. The main explorers involved in the discovery of Oceania were Diaz, Vasco da Gama, de Gonneville, Magalhaes, Alvaro Savedra, Mendana, Juan Fernandez, Luis Torres and Fernando de Quiros. De Quiros, for example, in his account of his voyages published in Seville in 1610 mentions many now familiar Pacific islands. Sixteenth-century Spanish navigators gave us the first indications of these islands' existence.

This should come as no surprise. Once America's gold was discovered, all Spain was agog with rumours of the existence of an *el dorado*, or country full of gold in the southern region. But instead of discovering mountains of gold, explorers' ships came to grief on the myriad islands scattered over its vast ocean. Europe, however, finding no mention of much coveted wealth in the gallant captains' logs, cared precious little about their discoveries. Consequently, many journals were simply not published or were left neglected and forgotten. De Gonneville, on his return voyage, had the misfortune to come across an English privateer (a not uncommon English occupation) in the South Atlantic. Not finding anything worth stealing, he wantonly destroyed the good captain's papers.

I mentioned in chapter one, volume one of this History, scholars' different theories regarding who discovered New Zealand. I suggested why, in my opinion, the country was discovered in the sixteenth century by an unknown French or Spanish explorer. I would refer the kind reader to my explanation.

Regarding this matter, Hursthouse, an English writer, comments, 'Might not de Quiros, holding on south (*from the New Hebrides**) in continued search of the gold land have been the real discoverer of New Zealand? At least, it is fairly conjectural that New Zealand was first discovered by some early Spanish navigator, inasmuch as there exists a remarkably correct Spanish chart of Dusky Bay, of very late date, and Dusky Bay was not a place Tasman, the recognised discoverer of New Zealand ... appears to have visited.'[1]

2. I should mention a very interesting fact on this subject. Dusky Bay, mentioned above, is situated on the south-west coast of the South Island, and is some forty kilometres long. At the far reaches of the bay, close to the shore, when the sea is calm the outline of a foreign-built ship can be seen lying buried on the seabed. No one can explain the shipwreck. In the middle of this century an English settler bravely dived down to it. He thought it was a foreign vessel, not having any similar features to British ships, ancient or modern. He said that it was wooden, solidly built and its timber resistant to sea water. The old ship still seemed sound and relatively intact in spite of being submerged for perhaps hundreds of years.

Local Maori have their own tradition regarding the ancient ship. One morning their forebears as children saw a large ship enter Dusky Bay. When close to shore it suddenly sank and disappeared beneath the waves. The crew swam to a nearby uninhabited island, but eventually died one by one. The Maori were unable to find out who they were or from whence they came. It is quite possible that local Maori menaced the unfortunate crew, making them seek safety on the islet. Otherwise they would surely have gone ashore on the mainland to get natives' help, rather than die from exposure and starvation on the miserable little island.[2] If it cannot be clearly stated who was the first discoverer of New Zealand, there is no doubt that the navigator, Abel Tasman, rediscovered it, gave it its present name and made Europe aware of the country's existence.

3. Tasman, a Dutchman, sailed with two ships from Batavia towards the southern hemisphere. After discovering the island south of Australia named after him, he sailed off in a north-east direction. On 18 September 1642 he anchored in a bay at the northern tip of the South Island, later called Tasman Bay or Golden Bay, near Farewell Spit. Two native canoes swiftly approached the ships. They heard a Maori on one of the boats blowing an instrument which sounded like a Moorish horn. The next morning a canoe with thirteen people on board approached within fifty metres of one of the ships. But neither the offer of

* Translator's note: The words in italics represent an addition by Vaggioli in Hursthouse's text.

food, clothing or trinkets could entice any natives to venture on board the anchored vessels. As soon as it returned to shore, seven other canoes full of Maori warriors set out towards the two ships. Some, with great trepidation, climbed on board the *Heemerkirk*. Tasman, who was on board the other ship some distance away, was alarmed that something might happen. He dispatched seven sailors in a longboat to warn the other ship's crew to be on their guard. As soon as the Maori saw the boat they began to yell furiously and they rushed at it, killing three sailors and mortally wounding another. Then they swiftly paddled away, carrying off one of the dead sailors.

Captain Tasman abandoned the idea of replenishing his food and water supplies. He weighed anchor and set sail, calling the place *Murderers Bay*. The Maori, gathered in large numbers on the shore, noticed the ships departing. They leapt into some twenty-two canoes and set off in pursuit. A man stood in the leading canoe holding an ornamental spear (symbol of a chief) while the others rowed strongly. As they drew near, Tasman ordered them to be fired on. A musket shot dispatched the chief. Other shot fell around the canoes. The Maori were stupefied by the sound of gunfire, which they had never experienced before, and they fled in panic.

Tasman headed north from the South Island and he sailed up the west coast of the North Island without landing, for fear of natives. He reached North Cape (which he named *Cape Maria Van Diemen* in honour of the Governor of Batavia's daughter). Continuing his voyage, he came across three small islands which he called the *Three Kings*. The country he discovered was called New Zealand, after the Dutch province of his birth. Tasman then sailed away in search of more hospitable shores. He reached the *Cocos* islands where he was able to take on food and water. This is a brief summary of the Dutch explorer's *Journal* published last century.

4. From Tasman's visit to Captain Cook's, more than a century later, there is no clear evidence whether any other explorers reached New Zealand. However, the Maori of Arapawa situated at the bottom of the North Island on the southwest coast have a tradition handed down by their ancestors. They say that well before Captain Cook's arrival a ship arrived there. Its captain was *Rongotute*. His men behaved so riotously ashore that the embittered natives took over the ship, killed and ate the entire crew. They then stripped the boat and left the hull on the beach. There were dinner plates in the booty. The natives broke them up and drilled holes in them and wore them as ear and breast ornaments. One of the pieces is said to resemble a *mere* (a Maori stone club). This was highly treasured and it is still in the possession of a member of the Ngatehine tribe. They also say that this was the first time they came across iron. They made adzes of the spike nails retrieved from the ship.[3]

5. Captain Cook, an Englishman, was sent to the southern hemisphere to make astronomical observations of the transit of Mercury over the sun.* He won renown for his five-month sojourn in New Zealand in 1769. The first sighting of land from his ship, *Endeavour*, in June 1769, was of the peninsula he called *Young Nick's Head*, near Poverty Bay on the east coast of the North Island, at 178 degrees longitude and 38.40 degrees latitude south. He stayed some time there.

From Poverty Bay he sailed north. He landed at Tolago Bay and then at Tauranga in the Bay of Plenty, so called because of the plentiful supplies he was able to get from local natives. Poverty Bay earned its name because he obtained so little there. Leaving Tauranga, he anchored at the first bay he came across in his voyage, where he observed the transit of Mercury, and he called the bay after it. He then set off for the Hauraki Gulf which he closely explored. Continuing up the coast, Cook reached the Bay of Islands where he stayed for some time.

Again raising anchor, he sailed around North Cape and he continued down the west coast of the island. Reaching Taranaki, he named its prominent, snow-capped mountain *Egmont*. Continuing his voyage, he reached the bottom of the North Island. After a brief stay at the northern tip of the South Island, Cook crossed the Strait now named after him. He continued his exploration of the North Island, rounding Cape Palliser and again sailing up the east coast as far as Hawkes Bay. He then turned south and explored almost all the lower east coast. After this, Cook set sail making directly for the northern-most part of the North Island, anchoring at Doubtless Bay.

During his voyage of exploration, Cook drew up a map of the country and he named many places, including capes, peninsulas and bays. The noted botanists Joseph Banks and Dr Solander, who accompanied him, collected 360 plant species from the many places they visited. To enable communication with the natives, Cook brought a Tahitian chief, *Tupaia*, with him, the Tahitian language being similar to Maori. Through Tupaia the captain and crew were easily able to trade with various tribes. They gave them pigs, chickens, cabbage seeds, potatoes, turnips and other vegetables, and showed them how to grow them. They also gave the Maori rum. They had no word in their language for it and called it: '*Te wai Toki i te rangi*[4] – *Cook's heavenly water*.' This expression became proverbial to signify any sweet drink.[#]

In the many dealings that Captain Cook had with Maori, he often suspected

---

* Translator's note: Cook was, in fact, sent 'to the Southwards of the Equinoctial line' to observe the passage of the planet *Venus* across the sun. This he accomplished in Tahiti. Later, in New Zealand, he observed the transit of Mercury. (cf. *The Dictionary of New Zealand Biography*, vol. 1, p. 90, Captain Cook entry.)

[#] Translator's note: This reference is probably sourced from Taylor (*Te Ika a Maui*, p. 207, 1974 facsimile edition) who describes 'Te wai toki a rangi' as passing into proverb 'for anything sweet'.

that they harboured hostile feelings towards him, while it was mentioned that generally they displayed trust and friendship. Only occasionally, when provoked, did they reveal distrust and aggression. In many situations during Cook's sojourn, Maori behaved in a civilised manner while the Europeans acted like savages. Indeed, Cook left New Zealand without any of his men being killed or even wounded by natives, while the British left them with ten to mourn and many more wounded as a result of their visit.

Dr Thomson rightly noted how very differently Captain Cook and Maori acted,[5] mentioning an unfortunate incident described by Dr Hawkesworth in *Cook's Voyage*, and by Te Taniwha, a native contemporary of Cook's who died in 1853, which should not be overlooked. Lieutenant Gore fired a musket from his ship at a Maori in a canoe who had stolen a piece of calico. The startled natives rowed away to get out of danger. They did not notice that Marutuahu had been killed because he was still in the same position. When they reached the shore they found that their companion, sitting on the blood-soaked calico, was stone-dead, the ball having entered his back. Several chiefs, investigating the affair, considered that he deserved to die, because he had committed theft. Therefore, they did not have to seek revenge on the foreigners for his death. Marutuahu, having paid with his life, was to keep the piece of calico he had stolen. His body was wrapped in it and he was buried. 'Singular to relate,' comments Thomson, 'Captain Cook landed soon after the murder, and traded as if nothing had occurred. Would Cook's ship's crew have acted thus if one of them had been so slain?'[6]

While Captain Cook was continuing his exploration of New Zealand, shortly after he left the Hauraki Gulf a French ship entered, anchoring at the mouth of the Waihau (Thames) river. It took on a cargo of spars and set sail again. The ship came across a fishing canoe driven out to sea by the wind. The captain took aboard its two young Maori paddlers. They went with him to France *where they were educated and learnt many useful things.** The same ship returned them two years later to New Zealand. The captain gave them some pigs and showed them how to rear them. They were also taught how to grow potatoes. This kind and generous captain's identity remains a mystery, and we only know about his visit through Te Taniwha, a contemporary Maori, mentioned above.[7]

Just before Captain Cook set sail from Doubtless Bay for Europe after completing his first voyage of discovery, he took possession of the country in the name of George III, King of England. He then raised anchor for his return.

6. Scarcely had Captain Cook departed than in December 1769 the French ship, *St Jean Baptist*, entered the Bay, having sailed from India under the

---

* Translator's note: Translator's italics. This information by Vaggioli is not contained in Thomson's account of the incident.

command of Captain De Surville. He landed at Mangonui, where he was warmly welcomed by the Maori and supplied with food and water. A fierce storm occurred a few days after their arrival. Several sick sailors who were ashore at the time tried to return to their ship. Their long boats, however, were driven back to the shore. Chief Nganui sheltered them in his own hut and gave them food for two days. When the storm abated, one of the rowboats was found to be missing. De Surville, with no clear proof, took it that natives had stolen the boat. They insisted on their innocence.

De Surville pretended not to bother about it. He invited chief Nganui to visit his ship, which he agreed to do. When he was on board, De Surville accused Nganui of stealing the boat, and he put him in chains. De Surville went ashore and burnt down the village. He then set sail, taking Nganui with him as prisoner. The poor chief, deeply upset by his harsh treatment, wept constantly for his family and kept on refusing food. After eight days he died of heartbreak and voluntary starvation. De Surville, however, was punished for his crimes. Eleven days after Nganui's death, he was drowned while trying to land at Callao, in Peru.[8]

7. Three years after Captain De Surville's unfortunate fate, another French expedition under the command of Captain Marion du Fresne reached the Bay of Islands. It comprised two ships: the *Mascarin* and the *Marquis de Castro*.* On 11 May 1772 they dropped anchor between two islands in the bay. The next day he had his sick crew members put ashore for a change of air to help them recuperate. The Maori made themselves out to be friendly and plied the sick men with fish and fruit. Du Fresne and his crew, in return, loaded them with gifts. Intimacy, friendship and confidence developed to such a degree between Maori and the French that sailors often slept in the village and Maori aboard ship. Du Fresne trusted the natives so much that his second-lieutenant, Captain Crozet, cautioned him about his foolhardiness. Du Fresne, however, took no notice of Crozet's wise counsel.

A month passed in this atmosphere of mutual harmony. It was noticed, however, that Maori had stopped visiting the ship. On their last visit a young woman appeared to be very upset as she was leaving the boat, but no one knew why. It appears that she knew that the Maori were about to slaughter the luckless Marion and his crew. That is why she was so distressed. On 12 June Du Fresne went ashore with sixteen officers and men, at the invitation of a chief whom the captain had befriended, to go fishing at Manawaroa Bay. By nightfall, Crozet and his crew were surprised that the party had not returned, but they did not suspect any misadventure.

Early the next day Crozet and sixty men went into the nearby forest to chop

---

* Translator's note: Spelt *Marquis de Castries* by Thomson.

down a large kauri tree. Shortly afterwards, a longboat with twelve sailors left the *Marquis de Castro* to gather firewood and fetch water at Orokawa. Suddenly, about midday, guards on board ship noticed a man running frantically along the beach. He dived into the sea and swam desperately towards the ship, reaching it exhausted. When the men pulled him aboard, terror-struck he told them that when he and his eleven companions went ashore that morning they were welcomed in the usual friendly way by the Maori. When they scattered, however, to gather firewood for the ships, the Maori suddenly fell upon them with spears, clubs and hatchets, slaughtering them. Only he had been able to escape. He hid in the bush and saw his companions being butchered. Their dismembered limbs were shared among the murderers, who quickly scattered with their spoils.

When they heard the terrible news, they were very alarmed about the fate of Captain du Fresne and his men. They immediately put the *Mascarin*'s longboat into the water and a large number of well-armed sailors jumped into it. As the boat approached the shore, they saw in the distance at the far end of Manawaroa Bay du Fresne's rowboat surrounded by natives. They decided not to go after their captain right then but to alert Crozet who was chopping down a large tree three miles from the beach.

When Crozet heard about the disaster he mentioned it to no one, but immediately he ordered his men to collect their tools and march to the beach.

As they withdrew, a crowd of heavily armed Maori followed, taunting them and exclaiming that Takouri had killed and eaten Marion du Fresne.

When Crozet reached the shore, he took a musket and drew a line in the sand, saying that anyone who dared to cross the line would be shot. Crozet's courageous behaviour enabled all his men safely to board the waiting boats. From them, in revenge, they fired off several rounds at the crowd of Maori gathered on the shore. During the night the sick sailors in the village were brought back on board ship. The next morning Crozet sent a large contingent of men to fetch firewood and water. They then burnt down the village, killing many of its inhabitants. The French also shot several natives seen to be wearing dead sailors' clothes.

At the same time, Crozet dispatched a column of well-armed sailors to ascertain Captain du Fresne and his companions' tragic fate. They found chief Takouri's village deserted. Takouri was seen fleeing in haste, wearing the captain's mantle. A basket was found in one of the huts containing pieces of human flesh. After setting fire to the village, Crozet returned to his ship.

He was certain that du Fresne and the officers and men with him had suffered the same horrible fate as the others; they had been treacherously slaughtered and eaten by natives. After naming the place 'Treachery Bay', he set sail and returned to France to tell about the expedition's unhappy end.

Reading this tale of horrible slaughter, one would assume, as Crozet maintained, that the Maori only pretended to be friendly to ensure that they could kill and eat their victims. But, in fact, this is not true. Now that their ancient customs, laws and beliefs are known, it is incorrect to impugn them with such a bloodthirsty and unscrupulous motive. When Maori befriended any one, they did so simply and sincerely. But only *usque ad aras*, that is, as long as they committed no sacrilege, violating *tapu*, or things considered sacred.[9] When foreigners took firewood from their cemeteries and sacred forests and water from sacred (*tapu*) springs and touched things declared tapu, which were not even to be approached, affection gave way to the most violent sense of revenge, causing the perpetrators of such terrible sacrileges to be killed. Maori strongly believed that their gods would punish them with death if they did not kill those guilty of violating their tapu. This was the real reason why they were slaughtered.[10]

8. Captain Cook returned to New Zealand in 1774 and spent some time at Dusky Bay on the west coast, near the bottom of the South Island. On this expedition he was accompanied by three scientists, namely the two Forsters (father and son) and Dr Sparrmann. They studied local plant life. Dr Forster estimated the native population to be about 100,000 people. Captain Cook sailed from there up to the entrance of *Queen Charlotte's Sound*, at the north-east tip of the South Island.

This time, too, Cook's visit had a fatal impact, many natives being killed by his crew. Cook sent off nine sailors in a longboat to gather edible plants for the crew. When they reached the shore, a native offered to barter a small stone axe with one of them. After examining it closely, the sailor would not offer anything for it or hand it back. The native, in seeking recompense, tried to get some of the bread and fish the sailors were eating, but they would not let him. A scuffle broke out and two Maori were killed. Before the sailors could reload their muskets, however, the natives fell upon them. They killed them and cooked and ate their bodies.

Maori ate their enemies after killing them, not because of hunger or any lack of food, but to show their hatred and contempt for their foe.

The following day a boat with well-armed sailors was dispatched to find their companions. When they discovered their sad fate they killed many natives, burnt down their huts and destroyed their canoes. After this incident, Cook returned to England.

He again visited New Zealand in 1775 and 1776. His last visit to New Zealand was in 1777. Cook came to a miserable end in Hawaii, in the Society Islands, where he was murdered by natives on 14 February 1779. He was only fifty years old.

9. Crozet's and Cook's voyages of exploration were followed by publication of their *Voyages* and those of the scientists who accompanied them. Alongside

descriptions of abundance and spectacular beauty discovered in New Zealand were tragic accounts of the bloody fighting and horrific slaughter that so often happened. Far from being lost and forgotten, these tales sold like hot cakes throughout Europe. It is impossible to describe the impression they made in the Old World.

Claims about the country and its qualities were exaggerated. It was vaunted as having a wonderful, extremely pleasant climate, where it was always spring. The vegetation was described as varied, lush and tropical. A wide variety of produce grew abundantly in its magically fertile soil. It was claimed that the country was so rich in natural resources that it would leave Europe for dead. Moreover, New Zealand had enormous tracts of forests with huge trees, providing excellent timber. Native flax was admirably suited for making clothing and it grew prolifically throughout the country. Large herds of whales and other mammals were to be found along its coasts. Many other features, too many to enumerate here, were described. This list of enticing features attracted many people and galvanised fortune hunters to want to set off immediately for this land of milk and honey. But a solid wall stood in their way, dashing their hopes.

The Maoris' incredible ferociousness and cannibalism posed an insurmountable obstacle. More savage than wild animals, they gleefully drank their victims' blood pouring from mortal wounds and filled their stomachs with their succulent flesh. Europeans saw themselves as mild and peace-loving in comparison. They could not gather courage to approach Maori without imagining that they would be horribly tortured, killed, cooked and eaten. As the fawn fears the tiger, every one is terrified of cannibals. Not only was the idea of ending up being eaten bad enough. But the mere thought of coming across graphic scenes of cannibalism froze the most stalwart Europeans' blood.

Because of the widespread fear of Maori ferocity, for many years European ships skirted New Zealand waters, even though they needed to take on food and water, and their crews could be decimated by scurvy. They preferred to suffer hunger, thirst and death rather than land and provide a meal for bloodthirsty cannibals.

Captain Vancouver in his voyage around the world, reached New Zealand in 1791, anchoring in Dusky Bay where there were very few natives. He had no stomach for landing anywhere else in the country. The French admiral D'Entrecasteaux, searching for *La Perouse*, arrived in New Zealand waters in 1793. He did not venture to anchor in New Zealand waters, for fear of the Maori. The naturalist on board urged on him the importance of collecting native flax plants, but to no avail.

10. The British government, however, although very aware of the climate of terror, cast a covetous eye on New Zealand, intending to claim it at the first

favourable opportunity. When the United States of North America proclaimed independence from Britain in 1783, England not only lost possession of a vast continent but also an ideal penal colony. One of Cook's companions, Sir Robert Banks, proposed to the British parliament that New Zealand would make a very suitable penal colony. Although Maoris' reputation as cannibals caused the proposal to be rejected as impracticable, the country was declared part of the British Crown, to be administered by the Governor of New South Wales, Australia. At the same time the British government established a penal colony at Port Jackson, where the city of Sydney now stands, appointing Captain Phillip as its first governor.

Phillip left England on 13 May 1787 with a small fleet of nine ships. There were 1017 people on board, comprising convicts, guards and soldiers. There were 787 convicts (595 men and 192 women). The expedition reached its destination without mishap on 20 January 1788. In February the following year many of the convicts and soldiers were sent to Norfolk Island, previously uninhabited. Norfolk Island lies not far to the north of New Zealand, and is part of the same group of islands.

As the convict numbers grew, there was a similar increase in Norfolk Island. By 1796 its population had grown to 889 people, most of whom were convicts.

The main occupations on the island were farming and mat and cloth-making from plentiful native flax. But their products compared unfavourably with the beautiful, prized woven goods Maori made from similar raw material. The authorities were puzzled by this and eager to find out how Maori did it. The governor used a despicable means to achieve this.

In 1793 he sent a ship to search the New Zealand coast and kidnap a Maori. When it reached the Bay of Islands, two natives were enticed on board. The ship then returned to Norfolk Island. But they gained nothing from what they did because one of their captives was a tribal chief and the other a priest. Both insisted they did not know how to dress flax because it was women's work. They did nothing on the island for six months and then returned to New Zealand to a rapturous homecoming. Captain King recompensed them handsomely for their shabby treatment, giving them seed, two young sows, two boars and maize.

Norfolk Island colony survived its first ten years, but it was seen as a rather expensive enterprise by the British government. Sydney, on the other hand, went from strength to strength. They realised that Norfolk Island had no farming potential because it had little arable land. Hopes for a textile industry using native flax were also dashed. For these and other reasons the Governor of New South Wales, who was responsible for the island, had most of the convicts returned to Sydney. Only the most hardened and dangerous convicts were to be kept on the island in the future. For some time the island continued to house several hundred dangerous criminals. Eventually the British government had all convicts removed and placed elsewhere. Only a few farmers remained on the island.

11. During the period described above, that is, from 1769 to 1800, Maori were continuously fighting among themselves, usually to settle insults. Because of this, factions, vendettas, bloodshed and cannibalism continued for generations. They told Captain Cook that they were always fighting and they sought his help to have a better chance of eliminating their enemies. Cook commented that if he listened to all his self-appointed friends he would have wiped out the whole country's Maori population.

Most natives, as is still the case, lived in the North Island, mostly along the east and west coasts. South Island Maori were much fewer and lived mostly in the northern area, along Cook Strait. Others were scattered throughout the island, in bays and near river mouths because they depended on fishing to survive.

Chapter Two

Origins of New Zealand Colonisation From 1800 to 1820

Summary. – 1. Australia's penal colony. – 2. Sealers. – 3. Pakeha-Maori. – 4. First Maori visits to England. – 5. Description of natives, 1808. – 6. Massacre of crew and passengers of the *Boyd*. – 7. Mainly British bloody reprisals. – 8. Anglican mission's establishment. – 9. Main aim of Protestantism and its founders. – 10. Exploits of first superintendent of New Zealand Anglican mission.

1. The British penal colony established in Sydney, Australia, in 1787 not only took root, but prospered and continued to grow year by year, thanks to its governors' influence. Shortly after the convicts' arrival, intrepid colonists, keen on seeking their fortune, began arriving in Australia from England. The colonial government gave them land and convicts to work it, undertaking to pay for their upkeep for two years. In 1801 the penal colony's population was 6508 people, comprising free farmers and convicts and excluding Norfolk Island's prisoners.

In less than fifteen years since its establishment, the colony had done so well in farming that it was more than self-sufficient. Trade was opened up with the mother country and neighbouring territories, making it one of the world's most flourishing colonies. Mention should also be made of sealers and whalers. Towards the end of the eighteenth century, as the colony grew, they began to frequent the east coast of Australia. They noticed that huge numbers of seals gathered there in the breeding season. At that time its shores were not yet invaded by hunters set on relentlessly and ruthlessly slaughtering defenceless mammals.

Whalers and sealers were not only mercenary and greedy, but also usually inveterate rogues and hardened criminals. They were thick-skinned and used to facing any kind of danger or hardship. The reader should not be surprised to learn, therefore, that while reports of Maori cannibalism filled Europe with terror, sealers regarded them simply as childish fears. They believed that it was most unlikely that they would be killed and eaten by savages, and if put in such a situation, they would sell their lives dearly. Casting fear aside, they were keen to sail wherever the greatest profits could be made for the least cost.

2. From the end of the eighteenth century, whalers frequently ventured into the Pacific Ocean to hunt whales and seals. They sailed close to New Zealand and

sometimes, out of necessity, they risked anchoring in inhabited bays to take on food and water. Whalers would land and trade peacefully with Maori. They were very careful and cautious to avoid foul play. The natives, consequently, were generally friendly towards them.

From several voyages in New Zealand waters, whalers believed that its bays, inlets and river mouths abounded with seals. They also believed that numerous whale pods frequented Cook Strait, and sounds and bays in winter, which is summer in the antipodes, to breed. They singled out particularly Dusky Bay, Banks Peninsula, Queen Charlotte Sound, Cook Strait, Hawkes Bay, Poverty Bay and offshore islands.

This very useful information became known at the beginning of the nineteenth century. Whalers then began to frequent coastal New Zealand, particularly in the South Island. Initially, they established friendly relations with the few Maori who lived there in poverty, growing little produce because of the scarcity of arable land, and dependent on fishing for their survival. From the beginning they welcomed whalers with open arms, while North Island Maori regarded them with caution and suspicion.

As long as whalers and sealers did not consider settling permanently in New Zealand, relations between the two races remained cordial. But when they decided to stay and make their living, things took a decidedly different turn, mainly because of European sailors' behaviour. This advance guard of civilisation, to be ironical, were mostly a ragbag of adventurers and villains from the dregs of European society. Some were sailors who liked a dissolute life, free from civilisation's constraints. Others were hardened criminals who had escaped from prison. Then there were freed ex-convicts as well as men of obscure origin with the education and manners of gentlemen.[1] A few were French but the majority were Englishmen and Americans.

You can imagine what Maori learnt about civilisation from this rat's nest of opportunists. They had no sooner settled at the bottom of the South Island than they schemed how to get native land and would use every guile to seduce Maori women. Consequently bitterness and bloodshed were engendered between the two races. Maori, quite rightly, refused to give up their land and their women to satisfy the rogues' insatiable appetites. When natives caught a European out, if they did not succeed in killing him on the spot, they killed and ate the first European they came across. Whalers in retaliation mercilessly killed the first savage they came across whether he was innocent or guilty.

As conflicts persisted, Maori realised that they were dealing with lawless, unscrupulous men with weapons to wipe them out if they stood in their way. They decided to negotiate and make peace with their new neighbours. Both parties agreed that the Maori would give the Europeans *Codfish* Island, west of *Stewart* Island, at the bottom of the South Island. They also gave them young women as wives.[2]

Europeans built wooden huts on the island and besides sealing they began growing crops. Their number increased as more sealers arrived. Consequently, many moved to Stewart Island or to the South Island, in spite of the earlier agreement with natives. Between 1816 and 1820 the number of sealers in New Zealand rose to one hundred. In 1814 a ship of 100 tons was built in Dusky Bay.[3]

3. There was also another kind of European emigrant in New Zealand, the *Pakeha-Maori*: foreigners who went native and embraced the Maori way of life and customs. Living among them, they became tribal members. They were sailors from merchant ships, frigates or whaling ships, and were similar in nature to sealers, described above. When their ships reached New Zealand, they took a fancy to Maori women and to Maoris' free and easy life style. They jumped ship and escaped, hiding in the bush. At first there were only a few *Maori-fied* sailors scattered among tribes. They adopted the native way of life and took a Maori wife. From 1804 two lived with Maori at *Kororareka*, in the Bay of Islands. By 1812 another five adopted a Maori lifestyle. By 1814 there were eight. By 1820 the number rose to fifteen and from 1824 numbers increased sharply, reaching one hundred and fifty by 1840.[4] They and sealers will be mentioned again later.

In the meantime, up till 1824, natives found *Pakeha-Maori* to be practically no use to them. Rather, they were seen as a burden. Besides giving them a wife and shelter, they also had to feed them. When natives adopted them into their families it was more from curiosity to see them close at hand and to get to know them, than for any other reason. After a few years, their curiosity would be more than satisfied and the wretches often ended up being treated as slaves. Quite often, if they were not made slaves, they were killed and eaten. Because of this, many sailors tried to get back aboard a European ship to escape slavery.[5]

4. During this period, some Maori visited Sydney and London by ship. *Te Pahi*, a Bay of Islands chief, was among the first. After visiting Sydney he returned home in 1804. In 1805 *Mohanga*, a slave, was taken by an Englishman to London. Matara, Te Pahi's son, also went to England in 1807. Similarly, Ruatara embarked on a whaling ship in 1805, reaching London in 1809. He returned to New Zealand at the beginning of 1814. Soon after he set off again for Sydney with *Hongi*, a young chief. (He will be mentioned later.) After staying a few months with Marsden, a Protestant minister, they returned to New Zealand with him and his colleagues at the end of the same year. These were the first natives to visit London.

5. By 1808 New Zealand Maori were much more at peace than they had been in the last twenty years of the eighteenth century. The main reason for the

positive change was that trade and commerce were firmly established. Besides sealers living in the South Island, many whalers visited the North Island coast annually trading blankets, hatchets, firearms, fishing gear and other items for pork, potatoes, spars and flax. Natives were so busy producing potatoes, pork, flax and similar goods to get the tools and weapons that they had little time for tribal vendettas, the fatal cause of their conflicts. Others worked for whalers. Because of their fearlessness as sailors, often they became harpooners. This is a highly skilled and dangerous job, involving killing a whale by harpooning it close to the heart.[6]

6. Good relations, which were becoming more evident between the two races by 1805, were suddenly dashed by a tragedy. This had a disastrous effect on both parties, but particularly on the natives. I am referring to the massacre of nearly all the passengers and crew of the British ship *Boyd* in 1809. This is what happened.

The *Boyd* left Sydney for England, intending to stop at Wangaroa, on the east coast of the North Island, to pick up a cargo of spars. The ship's complement was seventy Europeans and five Maori who were taken on board as sailors until Wangaroa, their home. Among them was *Tara*, son of a Wangaroa chief. He would not work during the crossing because he was ill. The captain refused him food and he was severely lashed, including twice publicly on the bridge. He did not cry out but he was so bitter about the insult that he was determined to seek revenge.

When the ship reached Wangaroa, Tara showed his raw and flailed back before a gathering of his father's whole tribe and told them how he had been ill treated and degraded. The tribe, in accordance with Maori custom, believed that if one of them was insulted, they were all affected; even more so in this case, when it was not a commoner but the son of a chief who had been insulted. They decided unanimously to avenge the crime. Nevertheless, according to Mr Nicholas's account, following his visit to Wangaroa in 1814,[7] the natives would probably not have carried out the eventual massacre were it not for the captain and his crew's provocative, unruly behaviour when they went ashore.

The Maori were infuriated by their conduct and fell upon them like hyenas on defenceless prey. They slaughtered them and then chopped them up, cooked and ate them. Those still on board suffered the same fate, except for a woman, two infants and a ship's boy. Tara himself saved the boy's life because he had been kind and considerate to him on the ship. The woman hid with the two infants on board and they were not discovered. Shortly afterwards, the four of them were rescued by Chief Te Pahi and Mr Berry, a British officer from a merchant ship anchored in the Bay of Islands, not far from Wangaroa.

Tara's hatred of Europeans, because of the captain of the *Boyd*'s brutal behaviour towards him, was not extinguished by his terrible act of revenge. It continued, after he became chief, for the rest of his life. On his deathbed in 1822, he exhorted his tribe to oust the Wesleyan Protestant missionaries and all Europeans from Wangaroa.

7. This ghastly, violent deed did not remain unpunished for long. Punishment unfortunately fell on Te Pahi's innocent tribe. They, as has been mentioned, hurried to rescue the four people. Te Pahi and his tribe lived in an unfortified village on a small island in the Bay of Islands. Five whaling ships happened to be in the Bay of Islands shortly after the Wangaroa massacre. Their crews were furious when they heard about it. Wrongly informed that Te Pahi was responsible, they gathered a well-armed force together and took the village by surprise, killing anyone they came across, whether man, woman or child. Thirty people were killed. Then they torched the village. Te Pahi managed to escape, badly wounded. Not long after he was killed in a fight with Wangaroa tribes hostile to him for rescuing the few survivors from the *Boyd*.

The Europeans' gentle mercies did not stop there, far exceeding the unlucky savages' brutal retaliation as they fought to save their lives. Few of the atrocities whites committed were mentioned by British writers of the period, so as not to provoke an outcry in Europe, or discredit their compatriots, or because no one would believe them possible. But from the few details provided, the rest can be imagined. If every crime committed by Europeans against Maori from 1809 to 1825 was known, it would represent such a black and disgraceful page of history as to make the fiercest savages in the world seem like lambs. Evidence will now be provided from reliable and trustworthy sources.

Rev. Ward, a Church of England minister wrote, '*A dark page** may be written on this subject. The Spaniards are very guilty, and the English colonists have not always been free of blame.'[8] He does not, however, reveal its contents, and almost appears to regret his indiscretion, retracting his criticism by adding, 'A better spirit and more enlightened views of colonization have characterized our younger colonies.'

Merchant ships visiting New Zealand from 1809 practised torture and unspeakable cruelties on natives and slaughtered them like so many wild animals.[9] A European gave a chief *corrosive sublimate* to poison his foes at a feast held to commemorate peace.[10] A British trader enticed a large number of Maori aboard his ship. He took them away against their will, landing them in enemy territory, where they were killed and eaten. Whalers, also, often seized Maori men and women, enslaving the men and treating the women to an even worse fate.[11]

During this period all visiting ship carried nets on board to snare Maori like animals.[12] In just two or three years (from 1814 to 1817), around one

---

*Translator's note: Italics are Vaggioli's.

hundred Maori were killed by Europeans in the immediate vicinity of the Bay of Islands.[13]

If in only two or three years *more than a hundred* peaceful natives were cruelly killed around Kororareka without a single European loss, the reader can well imagine how many more Maori were slaughtered in other parts of New Zealand, particularly in the South Island where the few Maori were in scattered coastal settlements.

Maori were much more numerous in the North Island, however, and did not take the slaughter of their brothers lying down. In 1816 when the brig *Agnes* went aground in Poverty Bay, natives killed and ate thirteen crew members. Only one managed to escape.[14]*

In 1820 a whaling ship foundered on the west coast near Wanganui. All except two sailors were killed and eaten. It was a time of terror and atrocities. Maori tried to seize as many European ships as they could, and wipe out their crews in revenge for the massacre of so many of their kin.[15] But the natives came off worse in the uneven conflict.

Besides seeing their lands stolen and their women raped or violated, they also had to endure being shot at. *Civilised* Europeans hunted down Maori as we in Italy would hunt rabbits. The miserable natives, particularly in the South Island, tried to escape into the bush and remote mountains, but even there they were cut down by bullets. Because of this, in just a few years the vast South Island was practically depopulated of Maori except in the Cook Strait area. Dr Thomson, wishing to be his compatriots' apologist for their massacres, concludes by saying, 'The idea of extirpating a race of cannibals stimulated Europeans to shoot New Zealanders; revenge and covetousness stimulated New Zealanders to slaughter Europeans.'![16]

Who were the new savages in kid gloves? They were European Protestants who with a bible in one hand and a musket in the other *planted civilisation* in New Zealand. They did the same shortly before in Sydney, Melbourne, Tasmania and other British colonies, accompanied by the complete extermination of the Australians and other indigenous peoples.

Instead of throwing stones at the Spanish for their atrocities in the Americas, British and Protestant writers should pause to wash their hands, dripping with Maori and Australian blood. I refer, in conclusion, to a report to Lord Durham by Dr Lang, a New Zealand Protestant missionary: 'We are used to speaking with righteous indignation about atrocities committed by Cortes, Pizarro and the *dissolute* bunch of Spaniards who followed these *rogues* to Mexico and Peru, but we forget that we ourselves in the nineteenth century have committed similar vile crimes in other countries. It took the same amount of time, thirty years, to destroy the indigenous peoples of Van Diemen's Land (Tasmania and

---

*Translator's note: Identified as John Rutherford by Thomson (p. 253).

New Zealand) *under the gentle yoke of Britain*, as it did to exterminate the natives of Hispaniola under the iron rod of Ferdinand and Isabella.'[17]*

By 1832 carnage had reached such a level in New Zealand that the British government the same year sought, albeit somewhat late, to put a stop to its subjects' barbarity. It passed a law giving supreme courts of Australia and Tasmania full authority to pass sentence on crimes committed by the British in New Zealand.[18] The British government hoped, with this law, to put an end to Maori being slaughtered with impunity. However, it was a dead letter because it had no legal authority in the country or any representative with the power to bring the guilty to court and account for their crimes.

8. Reading about these atrocities, one would naturally ask: Weren't there any Europeans in New Zealand willing to protest and put a stop to such shocking behaviour? Were there not from 1814 on Protestant missionaries in the Bay of Islands and elsewhere? What did they think about it, what did they do, and what on earth were they concerned about if not to make peace between the hostile parties? Were they not meant to be God's ambassadors of peace and harmony, preaching this message to all, especially to Europeans supposedly more able to understand God's commands and Christian civilisation's dictates? How is it that from 1815 to 1817 more than one hundred harmless Maori were massacred by Europeans in the very areas where Protestant missions were established and missionaries were toiling so zealously?

Gentle reader, let me explain the mystery. From 1814 Protestant missionaries had indeed set up a permanent base in New Zealand; in the Bay of Islands, to be precise, which was regularly visited by traders and whalers. But missionaries were intent on other matters than bothering about instilling humanity in their co-religionists, let alone mediating peace and harmony between the two races. A reading of this history will reveal the missionaries' true motives.

Before the ghastly *Boyd* massacre and the bloodier reprisals which ensued, the London Missionary Society decided to send missionaries to New Zealand and other islands in the Pacific. First, it sent a significant number of lay missionaries to Sydney. From there they were to be dispersed throughout the Pacific. Rev. Samuel Marsden reached Sydney in 1810. He chose Messrs King and Hall to set up a mission in New Zealand as soon as possible. But hearing of the *Boyd* massacre, he delayed sending the expedition until a more opportune time.

Rev. Samuel Marsden, who is recognised by the Anglican Church as founder

---

*Translator's note: Vaggioli's translation of this quotation from Lang is not entirely accurate and confusion is caused where he adds 'Tasmania and New Zealand' after 'Van Dieman's Land', which could suggest that the Maori alongside the Aborigines of Tasmania were exterminated within thirty years. Lang is clearly referring only to the latter.

and father of Anglicanism in New Zealand, was born in Yorkshire, England, in 1769. He was initially a blacksmith, like his father. He later studied theology and shortly before his graduation he was ordained a minister in 1793, and sent immediately to Sydney as the first and senior chaplain of the penal colony. His main priority in Australia was to secure a comfortable living for himself. He set about this so well, that in a short time he amassed considerable wealth, spending much of his time breeding large numbers of stock, particularly sheep. For several years he thus combined the occupations of sheep farmer and trader with that of preacher, while in the government's pay.

In the meantime, this worthy sheep breeder and pastor to his flock, was chosen by the London Missionary Society to found a new mission. In 1814 he believed the time was right to establish Anglicanism in New Zealand. 'He purchased the brig, *Active*, a vessel of one hundred tons, and with Messrs King, Kendall and Hall, their wives and five children, two sawyers, a blacksmith, a horse, a bull, two cows, sheep and poultry, he set sail from Sydney for New Zealand on 19 November 1814.'[19] According to another Protestant writer, 'They reached New Zealand safely with their wives, children, animals and farm labourers.'[20] They reached *Rangihu* in the Bay of Islands, setting up the first Anglican mission on 25 December the same year.

Mr Nicholas, Marsden's faithful companion on this and other missionary journeys, confirms that he was responsible for establishing the first mission at Rangihu. He chose and purchased from the Maori 200 acres (95 hectares) of the choicest land near the mission for 12 axes.[21] After completing a similar unsavoury deal, Marsden returned to Sydney in February 1815.

Mr Marsden returned to New Zealand in 1819 with more missionaries who were sent to *Kerikeri* in the Bay of Islands, setting up a similar mission to *Rangihu*. Up till 1837 Marsden made another five visits to New Zealand, establishing further Anglican missions like the first two. He died in Australia in 1838.

Samuel Marsden's iniquitous example of amassing personal wealth through breeding and selling sheep in Australia and buying vast amounts of land from New Zealand natives for virtually nothing was soon followed by fellow missionaries at Rangihu and Kerikeri. Dr Morison, a London Missionary Society historian and devout Protestant, and thus a reliable source, says that, 'By 1819 five *lay missionaries* (the combination of worker and missionary was not and is still not unusual among Protestant denominations) had bought 13,000 acres for 48 axes.'[22]

9. We will leave this subject for the time being since we will be discussing Protestant missionaries' and colonists' shady deals more fully later. It is, however, relevant to have a brief look at the fundamental principles of Protestantism, its purpose, the means it has used to attain its goals, and whether

it can make any real moral contribution to civilising ignorant savages. These considerations are vital for the reader confronted with evidence that most missionaries lacked the good character and abilities requisite for their vocation. He may not be so critical of them when he realises that Protestantism itself had no such requirements.

Indeed, scholars have studied and discredited the aims and hypocritical behaviour of the sixteenth-century reformers and their followers. Unfortunately, however, there are still, even in Italy, many ingenuous, deluded people who, when they look superficially at Protestant countries, believe that Protestantism is not damaging to faith and Christian morality, in comparison to Catholicism which they roundly condemn. Sycophants, totally ignorant of Protestantism's aims and its followers' immorality, have the gall to declare openly that it is more in tune with our times and social aspirations. From 1862, all kinds of riff raff, supported by the predominant spirit of revolutionism and secret societies, have devastated our lovely country, like a swarm of starving locusts. Their false teachings are in every town and now they have spread to villages, seeking followers from impressionable Catholic folk. I believe it is timely to alert Italians to Protestantism's false doctrines and immorality, by giving them a brief account of its lauded beliefs and moral precepts from writings and teachings of its founders and leaders.

Protestantism has no basic principles. It had none when it began, none as it developed and it will have none in the future. Its slogan and its very name distinguish it from other religions, affirming a total denial of any fundamental principles of belief. Protestantism began by protesting and it will always protest against the Catholic Church because it is the one true Church of Jesus Christ. The learned Balmes rightly comments that the Church was and is *unchanging*. That is, neither its faith, traditions, beliefs or moral teachings are subject to change. This is incontestable. The Catholic Church has not changed for nineteen centuries, from its birth up till the present. This provides 'indisputable proof that the Church alone possesses the truth, because *only truth is unchanging, being undivided.*'[23]

By upholding the principle of individual freedom to interpret the Church's teachings and Scripture, Protestantism undermines religious belief. According to this principle, anyone can believe what he likes. Consequently people are unwilling to be guided in their faith, and suit themselves. In Protestantism, 'Nothing is firm and clear. You cannot find the principles on which it is based. Its teachings are unclear and they shift at whim in every direction.'[24] Balmes continues, 'Its aims are vague and its intentions fickle. It examines every angle without making clear decisions. It follows new directions with no certainty, gaining nothing except getting more entangled in its ever more intricate labyrinths.'

At the bottom of their revolt against Christ's true Church, the real motivation of Luther, Calvin, Henry VIII, Elizabeth and her consorts, the fathers and founders of Protestantism, was *greed* and *unbridled lust*. To enrich themselves at the expense of churches, monasteries and nobles, these leaders of impiety found in the Protestantism they invented the perfect means to achieve their goal. They protested against Catholic faith and dogmas and declared them invalid. Then they confiscated churches' and monasteries' wealth and of those who did not accept their godless reforms. Similarly, property and valuables which for centuries had been used for religious worship and priests' stipends, as well as for the poor, orphans and hospitals, were by act of proscription handed over to Protestant leaders and their henchmen, to fatten their purses. Cobbett, although a Protestant himself, comments, 'Anyone can see, and particularly we English, that *a desire to get rich* was the real reason for the supposed Reformation.'[25] In his correspondence, Cobbett also states, 'It must be acknowledged that fanaticism, treachery, hypocrisy and pillage shared in despoiling our country.'[26]

Henry VIII, some years before his licentious love affair with Anne Boleyn, wrote to the princes of Saxony in 1525 about Luther's Reformation, 'There has never been such a subversive and evil faction seeking to do away with religion, abolish laws, undermine responsible behaviour, and subvert good government, as Luther's. It profanes the sacred and contaminates the profane.'[27]

It has already been mentioned that the Reformation's real aim, besides stealing property, was to indulge in fornication. Evidence of this can be found in their leader's and rabid followers' statements. It is well known that Martin Luther discarded his religious habit so that he could lead a dissolute life, indulging in every kind of filth. After often offering his partner to various followers, he eventually married her in a public ceremony. This is the man who became father and founder of Protestantism. Luther, too, allowed the Landgrave of Hesse to have two wives at the same time. When Henry VIII wanted to marry Anne Boleyn, the great Reformer suggested to him, as well, to have two wives.[28]

Calvin, the other major Reformer, was no better than Luther and fellow Protestants. There is evidence that he was often censured for his free-thinking and his loose-living. In the end, he was condemned for his excesses, as he gave full rein to lust.[29] Calvin, in his commentary on St Peter's Second Epistle justifies the Reformation in this way:

'Out of ten *Saints* you would be lucky to find even one who had become a *member* other than to be able to give full rein to gluttony and lust.'[30]

Baldwin, a Protestant jurist, wrote to his notorious confrere, Beza, 'Anyone passing by your dining room would be overwhelmed by the stench from your nightly carousing.'[31] And Froment, a Reformation leader in Geneva, mentions what new disciples were really looking for. 'Women are their gospel. As long as there is a good supply of stolen chalices and reliquaries, they and their wives have a merry time. When they have satisfied their desires, they clear off, leaving wife and children destitute, at the mercy of the poorhouse. Others take whores as their partners, pretending they are their wives. They, like the others, use them and then abandon them, stealing away from town.'[32]

I have already referred to the Protestant MP, William Cobbett. In a letter regarding the English Reformation he harshly criticises Protestantism, rightly commenting: 'I have to say that a genuine inquiry would convince my readers that these changes (reform) instead of being for the *better* have been for the *worse*. What has been called the Reformation was nothing more than the result of greed, hypocrisy and foul treachery, ensuing pillage and destruction. An enormous amount of English and Irish blood was shed in creating an edifice of filth and arrogance. The results, which still afflict us, are abject misery, endemic poverty, hatred and continuous conflict.'[33]

It would be better to pass over Queen Elizabeth's glorious achievements on behalf of Christianity. She chose not to marry so that she could freely indulge in clandestine love affairs. She confiscated the Church's goods, and the wealth of monasteries, hospitals, religious orders and Catholics for herself and her courtiers. Her persecution of subjects was like the bloody swathe cut by Turkish scimitars.

It has been shown that Protestantism arose from unbridled lust. It was fed by looting churches, convents and hospitals, and nourished by the innocent blood of people killed for refusing to accept it. For these reasons, Protestantism could not, cannot and never will be able to claim to be godly and a means to salvation. He who is the source of all justice and love would not sanction such outrages.

Thus Protestantism which by its very nature promotes indifference to religion and loss of faith, as well as the most abominable vices contrary to scripture and the natural law, cannot teach true Christian living to simple savages because it does not exemplify it itself. Protestantism can really only provide the false glitter of a material, pagan civilisation, solely intent on satisfying carnal appetites, greed and worldly pleasures.

But why bother discussing this further? You need only look at history to see what happened. Sneering and sarcasm will not affect it. Truth is unshakeable, like reefs swept by the sea, plainer to passing generations. Anyone who has studied the reformers' lives and the history of Protestantism clearly knows that Protestantism was founded simply to give licence to its founders' and disciples' false pride, adultery, lust, brutality and wickedness.

Protestantism founders, to gain an outlet for their perverse passions, in effect did away with the last *six commandments*. It is no wonder that their most loyal disciples, Protestant ministers and missionaries, followed their example in New Zealand and elsewhere. It is some small mercy that as missionaries they did not copy their forebears' feats and example to the letter.

10. Rev. Kendall, however, an Anglican missionary who accompanied Rev. Samuel Marsden to New Zealand in 1814, did follow the Reformation founders' example. He was not satisfied with his own share of 13,000 acres (6170 hectares) which he and four fellow missionaries bought from natives for forty-eight axes. He believed he could do better than that. Father Ottavio Barsanti writes, 'Being *the first superintendent* of *Protestant* missions in New Zealand, he promised the *Rangatira* (paramount chiefs) to live with them if they gave him a vast amount of land. The ingenuous Maori were not to know that Anglican missionaries were professional swindlers and did as he asked',[34] giving him 40,000 acres (19,000 hectares) of Hokianga land.

When Rev. Kendall obtained the land, instead of going to live in the Hokianga as he had promised the Maori, he left for England in 1822. When he arrived, he sold his property rights for merchandise to Baron de Thierry, a friend who was training as a Protestant minister. Since he had betrayed the natives, Kendall realised that New Zealand was no place for his apostolic zeal. He decided that it would be more opportune to transfer the benefits of his breeding and piety to another country. 'Calling himself an English chaplain, he went to Valparaiso in South America, and set himself up as a shopkeeper. His business did not flourish and he moved on to New South Wales, Australia, where he farmed in a settlement called Kiama. Finally, he was drowned in a ship sailing to Sydney with a cargo of cedar.'[35]* His confreres also tried to make their fortune and in other ways discredited the Gospel that they were meant to preach to these unenlightened people, as will be shown.

---

*Translator's note: Though sourced from Lang, Vaggioli's account of Kendall's death is slightly different: '... and he was at last drowned in a small coastal vessel bound with a load of cedar from his farm in Sydney.' (Lang, p. 105).

CHAPTER THREE

New Zealand in the Grips of Carnage and Mayhem From 1821 to 1830

SUMMARY. – 1. Chief Hongi in England. – 2. His atrocities. – 3. His final campaign and death. – 4. Arms and ammunition trade. – 5. Trade in Maori heads. – 6. Attempted New Zealand colonisation. – 7. European theft and exploitation of Maori tribes. – 8. French scientific expeditions.

The Maori, for all their ferocity, were also ingenuous and impressionable. One of the worst disasters to happen to them was to have as their first *models* of Christian civilisation sealers, whalers and other exploiters. They gave completely the opposite example. They came to New Zealand to get rich and do whatever they liked. They were mostly men who had escaped the gallows or were lifers on the run. However, an even worse misfortune to afflict Maori was to harbour as their first *teachers of Christian religion and civilisation* men devoid of both. They were not genuine teachers because they were either untrained or taught false doctrine. Also, Maori could see from their lifestyle and behaviour that they did not practise what they preached. They did not act in a civilised way because they considered only themselves, their own well-being, desires, interests and how they could set themselves up by exploiting Maori.

Thus, for many years, New Zealand history is nothing but a series of disasters, fuelled by a completely false impression of civilisation given to Maori, and fed by Europeans' greed for and pursuit of wealth, as exemplified by supposedly civilised Englishmen. Consequently, there can be no doubt that these were the main causes for the almost complete annihilation of a people who had every possibility of being educated and settled if only they actually had preachers who taught them and moulded them according to the true principles of Christianity.

1. An important man now appeared on the New Zealand scene. He was small, broad-browed with a martial bearing and darting, piercing eyes. Ambition, sheer physical strength and a spirit of revenge were the distinguishing features of his personality. He was so tenacious and courageous in his evil designs that he was never deterred by failure. Nor would he let any obstacles stand in his way.[1] *Hongi Hika*, like an ill-starred meteor, blazed a trail of destruction across the whole land.

He was a Ngapuhi chief, born about 1773 in the Bay of Islands. As a youth he distinguished himself in combat. Even as a child he had much influence over his peers, because he was a paramount chief's son, and he became even more powerful through his military prowess. Celebrated among his people for his exploits, he was made chief of seventeen villages. He then decided to travel. In 1814, accompanied by his friend Ruatara, another chief, he went to Sydney and stayed with Rev. Marsden, an Anglican minister.

After a few months in Sydney, Hongi and his friend returned home with Marsden and three other missionaries to found the first Protestant mission, as mentioned previously. Hongi promised to place the missionaries under his protection. Two months later, Marsden and Hongi went back to Australia. Shortly afterwards, Hongi returned home, solemnly declaring that he would be protector and patron of the Anglican mission. It also seems that about this time he became a Protestant, more from anticipated material interest than for any other reason. But, as Dr Thomson rightly notes, his roles of protector, patron and Christian did not prevent him from plunging into war and ruthlessly attacking tribes in the Bay of Plenty, Rotorua, Wangaroa and Hokianga.[2]

From the end of 1815, Protestant missionaries sent some natives to England to show devout British Protestants their wondrous works of conversion and thus obtain generous donations for themselves and their missions. They also hoped to persuade the Maori to become Protestants, bedazzled by England's wealth, prosperity and greatness, which they witnessed for themselves.

In 1819 Hongi found himself bored and restless, having defeated all his immediate enemies. Protestant missionaries, and Superintendent Kendall in particular, urged him to visit England. Hongi took their advice and told his people that he intended to go and see King George IV and bring back with him missionaries, carpenters, smiths, labourers and twenty soldiers to help him to run his territory.

When everything was ready, at the beginning of 1820 Hongi and a relative, Waikato, a young chief, together with the New Zealand Anglican mission superintendent mentioned earlier, set sail for Great Britain. They arrived safely in London. Kendall began to spread the news, as Mr Wakefield, a fellow Protestant mentions, that Hongi '*was a fine, devout Protestant.*'[3] Mr Hursthouse, another Protestant adds, 'This prized convert, Hongi, whom *brother* Kendall took all over the place, was nothing but a wolf in sheep's clothing. His behaviour, his finely tattooed face and *conversion* made him a sensation in hundreds of London's leading salons where he was lionised.'[4] Everywhere in London he was treated as a member of the aristocracy and 'his bearing', Rev. Taylor comments, 'was very dignified. When he was treated as a great man, he assumed the manner of a prince.'[5]

'During his sojourn in England,' adds Dr. Thomson, 'he charmed the religious world by acting the part of a devout Christian.'[6] King George IV gave him a private audience. He also showed him around the palace armouries, gave him a complete set of armour, several double-barrelled shot-guns and many other valuable gifts. Many other admirers also gave him similar generous gifts of arms, gunpowder and many sets of cutlery and farm tools. Dr Lee, a Cambridge University linguist, met with Hongi several times to help him write a Maori dictionary and grammar.

When Hongi was in England there was much talk of King George IV's proceedings against his consort, the Queen. The extent of mud-slinging and abuse in the ensuing public debate made it quite clear that if the Queen was a dissolute whore, her husband the King was no better. Chief Hongi, however, was meant to believe that the King was blameless, while his wife was nothing but a slut. Devout Protestants whose company he kept, as Dr Thomson mentions, reinforced their view with biblical quotations, saying to Hongi, '*A hated woman, when she is married, is a thing the earth cannot bear*,' and that '*a bad wife is as rottenness to his bones.*' But the savage was bewildered how a powerful man like King George IV could not control his wife without the assistance of the lords of the realm, while he himself managed his four* wives with no difficulty whatsoever.[7] A fine Protestant indeed with four wives! Luther, Henry VIII and the other founders of Protestantism would have been proud of him.

After living in England for a few months, Hongi and Waikato, his cousin, decided to return home. The British government gave them free passage to Sydney (Australia) on board an English naval vessel. When they reached the capital of New South Wales they stayed with their friend, Rev. Marsden, founder of the New Zealand Anglican mission. There they met Hinaki, a Thames chief and his friend, another chief.

Hardly had Hongi arrived than a native told him that while he was away from home a brother-in-law of his had been killed in a fight with one of Hinaki's men at Thames. When he heard this, Hongi immediately bought guns and ammunition. He sold all the King's and nobles' gifts and presents except the arms and gunpowder. With the proceeds he bought three hundred muskets and a good supply of gunpowder.[8]

Shortly afterwards, Hongi told Hinaki that he had learnt that his brother-in-law had been killed by a member of Hinaki's tribe. Poking out his tongue and grimacing wildly, he cried in a mocking and scornful voice, 'Make haste home, Hinaki, put your pa in a state of defence, for as soon as I can assemble my people I shall fight.' Hinaki tried to placate Hongi, but he would not listen to him. Meanwhile, Hongi and Hinaki ate together and slept under the same roof at Mr Marsden's. They made their return journey in the same ship without anyone being aware of Hongi's dark intention to exact ferocious revenge and exterminate Hinaki and his tribe.[9]

*Translator's note: 'Five wives', not 'four', according to Thomson.

Hinaki, realising that Hongi meant what he said, gave up hope of making peace with him. As soon as he returned home, he gathered his forces to prepare a defence against his implacable foe. Unfortunately, at this time no Maori tribes had firearms of any kind, fighting being in the traditional way with spears, clubs and stone adzes. Hongi and his warriors were the exception, having more than 300 muskets and powder to match.

2. In the meantime, towards the end of 1821, Hongi lost no time in calling together his warriors. Launching his war canoes, he and 3000 warriors entered the Hauraki Gulf. He reached the river Thames and drew up his forces in front of Hinaki's pa. Although he was related by marriage to the tribe he was about to attack, his keen desire to test out the efficiency of the deadly gifts he received in England and the arms he purchased in Sydney prevailed over any other consideration.[10]

Fierce fighting ensued between Hongi's and Hinaki's men. Hinaki, a fine-looking and very courageous man, was fighting a much better armed and larger force than his own. But the outcome remained undecided for a long time. Finally Hinaki, hit by four balls, fell.

Seeing this happen, Hongi rushed over to him and grabbing the clasp-knife given to him by the King of England, he gouged out an eye and gulped it down. He then stabbed him in the neck, and drank his warm blood, as it gushed forth from the dying man.

General slaughter followed. About one thousand members of the defeated tribe were killed. Most of the remainder were made slaves. Very few managed to escape into the bush. Three hundred of the slain were butchered and eaten by the victors on the battleground.[11] The massacre was so devastating that the area has remained uninhabited up to the present. These lands are now the Anglican Bishop of Auckland's property.[12]

Hongi returned home when the ferocious campaign was over. The canoes were full of prisoners and several slain enemy heads were stuck as victory trophies on the prows and sterns. Hongi had twenty prisoners intended as slaves in his own canoe. His daughter, however, who had lost her husband in the fighting, ran to the shore, pulling out her hair. Immediately her father's canoe grounded, she demanded *utu* (blood revenge) for her husband's death. Seizing the sword given to her father by King George IV, she leapt into his canoe and ordered the prisoners one after the other to put their necks on the side-board of the canoe. In the presence of the Protestant catechist, she beheaded the wretches with her own hands. Although they knew they were going to be killed they did not utter a word. Twenty-one more victims were killed, cooked and eaten. But she was like a thing possessed. She still believed that her husband's spirit had not been requited by the brutal killings. She grabbed a gun and went into the nearby bush and tried to blow out her brains, but she only shot herself in the arm. In her desperation to accompany her husband to Reinga (the next world) she made a rope out of flax and hanged herself from a tree.[13]

Immediately after this expedition, Hongi got ready for another raid. He assembled one thousand warriors and told *Thomas Walker Nene*, a Protestant Maori, his second-in-command and finest warrior, to conscript another 2000 men and to follow him. Hongi took to sea again to do battle with tribes at Mercury Bay and south of the Coromandel peninsula. Hongi had more than 300 muskets while his enemies had none. His victory was complete as he destroyed everything in his path and killed almost everyone in a once populous area.[14]

They say that when a tiger has tasted human blood it becomes even more bloodthirsty. The same can be said of Hongi. His massacres led him to commit even worse excesses. After devastating Mercury Bay he returned home briefly to gather fresh reinforcements. He then sailed off to attack the tribes that inhabited the Kaipara harbour on the west coast. Here, too, he defeated his enemies and wreaked terrible slaughter.[15]

In 1822, the following year, Hongi and a thousand warriors fought again in Thames against the *Ngatimaru* tribe. He landed opposite their *pa* at Totara on the left estuary of the river. Because the *pa* was so well fortified, Hongi and his men did not dare assault it, certain as they were to fail and suffer total defeat. To succeed, Hongi resorted to a cruel and cowardly trick, pretending to be a friend and telling the inhabitants that he and his men had come to pay them a friendly visit. The inhabitants of the *pa* did not suspect treachery and warmly and courteously welcomed Hongi and his men into the *pa* and prepared a lavish feast for them. Poor people! Their credulity led to their utter downfall! That night, while the host tribe slept peacefully, at a pre-arranged signal from Hongi his gang of murderers fell on the defenceless people, slaughtering them. Rev. Taylor mentions that about one thousand people died, but according to Dr Thomson only 500 men, women and children were killed, 300 of whom were cooked and eaten on the battlefield. Many prisoners were taken in the general flight.[16]

After this foul deed, Hongi returned home in triumph, but not to rest on his laurels. He was already planning another difficult campaign. A powerful tribe was entrenched on a small island in the middle of Lake *Rotorua*, about eighty kilometres inland from the Bay of Plenty. Chief Hongi decided to attack their pa and conquer them. But how was he to get the canoes needed across the lake to attack their defences? Hongi's extremely clever mind was not in the least deterred by a seemingly impossible task. He had the determination, and he would succeed.

So, at the beginning of 1823, without any further delay, he set off with all the canoes he could get hold of and with a very strong force he journeyed down to the Bay of Plenty. By way of the lake's tributaries the fleet neared

Rotorua. Unable to get any closer by water, he ordered his men to make a track which he himself stepped out through the forest. They dragged large tree trunks along it to the lake where they made war canoes capable of carrying sixty men each. This was a formidable task, involving incredible energy, difficulty and danger, but nevertheless it was achieved. Finally, when all the canoes were ready at the lakeside, he launched them. His warriors got on board and immediately paddled to attack what was up to then believed to be an impregnable pa. Again, with guns at his disposal, he was victorious. The pa's defenders were slaughtered and any survivors were enslaved.[17]

He returned with his canoes and prisoners by the same track he made getting to Rotorua. After a triumphal homecoming, Hongi soon undertook another bloody expedition. By spring, in September 1824, he was ready to attack two adjacent *pa* in the Hauraki Gulf area, now the settlement of Panmure, near Auckland. He took them and killed all who fell into his hands. But several inhabitants managed to escape and sought refuge among allies at *Matakitaki*, a well-known pa on the banks of the Waipa river on the west coast, about eighty kilometres from where the terrible rout occurred.[18]

The mere sight of the miserable fugitives, men, women and children, naked, haggard, starving, with no possessions, stumbling through mangroves, bush and swamps would have moved the most insensitive and coldest heart to pity. But not the merciless conqueror. On the contrary, he became angrier and even more aggressive. In his mad fury he determined to sail to Matakitaki and wipe them out. To get there would involve a 900-kilometre voyage travelling around the island by canoe. Hongi thought of a quicker way, namely to drag his canoes across the Auckland isthmus, adopting the same method he used the previous year.

Once he decided on his plan, Hongi got started. He travelled as far along the estuary as he could and then dragged the canoes the rest of the way across the isthmus. He refloated them on the Manukau Harbour, on the west coast. It took several months to carry this out and by the time he put his canoes back in the water it was February 1825. Immediately, he and his men left the harbour and sailed south-west, entering the Waikato river and then the Waipa. As he approached, the terrified Maori fled into the bush or retreated into their *pa*.

Matakitaki *pa* was built on a cone-shaped hill with sheer cliffs. Its base was surrounded by a wide, deep, obstructive trench. When they heard that the enemy were near, although they were terrified of Hongi, the people immediately prepared to defend themselves. But they hadn't a chance because they had no guns. As soon as Hongi reached the trench he ordered an attack. After a brief, desultory resistance, Hongi took the *pa*. As he entered through one way, men, women and children fled in confusion through another. In their mad panic to escape from the assailant's bloodthirsty clutches, they crowded and jostled together on the narrow hill-top and were forced off it, falling down the cliff into the trench below. It became full of bodies. More than a thousand people are believed to have perished. According to Dr Thomson, of the 4000 Maori at Matakitaki, 1400 were killed, others were taken prisoner and the rest escaped into the bush.[19]

During this time chief *Rauparaha*, who was to become famous in colonial history, was living with his tribe at Kawhia, about 40 kilometres from Matakitaki. Alarmed by Hongi's quick successes, he felt unsafe and he decided to move on. He and his people took whatever they could carry and travelled south down the coast looking for a new home. They settled at the bottom of the island, along Cook Strait, not far from Wellington, as it is now called.

Hongi's tigerish thirst for blood was still not satisfied. At the scene of slaughter by the Waipa river, he and his loyal lieutenant *Nene*, a devout Maori Protestant, christened *Thomas Walker Nene*, plotted fresh conquests. Returning to the mouth of the Waikato they turned south-west, voyaging down the coast. They attacked any *pa* or Maori village they came across and slaughtered the inhabitants. They continued on the rampage for several months, decimating peaceful tribes and sacking their settlements. Their raids took them as far as Wanganui, about 300 kilometres south. Hongi killed 1500 people and enslaved many more in the fighting. Dr Thomson notes that, 'After this major campaign Hongi returned home with a crowd of slaves. The women, who had remained at home, rushed out to meet the warriors, and those who had relatives slain during the expedition gave vent to their passions by murdering unarmed and unresisting slaves.'[20]

Hongi went on the warpath every year and he remained undefeated. His name caused terror wherever he went. He said that, like the King of England who was sole ruler of his country, he should be king of his own country.[21]

The powerful Ngatiwhatua tribe, some 20,000 strong, lived in the Auckland region. Hongi wanted them either subjugated or exterminated. He was determined to do this and, at the end of 1825, as soon as he returned home from the campaign just mentioned, he prepared to attack them. Fighting continued throughout the following years. Hongi launched several attacks on the defenders, often having to resort to hand-to-hand combat. Only his superiority in arms let him win. The noble Ngatiwhatua, after nearly three years of continual fighting, had to give in. Hunger, thirst, exposure, fire and especially Hongi's muskets killed many. A lot were taken prisoner and others fled into the bush. By 1860 there were little more than 400 remaining Ngatiwhatua survivors in the Auckland area.[22]

Hongi's favourite son was killed in 1826 in one of the fiercest battles in the Kaipara. In revenge, the savage cannibal plucked out the eyes of many wounded enemies lying on the battlefield and gulped them down. He was wearing the coat of mail and helmet the King of England gave him as protection against balls, since his enemy now had muskets, too.[23]

Firearms were needed to stop Hongi's slaughter and convince him of the futility of trying to subjugate the whole country. Maori soon realised this and badgered Europeans for guns. They began to get them and every year they collected more. The introduction of muskets into New Zealand soon brought about Hongi's demise.

3. Meanwhile, at the beginning of January 1827, Hongi declared war on an old enemy, Tara's tribe who lived at Wangaroa, near the Bay of Islands. Hongi's pretext for attacking them was that in 1809 they massacred and ate the *Boyd*'s crew. The real reason was to bring them under his control. Before leaving for Wangaroa, he invoked customary rituals to divine the outcome of his expedition. When the *tohunga* (priest) examined the bird's entrails he said that the omens were not auspicious and he predicted disaster. Hongi was not the sort of person to be put off by this[24] and he invaded the enemy territory. On 10 January 1827 he reached Wangaroa. First he sacked and torched the Methodist or Wesleyan mission founded by Rev. Lee and other missionaries in 1822. They barely managed to escape his evil clutches. They were so terrified that they felt equally unsafe when they reached the Bay of Islands, and immediately set sail with their wives and children for Sydney, Australia.[25]

'Thus,' concludes Wakefield, a Protestant, 'the fine, devout Christian showed himself for what he was, ambitious and bloodthirsty, and one of his first acts of devotion was to destroy the Wangaroa Wesleyan mission.'[26] Hongi showed that he was indeed a *fine, devout Anglican,* copying Henry VIII and Elizabeth who destroyed monasteries and Catholic churches to establish the Reformation. In fact, Hongi never laid a finger on any of the many Anglican missions in New Zealand. By destroying the Methodist mission, he was in tune with devout Anglicans, who regarded Methodists as heretics and apostates, to be shunned at all cost, and to be regarded in the same light as all the other 190 Protestant denominations and sects the Refomation has bestowed on the world up to the present. But back to our story.

When Hongi reached Wangaroa, the people dropped everything and fled into the bush. Hongi seized all the enemy canoes and ordered the *pa* to be attacked but it had been abandoned. Realising that Tara and his people had escaped into the bush, he pursued them and caught up with them in the forest between Wangaroa and Hokianga. Fighting began. Hongi won and many men, women and children were killed, but most still managed to escape. A horrible feast was made of the slain. The survivors fled to Mahungamuka. They got ready to face their ferocious enemy with guns now at their disposal to attack him.[27]

Hongi chased the fugitives and attacked them at Hunahuna. He did not assault the *pa*, but began firing from a distance. Straightaway an enemy ball whistled past his ear, making him aware that he was in deadly danger. He also realised that his enemy had efficient guns. He was wearing only the helmet of his suit of armour and he retreated to seek shelter behind a tree. From there he began firing at the enemy. When he shifted out to take aim and shoot at the defenders, a ball struck him. It broke his collar-bone, passed in an oblique direction through his right breast, and came out a little below his shoulder-blade, close to his spine. He suffered this injury towards the end of 1827 and it put an end to his devastating, dastardly career. Although Hongi lived for another year, his wound never healed and he had to abandon any further campaigning. When he breathed, the air escaped through the orifice with a hissing sound, which he made a subject of merriment among his friends.[28]

Three days before his death, ignoring Protestant missionaries' entreaties to prepare himself for death, he ordered his men to continue fighting and wipe out their enemies. The next day he had all his gunpowder brought before him. He looked at it and said to his people, 'You will be safe,' meaning that gunpowder would protect them. Then he summoned his sons. He gave his eldest son the coat of mail given him by the King of England and he distributed among the others all the guns and battleaxes he had. Then in a scornful, haughty voice he exclaimed, 'Who will dare attack my people after my death?' On the third day he had his tribe and allies gather around him and he addressed them: 'Do not worry about where your enemies come from, or how numerous or ferocious they are. Be brave! Then you will properly avenge my death. Be brave!' He continued repeating these words until he died on 6 March 1828, at the age of fifty-five.[29] Thus ended the life of Maoridom's fiercest enemy.

His body was dressed in his finest clothes and then laid out for three days in his hut for all to pay homage. He was in a half-seated position with his hair ornately decorated with feathers. Guns and all kinds of weapons were spread around his body.

Hongi was given an elaborate funeral. Three days were given over to the *pihe* or mourning chant, self-mutilation as a sign of grief, crying and wailing and firing muskets. In the meantime, confederate Hokianga tribes arrived. Forming a long cortege, the savage warrior's body was borne to the cemetery and buried amidst the clamour of the funeral *haka, tangi* or wailing and gunshots.[30]

4. Hongi's campaigns, massacres and string of victories were due almost entirely to the 300 or so guns which his warriors had as weapons from 1821. All Maori realised that having guns and powder was a vital necessity to defend themselves, tribe and family from extermination. They also realised that their traditional weapons and defences could no longer protect them from firearms, or give them any chance of victory.

No matter how strong or courageous they were, since they had no guns or ammunition they were sure to be defeated. They soon discovered that a mob of cowardly looters armed with muskets could beat any number of brave warriors armed only with spears, meres and tomahawks.[31]

Tribes were desperate to have guns and ammunition to defend themselves against their enemy or to attack with any chance of success. Every adult Maori male wanted a gun and considered himself fortunate and happy when he got one. Maori turned to whalers and other European traders visiting New Zealand, begging them to give them guns and ammunition. Europeans sold them at exorbitant prices and they had to pay in cash or goods. Since they had no money, natives traded in flax, pork, preserved meat, potatoes and anything else traders would accept, even land if that was what they wanted.

In London the extreme versatility of flax, as prepared by the Maori, was recognised, and it was eagerly sought on the London market. High prices were paid: about 500 francs a ton (or 1000 kilos). Since Maori were so desperate to have weapons, many Australians saw this as the ideal time to head for New Zealand and do a roaring trade. Not only traders but Anglican missionaries and all kinds of speculators set out, all intent on making a fortune at little cost. Trade begun in 1821 grew steadily until 1840. They brought over rum and other alcohol, obsolete muskets that had been lying forgotten in Sydney and London, magazines, gunpowder, axes, hatchets, knives and other similar goods. In exchange they took land and the kinds of goods mentioned above.[32]

European profiteers and traders were so unscrupulous and greedy that Maori had to give them thousands of hectares and hundreds of tons of flax for a few old guns or a little gunpowder. An English Protestant living assimilated among Maori wrote that, 'Traders gave natives rum, rifles, gunpowder, knives, hatchets and the like, and took as much as they could from them, having no scruples about their bare-faced robbery.' He added that, 'The poor innocent creatures thought that even a tiny piece of iron was priceless.'[33] Another Protestant wrote, 'The Maori would give traders a cargo-load of flax for a few obsolete guns.'[34]

The scurrilous arms trade increased so quickly that the Governor of New South Wales (Australia), who had jurisdiction of the British in New Zealand, feared its consequences for the two races. He tried his best to stop it, but was not successful. He then decided that the government itself should take over trade with the Maori. In 1824 it hired several ships which were sent to New Zealand with cargoes of guns and ammunition.

The government soon realised, however, that it was impossible to stop individuals from trading privately with Maori. It abandoned the project, leaving them free to trade openly.[35] For the next fifteen years New Zealand became the centre of daylight robbery of Maori under the guise of commercial trading.

The need for guns and ammunition brought a marked improvement in European and Maori relations. Maori required Europeans' cooperation to get guns and powder to fight Hongi. They overlooked the ill-treatment and unfair dealing they received from whites in order to get what they wanted. They knew full well that if they did not get on with Europeans they would not get guns, powder, clothes or anything at all. Inland tribes soon made peace with their coastal neighbours so as to have access to European merchant ships and thus get things they were so desperate to have.

The following are official statistics of imports and exports between Sydney and New Zealand from 1826 to 1829, published by the Governor of New South Wales in 1844.

Value of goods sent to New Zealand   Value of goods exported from New Zealand

1826	40,375 francs	1826	750,000 francs
1827	124,150 "	1827	1,575,000 "
1828	146,125 "	1828	3,146,550 "
1829	347,300 "	1829	3,387,150 "

These Sydney and New Zealand import and export figures represent only a portion of trade during this period. Account would also have to be made of the many whalers who had been doing much trading with Maori for some time, preferring New Zealand to other parts of the Pacific.[36]

In 1830 about 49 ships totalling 5,888 tons left Sydney for New Zealand and 36 large vessels loaded with flax sailed from New Zealand to Sydney.[37]

'In 1834,' Dr Thomson comments, 'a few muskets purchased from the natives a small shipload of flax; a blanket, the best pig in the country; and a fig of tobacco, 30 kilos* of potatoes. But after this date they began to know the commercial value of goods. Previous to the year1840, the munitions of war were solely in demand. After this period a market arose for tobacco, blankets, pipes, shirts, cooking-pots, trousers, gowns, cottons, hoes and spades.'[38]

5. Alongside steady trade in arms and ammunition, another nefarious trade developed, equally profitable for traders. I refer to trade in preserved Maori heads.

From 1820 Maori heads were available in England. The finely tattooed heads were so perfectly preserved that European scientists were very keen to have more for English and European museums. Museum directors paid handsomely for them. London became the centre for trade, naturally making handsome profits. They arranged for Sydney traders and whalers to buy them and they also set the price for heads according to their quality, state of preservation and tattoo design. This explains the origin of this abominable trade and why so many innocent natives were killed.

When traders bought flax they also endeavoured to get preserved Maori heads, paying a relatively high price for them, namely, a gun a head. Thus according to commercial principles, the availability of Maori heads increased

*Translator's note: The weight was 'sixty pounds' in Thomson's account.

markedly with the increase in demand from Europe.

'In the old days, a chief's head was preserved and venerated, but when Maori realised that they could have a gun a head, they began to collect enemy heads to sell to Europeans, killing slaves for their supply.'[39] Trade was fed by greed because heads were sold on to London merchants at a thousand per cent profit, and they in turn sold them to museums. Poor savages who had no idea of the trafficking that went on, traded them for guns and powder. Seeing the profits to be made, they eagerly set about preserving heads of fellow Maori who fell into their hands.

Traders, whalers, Anglican missionaries and other European profiteers were so keen to trade that demand could not be satisfied. Thus many Maori, especially those with distinctively tattooed heads, were ruthlessly killed by fellow Maori for their heads. Maori were driven to such unprecedented barbarity, without parallel among the wildest savages, by supposedly civilised Europeans.

'It is an indisputable fact,' writes Mr Fox Bourne, 'that a European arranged and paid in advance for a Maori to get the head of a Maori who was still alive when he saw him. He treacherously killed the poor native and a few days later he handed over the preserved head as agreed.'[40]

Rev. Taylor, an Anglican missionary, wrote that, 'So great was the demand for human heads, that many a murderous attack has been made solely to obtain heads for the market; and those who were the most finely tattooed were chiefly sought for. How many of the sins of these savage islanders have been participated in by their European visitors! Few are aware to what extent this abominable trade has been carried.'[41]

Many Maori were shrewder than their fellows, however, and realised the evil intentions of the traders in human flesh. They did exactly to them what they were meant to do to other natives. 'I have been told,' writes Taylor, 'that quite often the preserved heads were Europeans, sometimes the same people's who came to buy heads for the European market,[42] *or to be exact, the London market*.'* It was a terrible but fitting punishment for wretches who were a thousand times crueller than any wild savage.

It is impossible to say how far the infamous trade in Maori heads would have gone if in 1831 the following case had not been made public, revealing how disgusting, inhumane and illicit it was.

In 1830 when some Bay of Islands tribes were defeated with great losses by Tauranga tribes in the Bay of Plenty, the victors preserved the heads of the slain[#] and then sold them to the captain of *The Prince of Denmark*, bound for

---

*Translator's note: Translator's italics. The words in italics are an addition to Taylor's text, where Vaggioli is obviously emphasising British responsibility for the trade.

[#] The Maori method of preserving heads is described in vol. I of this *History*, part II. ch. V, page 287 and following.

Sydney. The ship called in at the Bay of Islands and many natives went on board to trade. The master of the ship in a state of tipsy jollity brought up a sack containing twelve heads, and rolled them on the deck. Some of the New Zealanders on board recognised their fathers' heads, others those of their brothers and friends. Appalling weeping and lamentations rent the air and the natives fled precipitously from the ship. The master, seeing his dangerous position, put to sea before the news of his *ghastly** cargo spread on shore.[43]

When news of the incident reached Mr Darling, Governor of New South Wales, he issued a decree banning the trade. He ordered anyone who had brought heads from the ship to hand them over immediately so that they could be returned to victims' relatives. He warned of the dire consequences for trafficking and ordered a thousand francs fine and publication of their name for anyone carrying out the loathsome trade.[44]

His prohibition and the public outcry that followed almost completely put a stop to the trade. In fact, an American expedition under the command of Commodore Wilkes visiting New Zealand in 1840 tried repeatedly to obtain Maori heads. Eventually they got two from the steward of an Anglican missionary brig in the Bay of Islands: 'The very last place,' said the commodore, that he could have 'expected to find such articles.'[45]

6. Trade in gunpowder, guns, preserved heads and other items mentioned above brought New Zealand to England's attention as a suitable place for British colonisation. There were many encouraging reasons for this. Vast amounts of land could be obtained from the Maori for practically nothing, thereby providing an opportunity to become very wealthy without effort. Land could be resold at tremendous profit. A handsome two hundred per cent profit could be made by trading European goods for New Zealand products. The climate, compared to fog-bound Albion, seemed to be always temperate. The country's natural resources promised enormous trade possibilities. And finally, freedom could be enjoyed in a country unfettered by restrictive laws. These were the factors which enticed people to hasten there. Many articles on the subject were published in London magazines.

All these material benefits had some effect on potential British colonists and in 1825 various schemes were proposed for colonising New Zealand but the little enthusiam that there was for colonisation at the time and an overriding terror of Maori cannibalism nearly killed the project. Nevertheless, that year, after a number of attempts, distinguished members of London society, including Lord Durham, formed a company to colonise the country. A ship was fitted out and in 1826 sixty colonists embarked and reached New Zealand at the end of the year.

*Translator's note: Translator's italics as 'ghastly' is an addition by Vaggioli.

The site chosen for a colony was near the mouth of the Hokianga, on the west coast of the upper North Island. Captain Herd, the company's agent, obtained a large amount* of land, since found to be only one square mile, or two and a half square kilometres, and two islands in the Hauraki Gulf near Auckland. Unfortunately, when the colonists landed, local natives were at war with Bay of Islands tribes. The newly arrived colonists were so terrified by war dances and alarming news of fierce fighting nearby that, after only a brief stop, nearly all of them quit the country for other more tranquil, hospitable shores. The ill-fated company lost half a million francs and was bankrupted.[46]

7. In Vol. I of this *History* comment was made on the importance to Maori of having communal ownership of land. For them women and land were enduring treasures. Women provided tribes with offspring to replace those who died. Land enabled tribes to survive. For centuries every tribe had its own territory to grow and harvest produce. Uncultivated land was used for snaring birds and gathering fern roots, and coastal areas were reserved for fishing, to feed the tribe. To deprive Maori of their uncultivated lands was therefore to take a vital means of support from them.

In the past, Dr Thomson writes, pieces of land were traded but right of ownership was not given up. Land exchanged in this way could not be given or traded with other tribes without the consent of the original tribal owners. The wisest of them had never before imagined that white men would value an article thus restricted, and which they could not take with them on leaving the country; and for several years after *the first purchases made by Anglican missionaries*[#] the natives ... did not believe they were relinquishing all rights to the soil forever.[47] This misunderstanding and unbridled greed in Anglican missionaries, traders, profiteers, cheats and swindlers as they got hold of vast amounts of land caused huge disputes, wrangling and strife between the races.

Between 1815 and 1825 purchases of land were made almost exclusively by Anglican missionaries. Trade in guns and ammunition also brought in many Australian traders, whalers and residents. From 1825 to 1829 between them they bought almost a million acres (470,000 hectares). In Kaitaka (Bay of Islands) and the Hokianga alone between 1825 and 1835 20,000 acres (9500 hectares) were *purchased*. Of this land, Thomson notes, 'Missionaries bought 17,000 acres (7200 hectares), or twenty-one square miles.'[48] The fact is that from 1815 to 1830, one million six hundred and sixteen thousand acres (767,600 hectares) were obtained or bought from the Maori, without including islands,

---

*Translator's note: Thomson's original version has Captain Herd purchasing 'a quantity of land' translated by Vaggioli as 'a large quantity' ('una gran quantita').
#The translator's italics represent Vaggioli's addition to Thomson's text. He simply mentions 'this period'.

and 40,000 acres obtained by the notorious Kendall.[49]

When it was widely known that New Zealand would eventually become a British colony, theft of Maori land become endemic. Land to Europeans there was like gold to the first Spaniards in Mexico. The oft-quoted Dr Thomson comments that, 'Greed for land gave rise to *land-sharks*, a breed of men who bought land from natives, exploiting their ignorance and ingenuity regarding its true value. Not only men whose sole purpose in life was to make money indulged in thefts, but included among them were Anglican missionaries, Mr Wentworth, an eminent Sydney lawyer, and Mr James Busby, the Government's Resident.'[50]

Statistics show that, from 1830 until the end of 1839, people acquired 12,360,000 acres. If the New Zealand Company's purchase claim of 20 million acres in 1839 were added to this figure, the combined total acquired in about ten years would be 32,360,000 acres (15,266,000 hectares). In 1840 alone it was boasted that a further 20,000,000 acres, or 9,500,000 hectares of Maori land were bought. Land grabbing by Europeans reached such a fever pitch that by the time Captain Hobson, the first Governor, arrived in 1840, purchase claims had risen to 45,976,000 acres, or 21,838,000 hectares, not including Stewart Island at the bottom of New Zealand, which was 1800 square miles, and other smaller islands. So already, half the country[51] or nearly 72 thousand square miles had been bought. There is no other record in history of such an outrageous theft of other peoples' land by Europeans.

Byirne* writes, 'From the outset these purchases were made for next to nothing: seeds, a gun, a little gunpowder, a few blankets, or some musket balls sufficed to buy tracts of land measured in miles by missionaries.'[52] Rev. Lang comments that Shepherd, an Anglican catechist, bought a large tract of land having a frontage from four to five miles on one of the navigable rivers in the Bay of Islands for two check shirts and an iron pot![53] These devout Protestants bought so much land for such trifling items that, according to Dr Lang, 'If the valuable live timber growing on the land so claimed, or possessed, were to be disposed of, it would be worth half a million sterling, or 12,500,000 francs.[54] Rev. Richard Taylor, who went to New Zealand in 1838, mentioned in 1845 that he had bought 50,000 acres, or 23,750 hectares, or more than 80 square miles from natives.[55] And yet Rev. Taylor in his book on New Zealand brags about his great zeal in preaching the Gospel to Maoris and saving their souls!

Rev. William Yate, another Anglican minister, described his confreres' lack of the spirit of poverty and self-denial, but he had the tact to say nothing about himself.[56] His silence, however, did not conceal *his own noble missionary efforts*. His *commendable* deeds are, in fact, *mentioned* in the records of England's

---

*The reference is to J.C. Byrne, author of *Twelve Years Wandering in the British Colonies, from 1835 to 1847*.

House of Commons: 'The House of Commons has been informed that Rev. William Yate forbade Maori to sell pork to whalers not because he disapproved of sailors, but because he wanted to buy Maoris' pork at a penny a pound and then sell it to whalers for five pence a pound.'[57] It also noted that, 'in the past many missionaries [that is, Anglican] indulged in this practice.' *Many missionaries* claimed ownership of pieces of land varying between one hundred and six hundred thousand acres in different parts of New Zealand.[58] Dr Lang, a respected Presbyterian minister, made this pungent, but very accurate observation, 'Protestant ministers in New Zealand were ringleaders of a powerful European conspiracy to rob and strip Maori of their patrimony.'[59]

Father Ottavio Barsanti, a Franciscan friar, rightly observes that 'England sends only idlers, vagrants, criminals, drunkards and cheats to its colonies. This is exactly what happened in New Zealand where the first Englishmen to step ashore were prisoners, fugitives from Australia, deserters and sailors who jumped ship to chase women. They were followed by another breed who called themselves *missionaries,* but, in fact, they were really *cobblers, shopkeepers, street-cleaners and opportunists*. According to Dr Lang, they started their missionary careers with adultery, rape, theft and murder, and once their missions were established they took over and became a law unto themselves as *lords of the manor.*'[60] Poor New Zealanders! Protestantism with its corruption and false values put into Maori hands the very instruments of their destruction. It will dispossess and impoverish them, finally ruining them and driving them to complete annihilation.

8. Between 1820 and 1830 there were two French scientific expeditions to New Zealand. The first arrived in 1824 led by Captain Duperry, commander of the corvette, *Coquille*. This was a botanic expedition. The second expedition took place in 1827 commanded by Captain Dumont D'Urville of the *Astrolabe*. This was a botanic expedition to the South Island and also engaged in mapping topographic features and the coastline. After a few months it sailed on to other parts of the Pacific.

Chapter Four

Inter-tribal Warfare, Unrest and Uneasy Peace From 1830 to 1835

SUMMARY. – 1. Causes of native fighting. – 2. Rauparaha's violent campaigns. – 3. European collusion in Rauparaha's cannibal atrocities. – 4. Fighting engulfs the country. – 5. Whalers. – 6. Pakeha-Maori. – 7. Rumours of French occupation. – 8. The British Resident and his achievements; A Maori flag. – 9. British troops' atrocities against the Maori. – 10. Anglican missionaries' proposal to be trustees of Maori land.

1. The thoughtless, nay stupid introduction of arms and ammunition into New Zealand by Europeans, far from having any benefit as some claimed, was a terrible crime. It caused incredible harm and bloodshed throughout the whole country. Giving Maori guns was like putting razors into babies' hands. With no appreciation of their danger, they would simply use them. And that is what happened to the Maori; having muskets only caused their mutual destruction. Dr Thomson comments, 'That very commerce which led to peace between the New Zealanders and their foreign foes rendered war for some time more frequent among themselves; and at no former period in the country's annals were conflicts so general as they were during the twenty years preceding the establishment of British rule.'[1]

There were significant reasons to explain the discord and ferocious fighting which raged from 1821 to 1841. First, Hongi's example. For seven years he caused slaughter and bloodshed throughout the region, reducing once heavily populated villages to desolation; secondly, the introduction of firearms which European profiteers plied natives with; thirdly, the ambition of several chiefs and, more importantly, revenge, or an eye for an eye, a tooth for a tooth, the erroneous view Maori had of natural justice which guided their behaviour. Divisions between tribes became greater. With every new incident wounds became deeper and fierce fighting broke out involving even remotely related kin. Truces were made but only to give a breathing space for more bitter battles. And peace, or rather the suspension of slaughter, was due not to any enthusiasm for peace-making but because both sides were exhausted.

Tui and Tere, two Bay of Islands chiefs, were among the most vicious exterminators of fellow Maori. Taking the advice of their Anglican missionary teachers, in 1818 they decided to visit England. Before leaving they wrote their friends farewell letters full of scriptural quotations and pious sentiment,[2] dictated no doubt by Kendall and King, their religious instructors. After a long voyage, on their return to New Zealand about 1821, they quickly put their *cherished piety and biblical knowledge* into practice by throwing themselves into ferocious fighting and vile cannibalism against fellow Maori. What strange goings on! During the day these devout Protestants shed innocent blood and gorged themselves on human flesh and in the evening they piously attended missionaries' services and lessons. Missionaries themselves commented on this.[3] It was just as well that their violent careers were short-lived and that they were struck down when they were wreaking most havoc. The country was well rid of two abhorrent creatures, loathed by all.

2. Besides Hongi, however, there was another frequently mentioned terrifying New Zealander, living in the lower part of the North Island. Rauparaha was paramount chief of the Ngatiraukawa tribe who lived on the west coast of the lower North Island, that is, Manawatu, Otaki and environs.

He was born about 1770. While still a child his father fell in battle. His mother just managed to escape with him and hid in the bush. The enemy chief was most upset at not getting hold of the child, and exclaimed, 'If I get that child in my clutches I will make a lovely meal of him to go with my rau paraha [a Maori vegetable]', or as we would say, 'with my salad.' That is how he got the name of 'rau paraha' and he was henceforth called Rauparaha in memory of his fortunate escape.

As a young man he was so fierce and bold that he struck fear and terror not only in subordinate tribes but also among his own relations. He surrounded himself with warriors like himself, and he was so aggressive that eventually the Ngatimaniapoto tribe with the help of an ally, chief Waharoa and his people, rose up against Rauparaha and his band of cut-throats and drove them out of the area. Rauparaha was forced to move away but he swore that when he had sufficient forces he would take revenge for the insults he suffered.[4]

He set out on his own for Wanganui. From there he sailed to Kawhia. His fame and reputation as a valiant warrior preceded him and he was ceremonially welcomed as chief of a major tribe. He very quickly gained chief Tuwhare and his tribe's friendship and became so influential that he was entrusted with supreme command of the tribe's forces. After Tuwhare's death he was to succeed him. He set about promoting his wish for revenge, persuading them to march against his former subjects on the pretext that they would gain glory in battle. A powerful war party was assembled. Under Tuwhare and Rauparaha's leadership they began their march, intending to take the whole 300-kilometre area from Kawhia to Cook Strait, at the bottom of the North Island.

When the invaders reached the Taranaki tribal area, the terrified defenders retreated to the security of their pa. But after an overwhelming assault they were routed. They had to flee into the bush to escape annihilation. The victors then reached the Wanganui river. The enemy's pa was on the opposite bank.

Rauparaha's men had no canoes and built raupo rafts to cross over and they immediately set about attacking Purua pa which fell to them.

Forty people were killed in the battle. The rest fled. From Wanganui they headed south, entering Rauparaha's former domains. Death and destruction were the order of the day and terrorised inhabitants fled to the safety of remote ranges and thick bush. Continuing their raids they reached Lake Wairarapa where they killed chief Rore and many of his men. They then marched down to Cook Strait, ever victorious in spite of a lack of guns. Once the invaders moved on, fugitives returned to their villages to repair the devastation as best they could.

Shortly after the victorious war party returned home, in 1825 truculent chief Hongi invaded their territory. He and his warriors camped by the Waipa river, not far from Kawhia. Rauparaha, now the tribe's chief, realised that he was too weak to offer the fierce cannibal effective resistance. He considered that he and his men should leave the area, which was vulnerable to Hongi's attacks, and return to live in the territory he had conquered, that is, the lower west coast of the island and the Cook Strait region. He would then be far from Hongi's campaigning, and also he could more readily obtain the guns and ammunition he was so short of.

Rauparaha met with the tribe and it was unanimously agreed to leave Kawhia as soon as possible, to avoid a risky battle with Hongi, and to proceed to Cook Strait. They would then waste no time in getting the arms they needed from whalers and European traders there. After the discussion they gathered their few possessions, put them in their canoes, and set off south in search of a new home.

When they reached Wanganui, Rauparaha chose a strong, well-armed war party and approached Putiki pa on the left bank of the river. In the absence of their husbands and menfolk, the few women left to guard the pa opened the gates showing warmth and respect in their welcome. As a customary sign of their friendship they prepared a lavish feast for their visitors. In recompense for the good women's hospitality and cordial welcome Rauparaha and his rabble fell on them, barbarously killing them. After this atrocity they continued their plundering trail of conquest.[5]

In the meantime, news of Rauparaha's imminent approach quickly spread south, carried by those who managed to escape the marauders. Coastal natives, already familiar with pitiless Rauparaha's tender mercies, were struck with terror at his approach. They did not wait but, gathering their few possessions, they immediately fled into the mountains or thick inland forests. The brigands arrived to find the villages abandoned. They sacked them and continued on their march, meeting no resistance. They pitched camp at Ohau, killing any local natives who had the misfortune to fall into their hands, and making frequent sorties against the Manawatu tribe, once Rauparaha's subjects.

When the Muaupoko tribe learnt of Rauparaha's massacre of their kin, they took up arms to avenge their deaths. A war party of 300 warriors assembled. It secretly moved to attack the cruel cannibal and took him by surprise, causing a rout in which one hundred of his men were killed. Rauparaha himself just managed to escape, leaving his musket, the only firearm he had, in enemy hands. Shortly afterwards, he was defeated again, losing some of his leaders and about a hundred warriors.[6]

The cruel conqueror realised that even with all the firearms and powder he got from Cook Strait whalers in 1824 he could not uphold his reputation as an unbeatable warrior. He needed a much greater quantity of guns and powder and he hastened to obtain them from the same source. He continued to increase his arsenal for several years. When he was well supplied he set out to engage his enemies.

They felt encouraged by reports of earlier victories over Rauparaha and they were unaware that his warriors were now better equipped. Again, they set out to attack him but they were routed with considerable losses. Nearly all Rauparaha's men had muskets, ensuring them complete victory over their enemies. This marked the beginning of a ruthless campaign against Rauparaha's fellow Maori, which lasted nearly fifteen years with hardly any respite, causing mayhem and slaughter everywhere. Rauparaha forced the submission of the Muaupoko and Ngatiapa tribes after nearly annihilating them. He then fought the coastal tribes of the lower North Island, on both coasts and along Cook Strait. Still not satisfied, he crossed Cook Strait, raiding and conquering tribes inhabiting bays, inlets and river mouths at the top of the South Island, wreaking horrible slaughter. Mere mention of his name caused so much terror that no tribe living within a 200-mile radius of the tiger's lair felt safe.[7]

Only the valiant Wanganui tribe stood up to cruel Rauparaha and his villains' aggression. This tribe also had guns. Rauparaha tried several times over a number of years to take the Wanganui pa. He had some success in his first battles, but he was never able to gain complete victory. Eventually he lost his advantage and he continued to be driven back with considerable losses. Finally the courageous tribe decided to settle matters once and for all. They levied all the warriors they could and rushed to the attack, determined to defeat Rauparaha or die. They attacked him so ferociously that they had total victory. Rauparaha himself came within an inch of being captured. After this ignominious defeat, although he continued to rattle his sabre, he had enough sense to leave the powerful, victorious Wanganui tribe alone in case he came off worse.[8]

Rauparaha was a very cunning man, ever intent on increasing his power and prestige. He entered into an agreement with Cook Strait traders to supply tribes with arms and ammunition only through him. He thus obtained a complete and exclusive monopoly on all guns and powder sold throughout the vast area. He became the sole means by which South Island Maori obtained guns and ammunition. Thus, any tribe wanting powder and guns had to come to terms with Rauparaha to have the new means of defence. Only Taranaki and Wanganui tribes would have absolutely nothing to do with the blackguard. Many tribes made peace with Rauparaha and traded foodstuffs, flax and other goods. 'He provided them with rum, tobacco, powder and the guns they needed.'[9] With this monopoly his influence over his native compatriots grew enormously.

Rauparaha's new career as gun dealer did not in the least prevent him from still pursuing for many years his erstwhile ideas of conquest and thirst for cannibalism. Tribes situated at the top of the South Island were especially affected, suffering death, destruction and annihilation.

3. In 1829, chief Pehi, a relative of Rauparaha, returned from England. He had foolishly been given a large quantity of guns and ammunition. He travelled to Banks Peninsula on the east coast of the South Island to trade guns for greenstone. But local natives barbarously killed him. According to Maori justice such a crime could not be absolved except by retribution, that is, by taking the head of the chief, Tamaiharanui. According to *ture maori* (Maori custom) the carrying out of the vendetta had to be done by the victim's closest relatives, namely Rauparaha and Rangihaeata. But how could such a risky thing be done? To kill a tribe's chief, either the whole tribe had to be wiped out or tricked by some ruse. This was practically impossible in a situation of mutual hostility, where everyone would suspect foul play. Fear not. Rauparaha will find Europeans venal enough not to hesitate to stoop to the most vile treachery, slaughter and foul play.

Two British merchant ships were anchored off Kapiti island, west of the bottom of the North Island, where Rauparaha and his tribe lived, to trade as usual in guns, flax and preserved heads.

Rauparaha proposed to Captain *Stewart*, commander of the brigantine *Elizabeth*, to give him a cargo of flax if he would take him and his henchmen to capture chief Tamaiharanui by a ploy and exterminate his tribe. The blackguard of a captain, sensing a handsome profit, jumped at the offer of this disgraceful deal. He took Rauparaha and eighty of his well-armed warriors on board. Among them was the slain Pehi's son. They set sail from Kapiti for Banks Peninsula, on the east coast of the South Island.[10]

When the ship anchored at Akaroa, according to a pre-arranged plan, Rauparaha and his men hid in the hold, so that no natives would see them. Local Maori quickly came on board to find out why the Europeans were there. Captain Stewart brazenly lied, saying that they had come to buy flax. He then asked them where their chief was. Not in the least suspecting any treachery from Europeans, they replied that he was in Wainui valley, a day's journey from Akaroa. Stewart, on hearing this, sent Cawel, the ship's boy, in the ship's lighter to invite the chief to visit the brigantine and inspect its cargo.[11]

Chief Tamaiharanui accepted his invitation. Three days later he came on board accompanied by his wife, daughter and several of his tribe, to a formal welcome by the crew. He then went down to the captain's cabin where Rauparaha and a good many of his cut-throats awaited him. Tamaiharanui immediately realised he had been betrayed but he remained calm and impassive, giving no indication of upset or discomfort. The two enemies stood silently staring at each other for a quarter of an hour. Then Hiko, the murdered Pehi's son, went up to him and pulled up his upper lip, saying, 'These are the teeth which ate my father!' Tamaiharanui was bound hand and foot and his retinue were all cruelly killed except for his wife and daughter. Like him, they were to be kept to grace the victor's triumphant return home.[12]

Rauparaha and his men went ashore the following day and attacked the tribe's defences. In spite of their courageous, desperate resistance, the fort was taken and a great many of its defenders were slaughtered, their bodies dismembered and put in flax baskets. After committing this atrocity, they returned to the ship laden with human flesh. (According to Taylor, they had 500 baskets full.) This was to be food for them on their return voyage of at least four days.[13] Once they were on board, Captain Stewart immediately set sail to return to Kapiti. Who could possibly describe the outrages these animals committed on the ship? Decency forbids a detailed description. Throughout the voyage the beasts gorged themselves on human flesh cooked in the ship's ovens. In between, their chanting and war dances were so violent that the ship shook. Chief Tamaiharanui, his wife and daughter, *Nga Roimata* (or *teardrops*), an exquisitely beautiful sixteen-year-old girl, were unwilling witnesses to the harrowing scenes.[14]

Chief Tamaiharanui was forced to witness disgusting cannibalism but he gave no indication of distress or concern. This would be regarded as a sign of weakness, which *ture* or Maori custom would not allow, and it would be regarded as unworthy of a Maori chief. His wife at his request strangled their dear daughter with her own hands. Both of them preferred to see her dead rather than made a slave. Rauparaha was furious that they had cheated him of such a valuable, beautiful prize. To revenge her death, the slavering jackel went up to the poor chief, slashed a vein in his neck and drank the hot blood gushing from the mortally wounded man. He then ran a red-hot ramrod through his body. In his death throes he added to his torments by mocking and abusing him. Tamaiharanui died a most horrible death without giving his tormentor the satisfaction of showing any sign of pain. His wife was killed later at Otaki.[15] These terrible atrocities were all committed on board a British ship, with the connivance and in view of a civilised English captain and crew!

'Stewart was given 24 tons of flax as blood money for his scurrilous service. He could have had more but he did not want to hang around waiting. Another captain also then at Kapiti island sailed away before Stewart and brought news of the event to Sydney. When later Stewart arrived in his brigantine, people pointed the finger at him as captain of the infamous *Elizabeth*.'[16] 'Stewart was summonsed to appear at the New South Wales Supreme Court for his part in the Akaroa natives' massacre. But he escaped punishment for lack of proof', according to Dr Thomson.[17] What a miscarriage of justice! Rusden, using documentary evidence, claims that witnesses to the crime 'were removed from the province and that really only Governor Darling wanted to uphold British honour by seeking Stewart's punishment.' Rusden also mentions that he was not brought to trial because witnesses had been allowed to leave and because of deficiencies in the summons procedure. He concludes by quoting findings of a special committee of the British House of Commons in 1836. It says that, 'Owing to inexplicable obstructions, neither Stewart nor his accomplices were punished because those who could have been witnesses were allowed to leave the province. Thus we see that an atrocious crime involving the slaughter of many people was committed by means of a British subject, and inspite of this, neither he nor any of his accomplices were punished.'[18]

Tamaiharanui's son succeeded his wretched father as chief of the Akaroa tribe. Realising that on his own he was not strong enough to fight Rauparaha and his allies, he approached the Ngaitahu paramount chief, a renowned warrior, and begged his and his valiant tribe's help to avenge his parents' murder. Ngaitahu jumped at such a good opportunity to grapple with their ferocious foe and immediately prepared for war, waiting for the right moment to attack Rauparaha. Soon they learnt that Rauparaha and tribal members were in the South Island, duck-hunting in their area. In a surprise attack the two chiefs and their warriors routed them completely. Rauparaha and forty of his people just managed to leap into a canoe and cast off frantically from the bank. But Rauparaha, seeing that the overloaded canoe was moving too slowly, threw twenty, including women, into the sea. He was thus able to save himself and a few others. All the others were killed without mercy.[19]

A defeated Rauparaha decided to wreak terrible revenge. He levied a considerable number of his warriors and allied tribes. They set off in canoes to attack the old warrior and his young Akaroa ally. Rauparaha very soon realised that he was dealing with a formidable foe. They were encamped at Orau-moa, a small bay completely surrounded by steep cliffs, with access only from the sea. Rauparaha approached the bay, landed and climbed to the top with his men. He ordered many of his warriors to clamber down to the bay. One hundred and forty warriors descended to engage the enemy, but they were killed one after another as soon as they reached the beach. The defenders left the following morning, quietly paddling home. Rauparaha was afraid that if he pursued them he would suffer a worse debacle than that of the previous day. Humiliated and disconcerted, he retreated with his warriors to Cloudy Bay.[20]

4. To satisfy his aggression and ambition, Rauparaha continued to fan the flames of discord and war, intensifying the fighting and slaughter not only at the top of the South Island but also at the bottom of the North Island. Rivalry, conflict and inter-tribal fighting increased so much in other parts of New Zealand that the foolish savages ended up locked in bitter combat until 1841, involving the whole country in slaughter and devastation.

Te Whero Whero, paramount chief of the Waikato tribes, was the bravest and most amibitious leader of the warring parties. He followed in Rauparaha's footsteps and for ten years he continued fighting enemy tribes far and near, terrorising them all.

Te Whero Whero started his campaign in 1830 by taking war to the Thames tribes. A bloody battle took place at Matamata and many on both sides perished. The Waikato tribe, however, was stronger and carried the day. After this victory, Te Whero Whero took on the Taranaki tribes on the south west coast. He continued fighting them ruthlessly and relentlessly for a good ten years, up till 1840. At first the Taranaki tribes put up a spirited defence, repulsing all attacks because there were three British sailors with them, bolstering natives' courage with their advice and example; more particularly because they had two small calibre cannons which wreaked death and destruction in enemy ranks. After a while the sailors stopped fighting for the Taranaki tribes and they began to lose ground. Te Whero Whero slowly dislodged them from nearly every bulwark. In 1834 he assaulted the main Taranaki pa and he took it after stout resistance. He himself killed 200 prisoners. Of those who managed to flee, some headed south and others hid in caves on the lower slopes of Mount Egmont.[21]

Chief Te Whero Whero was immensely pleased with his victories over the Taranaki tribe and decided to fight elsewhere. While still not ceasing hostilities with them, he rushed off to battle with Rotorua tribes, south east of the Waikato. His first campaign began in 1835 and lasted until 1841. Various battles and assaults on pas occurred in this period. But in spite of his successes, the fierce and seasoned warrior was unable to gain complete control. Nor was he able to subjugate the Taranaki tribes in spite of a ten-year extermination campaign.[22]

As Te Whero Whero's victories increased, he grew more ambitious. Ngapuhi warriors could not bear his arrogance and were also jealous of his infamous reputation as a bloodthirsty cannibal. Their commanders, Pomare and Kawiti, believed they were unbeatable even after Hongi's death. They decided to put an end to his unbearable effrontery.

Choosing 300 of their bravest warriors they left the Bay of Islands and moved to attack the Waikato tribes. Unfortunately, their previous victories on the battlefield led them to under-estimate their enemies' strength and the veteran Waikato commander's cunning. The 300 Ngapuhi were cleverly drawn into an ambush high up the Waipa river, far from their allies. Te Whero Whero suddenly fell upon them with a very large force and made mincemeat of them. Only ten managed to escape home to the Bay of Islands with the sad news of the disaster. Chief Pomare's head was preserved by the victors and kept by the Waikato tribes as a trophy of their great victory.[23]

The demon of discord and warfare seemed to rule the land during this period. Rauparaha continued his bloodthirsty southern campaigns, as mentioned earlier, and Te Whero Whero was still locked in conflict with his Taranaki and Rotorua enemies. From 1829 until 1832 Bay of Islands and Tauranga tribes fought in the Bay of Plenty. No great battles occurred in this period but there were frequent skirmishes, which wore both sides down. While fighting continued at Tauranga, two Ngapuhi sub-tribes came down in 1830 and fought a fierce battle on the coast. One hundred natives died on the battlefield and both sides suffered enormous casualties.[24]

This does not complete the list of inter-tribal battles. From 1835 until 1841, Bay of Plenty and Poverty Bay tribes were constantly fighting. So too were Taupo and Wanganui tribes. Civil war broke out in 1837 among Bay of Islands Maori. Fearing that this might affect Europeans there, the Governor of Sydney dispatched the warship *Rattlesnake*, commanded by Captain Hobson, to protect the *Kororareka* settlement. Europeans, however, were in no danger at all. The two conflicting sides had agreed not to fight there, to avoid any Europeans being injured or killed, even accidentally.[25] Battle was joined and both sides sustained considerable losses and injuries, prompting a mutually acceptable peace settlement. Such extensive fighting was mainly due to the introduction of firearms to the country. This caused general mayhem, slaughter and the destruction of entire families and tribes.

Rauparaha became even more rapacious in his murderous campaigns of conquest. In 1838 he forced members of the Ngatiawa tribe living near the Otaki river on the west coast of the lower North Island to migrate to avoid annihilation. They hired the English brigantine, *Rodney*, and sailed to make their home in the Chatham Islands, more than 500 kilometres off the east coast of the South Island. Thus they put themselves out of danger from the cut-throat. The islands became their adopted homeland. They have remained there and the present population is about six hundred people. Many whalers and their families also quitted Cook Strait region not to avoid being killed but to escape Rauparaha's excessive extortion.

During the twenty years of continuous fighting in New Zealand, from 1821 until 1841, it is estimated that 20,000 natives perished in one way or another.[26]

5. To soothe the gentle reader's spirit, perturbed by accounts of such terrible slaughter and bloodshed, we shall turn to more mundane matters which occurred during this violent period.

Sealers were briefly mentioned in Chapter Two. For some years they had good financial returns and even extraordinary profits, because of the huge numbers of seals they culled every year. But by 1825 sealing was scarcely profitable because of the enormous annual decline in the seal population. Sealers were forced to consider another trade and other fishing. They decided to turn from sealing to whaling and they established permanent whaling stations in New Zealand. There was no need to scour the Pacific for whales when they were to be found in abundance in New Zealand waters. They believed they could make handsome profits by hunting female whales which in summer frequented bays and inlets in great numbers to calve. Thinking only of immediate profit, they did not stop to consider that hunting female whales in calf would destroy stock in a short time and end further hunting not only in New Zealand but in other countries, since reproduction would be prevented. And that is what happened.

The first permanent whaling station was established in 1827 at *Resolution Cove* on the west coast at the bottom of the South Island. In a few years there were twelve stations between that place and Banks Peninsula. Others were established at Cloudy Bay and Queen Charlotte Sound and still more in the Cook Strait region of the South Island. Whaling stations were also established at the bottom of the North Island, Poverty Bay, the Bay of Plenty, Taranaki and on Kapiti island.[27]

Before they began building a station, whalers got exclusive rights from natives to hunt whales along a certain coastal area determined more or less by themselves. Once they had permission, they negotiated with Sydney traders to provide them the necessities for hunting and building. They guaranteed them a certain percentage of the net profit from hunting. Whalers then sent traders their products, that is, oil and blubber.[28]

Although whale hunting is considered exciting and glamorous, it is, however, very dangerous and calls for courage, expertise and considerable coolness from whoever takes it on. Because of this, Maori held whalers in high regard, and they were keen to be involved. As hunters they often displayed an incredible bravery and fortitude, rivalling and even surpassing Europeans.

There were twelve whaling stations at the bottom of the South Island. According to Mr Shortland, the average number of whales taken there in the thirteen years from 1830 to 1843 was seventy per year.[29] This does not take into account all the other stations. Thirty-nine whaling ships were counted one day in Cloudy Bay. Three hundred whalers had taken up living in New Zealand by 1840. They are not to be confused with those living on board ship, hunting whales from country to country, who often landed in New Zealand for a break and to take on supplies.[30]

Most of the whalers living in New Zealand had Maori wives whom they chose from the best native families. Young Maori women, like young Maori men, are handsome, and their beauty and fine physique often surpass our own country lasses, especially those from high-born families. These young Maori women were very keen to marry a whaler or European and their families considered such a union an advantageous and prestigious match. Before their marriage a kind of contract was made with the exchange of vows. The young woman promised to be faithful to her partner, to get up before dawn and prepare food for the whaler to take on board, to keep their hut clean and tidy, to mend her husband's clothes, to provide hospitality for visitors when he was away and to have his dinner ready for him when he returned the following evening from hunting. Her partner, in return undertook to provide her with European clothing, to treat her kindly, to give part of his profits to her parents and relatives, and to support in word and deed her father's tribe as if it were his own family.[31] The betrothed then lived together as though united in marriage.

Whalers regarded these marriages carried out according to Maori custom as civil marriages, with no solemn religious significance.

They provided no legal protection, especially to women. Offspring were not recognised as legitimate. Nor were family rights legally protected. Being Protestants, whalers had few if any religious scruples. They did not give a fig for their Church and only followed their own interests and basic instincts. These *civilised Europeans* had often deserted wives back home and had no shame in marrying respectable Maori maidens. They took advantage of the family's trust, leading them to believe that they were free to marry. When eventually they left New Zealand to settle elsewhere, they also left their wives and children behind. It is thus not difficult to appreciate the depths European morality had sunk to in New Zealand.

Young Maori women were affectionate, tender and very loving towards their white partners. Being ingenuous, affectionate and attractive, they generally gained the affection of the men they gave themselves to and they acquired quite a lot of influence over them. They often had to act as mediators in disputes between drunken whalers. They also, where they could, promoted good will between Maori and European. Sometimes they were able to change an habitual drunkard into a sober, even-tempered man. Whalers taught their wives cooking, mending and housework. They, for their part, showed a laudable eagerness and desire to succeed in everything they were taught and they dressed well to please their husbands as much as they could.[32]

Dr Thomson describes whalers' houses as being 'built of reeds and rushes over wooden frames, with two square holes furnished with shutters for windows. One side of the hut was provided with a huge chimney, and the other with sleeping bunks. In the centre of the room stood a deal table with long benches; from the rafters hung coils of ropes, oars, masts, sails, lances, harpoons and a tin oil lamp. Piled up in the corners were casks of rum, meat and tobacco; suspended against the wall were muskets and pistols; in the chimney hung hams, fish and bacon; on the dresser stood tin dishes and crockery and bottles; around the fire lay dogs, half-caste children and natives, relatives of the whaler's wife.'[33]

Not all whaling stations were the same size or had the same population. Te Awaiti in Queen Charlotte Sound, set up in 1830, had thirty huts.[34] Aparina settlement, founded in 1843, had twenty European males, one European woman and thirteen Maori women and two white children and thirteen half-castes.[35] The same year at Waikouaiti near Otago, there were eleven Maori women and fourteen half-caste infants. It can be assumed that other stations had a similar mix. In 1850 one hundred and seven Europeans were living in Stewart Island and in Foveaux Strait, most of whom were married to native women, and their grown-up daughters were also wives of Europeans.[36]

From May to October whalers were extremely busy hunting the leviathans of the deep and extracting their oil from blubber, sending it to Sydney traders. During the rest of the year, that is, spring and summer in the southern hemisphere, whalers idled away their time and moved around. Nasty fights broke out between them and Maori but whalers always got what they wanted because of their usefulness to natives, their Maori wives' intervention or their fighting prowess.[37]

Whalers were rightly accused of being responsible for introducing drunkenness, debauchery and civil marriage to Maori. Dr Thomson felt compelled to exonerate them, saying that, 'excessive drinking has often followed in the footsteps of civilisation and it is unfair to blame whalers for it.'[38] It is an indisputable fact that drunkenness has always followed in the wake of so-called British civilisation. It is not fair that blame should fall solely on whalers because nearly all foreigners who settled in New Zealand and visiting merchants and traders were just as guilty. Spaniards were the first Christian colonisers of far-flung heathen lands. Wherever they went they immediately built a church where all could worship the Lord Almighty, Creator of all things. However, the first building the British put up in any country they intend civilising is an inn or tavern, in honour of Bacchus. The contradictory British approach to introducing natives to civilisation shows the effect of Protestantism, exemplified by its founder Martin Luther's life and writings.

As for the other accusations against whalers, that is, introducing Maori to bad habits and marriages of convenience, Mr Thomson avoids the issue by stating that: 'civil marriages with natives were positive rather than negative.'[39] But this is contrary to fact, and he does not give even one reason to prove his point. Were he to tell the truth, he would have to acknowledge evidence to the contrary. Since, however, he himself was married to a Maori, is it any wonder that he would defend the practice. But that is not how to write history. Truth must be told. Immorality and casual marriages were introduced to New Zealand not only by whalers but also by whites living among Maori and by merchants and speculators who preyed on them for lust and lucre. Even Protestant ministers need to be included, as confirmed by Rev. Dr Lang and many other Protestant writers. Clear evidence will be shown in this book.

6. A similar kind of colonist to whalers was the *Pakeha-Maori* or Europeans who went native, as already mentioned. These *Maorified-Whites* (this is what the term *Pakeha-Maori* means) acquired a very great influence over tribes from 1824 to 1840 because of Maoris' general need for arms and ammunition and greedy European traders' for flax and preserved heads. Their numbers continued to grow, reaching 150 by 1840. But from that time their influence declined to such an extent that there were only about ten by 1853 scattered throughout New Zealand. It is important to explain at this point how their influence rose and then totally declined.

Thomson[40] mentions that, 'from coasting traders several Europeans proceeded into the interior to procure flax, and as they frequently lived in the country for several weeks until the cargo was ready, they provided themselves with wives. These dark-eyed women twined themselves round the rough hearts of these men, who, when the flax was ready, tore themselves away to the sea with regret; some, not having sufficient energy for this separation, remained in the country under an engagement with the traders to have cargoes of flax ready at certain periods.' They lived according to Maori custom and were called *Pakeha-Maori*, or Europeans gone native.

Europeans who were treated as slaves in 1820 were considered chiefs in 1830, and every inducement was held out to white men to settle in the country. Houses were built for them, land was given them. They were allowed to select wives from among the daughters of chiefs, and were not required to hew wood or draw water. In return for these royal privileges Pakeha Maori were required to barter pigs, potatoes, and flax for guns, blankets, tobacco and other articles.[41]

Some Pakeha-Maori of observation conducted their trade with great success and in strict accordance with native custom. They took into the interior large quantities of 'trade', which was distributed among the tribe for nothing; when the proper season arrived they asked their chiefs for flax, which was given without payment; and by this plan more flax was obtained than if article had been placed against article.[42]

From 1830 tribes which had no 'maorified' Europeans went to rack and ruin because they did not have the means to trade with Europeans. Maori considered a good Pakeha-Maori to be worth his weight in gold. By 1840 any tribe of note had its own European and there was evidence of this throughout New Zealand, even in remote places. These peripatetic traders were considered a tribe's property. Chiefs would debate among themselves the particular merit of their respective Pakeha-Maori.[43]

Although their fortunes rose quickly, they did not last long. By 1844 their influence over tribes was almost over, since British immigrants had settled in Wellington, Auckland and Taranaki. Maori also realised that their Pakeha were far less honest than newly arrived colonists. So natives began selling their produce to newcomers themselves, without using their itinerant traders and they found they did much better. Europeans living among Maori now lost their influence and had to consider their survival. Many left their tribe and, accompanied by their wives and children, they joined British colonists. Women without children returned to their parents' tribal home because often their husbands were poorer and worse off than Maori.[44]

A Pakeha-Maori who was also tattooed found himself unemployed and unable to make a living. He went to England and passed himself off as a New Zealand native. He made quite an impression and a living in provincial theatres. He married an English woman and returned with her to New Zealand. When they arrived, however, she went off with an American sailor, because his former Maori wife came after him, wanting to return.[45]

7. *Profiteers* and landsharks got vast amounts of Maori land for next to nothing, as was mentioned in the previous chapter. From 1831 they began scheming to make even more money, by selling on land got from their shady dealing to other Europeans at a massive profit. To foster their rampant speculation they needed to boost European migration to New Zealand. This could not happen unless the country came under the authority of a European power, preferably England, their homeland. This presented a serious obstacle. To overcome it, the rogues resorted to trickery and deceit, spreading false rumours. They obtained their goal, but not as quickly as they hoped.

They decided to spread a rumour throughout New Zealand that a French colony was about to be established in the country.[46] They let it be plainly known that the few French warships which cruised the Pacific visited New Zealand not for recreational or scientific pursuits, and that Captain d'Urville had more than surveying in mind when he mapped the South Island for two months in 1827. They claimed that various French whalers frequenting New Zealand waters may have seemed intent on whaling but their real quarry was to secure French occupation. These blatant lies were spread throughout the country and overseas to Australia and England, from whence they had been secretly disseminated in the first place. The real aim of these sycophants was to pressurise England into occupying New Zealand and make it a British colony. Thus they were carrying out their government's underhand, familiar manoeuvring, getting its agents to foment political unrest so that it would be forced to intervene and occupy a country, *for the good of humanity!* This has been, and, generally speaking, is still British policy. And it must be admitted that these tactics have almost always paid off.

In 1831 when European profiteers saw the French warship *La Favorite* anchor in the Bay of Islands, they rubbed their hands with glee, having an ideal opportunity to make Europeans and Maori believe their lies as the truth. The day after the ship's arrival they brazenly told Bay of Islands residents that the French government intended to take possession of New Zealand. They pointed to the French ship anchored within sight, as proof. In hushed, fearful voices, to be better believed, they said the captain had secret orders to carry this out. In fact, the captain neither had orders to occupy the county nor any notion that France wanted to take possession of New Zealand.

Once the cheap and nasty lie was started, it spread like wildfire among Europeans and Maori, and even to Australia. Kororareka residents who knew nothing about the French were told the most far-fetched, deceitful lies about them, and even more exaggerated untruths were spread among local Maori. They claimed that *Marion's tribe* (that is, Frenchmen, like the innocent, hapless du Fresne, barbarically killed by Maori in 1772 in the Bay of Islands) were about to fall on the Maori, exterminate them and destroy their homes, and that with French occupation natives would be certain to lose their lands and possessions. Their wives and daughters would suffer a shameful fate and if they were not ruthlessly annihilated, at the very least they would be enslaved forever. They needed to resist this horrible fate with all their might and stop *Marion's tribe* occupying the country. Speculators dreamt up these and other glaring lies to discredit the French. In fact, as has already been seen and will be further shown, exploiters had been doing these things to the Maori for years.

Maori literally believed the far-fetched stories. Hearing of their imminent death and destruction, they were thrown into terrible panic, believing that the end of the world was nigh. In an effort to escape the dreadful calamity of French occupation of New Zealand, 'they turned for advice,' as Dr Thomson mentions,[47] *'to their missionary friends, and they poured more oil on the fire.'* Anyone reflecting on the composition of the conspirators would not be surprised at this. Among them, missionaries posing as *good friends* of the Maori were pre-eminent. It was only natural that the gullible natives' trusted advisers would fuel the fire as they did, to lure them into the landsharks' trap. Missionaries, pretending to be on the Maori side, told them it was imperative to write to the King of England, begging him to protect them from the unscrupulous, bloodthirsty French.

Protestant missionaries in the Bay of Islands immediately prepared a petition on behalf of *'the native chiefs of New Zealand.'* In fact there were more than 500 sub-chiefs in New Zealand like the thirteen who signed the petition. How could thirteen be said to represent all the chiefs of New Zealand? The chiefs who signed the document begged King William IV of England to protect them from *'Marion's tribe'* (meaning the French) and to stop foreigners from seizing their lands.[48] At the same time, they complained to the king of the harm done to them by some of his subjects living in the Bay of Islands.

The British living at Kororareka, prompted by instigators of the lies, wrote to the King of England at the same time as the Maori, with the same intention, seeking his protection and prevention of another foreign power's occupation of New Zealand.[49]

Profiteers, not content with the success of their duplicity, sought the Governor of Sydney's support, to ensure their scheme succeeded. In fact, the Governor of New South Wales then wrote to the British Secretary of State that it would be expedient and vital to appoint a British Resident to the Bay of Islands to protect European and Maori, prevent fighting and discord between the two races, collect information on the development and progress of trade in the country, and to acquire appropriate influence over the Maori.[50]

8. To meet these needs, the British government appointed Mr James Busby, an Australian colonist, and dispatched him as British Resident to New Zealand. He brought King William's reply to the Bay of Islands sub-chiefs' petition.[51] In his letter, the secretary of state 'expressed on behalf of the king displeasure that New Zealanders had been mistreated by some of his subjects, and stated his determination to put an end to such abuses. The Resident also expressed his own eagerness to assist and support all tribes.'[52]

Mr Busby reached the Bay of Islands and set up residence at Kororareka in May 1833. On arrival he gathered the Maori together and gave them the secretary of state's reply on behalf of the king and presented them with gifts from the British government. The natives respectfully welcomed the Resident but Europeans described him as being like a man o' war without guns, or a man with no real authority. Certainly Mr Busby did not have a Resident's powers because he could not try, imprison or punish any felon. He was simply a representative of the British government without any power, and an annual salary of 12,500 francs and a 5000 francs annual discretionary fund for gifts for Maori. His real duty was to promote peace, watch the proceedings of other European powers in the country, furnish returns of New Zealand's progress and support the missionaries with his countenance.[53]

The London Missionary Society, popularly known as *Exeter Hall* after the residence in which it holds its meetings, is nothing other than a politico-religious society. It is under the control and patronage of the British government which uses it to serve its clandestine political aim of conquest. The society sends Anglican ministers and catechists overseas supposedly to convert people. In fact they are the society's and British government's emissaries and secret agents. With their help, wherever they settle, the government prepares the ground for later territorial conquest.

Anglican missionaries in New Zealand did not fail to promote their mother country's benevolence, but they concentrated more on their own interests. From 1814 to 1848 they used every possible means to increase and extend their personal influence and power over natives and Europeans in New Zealand, trying to bring them totally under their control. To achieve this, missionaries did their utmost to exclude any foreign power, including the British, from occupying the country, hoping that they alone would rule New Zealand and the Maori.

Thus, when the new Resident arrived, Protestant missionaries realised their danger, standing to lose with British occupation the unchallenged authority over the Maori which they had exercised up till then. They tried to prevent this calamity. Mr Busby had been ordered by his government to support the London missionaries completely. They took advantage of this to suggest to him that the best way to govern the country was to make New Zealand a free, independent state ruled by a native assembly of chiefs. Anglican missionaries guided and advised Maori in all their decisions and they alone spoke Maori. Thus they hoped to remain in complete control of the country, directing the native assembly and even Busby, the Resident, according to their wishes.

He welcomed their proposal and quickly set about implementing it. First, he suggested that Sir Richard Bourke, Governor of New South Wales, give Maori their own national flag and that Maori boats be registered as those of an independent state.[54]

The Governor of Sydney agreed to the Resident's proposal and he immediately sent the British warship, *Alligator*, to the Bay of Islands with three different flags for Maori to choose from. They chose one with stars against a striped background. With a few modifications, it was recognised at Kororareka by a 21-gun salute from *Alligator* as the national flag. The King of England was sent a detailed report of events which he ratified, recognising Maori right to complete independence. The Admiralty lords ordered their officers to recognise and respect New Zealand's national flag.[55]

At this time a plan for a European-style town on the foreshore to be known as *Russell* was drawn up. Maori called it *Kororareka* and a thousand Europeans were already settled there. A few months later, Busby, the Resident, proclaimed Russell capital of New Zealand. The township enjoyed the title for only a short period. Twelve years after its foundation, only a pile of ruins remained, and it never recovered. Presently it is only a small, miserable village with a scattering of Europeans. It was struck by the mighty hand of the Creator, as will be revealed in due course.

9. The British warship, *Alligator*, which, as mentioned above, recognised the Maori national flag with a cannon salute at Kororareka in the Bay of Islands, used the same guns a few months later to massacre and annihilate many innocent natives. They committed no other crime than remaining peaceful, keeping their word and asking so-called *civilised* Englishmen to keep their promises. Our description of events is drawn from British writers, biased against Maori and always defensive of their compatriots. The reader may form his own conclusions.

In April 1834 the *Harriet*, commanded by J. Guard, a former convict, was heading for Cloudy Bay on the East Coast of the South Island. He and his crew of thirty had been expelled from Australia. The boat was shipwrecked in a fierce storm off the Taranaki coast, in the same area where the township of

New Plymouth now stands. Local Maori treated the shipwrecked crew well and befriended them. *Inexplicably*, six days later, as Dr Thomson mentions, a brawl occurred in which twelve sailors and twenty-five natives were killed.[56] The incident was completely misreported by biased writers, particularly Protestant!

An inquiry regarding the sad event, however, ordered by the Governor of Sydney revealed that Guard and his men's debauchery caused the brawl.[57] The *Alligator* ship's doctor, Mr W.B. Marshall, an eye-witness, wrote to the British Secretary of State that the incident occurred after *'fifteen days riotous behaviour.'*[58]

After the terrible brawl, the surviving Europeans, that is, Guard, his wife, their two children and ten sailors, were made prisoner by Taranaki Maori. Captain Guard and some crew members were set free by promising to return with gunpowder as ransom for those remaining in custody.

Instead of keeping his promise, Guard went to Sydney and gave the colonial governor his account of what happened. He immediately dispatched the *Alligator* under Captain Lambert's command and a company of British soldiers of the 50th Regiment to free the prisoners. With the notorious Guard on board the ship set sail for the Taranaki coast.

Thomson writes that, 'When the expedition arrived the Maori freed the captive sailors and the two interpreters sent to parley with them promised the Maori they would get the promised ransom when Mrs Guard and her two children were freed. The soldiers then landed and formed up in battle line along the shore. Two unarmed Maori approached them. One said he was the chief holding the woman and children prisoner. He greeted Guard in the Maori way as an old friend and told him that his wife and children were perfectly safe and would be handed over when his people received the promised ransom. By way of reply, Captain Lambert seized the chief and dragged him on board *Alligator*. He was badly wounded and put in chains.'[59]

'A few days later, Mrs Guard and one of her children were freed by the Maori and the wounded chief had his chains removed and he was released. A short time later the other child was carried to the beach on the shoulders of the chief who had been looking after him. He asked to take the child on board himself and collect the promised ransom. He was told he would be given nothing. Hearing this he started back towards the village but he had only gone a few yards when he was shot in the back. The poor man fell groaning to the ground while the child kept clinging to the dying man's neck as though he were a dear friend. He was prised off him and carried on board. The dead man's head was cut off and kicked about by soldiers. Mrs Guard realised that the head was their loyal friend and protector's. The ship's cannons then began to bombard the Maori and their homes. They destroyed their two settlements, many canoes and killed several natives. The troops re-embarked and the expedition returned to Sydney.'[60]

The Taranaki campaign was a real disgrace to the army, England and so-called *British civilisation*. It was not an expedition motivated by civilised men seeking justice but a punitive raid by ruthless marauders and pirates, happening in this century! A House of Commons committee indeed later expressed its disapproval of the expedition's actions. It commented that the Maori kept their word, but the British did not keep theirs. They blamed them and particularly the former convict, Guard, who had the audacity to say that the best way to civilise Maori was to shoot them down![61] Notwithstanding this vindication of Maori innocence, the guilty went unpunished and the poor New Zealanders received no compensation or reparation for the harm, destruction and slaughter inflicted on them. Reading this account, gentle reader, you may think we exaggerate. Protestant Albion, this citadel of humanity and civilisation, would like to subject our beloved Italy to the same condition. Consider what has happened to noble, wretched Ireland, the practical extermination of Australian aboriginals and New Zealanders and most recently the fate of Uganda in the dark continent! Woe to the weak and conquered!

10. Protestant missionaries claimed to be Maoris' ardent protectors. Instead of rushing to defend the poor, unfortunate Taranaki Maori as they should have, they did not say one word against the atrocity. They had another more important matter on their minds.

They were aware that Europeans in New Zealand and Sydney colonists and traders were following their example of getting vast amounts of land for next to nothing. This practice threatened to become even more widespread. They feared, with good reason, that speculators would continue to get as much Maori land as they could, reducing them to destitution. When they had the whole country in their hands, they would badger the British government to take formal possession. Protestant clergy did not welcome either action since they wished to remain in sole charge of New Zealand, guiding, controlling and ruling the Maori.

In the meantime, in December 1835, to ward off this serious threat, the chief missionary, Rev. Henry Williams, who had already got hold of 23,000 acres, or 11,000 hectares of Maori land, 'sent the Governor of New South Wales and the Secretary of the London Missionary Society a trust proposal or "A Deed of Trust of Land belonging to Natives". In the memorial attached to it, Williams requested that Bay of Islands Anglican missionaries be made trustees of lands which Maori wished them to preserve from the intrigues of rapacious profiteers.'[62]

If a proposal of this kind had been made by honest men of repute and integrity it would have been considered well-intentioned and meritorious and possibly a valid means of rescuing natives from whites' abuse of power and insatiable greed. But since it came from the same men who were the first exemplars to speculators of how to rob Maori of their best land, it was a shameful farce. Perhaps they thought that their thefts were completely unknown outside New Zealand. But they were quite wrong because there was considerable awareness of them both in Australia and England.

On receiving Rev. H. Williams' proposals, the Governor of New South Wales and the London Missionary Society were astounded, knowing as they did the principles which drove New Zealand missionaries. In reply to the memorial, the Governor of New South Wales and the London Missionary Society formally refused to sanction Rev. H. William's bizarre proposal.[63] They would have done even better and performed a valuable service for Maori and mankind had they bluntly forbidden anyone to continue robbing natives of their land.

Chapter Five

Political Unrest, the Catholic Mission From 1836 to 1840

Summary. – 1. Baron de Thierry's aspirations and proclamations. – 2. Proposal for a Maori constitution. – 3. The Baron's achievements and death. – 4. European and Maori skullduggery at Kororareka and elsewhere. – 5. The Kororareka Association. – 6. British government's concerns about New Zealand. – 7. Catholic missionaries; Vicar Apostolic of Western Oceania. – 8. Undermining of Catholic missionaries. – 9. Catholic missionaries' arrival; obstacles and achievements. – 10. Their early successes. – 11. New missionaries and missions. – 12. Catholic and Protesant religion statistics. – 13. The New Zealand Company. – 14. New Zealand Company's devious dealings. – 15. Larceny. – 16. Harmful effects on the Maori.

1. While British cannons, manned by rogues rather than decent soldiers, blasted devastating salvoes on innocent and peaceable Taranaki tribes, in London an ambitious misfit was trying to find a way to become a person of consequence. He was of noble descent, cultured and elegant. For some years he had been seeking desperately to find a path to fame, and perhaps even, dominion. His name was Baron de Thierry.

He was born into a baronial, well-off family in Somerset, England towards the end of the last century. His father was also born and raised there, although their forebears were French immigrants. After de Thierry's ancestors moved to England, their children and other relations born there embraced Protestantism and became British citizens. In keeping with his position, the father had his son Charles educated in one of the foremost English public schools.

Having completed his schooling, young de Thierry began his career as an attache to the Portuguese embassy in London, and at the Congress of Vienna he was admired for his excellence as a musician. A few years later, bored with his embassy position, he entered a British Regiment of Guards, and was made an officer. Not content with this either, after a while he quit the army and married the daughter of an Anglican archdeacon. The marriage allowed him the opportunity of mixing freely with Anglican dignitaries and gave him the prospect of finding a lucrative, comfortable position. With the patronage and support of his father-in-law, the Archdeacon, de Thierry considered embarking on a career as a Protestant minister. Accordingly, he entered Queen's College, Cambridge, to study Protestant theology, and later be ordained a minister of the state church. Young de Thierry had frequent contact with Anglican ministers and he was fully aware of missionary work being carried out by Anglican ministers in New Zealand, that is, swindling natives of enormous amounts of land and their intention of ruling the country themselves for their own benefit. He was eager to follow their example.

At Cambridge, instead of studying Reformation theology, in 1822 he had a number of meetings with Chief Hongi and Rev. Kendall, hoping, like Kendall and his missionary colleagues, to exploit Maori land. De Thierry himself informs us that with Chief Hongi's approval, he gave Rev. Kendall goods worth 26,000 francs for him to buy on his behalf the upper part of the North Island, from the Auckland isthmus to the top of the island, that is, about eight million hectares. Rev. Kendall, as has already been mentioned, was one of the first to swindle Maori. He eagerly accepted the Baron's offer and promised him to settle the deal in London at the Missionary Society.

And what did the scoundrel, Kendall, do? He sold all the merchandise in London, pocketed the money and handed over to de Thierry the transfer deed given him some years ago by three Hokianga chiefs, of 40,000 acres (19,000 hectares) in the Hokianga, on condition *that he lived with them*. He told the Baron that that suited him perfectly. He altered the deed, making the purchaser Baron Charles Hippolytus de Thierry, of Somerset, England, residing at Queen's College, Cambridge. To make it look as if de Thierry was responsible for the fraud rather than himself, Kendall added that de Thierry in payment for the deed gave him only thirty-six axes. But even if that were true, the transfer was a real swindle because Hokianga Maori gave him the land on condition that he went and lived with them. Since he did not fulfil the condition, the transfer was null and void. Thus, de Thierry who thought he had swindled Maori of their land was robbed by Rev. Kendall.

Against this background, the young aspirant to Anglican orders prepared himself to become a missionary. Having completed the necessary studies he presented himself as a candidate for ordination. He was not found suitable, however, because he failed his exams and he was therefore rejected.

Having lost any chance of lucrative ecclesiastical stipends, he tried many other ways of making his fortune but nothing came of them. Then he remembered his grand purchase twelve years earlier of vast domains in New Zealand. This put into his head the idea that he was a great lord, even a potentate, and he decided to take possession of his realm. After secret preparations, he gathered his possessions and set sail from England with his family for the Pacific.

At the beginning of 1835 Baron de Thierry reached Tahiti. From there he hastened to write to Mr Busby, New Zealand Resident, informing him of his intention to come and take possession of his vast domains and establish his independent sovereignty. He mentioned that he had already informed the Kings of England and France, and the President of the United States of America of this intention. At the same time he sent a declaration to the Maori in which he proclaimed himself, 'Charles, by the grace of God, Sovereign Ruler of New Zealand and King of Nuhuheva.' The small island of Nuhuheva is in the Marquesas group. In the declaration he announced that he was waiting for a warship from Panama to take him to New Zealand to back up his authority. All the natives and inhabitants of New Zealand would be placed under his protection. He also sent European colonists and Protestant missionaries a detailed description of his possessions and he outlined his plan for future government, promising generous salaries to missionaries willing to serve as magistrates under his rule.[1]

The Baron's proclamations, far from advancing his poorly conceived enterprise, caused its abortion.

Busby, the Resident, Protestant missionaries and British colonists, particularly profiteers and landsharks, were shocked and horrified by de Thierry's declarations. They were shaken not because they were actually afraid of the Baron's power, which was inconsequential, but because of the rumour, albeit false as it turned out, that de Thierry, being of French origin, was a secret agent of the French Government. They feared he would get control of the country by a surprise attack and hand it over to France, Great Britain's implacable enemy. This bizarre rumour was spread throughout New Zealand and overseas, and many English writers regarded it as factual. But no proof has ever been produced of the supposed secret mission entrusted to de Thierry by France. Rather, from what has already been mentioned, the rumour was false, and the farce as it played itself out will make this even clearer.

Even if it were possible that France had designs on New Zealand, it is hardly likely that she would have used a pathetic British citizen like Baron de Thierry as her agent. Even if France was keen to use him she would certainly not have left him without support, ships, men and especially money to achieve her intent. At that time (1834-1838) France had no lack of frigates, cannons, troops or ammunition for such an enterprise. In fact, it is undeniably true, even to France's enemies, that she did not lift a finger to support the fiasco. It is evident that it was the ambitious Baron's own initiative to become a crowned head. Instead he ended up a royal clown.

2. After the initial shock of de Thierry's proclamations, the Resident sought advice from his loyal Anglican missionaries on what to do in the perilous situation. He immediately got the Protestant press at Kerikeri to print manifestos in Maori and English, rejecting Baron de Thierry's claims, and they were widely distributed. He also appealed to British colonists' loyalty to the mother country against foreign usurpation and an adventurer's designs. At the same time he announced his intention to summon all Maori and tell them of the Baron's threat to their recognised independence and inform them of how de Thierry

could be shown the futility of his design.

Mr Busby saw in the Baron's aspirations a propitious occasion to realise a plan, which he shared with Protestant missionaries, of establishing a national native government, under the British Resident's supervision. With his approval, in October 1835, thirty-five northern New Zealand chiefs met with Protestant ministers, and made a declaration of independence. They called themselves '*the United Tribes of New Zealand*' and announced that they would meet annually to make laws for the adminstration of justice and preservation of peace. All tribes living south of the Bay of Islands were invited to join the federation of northern chiefs. The native parliament petitioned the King of England for his protection and patronage.[2]

The '*United Tribes of New Zealand*' gathered at the Congress approved the following constitution, which remained a dead letter.* 1. Supreme power and authority over the islands of New Zealand were invested in hereditary chiefs as a collective body. 2. An executive body would be established, presided over by the British Resident. 3. Justice would be administered by European and Maori judges and British and Maori laws would be united in one system. 4. Anglican ministers would be supported from the sale of land. 5. The Congress would control finances but the British government would provide loans. 6. A body of soldiers would be maintained from state funds, composed of natives and Europeans, to protect citizens and maintain law and order. 7. Lands not occupied by Maori and not yet sold to Europeans would be public land. 8. New Zealand would be divided into districts, each being presided over by a chief and a European as district judges. 9. Setttlements which had a thousand inhabitants would have certain privileges and exemptions. 10. The country would be divided into provinces, each with its charter of privileges and exemptions; each would be governed by a Council composed of Europeans and Maori, elected by the people of the province. 11. This form of government and constitution was to remain unaltered and in force for twenty-one years, after which each province and local district would send members to form a National Assembly to legislate for the future government of the country.[3]

The independent tribes' constitution was not, nor could it have been, the work of savages like the Maori, incapable of formulating a constitution of this nature, which, although it bristled with thorny, insurmountable practical difficulties, nevertheless had the merit of being concise and clear. It was entirely the work of Protestant ministers who had not neglected to put in a clause for

---

*Translator's note: Vaggioli's reference to and representation of the Declaration of Independence is substantially different from the official version which contains four clauses expressing broad principles (cf. *Facsimiles of the Declaration of Independence and the Treaty of Waitangi*, R.E. Owen, Government Printer, Wellington 1960). Vaggioli's version is extremely detailed and reflective of a bi-cultural approach to rule.

their own benefit, still not content with what they had taken from the natives.

Mr Busby, Protestant ministers' obedient lackey, gave his approval even before details of the Constitution were presented for discussion by chiefs meeting at the Congress. Anglican ministers were hardly concerned that the constitution was practically unworkable. For them the main point was that the Maori would be independent and self-governing, meaning they would remain at the head of the Congress of chiefs and executive government, free to run the country and control Mr Busby, British Resident. Thus they were particularly pleased with their work and they hoped to convince Britain of the necessity of leaving New Zealand completely independent. But Britain listened, studied the proposal, said nothing and quietly planned to disillusion them.

3. After his famous proclamations, Baron de Thierry gave no sign of life. He was awaited in New Zealand with trepidation from one moment to the next, but there was no sign of him. Eventually, in March 1837 he sent another proclamation from Sydney to New Zealand Europeans, in which he again revealed his intention of visiting his dominions and of taking possession of them by peaceful means, and hoping for their cooperation. He and his family set off for the Hokianga with about a hundred men and he arrived in March 1838. He raised his own flag and then landed, proclaiming himself Supreme Ruler of the country.

The poor Baron soon realised his illusion. The few Europeans there, following Busby and Protestant ministers' orders, opposed him with all their might. Maori not only laughed at his assumed title of Supreme Ruler of the country, but refused to recognise the right to 19,000 hectares he claimed to have acquired from Kendall, the Anglican minister, because the latter had not *fulfilled the condition that was the basis of the transfer*. Notwithstanding this, de Thierry began to build a coach road to connect the Hokianga to the Bay of Islands, but very soon, lacking necessary funds, the men whom he had brought with him from Sydney abandoned him and went to Kororareka.[4]

Within a short while, the wretched Baron found himself alone, abandoned and even reviled by his own compatriots. However the compassion denied him by them he found among the Maori, who allowed him to build a home among them and to have a few hectares so he would not starve.[5]

The unfortunate de Thierry lived for some years quite humbly with his family in the Hokianga. Eventually tiring of the rather solitary life, he wandered off around the Pacific. Finally he settled in Auckland, where ignored and unrecognised he died in 1865, leaving his family almost destitute.

From this brief summary of Baron de Thierry's exploits, the astute reader will be in a position to adduce whether this saga could represent a plot and involvement of the French government under the reign of Louis Philippe. Others will draw the conclusion they prefer.

4. A rich, abundant whale harvest, lucrative trade in munitions and flax, easy pickings through exploitation of Maori land, as already described, together with Europeans' unrestrained debauchery and thuggery, attracted every year more and more whalers, traders, profiteers, ex-convicts, usurers, drunks and scum of every kind from every corner of the globe. People behaved exactly as they chose because in New Zealand there were no laws, government, magistrates or police to make them conform.

Loathsome lechery and lawlessness were prevalent almost everywhere whalers and European migrants settled, particularly at Kororareka in the Bay of Islands where colonists and Maori were more numerous and because it was also the busiest trading centre. The natives, like ingenuous children, followed the examples of corrupt, lawless Europeans they came in regular contact with. The settlement of Kororareka, which in 1832 had hardly a thousand European colonists, was a sewer of sinfulness. Injustice, brawling, cursing, gambling, drunkenness, extortion, rape, treachery, quarrelling, and outrageous public immorality reigned unchecked.

There is no doubt that the Bay of Islands provides the most magnificent sheltered natural harbour in the world. It could easily accommodate all the fleets of Europe. Up till the beginning of the nineteenth century, mostly whaling ships visited, particularly those frequenting the North Island coast. It was their favourite place for replenishing supplies. It had a lot of advantages, including numerous suitable anchorages, an abundance of potatoes, pork, preserved meat and other goods. Many Maori lived along its delightful shores and river banks, which gave ready access to foodstuffs and other provisions.

Merchant ships trading in flax, guns and powder and whaling ships found shelter from storms and gales in the vast bay's beautiful inlets, and sailors 'had a riotous time.'[6]

In 1833 at Kororareka Busby designed a plan for a much grander town, changing the native name of Kororareka to Russell, and he declared it the capital of New Zealand. There were about a thousand European inhabitants. More than a hundred whaling ships from England, France, America and Australia anchored annually in the harbour, without counting merchant ships.[7]

It would be impossible to describe the wicked, dissolute life Europeans led at Kororareka for some ten years. It caused infinite harm to Maori living among them, exposed to such a terrible example. I would shrink from describing their obscene behaviour.

It might be claimed that this is all exaggerated, to denigrate the British. Anyone believing this would only need to read the sordid descriptions given by two Protestant British historians (others could be mentioned); namely, Dr Arthur S. Thomson[8] and Mr Charles Hursthouse.[9]

Mr Hursthouse writes, 'There was no magistrate, police force, law and order, or religion at Kororareka', and he adds, 'the kind of colonisation found at

Kororareka was repeated elsewhere. Many small whaling stations near Cook Strait and Foveaux Strait and along the east coast were little, flourishing replicas of Kororareka.[10]

'Year by year at Kororareka disorder and immorality grew at the same rate as the influx of newcomers looking for drink and debauchery. By 1837 there were an Anglican church, five hotels, countless grog shops, a music hall, many billiard saloons, gaming rooms and numerous houses of ill-repute.'[11]

A Protestant minister, Rev. Ward, mentions that in 1837, 'more than 1000 Europeans were settled in Russell and that 131 merchant ships, many quite large, visited the Bay that year. Local inhabitants were seriously exposed to harm and danger by the influx of visiting sailors. Many native girls were made available by chiefs for prostitution. *Nothing was safe*; neither property nor peoples' lives.'[12] 'It was impossible,' adds Thomson, 'that a community comprising sailors of various nations, escaped or pardoned convicts, traders, sawyers, all kinds of ruffians and Maori, could live together, sober or drunk, without coming into major conflict, particularly *knowing that British sailors go ashore for debauchery, brawling and to cause havoc.*'[13]

Because of the mayhem at Kororareka, from 1832 there was such intense conflict between European and Maori that often it was on the point of erupting into all-out fighting. Disputes and brawls between the two races were mainly caused by the sale of land to Europeans.[14] Sales were frequently made in an utterly shameful and despicable manner, as has been attested by early settler eyewitnesses.

This was the most commonly used method: *Land-sharks* would have lawyers in Australia prepare neatly drawn up deeds of purchase. They would then spend time with Maori landowners, plying them with as much rum and tobacco as they wanted. After a few months daily dosing they promised to keep them supplied if they gave them the land they wanted. If they refused, they were requested to immediately pay for the rum and tobacco given them. Since the wretches did not have the means to pay, quite often they forfeited their land. Many signed over their land when they were drunk and if anyone steadfastly refused, they got him well and truly drunk and made him scribble a signature on the deed. That is how purchases were made in a perfectly legal manner! No wonder endless disputes resulted from these contracts.

While morality, law and order, and fair play were openly ignored at Kororareka, what was Busby, the British Resident, doing to instil some order among the stupid, wicked people? He made sure the British flag was flapping in the breeze at his residence and he enjoyed a salary of 12,500 francs. He looked around him, saw what was going on and kept silent, since he was powerless to suppress disorder and close down the brothels contaminating the area.

But, one might say, the Kororareka district was Anglican missionaries' main centre. What on earth were they doing? Why didn't they take any initiative to instil law and order and honesty, which were held in such contempt? Were they asleep? No. They were not. On the contrary, they were busy stealing Maori land, and were up to their own tricks.[15] No, they were not sleeping. They were scheming to spread crude, wicked lies among Europeans and Maori about Catholic missionaries even before they landed in New Zealand!

5. At Kororareka, meanwhile, things went from bad to worse. A few decent citizens did their best to maintain a modicum of law and order and good behaviour, but in vain. Finally, after a particularly violent brawl in May 1838, every one could see the necessity for a solution. Accordingly the most responsible colonists called for a general meeting of all inhabitants to find a practical way to administer justice and protect citizens and property.

As a result of their meeting *'the Kororareka Association'* was formed in June 1838 with a president, vice-president, secretary, treasurer, and an executive committee elected by local residents. They comprised the administrative council. The association's jurisdiction extended over the Bay of Islands area inhabited by Europeans.[16]

Members of the executive committee examined charges, heard witnesses and accused, and their sentences could not be appealed. Those breaking the law were fined. More serious crimes, including a refusal to pay established debts, were punished by expulsion from the association's territory. The most serious offenders, before being expelled, were publicly humiliated by tarring and feathering and then drummed out of town. The association's charter recognised the British Resident's power to punish offenders found guilty by the association, but Busby had so alienated settlers by his arrogance and refusal to recognise the association, that the executive council reserved the right to punish them.[17]

The association's charter had fifteen articles, similar in spirit to the American Lynch's law. Article 13 gives an indication of how it operated. Each association member was required to provide a good musket, a bayonet, two pistols, a sword, and twenty charges.[18] The association, far from maintaining law and order, was more like a gang of villains taking the law into its own hands. Even so, their bizarre laws were better than no law at all.

To give an idea of how the association administered justice, let us look at how they used tarring and feathering and expulsion, as described by Swainson, Rev. Ward, Thomson and many other writers. A European culprit arrested in the evening would be put overnight in a cell normally used for sailors. In the morning he would be stripped, and tarred and feathered with *toitoi (Arundo australis)*, a swamp plant. In this ridiculous, degraded state he was led along the foreshore preceded by two men with pipe and drums playing the *'Scoundrels' March'*. He would be followed by a big crowd of drunken Europeans and bemused Maori. The culprit was then put in a canoe with the musicians and taken to the opposite shore, outside the association's territory. He was left there with the threat that he would suffer the same fate if he ever returned to Kororareka.

6. While the Bay of Islands was beset by so many disconcerting events, in Britain many people were considering the colonisation of New Zealand. The British government, alarmed by false public rumours of an imminent French occupation of New Zealand, could not make up its mind whether the time was right to declare the country a British colony or to await the outcome of events. The matter was raised in the House of Commons and two committees were successively appointed to deal with it. They reported that the islands presented a magnificent opportunity for colonisation. But nothing happened for the time being.

In 1836 there was further agitation to colonise New Zealand because it became known that Catholic missionaries, seen as agents of the French government, intended going there. A committee was set up in London to gather accurate information about the New Zealand situation. But the Anglican Missionary Society, heeding its New Zealand missionaries' advice, urged the government 'to protect Maori from European influence, saying they would destroy all the good missionaries had done!'[17] As has been mentioned, this 'good' consisted in robbing them of their land and scandalising them in a thousand different ways, behaving in the same way as emigrants and profiteers.

The London Missionary Society's unfounded claims impelled the House of Lords in 1837 to appoint a special committee to investigate the situation in New Zealand, and if appropriate regulate British settlement. The committee gathered information and published a 367-page report. It recommended ministers of the Crown to assist Maori in their progress towards civilisation but it did not at all discourage emigration to New Zealand.

While the British Cabinet committee was doing its research, Busby and missionaries cast a jaundiced eye on the Kororareka Association's role of maintaining law and order. The association took no notice of them. They then wrote to the British government informing them of how it was acting without their approval. The government was surprised and alarmed and 'saw a need to establish British authority in New Zealand and prevent the Kororareka Association from setting up a republic, ruling the country with the support of the "United Maori Tribes", and causing England to lose a colony.'[20]

Accordingly, in December 1838, Lord Glenelg recommended his government to send a consul with full powers to New Zealand. But for the time being his recommendation was ignored.

7. Up to 1833, the Cross of Christ, glorious symbol of human redemption, had not been planted within Oceania's vast reaches. But the hour of divine mercy

was at hand for its many peoples living under the shadow of paganism. That year, Pope Gregory XVI, Christ's Vicar and St Peter's successor, established an Apostolic Vicariate in Oceania, entrusting its many islands to the Picpus Congregation of the Sacred Heart of Jesus, and appointing Monsignor De Solages as its first Vicar.

On Holy Trinity Sunday, 1835, Pope Gregory divided the huge area into two vicariates, Eastern and Western Oceania. The Picpus Congregation had the former, its territory being from the American coast to 155 degrees longitude west of Greenwich.

Western Oceania's vicariate extended from the boundary of Eastern Oceania's vicariate to the Australian coast, or from 155 degrees longitude west to 155 degrees east of Greenwich. It encompassed the numerous archipelagos and islands above and below the equator, and included New Zealand.

The Propaganda Sacred Congregation deliberated over whom to entrust the new vicariate to. After considerable reflection, it was given to the Marist Fathers, a new French Order, recently established at Lyons. Rev. Father Jean Baptiste François Pompallier was chosen as the vicariate's first apostolic vicar.[21]

He was born on 11 December 1801 and came from a devout, well-to-do family. He studied arts and science diligently at Lyons and completed his theological studies with great distinction, combining deep piety and scholarship. After ordination as a priest, his archbishop appointed him as curate and then parish priest, offices he discharged with great zeal and to his superiors' satisfaction. They testified to Propaganda's Sacred Congregation that he was a learned, prudent, pious man, devoted to saving souls.[22]

Although Monsignor Pompallier was only thirty-five years old, he was advised at the beginning of 1836 of his appointment as Bishop of Maronea *in partibus infidelium* and Vicar Apostolic of Western Oceania. He went to Rome and he was consecrated bishop on 30 June that year. From Rome he travelled to Livorno where he embarked for Marseilles and from there he returned home to Lyons.

He immediately began purchasing altar equipment and seeking grants and donations to build chapels in the vast, remote vicariate. The Marist Order gave Mons. Pompallier four missionaries, namely, Fathers Chanel, Chevron, Bret and Servant and three lay brother catechists, promising to send more missionaries later. The apostolic vicar obtained money for the cost of the long voyage from the Propagation of the Faith's Lyons and Paris committees. He and his new confrères departed from the port of Le Havre (France) on 20 October 1836 on the sailing ship *Delphine* bound for Valparaiso in South America.

When the ship arrived off Madeira in the Canary Islands, it was realised that the ship's rudder was severely damaged from high seas. It was necessary to dock at Tenerife and repair the damage. They landed at Tenerife on 10 January 1837. A new rudder was fitted and they set sail again at the beginning of March for Valparaiso. But another unfortunate, even sadder, accident struck the little band of missionaries. During the crossing Father Bret suffered a stroke and just as they were crossing the Equator he died peacefully in the arms of the Lord, in the presence of his bishop and beloved confreres, who tearfully mourned his death. The others safely reached Valparaiso towards the end of June.

Our missionaries left Valparaiso in the first half of August on board *Europe*, an American ship, bound for the Sandwich Islands in the Pacific. They arrived safely and in good time, with favourable weather and steady winds. They departed again quickly on another ship bound for the Samoan Islands which were part of the new vicariate.

On 1 November 1837 they landed on the island of Uea or Wallis which is part of the same group, and lies at 178 degrees longitude west of Greenwich and 12 degrees latitutude south. Monsignor Pompallier found the islanders peaceable and friendly and established his first mission, leaving Father Chevron and a lay brother catechist there.

Monsignor Pompallier and his little band went from Wallis to Futuna, another island, about 200 kilometres southwest of Wallis. He established another Catholic mission, leaving Father Chanel of the Belley diocese (France) in charge with a lay brother, and appointing him the far-flung islands' Pro-Vicar. A short time later, on 28 May 1841, Father Chanel shed his precious blood for the Faith, becoming Oceania's first martyr.

Out of the missionary band the only ones left were His Excellency, the Bishop, Father Servant and a lay brother. Farewelled emotionally from Futuna by their dear companions, they set sail again on the same ship, bound for their ultimate destination, New Zealand. Let us now leave them to Providence, their guide, while we cast an eye on events in their adopted country, which they would soon reach.

8. Rumours soon reached England of the Pope's establishment of a new Western Oceania vicariate, his intention to entrust it to a French Order, and the appointment of a French priest as first apostolic vicar, to reside in New Zealand. The London Missionary Society was most upset. They immediately sent the news to their New Zealand colleagues so that they could use every means to protect themselves and poor Maori from the imminent invasion of 'papist superstitions'.

Their instructions reached Kororareka three months later, in spring 1836, and struck like a thunderbolt, causing the heretics enormous consternation. They immediately repeated the false rumours they had earlier spread in 1832 of an imaginary French occupation. They had the cheek to claim that King Louis Philippe supported Baron de Thierry's aims, and that the appointment of a French priest as Roman Catholic Bishop of New Zealand 'was clear proof of the imminent occupation of the country by the French.'[23]

Thomson, a great apologist for his missionary colleagues, wrote, 'Many of these saintly men were fearful of the establishment of a Roman Catholic mission, and of possibly losing their homes, and anxious that the country should remain under British protection. In 1835 they sent a petition "of *British colonists in New Zealand*" to King William IV, seeking his protection as British subjects.'[24]

The petition was presented to Parliament by the secretary of the London Missionary Society. But Cabinet criticised the missionaries for dabbling in politics instead of attending to religion and education. The secretary of the Church Missionary Society, to exonerate his colleagues, replied that they signed the petition not as missionaries but as private citizens.[25] This excuse only increased the missionaries' blame.

Meanwhile, by spring 1837 New Zealand Protestant missionaries had already been informed by London that Monsignor Pompallier and his companions had embarked from France for New Zealand, travelling via America. The heretics went to great lengths to persuade Maori to totally oppose the *Papists*, to stop them setting foot in the country, or to drive them out if they dared to land unbeknown to them.

The ingenuous, simple folk were easily influenced by people with more knowledge than themselves. For a quarter of a century they heard only of Protestantism, which was constantly praised for its beauty, righteousness, moral superiority and material achievements. And so they believed all they were told. Now they were told the *terrible* news that Catholic missionaries were coming. Protestants, rightly fearing that their work would suffer considerably, to secure their position and prevent the new missionaries from helping natives, lied vehemently to the Maori so they would hate the missionaries and their religion even before they arrived.

They convinced guileless natives that Catholic priests were really ferocious, bloodthirsty barbarians and despicable men, universally loathed, whose secret intention in coming to New Zealand was to take over their country, kill them or, at the very least, enslave them. Their religion, they said, consisted of nothing but idolatry and superstitious rituals invented by the Devil; they dressed strangely. Honeyed words came from their lips but in their hearts they harboured intentions of rape, slaughter, destruction and murdering every Maori in New Zealand. Wakefield, a Protestant, mentions that the natives were urged by Protestant missionaries to believe that if Catholic priests were allowed even for an instant in their midst they would all be slaughtered or, less drastically, be driven out of their own country.[26]

Protestant preachers were so determined to lie to poor New Zealand savages about Catholic missionaries that Dr Ernest Dieffenbach, a naturalist and Lutheran, remarked accurately, 'Native Protestants regarded their Roman Catholic brethren as the devil's spawn.'[27] This was no figment of Maoris' imagination. This is what their religious teachers taught them.

Do not be surprised, dear reader, living in an enlightened age such as ours, that New Zealand Maori were fed such a pack of lies. The same Protestant ministers were determined to make rude British emigrants believe them too. Note the comment of Strachan, a Protestant minister, in 1853: 'Satan set about shoring up his natural fortifications by a new importation of helpers from France!'[28] Notwithstanding his remark, it has already been seen, and further evidence will be shown, who really were Satan's willing helpers in New Zealand. Catholic priests' sombre robes were and always will be abhorred by the Prince of Darkness.

9. Meanwhile, the two apostles of the Cross, unaware of the extensive scheming against them and the Catholic Church, drew closer to the field of their missionary endeavours. At last, after long awaiting the 'ferocious pirates', Bay of Islands' inhabitants saw them arrive on 10 January 1838. Monsignor Pompallier, Fr Servant and Michael, a lay brother, landed in the bay.

True preachers of the Gospel, they arrived unarmed, with no military backing, without family or servants, with no human help and sustained only by their trust in God. They were viewed suspiciously by the British Resident, with malevolence by Protestants of every denomination, and feared by natives. These were men who had neither possessions nor money. They were messengers of a doctrine detested by the powerful, degenerates and prophets of doom. Their doctrine condemns lying and greed, hypocrisy, corruption, theft, immodesty and all other vices, whether committed by weak or strong, rich or poor, elegantly clad lords in carriages or peasants and ragged, barefoot savages.

'The shoddily clothed missionaries,' wrote Bright, a Protestant, 'far from captivating Maori, did not attract them in the least,' and he added, 'in natives' eyes, being a good trader showed a person's worth.'[29] But this was not what really mattered. In their first speech to Maori the Catholic missionaries declared that they had not come to trade earthly goods since they had none and they were not interested in this. They came simply to bear witness to the gospel, their only aim being to save souls.

This was enough to convince the savages that if they took sides with these poor missionaries they had no hope of material gain. Rather they had everything to lose by offending their wealthy patrons and masters. And so they stood by, awaiting their orders.

Meanwhile, after landing, the missionaries sought lodging at Totara where there was a European settlement including about fifty Catholics, nearly all sons of glorious Ireland. One member of this noble, valiant and truly Catholic nation immediately offered his Excellency the Bishop and his colleagues his best house for their personal use. I regret that I could not ascertain the benefactor's name, which should be handed down to posterity. Part of the house was set up as a chapel for mass.[30]

From the moment they set foot on land, the missionaries practised their sacred ministry among Hokianga's European Catholics, most of whom were delighted to receive the blessed sacraments. On Sundays, Catholics hastened from remote areas to hear mass and listen to the Word of God. Even natives approached the Catholic chapel drawn by curiosity. They were enchanted by the rituals and delighted with the singing, which impressed them greatly.[31]

The Devil, however, took no pleasure in the new missionaries because they had begun to attack his dominion over the country, and, fearing worse to come, he tried to get them thrown into the river or at least driven out. He chose as the detestable instrument of his wicked design Protestant misssionaries to get Hokianga natives to commit the dark deed. Providence, however, was watching over His servants.

Monsignor Pompallier describes events in a letter he wrote from the Hokianga to the Marist Superior in Lyons, dated 21 May 1838:

'I mentioned earlier that by the time of our arrival, rampant heresy had done all it could to ensure our persecution. In fact, at daybreak on 22 January, about twenty savages led by chiefs suddenly appeared in front of our house with the intention, we later learnt, of *destroying religious vessels and hurling the Bishop and his priest into the river which ran by our house.* We had only been in the Hokianga about eleven or twelve days, and we hardly knew a word of their language. Thus it was impossible to raise a word in our defence. But the Almighty, without Whose permission, not a hair on one's head can be harmed, did not want us to be martyred. He saw to it that on that very day, three or four European Catholics who knew Maori happened to be passing by. Thus they were able to dissuade the natives from carrying out their wicked intentions.

'After a discussion of two and a half hours, God, in Whose hands rests man's fate, changed our aggressors to such an extent that they recognised the injustice of the act *which heretics persuaded them to do*. They came and shook our hands and even seemed ready from now on to defend us whenever necessary against the original instigators of their anger. The heretical ministers, however, were not put off by this and in our first months in New Zealand we were constantly threatened. Hence, while resigning myself to God's will, I have not shrunk from using every means to destroy lies spread against us.'[32]

The venerable Prelate concluded his letter saying, 'I am pleased, however, to mention that the British authorities in Sydney and the Bay of Islands were most critical of the rough treatment some wanted to use to expel us. The result was that it caused the heretics to be discredited and brought us appreciation and affection.'[33] Once again the Cross of Christ overcame Satan's rule!

10. Catholic missionaries from the moment of their arrival gave urgency to their task of evangelisation. Besides the spiritual care of European Catholics in New Zealand, they immediately set about learning the native language, which

was absolutely vital for the exercise of their Maori ministry. Their laborious efforts were soon rewarded with happy results. God seemed to be repeating the Pentecost miracle of his apostles in Jerusalem. In less than ten months from their arrival in the remote land, they could speak Maori quite well.

As well as studying the language, they began building a wooden residence on a four hectare block of land, given them for the mission by a local European Catholic. Part of the house was set aside as a chapel for mass and the administration of the sacraments until they had the means to build a wooden chapel on the same plot, for which European Catholics had already donated the Apostolic Vicar 1500 francs. The rest of the house, comprising only three small rooms, had to serve as sleeping quarters and workshop for the missionaries. Cooking was done in a small shelter outside. It was more than adequate for their simple fare of a few potatoes and a little fish or pork, and water.[34]

Notwithstanding their varied tasks, they worked zealously for the salvation of souls. Father Servant, on 22 May 1838, less than five months after their arrival, wrote, 'We have already baptised fifteen infants and adults, including a chief who had long desired baptism and had been duly instructed in the articles of the Faith. Monsignor gave him the name of Gregory. A paramount chief's daughter was among the converts and christened Maria. Twelve marriages were also celebrated as well as a European child's funeral. A cross was placed on his grave. It was the first to be erected in New Zealand. Now that we have overcome our first difficulties, a great number of chiefs, including some with considerable influence, show themselves very well disposed towards Catholicism.'[35]

In the same letter, the holy missionary adds: 'With the little knowledge that I have so far gained of natives' favourable regard, I believe that to convert them spectacular miracles are not necessary. The good example of our endeavours, zeal, lack of worldliness, the practice, in short, of missionary virtues would be seen as really marvellous to these poor savages. They would soon then be ready to receive religious instruction. Examples of charity, so new to them, would produce an incredible effect, similar to the miracles our divine Saviour promised his Apostles.'[36] The reason for this was that they had never seen heretical missionaries display such virtues.

Protestant ministers certainly vilified Catholic missionaries and their religion, but the facts spoke for themselves. Monsignor Pompallier, writing from the Hokianga on 21 May 1838, commented, 'People everywhere are beginning to realise that Catholics do not adore images, as heretical ministers keep repeating. They have done grave damage to themselves with this false accusation, and are now seen to be either ignorant or ill-intentioned.'[37]

But this does not represent all that Bishop Pompallier did. Mention should be made of his missionary trips and journeys for the salvation of souls. Writing from Kororareka on 10 November 1838 to the Propaganda Congregation, he said that in ten months, 'he baptised 44 Maori, mainly chiefs and their wives and children. Up till now I have only visited the Hokianga, Bay of Islands, Mongonui and Kaipara. There are about 120 European Catholics in these districts and about five or six thousand Maori wishing to be baptised.'[38] To visit these areas the Prelate had to cover more than 600 kilometres mostly on foot. One can readily appreciate that accomplishing all this in such a short time was an extraordinary achievement.

But let us leave Monsignor Pompallier, in a letter dated 28 August 1839, to describe his missionary journeys. 'I can assure you that New Zealanders are very fond of us offering, especially high ranking chiefs, to accompany me in my long travels, undertaking to carry my portable altar, mass kit and luggage of my fifteen or twenty travelling companions. Sometimes I almost laugh seeing myself in the middle of nowhere with a bunch of tattooed, half-naked former cannibals armed with clubs or guns. You would think they were a bunch of cut-throats. In fact, they are like gentle lambs following in the footsteps of the Pastor to whom Jesus Christ has deigned to entrust them. There is nothing they will not do for me since they have the utmost respect for my office. They prepare my meals and out of respect, set me a separate eating place.

'On reaching a river or swamp, they vie to carry me on their shoulders. The leading chief appropriates this role, and in this, as in everything else, his word is law. By nightfall, if we have not come across a hut, they make me a shelter in no time at all out of branches and fronds. They quickly make a good fire and after settling down, they pray. Then I give a brief talk and a hymn follows which they sing melodiously and with much feeling in their language in the silence and solitude of the bush. Finally, I make the sign of the cross over them and we get ready for bed. It often happens, that instead of going to sleep, I am asked questions and discussions on religious matters follow long into the night. Such, briefly is an account of my activities in New Zealand.'[39]

But what is even more surprising is the loyalty and devotion of Maori converts to Catholicism to their priest and pastor. Father Servant commented on this in a letter from Hokianga dated 15 October, 1839. 'When rumour spread that Protestants wanted to evict us from New Zealand, many natives rushed to Monsignor Pompallier's and stayed for several days awaiting the heretics emissaries. "Bishop," said a leading chief, "you have forsaken your country and your family to bring us to the light. Stay, please stay, we are all here to protect you, and we will die to the last man on your doorstep before anyone can lay a hand on you." But God watched over us, making their generous resolve unnecessary.'[40]

11. While Monsignor Pompallier and Father Servant worked alone so energetically in our heavenly Father's vast vineyard, Providence ensured that more missionaries would be sent from France. With enormous pleasure at the end of 1838 they witnessed the arrival of further missionaries to give them

practical support in converting natives' innocent hearts. In 1839 another group of zealous missionaries arrived. By the beginning of 1840 there were fourteen Catholic missionaries and fourteen assistants or catechists in New Zealand, not counting those in other parts of the vicariate.[41]

As soon as he had missionary reinforcements, the vicar apostolic immediately set up a new mission at Kororareka, or Russell, in the Bay of Islands. In 1839 he left two priests in charge of Hokianga while he and the others went to Kororareka. He transferred his bishopric there. At that time, Kororareka was the main centre where colonists, traders, European whalers and many natives gathered to sell their goods. Since it was also established as the country's capital in 1833, it was appropriate to set up the Catholic bishop's main residence there.

In fact, Kororareka at the time was the most suitable place for this. It was on the shore and even large ships could tie up near the beach. This was not possible at Hokianga. It also provided easier access to essential supplies from Europe. The bishop also felt that it was more suitable to exercise his apostolate among Europeans and natives there. It was fitting too that the vicar apostolic, embodying justice, morality and decency should make his home in little Babylon and root out its degraded society's teeming vices.

In fact, shortly after Monsignor Pompallier and his missionaries took up residence at Kororareka, social life began to improve and disorderly behaviour began to decline noticeably. This greatly satisfied His Excellency the Bishop and upright citizens.

Meanwhile the zealous vicar apostolic continued putting much effort into spreading missions. In just four years (from 1838 to 1842) from his arrival, he established twelve mission stations in New Zealand, ten of which had a missionary residence. The names of the different missions are as follows:[42]

Kororareka. This mission was established in 1839. By 1841 it had a wooden chapel, a wooden twelve-room residence which was the vicar apostolic's bishopric and housed two pro-vicars, the Marist father provincial, a priest in charge and lay-brothers; a second wooden four-room house with a barn or warehouse of the procurate. It housed the procurate's lay-brothers and contained a printery; a third wooden dwelling was used as a temporary school for many European and native children; a piece of land bought for a boarding school and infirmary; a 135-ton brigantine bought for 40,000 francs, indispensable for the vicar's long voyages to visit far-flung New Zealand missions and scattered in the Pacific. There were eighteen tribes needing conversion living in the mission area. They had just two raupo chapels.

Hokianga. This was the first mission, established in January 1838; it has two missionary priests and a lay-brother to evangelise the whole area; it has a wooden chapel. There are twenty local tribes. They have a small church and two raupo chapels. The mission was donated twenty-two hectares.

Wangaroa, north-west of the Bay of Islands, has a missionary priest and a lay-brother. They live in a wooden hut and have a raupo chapel. They are responsible for eight tribes. This mission also includes *Mongonui*, north of Wangaroa, containing five tribes, with a raupo chapel. The missionary had a boat for travelling.

Kaipara. Situated south of the Hokianga, it had a missionary and a lay-brother, using native huts for residence and chapel. They cared for eight local tribes. The mission had a boat for missionary trips.

Waitemata and the Hauraki Gulf. Established at the beginning of 1840, the mission had a priest and lay-brother. There were thirteen tribes in the vast area and seven raupo chapels. At the end of 1840 a town plan was drawn up for Waitemata. It was to be called Auckland and made capital of New Zealand. The British government gave the Catholic mission a block of land about 2000 square metres for a church and schools for the future European Catholic population. A similar allocation was made for Protestants.

Tauranga, in the Bay of Plenty, founded in 1840, had a priest and a Marist lay-brother. They had two raupo huts at Tauranga and another at Mounga-tapu. They ministered to six tribes who had three raupo chapels. The missionaries owned a boat.

Maketu, situated south of Tauranga in the Bay of Plenty; a missionary priest and a lay-brother lived there. They had a raupo hut and a boat and ministered to nineteen needy tribes.

Opotiki, south of the Bay of Plenty, had a priest and a lay-brother. They ministered to eight tribes. There was a large raupo chapel at Opotiki.

Waikato and Matamata (in the Piako district interior). The two missions were administered jointly for lack of missionaries. A priest and lay-brother ministered to 18 tribes.

Akaroa, on Banks Peninsula in the South Island. It was established on 15 November, 1841, for 57 French Catholics who emigrated there on 15 August 1840. There were two priests and a lay-brother.

Port Nicholson (Wellington), in Cook Strait, visited in 1841. There were three tribes, 400 British Catholics, mostly emigrants, and a raupo hut used as a chapel. His Excellency, the Bishop, promised to send them a missionary as soon as possible.

Terakako (Mahia Peninsula), situated on the east coast of the North Island. There were 20 tribes in the area. The two missions had no resident priest, but were visited regularly by a missionary.

12. New Zealand religious statistics, November 1841: The Catholic Church established in New Zealand less than four years previously had fourteen missionaries including His Excellency, the Bishop; fourteen Marist brothers and twenty native catechists. There were 822 European Catholics and 1000

Maori Catholics. Protestant statistics, after twenty-seven years since establishing missions (all denominations): forty-one Protestant ministers, many catechists or native preachers (exact number unknown); 2050 European Protestants, 6000 Maori Protestants. Dr Thomson comments that from 1818 to 1838 British Protestants spent not less than *'200,000 pounds'* or five million francs on their New Zealand missions.[43]

13. In England, meanwhile, an ex-convict not long released from Newgate prison for abduction, was busy drumming up support for a plan to colonise New Zealand.[44] He concealed his name and personal details, encouraging and using others to do his work. In 1837 he persuaded some influential Londoners, including Francis Bering, a Jew, and Lord Durham to found the *'New Zealand Association'*. They became its main directors.

The association's aim was to persuade the British to emigrate to New Zealand, to convince them of business opportunities and, above all, to implement systematic colonisation. The association's directors urged the British government to protect the natives and to sell New Zealand land at a fixed price of a pound (25 francs) an acre. (A British acre is about 4400 square metres.) Meanwhile association members held frequent meetings to discuss the best means of establishing a British colony in New Zealand.

At first, the British government appeared to support the asssociation, but soon it reversed its position, stating that if it were a trading company it would have supported and promoted it, but not as an association. The directors replied that they could not change its nature, because they intended to exclude personal profit. Seeing that it could not achieve its aim, the association presented a draft law to Parliament in 1838 seeking to 'establish in New Zealand a provincial government system under the control of 16 commissioners'. To achieve this, they sought the support of the Duke of Wellington and Dandeson Coater, secretary of the London Missionary Society. The Duke of Wellington said that he believed England had enough colonies, but nevertheless he promised to lend his support. Coater, however, was opposed to any colonisation and said he would use every means to stop the project.[45]

Protestant missionaries were anxious for New Zealand to remain under their direct control. They ensured that the British government followed their recommendations. When the association's proposed law was debated, it was defeated by a sound majority. After this reversal, the association was dissolved.[46]

Notwithstanding the British government's clear opposition to the association's bizarre colonisation scheme, Gibbon Wakefield, Miss Turner's evil abductor, was not in the least discouraged. He was determined to push his scheme, come what may. In fact, at the beginning of 1839, while remaining incognito, he formed *'the New Zealand Company'*, appointing Lord Durham as managing director. In London many other influential people also signed up.

Wakefield was not deterred by the opposition of the government, the London Missionary Society, or the colony's Protestant missionaries.[47]

The new company's aim was to send emigrants to New Zealand; to establish settlements and towns, build factories and provide free passage for farm workers and labourers keen to migrate from England to New Zealand.

Wakefield was the driving force behind the enterprise. Hearing that the government would not authorise the company to colonise New Zealand, he decided to force the issue. Before the directors' announcement of the company's establishment and its aims, he dispatched the *Tory* with emigrants for New Zealand. It left secretly on the evening of 20 May 1839 with Colonel William Wakefield, Gibbon's brother, on board. He was appointed Principal Agent of the company. The ship carried merchandise, gunpowder, muskets, bullets and trinkets as payment for the vast amounts of land they wanted. He was ordered to buy all the land he could, and to establish settlements, townships and farms.[48]

Two days after the ship's departure, the directors announced in newspapers the formation of the New Zealand Company and published a detailed prospectus. Lord Durham also immediately sent a copy to the secretary of state, declaring that the company had already acquired vast amounts of land and that the ship presently heading for New Zealand was to buy more. The British government was astounded at such provocative behaviour. It informed the company's directors that the expedition was illegal and it did not have its approval. They admitted their wrong and sought the government's pardon and support, saying their motives were innocent. The government said that it was satisfied with their apology.[49]

After this, the British government lost no time, on 15 June 1839, in extending the boundaries of its New South Wales colony to include any area of New Zealand claimed as sovereign territory. It appointed Captain Hobson R.N., as British Consul, ordering him to leave immediately on the *Druid* for New Zealand and make it a British colony. When this was done, he was to be acting-governor.[50]

14. In the meantime, the company's directors persuaded many people to invest money, and a capital float of £100,000 (2,500,000 francs) was set with 400 shares at £25 (625 francs).* This was immediately paid up. Consequently, in June that year in London, the company announced the sale of 110,000 acres of New Zealand land before they even bought them. This was land they anticipated buying from the Maori. They divided it up into 100 acre (48 hectares) rural blocks, and one acre (about half a hectare) town lots in areas. These lots sold like hot cakes at a pound (25 francs) an acre. Sales were made on the condition

---

* Translator's note: There is an error in Vaggioli's account of the number of shares. It should be 4000 not 400 (cf. Patricia Burns (1989), *Fatal Success: A History of the New Zealand Company*, p. 106).

that for every £101 paid out,* £75 could be reclaimed for family and servants' travel costs to New Zealand.[51]

The company under the clandestine direction of Gibbon Wakefield not only unashamedly sold land it did not own, but deceived the public with false information and reports. To recruit emigrants they published in London a 'New Zealand Journal' in which they made exaggerated claims about the country. As if this was of no consequence, they paid many British journalists considerably to publish articles praising New Zealand. Accordingly, they wrote fulsome, extravagant descriptions, often completely false. The company, at the same time, launched a publicity campaign in London with grand plans and illustrations of *Hutt* valley, Port Nicholson and environs, to further encourage people interested in migrating.

Many English and Scottish workers, excited by the advertising, flocked to London to draw lots for land the company claimed it had to sell, but which it had not bought.

Meanwhile, on 30 July 1839, the company announced the sale of 50,000 acres (24,000 hectares) in blocks of 100 acres each, at one pound an acre, to be paid in cash. The company, in exchange, gave purchasers land-orders for New Zealand land. Almost all the land was sold by the company and from May 1839 until January 1840, 1125 emigrants, nearly all English and Scottish, left for New Zealand. 'Irish were not encouraged to emigrate because the Company considered them to be "troublesome and dangerous".'[52] They did not want Irishmen because of their Catholicism. This did not suit the company, which comprised Jews and Protestants.

16.# The first emigrants and principal agent left England for New Zealand in May 1839 on the *Tory*. On 16 August 1839 they landed in Queen Charlotte Sound, at the top of the South Island. Colonel Wakefield also visited Admiralty Bay. The ship then cast anchor on 20 September in the magnificent harbour of Port Nicholson, now called Wellington, in Cook Strait. Many Maori went on board and the company agent displayed merchandise he had brought with him on the bridge. He hoped the natives would be enticed to sell land for it.

While natives admired the goods, Wakefield, standing on the bridge, asked an old whaler called Barrett, his interpreter, the names of the valleys, rivers, harbours, sounds, islands, coastal areas, hills, promontories, and everything in sight. He noted them all down and then asked the Maori if they were willing to

---

* Translator's note: According to Burns (1989), those who bought land-orders were entitled to a 75 per cent rebate on travel costs for themselves, their family and servants.
# Translator's note: There is no inclusion of the heading '15.' in the original Italian text. It has obviously been inadvertently omitted.

sell it all to him. He said that he would give them a good deal of the merchandise on display. The poor, ingenuous savages agreed. The company agent set to work getting them to sign prepared deeds of sale he had handy.

It is deeply distressing to consider how a supposedly civilised people were capable of such pillage and theft, evidenced in the deals Colonel Wakefield carried out over three months to get the land which was so precious to the Maori. They were completely ignorant of the real meanings of the transactions, and were only interested in acquiring arms and ammunition to defend themselves from their enemies. The company agent embodied a greed for native land which would stop at nothing, neither bothering to find out the real owners or whether there was enough left for their survival. How many crimes are committed through covetousness! But as you sow, so shall you reap.

Three months after his arrival in New Zealand, Colonel Wakefield wrote to the London directors that he had purchased land the size of Ireland, from 38 degrees to 43 degrees latitude south on the west coast of both islands, and from 41 degrees to 43 degrees on the east coast, or about 10,000,000 hectares. Purchase deeds were modelled on those used by New Zealand Protestant missionaries for buying land. The three deeds were signed by fifty-eight chiefs. In the first deed, a tenth of the land was made a native reserve. In the other two deeds there was no such mention.[53]

The company agent, for the purchase of the 10 million hectares, gave the Maori goods he valued at £8,983 (224,575 francs). In fact, they were not worth a third of the amount. Even accepting the value was true, Wakefield would have paid *only two centimes a hectare for the land!* If, also, one considers the main items traded, it is obvious that the transaction was a farce, like nearly all previous dealings with natives by Protestant missionaries, traders and other thieves. The following is a list of trade items: '200 old flintlock muskets, 16 single-barrelled guns, 8 double-barrelled guns, 15 shotguns, 18 barrels of powder, 2 cases of cartridges, 4 cases of lead for making bullets, 24 gunshot moulds, 1500 flintstones, etc., etc.'[54] If Wakefield had an ounce of good sense he would have realised that deadly weapons should never have been put into native hands. The time would come when the arms would be used against the company and its offshoots.

On 30 September 1839, Colonel Wakefield took formal possession of the harbour and Port Nicholson. He hoisted the New Zealand flag from the highest flagpole, accompanied by a gun salute. Maori entertained Europeans with a war dance, waving their newly acquired muskets. British colonists toasted local chiefs with *champagne*. Thus was concluded the New Zealand Company's first shameful theft. Painful repercussions for it would follow.

Chapter Six

New Zealand, a British Colony, Migrants' Arrival From 1840 to 1844

Summary. – 1. Governor Hobson's arrival in New Zealand, Sovereign's decrees. – 2. Treaty of Waitangi. – 3. Discussion of its validity. – 4. New colony's militia. – 5. Migrants' arrival in Wellington. – 6. Colony's new capital. – 7. French migrants in Akaroa. – 8. Migrants' arrival in Wanganui, Taranaki, Manukau and Nelson. – 9. Hobson's death; Shortland's administration. – 10. The Wairau massacre. – 11. Governor Fitzroy's peace-making attempts. – 12. Land purchase claims and concessions made by the government commission. – 13. Protestant missionary claims and concessions made to them. – 14. Country's situation by end of 1844.

1. While Wakefield, the company's agent, was busy robbing the Maori, towards the end of December 1839, Captain Hobson, the new British Consul, arrived safely in Sydney after a long voyage on H.M.S. *Druid*. On 14 January 1840 he was sworn in as Lieutenant Governor by Sir George Gipps, governor of the colony. He gave him wise counsel and guidelines for governing the new country. On 19 January, accompanied by a treasurer, a customs officer, a magistrate, two clerks, a sergeant and four troopers, he set sail for New Zealand, reaching the Bay of Islands on 29 January 1840.[1]

Following his arrival, the office of the British Resident, represented by Busby, was dissolved. The new British representative on landing at Russell was cordially welcomed by local people. Two days later, he held a meeting of Europeans on the foreshore near the township, and had two government decrees read out. The first declared that from that day New Zealand would become part of the New South Wales colony. The second confirmed Captain Hobson as Lieutenant Governor of any areas in New Zealand which would later be added to Her Majesty's British dominions.[2]

At the same time he promulgated two royal decrees. The first stated that any British subjects living in New Zealand would be placed under the authority and rule of the British government, as part of the colony of New South Wales. The second declared that Her Majesty the Queen would not recognise Europeans' legal entitlement to land unless it had been examined and confirmed by the government. To implement this, the Governor and the Sydney Legislative Council would appoint a commission whose task would be to investigate all land purchases made up to then. In the meantime, from henceforth it was forbidden and illegal to buy Maori land. 'The second Royal Decree,' Dr

Thomson comments, 'dismayed residents, dealing a mortal blow to those who had acquired huge amounts of native land for *next to nothing*.'[3]

2. There remained, however, for Captain Hobson a particularly important task to carry out; to proclaim the annexation of New Zealand as a British colony, by getting the Maori to cede their country to England. Once this was done, he was to govern the new colony as Lieutenant Governor. The instructions given him by Lord Normanby included a detailed direction on how to carry out negotiations with the natives and he was to complete proceedings as soon as possible.[4]

When Hobson reached Kororareka, he immediately noticed numerous large bands of well-armed chiefs and warriors 'and realised how powerless he was in comparison. He knew then that he could not declare the country a British colony without practically unanimous native consent. Requesting this without antagonising them would be a difficult and dangerous task.'[5] British intrigue, Protestant ministers' support and several sweeteners would together triumph over all obstacles and beguile Maori ingenuousness.

Captain Hobson immediately sought Anglican missionaries' advice and support, particularly Henry Williams's. 'He told him that he had been authorised by the Government to turn to him for assistance. Similarly, the Protestant Bishop of Australia sent letters to Williams strongly urging Anglican missionaries to use their influence to persuade chiefs to cede the requisite sovereignty of the country to the Queen.'[6]

Rev. Henry Williams and his colleagues were willing to cooperate and an agreement was reached to call for a general Maori assembly on 5 February. On 31 January 1840, only two days after Hobson's arrival, the Anglican press issued several copies of a manifesto in Maori in which Hobson called for a general assembly of all natives in the area at the mouth of the Waitangi river, to present them a treaty proposal for their consideration. Copies of the manifesto were widely distributed to spread news of the assembly.

Mr Hobson had the treaty prepared in English. He then requested Williams to translate it into Maori and have copies made.

The meeting day was perfectly fine and the meeting place beautiful and most pleasant. The superstitious, however, foresaw an unhappy outcome because they were to meet at *Waitangi*, meaning *weeping waters*.[7] Fifty chiefs and their followers assembled.

A large marquee, decorated with flags, was erected. At noon, Mr Hobson entered accompanied by Captain Nias and officers of H.M.S. *Herald*, Busby, heads of the Protestant and Catholic missions, and most of the local Europeans. Proceedings took place on a platform set up under the marquee, the natives seated in front and the Europeans behind. After a brief pause, Hobson rose to his feet and addressed the chiefs, concluding by saying that they could completely trust in the good faith of Her Majesty's Government.[8] Rev. Williams acted as his interpreter. He read out the treaty text in Maori and he explained it to the natives clause by clause. Hobson then asked the chiefs to sign it on behalf of their respective tribes.

A discussion among the Maori ensued. 'Twenty chiefs spoke in favour and six against. Opponents said the treaty would deprive them of their lands, and that while everything seemed plain and straightforward, beneath the fine promises lurked deceit. The speeches so moved the native audience that it seemed likely that the proposal would be rejected. Finally, chief Walker Nene spoke in favour of the treaty. But Hobson, seeing the debate had aroused strong feelings, allowed the natives twenty-four hours for discussion, so that tribes could examine the proposal closely. The following day, without further ado, forty-six chiefs signed the treaty. The first signature to appear on the document was chief Kawiti's, one of the main leaders in the 1844 rebellion.'[9]

The following is the actual text of the Treaty of Waitangi:

'Her Majesty Victoria Queen of the United Kingdom of Great Britain and Ireland, etc., etc., etc.

ARTICLE THE FIRST. The Chiefs of the Confederation of the United Tribes of New Zealand and the separate and independent Chiefs who have not become members of the Confederation cede to Her Majesty the Queen of England *absolutely and without reservation* all the rights and powers of Sovereignty which the said Confederation or Individual Chiefs respectively exercise or possess, or may be supposed to exercise or to possess over their respective Territories as the sole sovereigns thereof.

ARTICLE THE SECOND. Her Majesty the Queen of England confirms and guarantees to the Chiefs and Tribes of New Zealand and to the respective families and individuals thereof the full exclusive and undisturbed possession of their Lands and Estates Forests and Fisheries and other properties which they may collectively or individually possess so long as it is their wish and desire to retain the same in their possession; but the Chiefs of the United Tribes and the individual Chiefs yield to Her Majesty *the exclusive right of Preemption* over such lands as the proprietors thereof may be disposed to alienate at such prices as may be agreed upon between the respective Proprietors and persons appointed by Her Majesty to treat with them in that behalf.

ARTICLE THE THIRD. In consideration thereof Her Majesty the Queen of England extends to the Natives of New Zealand Her royal protection and imparts to them all the Rights and Privileges of British subjects.

(signed) W. Hobson.

Now therefore We the Chiefs of the Confederation of the United Tribes of New Zealand being assembled in Congress at Victoria in Waitangi and We the Separate and Independent Chiefs of New Zealand claiming authority over the Tribes and Territories which are specified after our respective names, having been made fully to understand the Provisions of the foregoing Treaty, accept and enter into the same in the full spirit and meaning thereof in witness of which we have attached our signatures or marks at

the places and the dates respectively specified.
(The signatures of the chiefs follow.)

Done at Waitangi this Sixth day of February in the year of Our Lord one thousand eight hundred and forty.'

Three Anglican ministers, the brothers Henry and William Williams and Rev. Mounsell and three of Hobson's officials hurried through the country taking several copies of the treaty for signing by chiefs who did not attend the gathering. After nearly five months of feverish activity they managed to obtain 512 signatures in all. How did they achieve this? Dr Thomson, a reputable source, provides the answer. In his words, 'The majority of the signatories were handed over a blanket and tobacco as gifts.'[10]

While this was going on, Captain Hobson, on 21 May, proclaimed British sovereignty over the North Island, invoking the Treaty of Waitangi, and over the South Island, by right of discovery. To remove any doubt about sovereignty of the South Island, on 17 June the same year, Major Bunbury proclaimed that it was under the Queen's authority 'in virtue of the treaty of Waitangi.'[11]

Rusden, Catholic missionaries' enemy and Protestantism's champion, mentions that once Hobson had the signatures he wrote a letter to the local Anglican Missionary Society thanking them 'for their most zealous and fruitful collaboration in this matter.' In 1841 in the Legislative Council he publicly declared that if he had not had their assistance, 'he would not have been able to make New Zealand a British colony.'[12]

3. When we examine the Treaty of Waitangi, we find it extremely *biased* in favour of the British government and extremely *contemptuous* of the Maori. Indeed, Article II gives the British government the *exclusive right of pre-emption* to buy any land Maori wished to sell. Thus it established a monopoly as land purchaser, able to buy land at ridiculous prices and sell it on to settlers at 26 francs or more a hectare. It thus became the unique and absolute agent of native exploitation. Article III accords the Maori all the privileges of British subjects. This was really so only on paper. In practice they were forced to observe British laws of which they had no knowledge and if they unwittingly transgressed, they were imprisoned without pity and even hanged.

Having noted this, let us turn to the same Protestant writers and Maori sources for their opinion of the treaty.

According to Thomson, 'the treaty of Waitangi was considered ridiculous and farcical by many Europeans who saw it as trading sovereignty for blankets.'[13] Hursthouse, another Protestant, called it a 'Blankets Treaty'.[14] A House of Commons committee described the agreement as an 'ill-judged act'.[15]

The Maori were wickedly deceived mainly by Protestant missionaries, headed by Rev. Henry Williams, the treaty's arch-manipulator. One of his colleagues, Rev. Ward, wrote: 'The Maori turned to them [Protestant missionaries] for explanation and advice regarding the treaty and, re-assured by them, they acquiesced and signed,'[16] but, it should be noted that what they led the simple folk to believe was quite different from what was expressed in the agreement, as will be seen.

Dr Thomson, an English Protestant and man of integrity, comments, 'Few of the natives understood the nature of the treaty. Nopera, an astute chief, said: the shadow of the land passes to the Queen but we retain the substance. All those who signed it believed that their lands would remain theirs. *None* realised that the treaty exposed them to the danger of being hanged or imprisoned for transgressions against British law of which they were totally ignorant.'[17]

Maori opposition to the treaty was also found outside the document's signatories, who were small in number and not paramount chiefs. There were more than 3000 principal and sub-chiefs in New Zealand out of a native population of more than 100,000. Another unbiased Protestant, Terry, mentions that on 12 February 1840 Hobson went to the Hokianga to have the treaty signed. He met with between 400 and 500 chiefs of differing rank in a native gathering totalling 6000. *All of them* showed their repugnance and opposition to the treaty.[18]

At that time, 'seven chiefs staying in Sydney (as the rabid Protestant Rusden writes) were invited to Government House to sign a declaration accepting the Queen as their sovereign. They went, listened to the document being read out and were each given ten pounds (250 francs). They promised to sign another day and then disappeared.'[19] 'Chiefs who refused to sign,' notes Thomson, 'ridiculed those who did sign as lackeys.'[20] Hobson, in a despatch to the Colonial Secretary in London, commented, 'The Treaty of Waitangi was received with mixed feelings by the people it was proposed to.' This was confirmed by Mr Swainson, another staunch Protestant.[21]

Father Barsanti, a Franciscan, concluded that, 'The history of New Zealand confirms that the Treaty of Waitangi lacked the necessary conditions for transferring dominion of the country to the British Crown and making the Maori British subjects, for the following main reasons:

> 1. The Maori who signed the Treaty were only some Northern chiefs and they were not Rangatira, or paramount chiefs, or as the Maori would say, *Rangatira Nui*, but sub-chiefs. The others refused to sign.
>
> 2. Because Maori objections to the treaty were not considered.
>
> 3. Because the British, not yet conversant with Maori, used words in a different sense from what Maori understood by them.
>
> 4. Finally, because people present at the great assembly maintain that the key point

of *complete cession* was not read out to the natives. Acting in ignorance, they were not able to see and examine the treaty's intention, but had to trust in the *good faith* of the British Crown's officials.'[22]

Undoubtedly, the Maori were wickedly deceived in this by Protestant missionaries and the British government's officials. One of them, ex-Resident Busby, wrote: When the Treaty of Waitangi was later re-examined by the natives without European interference, it caused them considerable alarm because of its implications. They decided to get together and kill the British and take their wives. But native catechists opposed the plot and prevented a horrible crime.[23]

The great majority of natives never endorsed British sovereignty over New Zealand. Rather, they opposed it constantly in combat in the *Wairau* massacre in 1843, *Heke's* uprising in 1844, *Kororareka's* destruction in 1845, the battle of *Ruapekapeka* in 1846, fighting in Wanganui in 1847, the creation of Maori sovereignty in 1857, and fierce campaigning in *Taranaki, Waikato, Wanganui* and *Tauranga*, lasting from 1860 to 1870.

4. Storm clouds gathering over Cook Strait, the scenes which occurred at the Waitangi gathering and growing Maori opposition to the British demand of sovereignty convinced Hobson that without military support he could not maintain law and order. Accordingly, once he proclaimed British sovereignty, he urgently wrote to the Governor of Sydney for soldiers. Shortly afterwards, two companies of the 80th Regiment arrived in the Bay of Islands. Their services were very soon called for to restore order in frequent clashes between natives and colonists.[24]

In the meantime scientific exploration was quietly being carried out in New Zealand. An Antarctic expedition under the command of Captain William Ross arrived at the end of 1839 and stayed until 1843, carrying out scientific research. Botany is indebted to the eminent Dr. J.D. Hooker for his classic work on *The Flora of New Zealand*, in which he assembled and catalogued all native botanical plants known up till then. This probably remains the definitive work on the country's flora.[25]

5. On 22 January 1840, the first ship carrying New Zealand Company emigrants anchored in Cook Strait at Port Nicholson, at the bottom of the North Island. Before the end of the year, 1200 English colonists had landed.

The terrible disappointment emigrants felt when they arrived is indescribable. Aware that their homeland was on the other side of the world, they realised there was no hope of ever seeing it again. Recognising that they had each paid the company for 101 acres (about forty hectares), they saw no sign of their land. They might have found solace in tilling their own soil, but where was it? They thought that they would at least have basic necessities for living, but there was nothing. They cast their eyes over valleys, hills and mountains; their future home, and they saw only wasteland and bush; not a single house or any indication of civilisation, peopled by surly, shiftless savages. At this heartbreaking realisation, they were filled with remorse and many wept for the homeland they had left.

Colonel Wakefield tried to cheer them up, and eventually they established holdings in a settlement previously chosen by Wakefield, calling it *Britannia*. The colonists took heart, pitched tents, built huts and temporary homes with Maori help, and began sowing nearby land for their needs. The natives were friendly and taught them how to build huts and sold them potatoes and pork. Thus the two races lived in harmony.

The *Britannia* settlement at the entrance to Hutt Valley was found to be unsuitable, proving to have difficult sea access. In March 1840 at a colonists' meeting it was decided to transfer their settlement to the opposite shore, to a place called Te Aro by the natives. This was done. It is now known as *Wellington*, which is today a beautiful town and the capital of New Zealand.

Unfortunately, natives grew crops there and they were strongly opposed to its settlement by colonists. They denied they ever sold the land and they told the Europeans that they were wrong to take other people's property. However, the colonists took no notice and built their huts on their land. The Maori offered no physical resistance because they were advised by collectors of signatures for the Treaty of Waitangi that the government would send down a magistrate to see that justice was done. This was the first time that migrants usurped others' land. Unfortunately, it was not the last.

Natives' complaints regarding theft of their land by colonists in Wellington drove more thoughtful migrants to investigate the British company's purchases. They discovered that the notorious Colonel Wakefield had bought for virtually nothing 20 million acres (9 million hectares) from 58 Maori of different tribes. Ten thousand natives lived in the huge area, all of whom were legitimate landowners since, according to Maori law, each had a right to a share and could not be deprived of it without his personal, explicit consent. Otherwise the sale was invalid. They found that whalers and Protestant ministers before Wakefield had bought some of the same land and that purchases made in such fashion by the company were called 'daylight robbery' by the Maori.[26]

6. Meanwhile, Governor Hobson was looking for a place to establish a new capital in the Bay of Islands. He wanted to get cheap land, but this was rather difficult because Maori had relinquished nearly all their land to Anglican missionaries and colonists. If the latter were to sell it to the governor, they would charge him an exorbitant price. Thus he realised that he would have to look for a suitable, cheap site elsewhere.

In 1796 Captain Cook, visiting the area for the first time, recommended that the Hauraki Gulf would provide a suitable European settlement location. Mr Hobson visited the area. He found that the land was occupied by Maori. Nevertheless, he chose a site for the new town and for a nominal sum he acquired nearly all the isthmus and surrounding area. On 19 September 1840 he raised the British flag and called the new capital *Auckland*.

To tell the truth, this is one of the finest and most pleasant areas in the colony. It is better situated for sea and land trade on both coasts than its sister towns. Auckland lies on a narrow isthmus, nearly in the centre of the North Island. Because of the numerous bays in the Hauraki Gulf it provides communication by water to remote, inland areas. It is surrounded by arable, but not very fertile, land. One could compare it to Corinth for trade and to Naples for the beauty of its harbour. The population of Auckland and district in the 1886 census was about 60,000 Europeans. Now it is about 65,000.

That same year, 1840, the Queen approved Auckland as the new capital and in January 1841 Governor Hobson transferred his residence there.

The first sale of land by public auction took place in Auckland in April 1841. The auction was publicised months before in Sydney and attracted a great number of speculators. Forty-one one-acre town lots were sold at an average of 14,800 francs each. The following September a similar sale produced 1125 francs an acre for suburban lots and 75 francs for country blocks.

Sales were authorised by the Crown in 1840. It was decreed that all Crown lands were to be sold at a set price. Later the secretary of state ordered that town and suburban lots should be sold for not less than a pound (25 francs) an acre, and permitting the governor to gift Crown land to private individuals and public bodies. Later, when New Zealand had its own constitution, these terms were changed and prices adjusted according to the area and particular features.

7. In August 1840, a French whaling ship, *Conte de Paris*, with seventy-seven migrants on board, arrived at Banks Peninsula on the east coast of the South Island. They landed on the shores of *Akaroa* harbour where they built huts and wooden houses on land bought in 1838 from local Maori.

Banks Peninsula was formed from volcanic activity, and is a pleasant area. French colonists cultivated the land well and planted fruit trees and vineyards, transforming the area into one magnificent, fertile garden. Today it is renowned as one of the most beautiful places in New Zealand.[27]

This is how French emigration to Akaroa occurred. In 1838, Mr Langlois, captain of a French whaler, bought 30,000 acres (about 13,000 hectares) at Akaroa and environs from Banks Peninsula Maori. It was agreed that part of the purchase price be paid immediately. This was done, and the remainder was to be paid on Mr Langlois' return. The captain returned to France the same year, and sought partners to fund French colonisation. He succeeded in establishing a partnership with two Nantes firms, two in Bordeaux, and with two members in Paris. Thus the 'Nanto-Bordelaise Company' was formed. In 1839 it sent Langlois and migrants to Akaroa. They arrived in August the following year, paid the natives the balance of the agreed price in merchandise valued at 10,000 francs and the Maori gave Langlois the purchase deed for the land acquired two years previously.

From the moment of their arrival, the French migrants were fiercely opposed by Governor Hobson, his officials and agents. They wanted them to abandon the Akaroa settlement. So they spread the rumour that Langlois had not paid the Maori and that his deed of purchase was invalid because it had been made after the proclamation of British sovereignty over the country. The truth, however, was that the purchase was made in 1838 and therefore valid, and that he paid the agreed price. In fact, there is written evidence that Langlois was much fairer and more honest towards the natives than all the other speculators, including Anglican ministers.

The colonial commission ordered by the governor to examine all purchases made before 1840 tried to invalidate the Nanto-Bordelaise Company's Akaroa purchase. It turned to the British government, and at the request of the prime minister, a London commission considered the French company's transaction. After examining documents provided they were satisfied that the Nanto-Bordelaise Company spent £11,685 or 292,125 francs for the land purchase and colonisation of Akaroa. Therefore, the Nanto-Bordelaise Company, according to Lord Russell's edict '*was entitled to*' four acres for every pound spent on the settlement, in accordance with the same conditions established for the British New Zealand Company.[28] The French company therefore had the right to 46,740 acres rather than the 30,000 acres at Akaroa it claimed. But the government let it have just the 30,000 acres it requested.

The colonial government's systematic opposition to French migration caused the immediate suspension of the plan to send more colonists to Akaroa. The Nanto-Bordelaise Company was held ransom in a myriad of ways, for years receiving fine promises which came to nothing. Eventually, it grew tired of the unfair struggle. Without waiting to find out the British government's London commission's decision, which, as was mentioned, recognised its legitimacy, it sold its rights to Akaroa to the British New Zealand Company on 4 July 1849, under ruinous terms, for only £4500. The colonial government[29] was extremely pleased with the sale and the French company lost 200,000 francs according to its enemies, and 800,000 according to the company.

Nine years opposition, ending in the sale of the French company's rights, completely ruined the Akaroa settlement. Most of the seventy-seven French migrants, disgusted by their unfair treatment, left for other lands. A few settlers remained, and their offspring have intermarried with British colonists.

Up till 1840 New Zealand was part of the New South Wales colony, but then the British government made it an independent colony. Hobson was appointed governor. Its three islands, North, South and Stewart were called New Ulster, New Munster and New Leinster, but after a brief period these titles fell into disuse and they were called the North, South and Stewart Islands. An executive council was set up comprising the governor, his secretary and colonial treasurer, together with a legislative council comprising the above-mentioned officials and three senior justices of the peace. District magistrates, a chief justice and a Crown solicitor were also appointed. A Protestant bishopric was created, and Rev. George Augustus Selwyn, a man of fine qualities and vision, was made the colony's first bishop.

The first meeting of the Legislative Chamber took place in Auckland in May 1841. The governor opened it and a number of decrees were issued. 'While meetings appeared to be democratic,' Dr Thomson comments, 'in fact, however, the Governor made the decisions.'[30]

8. Towards the end of 1840, 200 British colonists in Wellington found themselves reduced to dire poverty because arable land was eighty-three kilometres away from their settlement. They decided to emigrate to Wanganui on the west coast, 190 kilometres north of Wellington. When they arrived, they settled six kilometres from the mouth of the Wanganui river, navigable only with small craft. They called their settlement Petre. Later the township that grew up was called Wanganui.

Colonel Wakefield, the British company's agent, claimed he had bought nearly all of Wanganui and part of Taranaki from local Maori. This was not true. There were many Maori living in Wanganui; the land was fertile and there was coastal communication with Wellington.

In 1841 another group of migrants went to Taranaki, north of Wanganui. The first settlers arrived in May and the rest in September. They were sent to New Zealand by an English association called 'the New Plymouth Company'. They settled near the coast and called the area where they pitched tent New Plymouth. Taranaki is known as the garden of New Zealand for its natural beauty and fertile soil. Since it was not endowed with a natural harbour, the colonial government with the support of the New Plymouth council built a harbour for the township. Recently New Plymouth and Wanganui have been opened up by rail communication with other North Island towns.

Towards the end of the same year, twenty-seven Scottish migrants arrived in the Manukau harbour, on the west coast of the North Island, in the Auckland area. They landed and tried to settle. However, the New Zealand Company had no legal title to any local Maori land. The governor gave the newcomers land in other areas, and bought up a good part of the area for himself from the Maori.

Meanwhile, in October 1841, two large British ships arrived at Tasman Bay, at the top of the South Island, opposite Cook Strait. The numerous migrants were looking forward to claiming the land they had earlier bought in London from the New Zealand Company.

Local Maori opposed their landing, vehemently denying they sold land to Colonel Wakefield. Captain Arthur Wakefield, the company's new agent at Nelson, and brother of the unscrupulous colonel, promised the natives that his brother would give them presents once the migrants had their land. The natives argued about the proposal among themselves, but the majority agreed to it. Surveyors and emigrants were thus able to disembark. They chose the site of their future town, later called *Nelson*, and they began to settle in the bay area.[31]

The new arrivals were very happy with the mild, pleasant climate, and the magnificent harbour at their doorstep, although it had a difficult entrance. A superb natural reef enclosed it. The local land was also very fertile.

The Maori realised that they had blatantly been robbed of their land by the New Zealand Company. They became further disillusioned with British colonists, many of whom became even more insolent, not only treating the poor savages with contempt, but regarding them as a local pestilence, preventing the settlers from getting land to which in fact they had no right. Deep antagonism thus grew between the two races living side by side.

In Wellington, colonists had taken possession of land which was not theirs, in spite of Maori protests. Seeing their justifiable objections had no effect, they let Europeans know that they would retaliate to assert their legitimate rights. Things got so bad that both sides committed secret murders. The British burnt down the Maori settlement of Te Aro by stealth. In reprisal, outraged natives at night demolished huts built by the colonists by day on their land. To put a stop to the clashes, the Wellington magistrate had a warrant issued for chief Rangihaeata's arrest, but no policeman had the courage to execute it. Thus discord increased between the two races.[32]

Things were no better at Wanganui than in Wellington. Wakefield, the unscrupulous company agent, put emigrants on land he claimed to have bought. The Maori formally denied they had ever sold any of their ancestral lands, and told the intruders they would take up arms if they dared to occupy it.

In Taranaki, things were even worse. In the fighting which took place between 1825 and 1834, local tribes were taken into slavery by the fierce chiefs, Rauparaha and Te Whero Whero. In 1839 and 1840 Wakefield bought the whole area from the few natives still living there for next to nothing. In 1841, more than a thousand freed slaves returned to their Taranaki homeland and found that they had been sold out for trinkets. They said that they did not recognise the sale and requested the migrants to leave. They took no notice and consequently many disputes arose between the two races. Eventually, Governor Hobson bought the whole vast area for £400 (10,000 francs) from Te Whero Whero on the basis that the bloodthirsty cannibal had got it by right of conquest in 1834. Thus, the unhappy owners were stripped of their ancestral lands and had to be content that nothing worse happened. Hostility between the two races was to last for many years to come.[33]

At Nelson the situation got more and more complicated. Colonists discovered coal deposits at Murderers' Bay and began mining. Local natives denied selling the land and refused gifts they were offered in payment. Europeans continued mining coal, but natives stole it at night. Consequently, the Nelson magistrate ordered a chief to be arrested. He was then sentenced to a fine or face imprisonment. The chief, believing he was in the right, refused to pay, but his wife secretly paid and he was freed. The dim-witted magistrate was very pleased that he had taught British law to the *cowardly niggers*, as colonists called poor Maori. But they did not realise that while they were slow to revolt, they were not easily quelled.

Thomson wrote that, 'While Company emigrants were teaching Maori English law at the expense of justice'[34] and legality, similar disputes caused by European occupation of native land were occurring further north, namely, at Kaipara, Mongonui and Wangarei.

9. In the midst of all this trouble and unrest, Governor Hobson who had suffered a stroke shortly after arriving in New Zealand, died in Auckland on September 1842 at the age of forty-nine. He had governed the colony for only thirty-five months. His remains are buried in the Auckland Anglican cemetery.

Colonists' and scholars' verdict on Hobson's rule was that, notwithstanding his impartiality and good intentions, because he had spent thirty years in the British navy, he was seen as unfit to govern a burgeoning colony. Weak-minded, he allowed himself to a large extent to be controlled by Anglican missionaries whose policies, declared Mr Hursthouse, 'led to fighting, ruin for thousands of colonists and degradation for countless Maori.'[35] The country was brought to the brink of ruin. Europeans, therefore, strongly opposed Hobson and petitioned the British government for his recall to England. The strength of opposition to him and illness caused his premature death.

On Hobson's death, Mr Willoughby Shortland, colonial secretary, assumed the role of acting-governor, and he held the office for fifteen months. He was a vain man and, once in office, he became arrogant, following his predecessor's policy. After the new governor's arrival in December 1843, he was sent to govern another British colony. During his short term as governor he encountered major problems because of ever-increasing disputes between the two races, raising serious concerns for the future.

10. Finally, the whirlwind struck, in the South Island. A bloody massacre occurred in the *Wairau* valley, south-east of Nelson, in what is now the Marlborough district. Events occurred as follows:

The New Zealand Company claimed it had purchased land in the valley, but local natives denied selling any. Captain Wakefield, company agent, took no notice of Maori opposition. In April 1843 he sent surveyors to survey the land. This upset the natives. Local chiefs, Rauparaha and Rangihaeata, informed Wakefield that they would rather die than give up their rights. The agent feigned ignorance and had the surveyors continue. Rauparaha then had pegs and surveyors' equipment removed from huts built in the valley and he burnt them down. To their protests he replied that the material used to build huts was taken from his land and he therefore had the right to do what he liked with it. When news reached Nelson, Magistrate Thompson, whose role was *protector* of Maori as well as the colonial government's representative in Nelson, ordered the arrest of chiefs Rauparaha and Rangihaeata for arson.[36]

The magistrate and Wakefield, the Crown solicitor, Captain England, five other citizens and forty constables and militia boarded a brigantine to carry out their dangerous mission and set sail for Cloudy Bay, and thence for the trouble spot. On 17 June 1843 they reached the Wairau valley. After a few hours march they arrived at their destination. Rauparaha and 100 warriors were encamped. The magistrate and his men approached the native camp. The following conversation took place between Magistrate Thompson, who acted as interpreter, and the chief. Although Rauparaha had converted to Protestantism he had not abandoned his ferociousness and aggression.[37]

– Oh! said the magistrate, where is chief Rauparaha?

– I am here, said the chief, standing up. What do you want of me?

– I have come to arrest you and Rangihaeata for burning down surveyors' huts.

– I have not burnt down anything belonging to Europeans, replied the savage. The huts were built from timber taken from my land, and I can do what I choose with my own possessions.

– And where is Rangihaeata? asked the magistrate.

– Rangihaeata, who had been sitting in silence, jumped to his feet and replied scornfully, I am here. I am at home on my own land. I do not go to England to meddle in your business.

– Leave this to me to sort out, said Rauparaha to his brother-in-law.

– Rauparaha, said the magistrate, I implore you to surrender if you wish to avoid more serious consequences.

– I do not want to go to prison. I wish to remain here. I have done no wrong. If you think you have a case, take it to court. Lay a charge. I do not mind. But I will never be treated like a slave.

– If you don't surrender, I will have my troops open fire.

– I hope, replied the cannibal drily, that you would be intelligent enough to see the consequences.

At this point the magistrate pulled out handcuffs and Rauparaha put his hands under his cloak.

Then the magistrate turned to his men and exclaimed: 'Soldiers! Fix bayonets, arrest the chiefs!' Captain England advanced at the head of his troops. A soldier fired and Te Ronga, Rauparaha's sister and Rangihaeata's wife, fell gasping to the ground. In the confusion that followed, Rauparaha was heard shouting: 'The light must die! Daylight is no more! Welcome death's embracing gloom!'[38]

At the signal for attack foolishly given by the Europeans, the natives fired on their assailants. Terrified by the Maori resistance, they tried to flee, but they fell on them, massacring them horribly. Of the British force, twenty-two were killed and four wounded. The others managed to flee or hide in the bush. Magistrate Thompson, Captain Wakefield, the company agent, Richardson, the Crown solicitor and Captain England were among the dead. Maori suffered five dead and eight wounded.

Who should be held responsible for the massacre? Colonel Wakefield, who by his unjust claims and thefts intended to strip natives of their land; the company for supporting its agent's injustices, and Magistrate Thompson and other Nelson officials for attempting to subvert justice with brute force. When Lord Stanley, colonial secretary in London, heard about the unhappy event he said, 'Those who unfairly make war against barbarous tribes have no right to complain about their atrocities in reprisal.' Mr Fox Bourne was right in saying that European conduct at Wairau 'was clearly illegal, unjust and foolish.'[39]

Rauparaha and his Wairau kin barricaded themselves at Otaki, near Wellington. He told his compatriots what had happened, showing them the handcuffs that were meant for him. News spread by word of mouth throughout the island, heartening exploited natives. In their eyes, British military prestige had been dashed and their sympathies were with the two brave chiefs. Rauparaha, fearing British reprisals, declared that he would wipe them all out if any of his kin suffered harm because of his actions at Wairau.

Maori were proud of Rauparaha's success and predicted further victories against their enemies when in 1843 they saw a spectacular comet and witnessed a severe earthquake in the Wanganui district. Furthermore, headstrong warriors wanted to take on the British troops. Nelson and Wellington colonists' reaction also raised natives' hopes. When they heard about the disaster they were filled with utter terror.

Knowing that Rauparaha was in the Wellington area, colonists were very anxious, fearing that he would pounce on them at any moment. Frantically they sent messengers to the acting-governor in Auckland, and to Australia and Tasmania, requesting soldiers to protect them against the Maori. Shortland considered the Wairau massacre as a native warning to rapacious colonists. Fearing for Auckland's safety, he ordered Europeans in outlying areas to come to town for greater security. He immediately sent fifty-three soldiers of the 96th Regiment to Wellington, appointing Major Richmond as southern chief magistrate. At the same time the British frigate *North Star* reached the port of Wellington from Australia with a company of soldiers of the 80th Regiment.

Boosted by the troops' presence, colonists requested local magistrates to avenge their compatriots' deaths by hanging Rauparaha and Rangihaeata. But they had more sense and were unwilling even to arrest them, fearing this would lead to open warfare and the colonists' annihilation. Denied their revenge, they execrated the Maori race. An indignant Colonel Wakefield, prime cause of all the harm, declared that the time would soon come when, with an increase in British colonists, there would be thorough revenge.[40] His prediction, as we shall see, would come true twenty years later, to the discredit of so-called British civilisation.

When news of the Wairau disaster reached England, people considered that New Zealand was not safe for Europeans to settle, and emigration was suspended for some time. The New Zealand Company, which in less than three years had sent forty-four shiploads of migrants for Wellington, Wanganui, Taranaki and Nelson, stopped sending new migrants.

11. In the meantime, the British government was considering who to send to succeed Hobson after his death. Sir Robert Fitzroy, a naval captain, was chosen for the difficult post. He arrived in Auckland in December 1843. As soon as he landed in New Zealand he made a brief, reassuring speech, saying, 'I have come here to do the best that I can.' In fact, during his brief term of office, he showed that he was fair-minded, impartial, a peace-lover and well-disposed towards the unfortunate, despised natives. A governor with this temperament was hardly ideal for most of the British. They wanted someone who thought and acted quite differently.

The following day, the governor held a public reception at which Maori made two addresses. In the first, they complained about not having the right to sell people their land; in the second, that tobacco was too expensive.

On 18 January 1844, Governor Fitzroy embarked for Wellington to investigate the cause of the Wairau conflict. At a public meeting, colonists demanded revenge on their companions' killers. Natives protested about white hostility towards them.

He went from Wellington to Nelson. After hearing an account of the Wairau debacle, he criticised the magistrates for ordering the two chiefs' arrest as arsonists. '*Arson*,' said the governor, 'means burning down another's home. It is not *arson* to burn down one's own home. The natives never sold the Wairau block. The hut that was burnt down was built on native land with materials belonging to them. Hence it was not an act of arsonists and the arrest warrant was illegal.' His speech incensed the Europeans. Some magistrates resigned and said that the governor was insane. His visit to Nelson, far from reducing the acrimony between the two races, only increased it.[41]

Captain Fitzroy travelled from Nelson to Waikanai to question Rauparaha. He found him entrooped with 500 natives. The governor said he had visited Wellington and Nelson to discover the truth about what happened at Wairau. Now he had come to hear Rauparaha's account, so he could reach an objective judgement concerning the disaster. Rauparaha described in minute detail what happened, and concluded by saying that at least twice Magistrate Thompson ordered his men to fire on the Maori. When the eloquent chief finished speaking, there was an half hour of complete silence, as the verdict was awaited. The governor said, 'The Pakeha (colonists) were wrong to build huts at Wairau and to arrest you, because you were not guilty. Since Europeans attacked you first, I will not seek retribution for their deaths.' After this, the governor left the native camp and returned to Auckland.

Company agents and colonists, hearing about the Maori pardon, flew into a rage, 'howling with fury, according to Kennedy, and denounced the governor's behaviour as cowardly and unfair. They said that he was biased, and tried to discredit him as much as they could.'[42] For these fine folk, justice came out of a gun or cannon. Fortunately, Captain Fitzroy did not share their thinking.

From 1840 only the colonial government could legally buy Maori land. Since the previous Governors Hobson and Shortland had exhausted their funds, little land had been acquired from Maori. As they were short of money they complained to Fitzroy but at that time he would neither buy their land or permit individuals to buy it.

The governor then decided to placate the natives and also restore his exhausted finances. In March 1844 he gave Europeans permission to buy land from Maori on condition that purchasers paid the government 12 francs and 50 centimes for every acre bought. This was plainly unfair.

The new system was used for a while, but it did not suit sellers or buyers. Maori did not like it because they were constrained either not to sell or at a minimal price to avoid the large tax. Europeans felt similarly, because they wanted to pay nominal amounts for land and nothing to the government. General dissatisfaction arose particularly among natives. They claimed that through its taxation the government did not recognise their property rights. They drew the conclusion that the Treaty of Waitangi was a fraud and that their lands were no longer theirs. In October that year, to placate both sides, the governor decreed that buyers would have only to pay 10 centimes an acre to the government.[43]

It was mentioned earlier that Hobson instead of recognising Taranaki slaves and fugitives' rights approved Te Whero Whero's right of conquest. The dispossessed natives did not remain compliant. In 1844 they reoccupied some of their disputed land. The commission set up to examine purchase deeds said that the New Zealand Company could claim 60,000 acres. Governor Fitzroy, however, decided it should have only 3500 acres, and recognised the slaves' and fugitives' right to the rest. His decision was most unpopular among colonists, but the governor acted justly.

12. As has been mentioned elsewhere, up to 1840 many British and some Americans tried to plunder as much Maori land as they could. They acquired the land for trinkets and baubles, for old muskets, a little gunpowder and such like. Dr Thomson writes that greed for New Zealand land was not just restricted to traders and venous individuals openly flaunting their wealth and possessions. Protestant missionaries, members of Sydney's gentry including the well-known lawyer Wentworth, Mr Busby, former British Resident, and directors and agents of the New Zealand Company had their fingers in the pie. They claimed to have acquired 45 million acres (equivalent to half of Italy) from the Maori.

In 1840 the British government decreed that all purchase deeds regarding Maori land would be invalid unless approved by governmental commission. Accordingly, the Sydney government quickly appointed a three-member commission who travelled to New Zealand that year. They announced that all requests for approval had to be sent within six months to the government in Auckland, and that no individual could have more than 2560 acres, or four square miles.

The commission also gave a schedule of land values according to the time of purchase. Put in monetary or commercial terms, this was as follows: for land bought before 1824, 60 centimes an acre; for land bought between 1825 and 1834, between 60 centimes and 2 francs; for land bought in 1835, between one and two francs, 50 centimes; land bought in 1839, from 5 to 12 francs an acre. Merchandise given in payment to Maori was put at three times the Sydney value.[44]

The commission discovered that deeds of sale were prepared in England and Sydney with the amount of land left blank. They were then sent to New Zealand agents. It was discovered that a Sydney law clerk prepared a huge number of the documents and he sold them in New Zealand for 125 francs each. As has already been mentioned, in many cases Maori had no idea that they had sold their land. Often there were multiple purchasers of the same land. Fishing permits conceded in certain coastal areas were converted to title deeds for miles and miles of surrounding land. Huge tracts of land, identified by longitude and latitude, or main river boundaries were bought for trifling amounts, set out on a scrap of paper. Purchasers also inserted the extent of their purchases after obtaining signatures. Many chiefs sold land that was not theirs. Finally, the whole of the South Island was bought from a few natives who happened to be in Sydney in 1839.[45]

Of 26 million acres claimed to have been legally bought by 1200 individuals, not including New Zealand Company purchases, the governmental commission approved only 100,000 acres. It returned the rest to its rightful owners. The New Zealand Company, which argued it had bought more than 20 million acres (by manipulation and deceit), only obtained from the commission, at the government's insistence, 122,900 acres in Wellington and Nelson; 40,000 acres at Wanganui and 3500 acres at New Plymouth in Taranaki. It had to return the rest to the natives.

13. Most ministers, missionaries and Anglican catechists in New Zealand had huge amounts of Maori land purchased for less than all the other fraudsters put together paid.

It should be mentioned that when the London Foreign Missionary Society sends ministers and missionaries overseas, it guarantees not only to support them but also their families and pays them a stipend according to their position, so that they can maintain and educate their children appropriately. The stipend also increases according to the size of the family. To make this commitment less onerous, when the society began sending missionaries to New Zealand, it gave them permission to obtain sufficient Maori land to raise their families adequately.

This was the most foolish thing the Church Missionary Society agreed to. In no time at all, missionaries took so much advantage of this that they took over huge amounts of land. On their missionary journeys, they searched out the most productive area, the finest locations and places with best ease of communication, and later they returned there to live. They then opened trading posts and did business with Maori as though they were traders born.[46]

These reverend gentlemen were invited by chiefs to settle among them. They consented after obtaining as a token of their good will *as missionaries* huge amounts of the land they had already espied. This was to cover all their present and future needs. And it was not long before they began to collect donations and impose tithing on the poor natives. The government also, to overcome Maori resistance to British imperial expansion and promote emigration, used missionaries' influence to acquire land for its own use. They were, accordingly, paid handsomely from state funds.[47]

A missionary, who is still alive, told natives one day that he needed a piece of land to build a native school. He obtained several thousand hectares of good land from the simple folk. Instead of building the school he used it to graze large herds of his sheep and cattle. Only several years later did he build a school on just a small piece of the land. Another well-known New Zealand Anglican minister had 450 hectares given to him to build a Maori school. Before obtaining this land he got a beautiful piece of lakeside land from the Maori. Once he had the extra land, he still did not build the school. To this day the priestly farmer tends to sheep rather than pupils.[48]

Other Protestant missionaries, like Shepherd, bought land from natives for next to nothing. Dr Lang, a Protestant minister, mentions that Shepherd, 'bought a great amount of land (about thirty-five square kilometres) bordering a navigable Bay of Islands river for two shirts and an iron pot.'[49]

'Rev. Henry Williams, archdeacon of Tukerau, became owner of all the land from Kororareka to the Hokianga, and he used similar means to Shepherd's. This can also be said of his brother, W. Williams, bishop of Waiapu and similarly of Maunsell, archdeacon of the Waikato. Many others could be mentioned, but these few examples will suffice.'[50]

Before the commission's inquiry into land acquired by saintly Protestant stalwarts, they strongly insisted they had fairly *bought* more than 600,000 acres, or more than 2400 square kilometres, from the Maori. But when they realised that their claims would come under the commission's scrutiny, they reduced the amount to 216,763 acres. If the commission had been firm and enforced strict, true justice it would have quashed all their purchases and not allowed them an inch of land. This did not happen because under the governorship of Hobson, Shortland and Fitzroy missionaries were all powerful. Rather, because of ministerial intervention, the commission had to dispense with the regulation of not allowing any person more than 2560 acres.

Dr Thomson, a devout Protestant and fervent defender of his church and ministers, provided the names of twenty-two of these ministers, their claims and concessions by the government commission, together with purchases made by the Anglican Missionary Society and missionary families. The most important are listed as follows: 'Rev. Richard Taylor requested 50,000 acres and was allowed 1,704. Rev. Henry Williams, so intent on getting the Maori to sign the Treaty of Waitangi, and later made an archdeacon, requested 22,000 acres and was granted 9,000. Rev. W. Williams, his brother, a few years later made Anglican Bishop of Waiapu, claimed he had bought 890 acres and was allowed this amount. C. Baker requested 6,242 acres and was granted 2,560. G. Clarke requested 19,000 acres and received 5,500. R. Davis wanted 6,000 acres and was granted 3,500. W.T. Fairburn claimed the right to 20,000 acres and was granted 2,560. S.H. Ford wanted 8,400 and got 1,757. J. Hamlin requested 6,774 and received 3,937. J. Kemp claimed 18,552 acres and got 5,276. J. King requested 10,300 acres and was granted 5,150. J. Shepherd wanted 11,860 acres and got 5,330. Ten other ministers together claimed 18,880 acres and received 16,449. The Anglican Missionary Society requested 11,665 acres and got nothing. Missionary families claimed to have purchased 6,200 acres and received 3,100. Total claims amounted to 216,763 acres and the Commission approved 66,713.'[51] Mention has been made only of Anglican missionaries who went to New Zealand before 1838. There are no official statistics regarding later purchases.

Maori were willing to generously cede land and sovereignty to Protestant missionaries on condition that they received *valid payment and the clear, substantial benefits* they were promised. Father Barsanti rightly comments: 'When the poor, deluded savages saw ministers becoming prosperous at their expense; when they witnessed their families grow and spread while their own continued to decline; when, in short, conditions deteriorated altogether and they realised they were heading for extinction instead of reaping clear and substantial benefits, they then lost all their trust and respect in ministers. They called them *money-hungry sharks* and their religion a cloak used to conceal their greed, deceit and baseness.'[52]

When the Maori discovered their so-called friends' deceit, they tried to repair the grave damage. Most chiefs were desolate at the realisation of their desperate situation and addressed their tribes: 'Oh! What can we do? Look! We are losing our mana. Our ancestors' lands are passing into foreigners' hands. If we continue to allow these predators to live here we will lose everything, and we will not even have enough land to bury our dead!'[53] Their patriotic lament was the prelude to a long, ferocious struggle against their oppressors, as we shall see in due course. The outcome, however, for the brave, honest and valiant people worthy of a better fate, was mayhem, ruin and slaughter.

14. Before concluding the chapter, we should briefly mention New Zealand's social, commercial and financial condition by the end of 1844.

According to the 1841 census conducted by Mr Edward Helswell, the total Maori population was 107,219. Only 4424 lived in the South Island; the rest inhabited the North Island.[54] The European population, including migration figures from 1839, was 12,447 by the end of 1844. There were 2754 in Auckland; 531 at Kororareka (Bay of Islands); 179 at Hokianga; 1155 at New Plymouth in Taranaki; 197 at Wanganui; 4347 in Wellington; and in the South Island, 3,036 in Nelson and 245 at Akaroa.

Colonists who settled in the upper half of the North Island were mostly migrants from Australia. The others came directly from England. Their occupations were as follows: At Russell there was the whaling industry. In the Hokianga they milled timber. In Auckland the population was mostly employed as clerks or workers for government departments. At Akaroa they farmed, planted vines and were orchardists. Elsewhere they made a living as best they could. They had not been able to get farmland because of disputes between the two races. Eventually they hoped there would be a solution to the problem and that they could begin farming. The military presence comprised 150 soldiers of the 80th Regiment.

Most European homes were wooden. There were also many raupo huts. The government, however, banned them because of fire risk.

There was no shortage of labour. Being short of money, few were able to set themselves up in farming. The New Zealand Company organised road construction and labourers, besides their upkeep, received 19 francs a week. Carpenters and masons were much in demand and they received 100 francs a week.

European and natives' staple diet was pork and potatoes. Maori supplied pork for 70 centimes a kilo. Beef was rarely available because of the scarcity of cattle in New Zealand. It was sold at three and a half francs a kilo and mutton at two francs, fifty centimes. Chickens cost seven and a half francs each, and eggs between seven and eight francs a dozen. The common beverages, besides water, were gin and rum, which were plentifully consumed.

During this period, Maori were generally at peace among themselves, but they were disturbed by the colonial government's and European usurpation. Nevertheless they believed that they could protect themselves against their encroachment. During 1840 and 1841 they traded pork and potatoes for pipes, tobacco and other domestic articles. Later, in settlements they invariably demanded money for their produce, but inland they continued to trade in the usual way. Those who embraced Protestantism were less hospitable than the others and, according to various Protestant writers, 'religion consisted for them more in words than deeds.'[55]

Colonial revenue came from British government subsidies, duty on imports, and particularly from taxes on tobacco and blankets, much in demand by Maori, and finally from government profit from selling native land to Europeans. In 1844 revenue from duty was 277,500 francs. Total income for the year, including duty, was only 593,275 francs while expenditure amounted to 1,353,650 francs. The governor had to issue debentures for 760,000 francs to settle the deficit.[56]

Hobson left the colony in a deplorable financial condition. In his 35 months' rule, in spite of the British government's million and a half subsidy and the million collected from land sold in Auckland in 1841, he left the country on the brink of ruin.[57] In 1843 Governor Fitzroy found himself similarly strapped for cash. The government was not only in a most embarrassing financial position, but it had exhausted its funds and employees' and soldiers' wages were several months in arrears, with a deficit of 500,000 francs.[58]

Nine weekly papers were published during this period: one at Russell in Maori; the rest in English, namely, two at Russell in the Bay of Islands, four in Auckland, two in Wellington and one in Nelson.

CHAPTER SEVEN

Unrest Throughout the Country From 1845 to 1850

SUMMARY. – 1. Chief Heke. – 2. Heke destroys Kororareka.– 3. Government declares war on Heke. – 4. A new governor. – 5. Fighting against Heke continues. – 6. Fighting in Wellington. – 7. Uprisings in Wanganui. – 8. The 'Fencibles'. – 9. New migrants in Otago. – 10. 1848 earthquake. – 11. Proposal for an autonomous New Zealand government. – 12. Colonial statistics, 1850-1851.

1. Because of Governor Fitzroy's incompetence, European colonists' greed, and the duplicity shown towards natives, New Zealand was in the grips of internal upheavals which presaged considerable trouble ahead. Fitzroy, in attempting to bolster Treasury's exhausted coffers by imposing taxes and duty on all imports, particularly inflamed northern Maori discontent, so much so that horrendous conflict seemed inevitable.

The number of whalers visiting Kororareka, New Zealand's main trading centre, declined dramatically because of customs duties. Up till then whalers provided Maori with a steady, lucrative trade. Tobacco and blankets, which previously they could afford to buy at reasonably low prices, not only leapt hugely in price, but became scarce.

Maori chiefs reflected on the change in circumstances. They believed that they had now lost all their influence with Europeans and that a new force, completely outside their experience, had sprung up in their midst, paralysing their traditional trading system. An American colonist at Kororareka, well known to the natives, fanned the smouldering embers, telling them that the British flag flying from a Kororareka hill symbolised the power destroying the country's trade and keeping whalers away. His words made an impression on the natives. Later, when they had only tattered blankets and hardly any tobacco, they felt convinced that the British flag was to blame and that if it were removed former days of peace and prosperity would be restored.[1]

One who was most affected by the worsening situation was *Hone* (John) *Heke,* a Ngapuhi chief who lived at Kaikohe, not far from Kororareka. He was born in 1808 of a sub-tribe, and from the age of sixteen he participated in the fierce campaigns of Hongi, his ferocious chief. As a young man he distinguished himself by his mental agility, courage and military prowess. When he was nineteen Hongi gave him his much coveted daughter in marriage. Through this splendid match Heke acquired prestige among his people and Hongi's magical influence when he died. An illustration of the couple is depicted on the opposite page.

From his early youth the new chief was taught by Anglican missionaries and he soon surpassed all in his knowledge of the Protestant Bible. In 1833, when he was about twenty-five years old, he was solemnly baptised. Heke was regarded almost as an elder of the Anglican church and as a great chief, as Protestant ministers described him, 'who excelled others in his knowledge of the scriptures.'[2] From the time of his baptism up till 1842 the 'distinguished Protestant missionary' did very good business with whalers visiting Kororareka, 'trading pork, potatoes and other local produce and young women slaves.'[3] He wrote to the Queen of England that his people were quite confused about the various religious beliefs established in the country. 'When the first missionaries arrived,' he said, 'they declared that the Church of England was the one true church. Now, however, there are three churches saying the same thing! How can we know the truth?'[4] If Heke were alive today, what would he now say, with more than 100 Protestant denominations in New Zealand?

Dr Thomson mentions that 'as an older man Heke returned to his former beliefs and relished debating religion, disputing the truth of the Bible and using Christians' [Protestants'] own arguments against them. He had no liking for Europeans and loathed the English. He compared them to Egyptians at the time of Pharaoh, and Maori to the oppressed Israelites. He claimed that natives were colonists' slaves, and as proof, said that many Maori worked for the British, but never vice versa.' He said to his tribe: 'Up till 1841 you were well clad; now you have only threadbare blankets to cover your bare skin. Before, you smoked choice American tobacco; now you are forced to smoke dry leaves.'[5]

Heke was not keen on fighting, knowing its harmful effects on trade, and he liked making money. Nevertheless, he enjoyed a reputation as a valiant warrior. Wishing to become famous like Hongi, his father-in-law, he took advantage of general Maori discontent to increase his prestige among his people.

Lord, an Englishman, lived with a woman from Heke's tribe at Kororareka. One day, in a rage, she called Heke *a pig*. To avenge the insult, he collected 100 men and went to Kororareka. He ransacked Lord's house and returned the woman to her tribal home. Lord offered him a cask of tobacco as recompense, providing she was returned to him. Heke agreed but Lord reneged on the deal. Further insulted, Heke and his warriors went back to Kororareka, sacked a few houses and cursed the Europeans.[6]

Two days later, on 8 July 1844, Heke gathered his mostly Protestant warriors, telling them to place themselves under divine protection and to pray to the Christian God and *Tumatawenga*, their god of war. They then performed a war dance, climbed the hill, chopped down the flagstaff and pulled down the British flag, burning it on the spot and took away shot used to signal ships' arrival in the harbour.

Their brazen declaration of war shocked the governor who had only ninety

Chief Heke and his wife, 1845.

soldiers in Auckland. He sent urgent dispatches to Australia, requesting soldiers, arms and ammunition. At the beginning of August, 180 well-armed soldiers under the command of Colonel Hulme of the 99th Regiment reached Kororareka with two field guns and 30,000 cartridges. They encamped at Kororareka. The governor and soldiers arrived from Auckland on board the warship *Hazard*. He ordered the troops to pursue Heke inland.[7]

While troops were landing at Kerikeri, local chiefs urged the governor not to fight, promising to pay for the flag themselves and to be guarantors for Heke's future good conduct. They immediately placed ten old muskets at the governor's feet, which he accepted as payment, promptly returning them. A meeting of Maori was held at which twenty-five chiefs sought the governor's pardon for Heke's action. Heke however did not attend, even though he was only ten miles away. Nevertheless, he sent a letter requesting the governor's pardon for taking the flag down, but he added that the flagstaff was his property. The timber had been taken out of the bush by natives as a flagstaff for a New Zealand or Maori flag, not the British.[8]

The governor accepted Nene and the other chiefs' promise to keep the peace and he sent the soldiers back to Australia. He had a new British flag raised on the same spot. Realising that customs duties had done the country more harm than good and upset the natives, the governor declared Kororareka a free port. His decision pleased local Europeans so much that they lit all the candles they could find, providing a brilliant spectacle.

Thomson writes, 'the colony had never been in such dire straits. The grave financial problems of 1843 were aggravated the following year. The governor could not remedy the situation for lack of funds. Government employees remained unpaid. Customs revenue decreased continually. 400 certificates of title languished in the colonial secretary's office because owners had no money to claim them. Discontented Maori throughout the country stirred, threatening revolt. Europeans were confused, humiliated and afraid. For several days, Heke and 100 men insulted Kororareka residents with impunity and Auckland settlers refrained from manoeuvres for fear of inciting the natives. Further south, the New Zealand Company stopped road building for lack of funds and colonists were in a parlous state. In Nelson, hunger forced colonists to dig up potatoes which they had just planted.'[9]

To prevent the colony's ruin and complete collapse, the Legislative Council passed a law in October 1844 authorising Governor Fitzroy to issue treasury bonds to meet the deficit and it passed another law abolishing customs duties, replacing them with a land tax.[10]

Towards the end of the year, news reached New Zealand that a British Cabinet committee had declared that the Treaty of Waitangi was rather imprudent and unwise, adding that all land not actually occupied by Maori was the property of the British Crown.[11] This foolish decision upset Maori very much. The governor and Anglican missionaries had always led the Maori to believe that the treaty was for their benefit, to preserve their rights over their lands and property. They saw the British government's decision as injurious and oppressive.

Chief Heke took advantage of native discontent, the British government's unfair claims and colonists' provocation to convince the uncommitted and encourage tepid supporters to take up arms and resist usurpation. He also wrote to Governor Fitzroy that he was now convinced that Maori would be stripped of their lands like the unfortunate Australian natives.

In 1883 Rusden, an historian, had the nerve to write: 'French Roman Catholics sowed the seeds of discontent and told the Maori that the British flag was the cause of all their woes.'[12] Rusden's claim is an impudent lie. This can be seen from his earlier reference to Governor Fitzroy's dispatch to Governor Gipps of Sydney, which states: 'The lies told by *treacherous, deceitful British subjects* caused the discontent and unrest.' Rusden, like so many other Protestants who loathe Catholicism, shamefully betrays the truth, falsifying history and contradicting himself.

2. At the beginning of 1845, Heke and his men took up arms and began hostilities by destroying the properties of two British settlers, Hingstone in the Bay of Islands and Mellon at Matakana, because they were occupying land which Maori claimed they never sold them. They then went back to Kororareka, tore up the flag, and chopped down the flagstaff, without meeting any resistance.

Immediately the governor issued two decrees. In the first, he promised £100 (2500 francs) for the arrest of natives who damaged Messrs Hingstone's and Mellon's property. In the second, he offered another £100 to the person who captured Heke. The decrees had no effect, except that the second angered the enemy even more. 'Is Heke a pig,' they asked, 'to be bought and sold?' Chief Heke was not in the least frightened. To match the governor, he offered a reward of £100 in land to the person who brought him the governor's head.[13]

The governor sent a detachment of soldiers to Kororareka to raise the British flag again. This time the flagstaff was sheathed with iron, secured to the ground with chains and surrounded by a solid fence. A blockhouse was built beside it, to house a detachment of soldiers sent to keep watch and defend the flag. This foolish act confirmed Maori in the belief that the flag kept ships from the bay. 'See,' said Heke to his men, 'the flag shows who is in control. Otherwise, why keep on trying to keep it flying?'[14]

Meanwhile in Auckland, on 4 March 1845, the governor in opening the Legislative Council announced that colonial revenue was increasing and that were it not for damage done by an irresponsible press, the country would be at peace. But colonists no longer believed him and sent a petition to the Queen requesting soldiers and money, stating that the natives were becoming insufferable because of Captain Fitzroy's appeasement policy.[15]

When the British flag was raised a third time, chief Heke openly declared that he would not allow it to continue flying. Since Heke never failed to carry out his intentions, settlers and soldiers trained privately for battle and took up the best defence positions in readiness for hostilities. There were just over 500 Europeans living at Kororareka. Captain Robertson of H.M.S. *Hazard* and a company of marines with a cannon took up their position near Monsignor Pompallier's residence. Twenty foot soldiers were sent to defend the flagstaff, other soldiers and armed settlers with three cannons were stationed half-way up the hill and the rest of the infantry and marines and volunteer settlers occupied a barricaded house in the settlement.

At the beginning of March, knowing that Heke and Kawiti, his loyal ally, had taken up arms and were near Kororareka, Walker Nene and some other chiefs went to Heke and begged him to cease hostilities, saying that if he persisted in fighting the British, they would have to oppose him and fight on the whites' side. Heke did not listen to them as he was determined to free his people from British slavery.[16]

'There were 500 mostly Protestant or heathen armed Maori as well as a few Catholics related to Protestant chiefs who were forced to take up arms. God allowed there to be some Catholics among the rebels to prevent worse things happening. They easily got their relatives to promise that the Catholic Bishop and his residence would be respected. In fact, a few days before hostilities began one of them, in the name of the rebel chiefs, went to Bishop Pompallier and promised protection if they were victorious. He was told not to leave his house, which only his presence would protect. The Prelate, after exhausting every means he had to reconcile the two races, turned to pray to the Lord to have mercy on the people who were about to come to blows.'[17]

In the meantime, skirmishes occurred and Lieutenant Philpott was taken prisoner. At first, the Maori took his two pistols off him, then gave him one back and released him, warning him to make sure that he was not caught again.[18]

The following Sunday, an Anglican missionary visited the rebel native camp to preach, taking as text for his sermon St James' words, *'Whence come wars and conflict?'* At the end of the sermon, Heke recommended the preacher to give the same sermon in the British camp 'because, he said, it applies more to them than to us.' In proof of his sincerity and real desire for peace, he told the preacher that he had let Lieutenant Philpott go unharmed.[19]

On 11 March 1845 before dawn, Captain Robertson's position was attacked by 200 natives under Kawiti's command. At the same time, soldiers defending the flagstaff were assaulted by Heke and his men. They overcame them and hauled the flag down again. Captain Robertson defended his position strongly but seeing soldiers running headlong down the hill, he ceased firing and retreated. The British troops withdrew to Polack's stockade. With settlers' assistance and the *Hazard's* cannons, they defended their position for three hours shooting at the enemy concealed in the surrounding hills.[20]

The commander of the American warship *St Louis* which was in port, had great difficulty in keeping his troops, many of whom were English, uninvolved. Shooting continued on shore. A courageous settler offered to climb the hill and retake the flag, but he was refused permission. Meanwhile, women and children fled in terror to the shore. Rowboats and canoes took them to ships. When their embarkation was almost complete, a huge explosion was heard. The enemy had blown up the settlement's magazine. The British held a council of war, and it was decided to cease combat and abandon the village.[21]

During an armistice Maori requested to gather their dead and wounded, settlers and soldiers embarked on the warships *Hazard* and *St Louis*, the whaler *Matilde* and the schooner *Dolphin*. Concealed in the hills, the enemy amazed at their victory, observed the fugitives. When they saw that they had all embarked they performed a war dance, entered the township and sacked it. Some stuffed themselves with sugar and others got drunk on rum. In their victory, though, they showed a humanity and decency which civilised people do not possess. They allowed settlers to return and collect their valuables. Heke himself gave a woman and children safe conduct.[22] The Catholic bishop and two priests and Selwyn, the Protestant bishop, attended the wounded. Then the Anglican bishop and his ministers fled the township with the settlers.

After sacking the settlement, the Maori torched it and the whole township was burnt down, except the Catholic Church, the bishop's residence and fifteen nearby houses. The bishop told the victors that they probably could not burn them down without destroying his property too. 'It is hard to believe, said MacKillop, a Marines' sub-lieutenant, but it is absolutely true that nearly all the natives taking part in Hone Heke's campaign against the British government in the Bay of Islands, were Protestant.'[23] Indeed, as Protestants, they did not spare the churches or homes of their ministers, nor Bishop Selwyn's residence. Colonel Mundy commented that, 'In the Kororareka conflagration the *only* part of the town spared by rebels was in the precincts of Bishop Pompallier's residence.'[24] The saying, 'As you sow, so shall you reap,' is very true.

'Monsignor Pompallier, two priests and a few catechists were the only inhabitants of the deserted settlement. The Bishop gave refuge to the school teacher and his family. He was a retired soldier who had been requested by the authorities to lead settlers' resistance. After the rout, he and his family sought refuge in the Catholic mission. The Maori recognised him and wanted to take him and his family and kill them, but the Bishop intervened. He dissuaded them, telling them that he acted under orders, and that every one has to recognise authority and that therefore after the battle he deserved protection. But he felt that he was only safe in the Bishop's house and if he ventured outside he would be killed. The following day, therefore, Monsignor Pompallier put him and his family in his own canoe and he safely rowed out to the ships with the rest of the Europeans.'[25]

'The Bishop and his missionaries remained to protect the mission's physical and spiritual interests. What an unhappy time for a Shepherd! The pen was wide open and the sheep all fled. After burning down the township the victors returned to their tribes, five or six leagues from Kororareka.'[26]

During the fighting which lasted five hours, eleven Europeans among the infantry, marines and volunteer settlers were killed and twenty wounded, including Captain Robertson and Lieutenant Morgan. Natives suffered thirty killed or wounded. Property losses, including destruction of wooden houses, were estimated at one million, two hundred thousand francs.

On 13 March, two days after the battle, settlers and troops set sail for Auckland, about 200 kilometres from the disaster area. In their consternation, people likened their misfortune to the famous 1812 burning of Moscow.

This Maori victory increased Heke's prestige enormously among natives. His name was now on everyone's lips. They became convinced that settlers could not protect themselves on their own, and the aura of British military invincibility was gone.

Kororareka residents accused the soldiers of cowardice and complained that they evacuated the town unnecesarily. Because of the accusations, the only two subalterns of the 96th Regiment in Auckland were tried by court-martial. The lieutenant was honourably discharged, and the standard bearer, a callow youth, was reproved for leading the soldiers' retreat from their trench without his superior's order, leaving the flag in enemy hands.[27] Many believed Kororareka fell because soldiers and settlers panicked. Others, more correctly, saw it as retribution for evils and crimes committed there, as mentioned earlier.

When Kororareka's distraught and horrified settlers, crammed like sheep in their ships, reached Auckland, local people were panic-stricken. Their terror further increased when news arrived of Heke's intention to attack Auckland by the next full moon. Settlers in outlying areas, fearing a racial war, retreated to the town, and many fled the colony. The Britomart barracks were reinforced with trenches and loopholes. Two more blockhouses were erected; Fort Liger was built and windows in the Anglican church were strongly shuttered. The governor immediately ordered the formation of a militia to defend the settlement and 300 men were enlisted and trained.[28]

Every day Heke became more of a spectre in people's minds. Sentries were constantly on guard watching from ramparts for the enemy. But they had no intention of attacking Auckland which lay close to the domains of their implacable enemy, Te Whero Whero. Recognising Auckland settlers' consternation, chief Te Whero Whero indicated his willingness to defend the town against Heke. The Ngatiwhatua tribe occupying the Auckland posed no threat because they were engrossed in kauri gumdigging. Its value had risen dramatically after it fetched good sales on the American market. When news of the disaster reached Wellington and Nelson, settlers began to build defences and also raise a militia.[29]

Meanwhile, in the Bay of Islands the enemy was far from dormant. 'Monsignor Pompallier and his colleagues had remained three weeks in the midst of Kororareka's ruins without any human protection. Suddenly one evening they were told that at daybreak the next day a great many Maori were coming to attack the bishop's house. They intended to leave no European house standing or any European alive, and thus avenge the deaths of chiefs killed in battle. The Bishop's and his missionaries' lives would serve as compensation. An oracle told them that the gods needed holy people as victims in expiation for the bloodshed.'[30]

'The news,' Father MacDonald continues, 'was unfortunately true. At dawn six large canoes, some of which contained more than 30 armed men, approached the shore. They were half-naked, rowing vigorously and yelling their customary, blood-curdling war cries. Face to face with sacking, arson and death, there was no way out by resistance or flight. The Bishop exhorted his companions to place their trust in God and be prepared to sacrifice their lives if it was His will. Providing an example of resignation, the prelate began quietly to recite the holy Rosary.

'Meanwhile, the canoes rapidly came closer and were only fifty paces from the shore when *Peata*, a Catholic widow of a chief, whom Providence brought there as if by chance, ran down to the beach. In a very loud voice she cried out to the attackers: *"As brothers you are welcome; if you are traitors, I am ready for you."* At these words from a person Maori regarded as a queen, the canoes stopped as if by magic. The men were dumb-struck and the chiefs stopped to discuss the situation. Shortly afterwards, their leader asked *Peata* how many men there were ashore to oppose their landing. *"There is only me*, replied the intrepid woman, *only me between you and the Bishop's house."* It was as if she were saying: It is a woman who is blocking your way but if you refuse to heed her, she has subjects who will avenge your trampling on her authority. The assailants, realising that they could not pass without signalling a declaration of war against a very powerful tribe, turned their prows further down the coast. On disembarking, a contingent of about 150 Catholic natives armed with rifles suddenly appeared. These defenders were quite unexpected. During the night they had hurried to set up an ambush behind a hill near the house and observe enemy movements. When they saw them disembarking they rushed over to welcome them as friends or repel them according to whether they abandoned or pursued their intention to attack. Chiefs began to parley and they made peace. Warriors of both sides embraced and their women hastened to prepare a feast as a sign of reconciliation.

'As a pledge of this change of heart, the attackers' leader proffered the Bishop his dogskin cloak and placed his double-barrelled shotgun in his hands, signifying that having his firearm in his house would provide the Bishop his protection. Finally the two groups returned to their respective tribes.'[31]

Once Monsignor Pompallier settled the mission's affairs in the Bay of Islands, at the end of the year he transferred his bishopric to Auckland, leaving a missionary and a few assistants at Kororareka, now known as *Russell*. Kororareka has never recovered from its ruin. It is now more than fifty years since its destruction and the present European population is little more than a hundred.

3. The governor, now convinced that peace could only be restored by force of arms, requested troops and ammunition from Australia. He summoned the council and acknowledged his mistake in attributing the cause of unrest to customs levies. Moreover, since Wellington and Nelson settlers had refused to pay the property tax established the previous year, because they had no representation on council, the governor cancelled it and reinstated customs duties. Little revenue was obtained from this source and there was a desperate shortage of funds, forcing Captain Fitzroy to enter into further deficit and issue more debentures than he had authority to. On 20 April 1845 he dismissed the council in preparation for war, which he declared, promising it would be conducted *'with justice and clemency.'*[32]

The rebel leaders, Heke and Kawiti, realised that they would have to fight for their very lives. In vain they sought allies among distant Maori tribes and principal chiefs. If all or the majority of Maori had fought together for independence, it would have spelt the end of the British in New Zealand. They would have had to leave the country or be annihilated. But the lack of harmony between main tribes, the personal ambitions of the most powerful chiefs, and the generous promises of the government and Anglican missionaries to those who sided with the whites, caused widespread divisions among the Maori. Rauparaha in the South, pursued his own course. Te Whero Whero, in the centre of the island, was against Heke and on the government's side. In the north, some tribes declared their neutrality while several others joined Walker Nene in fighting for the British against their fellow Maori. In spite of their abandonment, Heke, Kawiti and a few other chiefs did not at all lose heart. They prepared defences building a pa or native fortifications inland and awaited the British soldiers and their native allies.

Once troops from Sydney reached Auckland, on 3 April 1845 an expedition under the command of Colonel Hulme set sail for Kororareka. They landed and a guard of honour raised the British flag and martial law was proclaimed. The British began their campaign with treachery. Pomare, a chief who took part in sacking Kororareka, was tricked into being captured when British soldiers appeared waving a white flag. His pa and village were then burnt down. Pomare was imprisoned in Auckland and after a few months he was freed and given a canoe as recompense for the wrongdoing.[33]

News came that the enemy were at *Okaihau pa*, twenty-seven kilometres away. The expedition returned on board and on 3 May disembarked at the mouth of the Kerikeri river. There were 830 troops, comprising 430 infantrymen and marines, and 400 armed native allies. To distinguish themselves from the enemy, natives wore a white band around their head. They had no means of transport. Every soldier carried thirty cartridges and five days' rations in his kit. After four days difficult marching they reached the pa. If chief Nene and Ruhe, who was neutral, had not provided food for the troops, they would have gone hungry. Ruhe needed to drive pigs for the soldiers through the enemy camp. He requested Heke's permission, which was immediately granted. They did not want to violate a Maori custom by fighting starving men.[34]

Okaihau pa lay at the end of a narrow plain, flanked by bush-covered hills, near a large lake. It had two wooden palisade enclosures and an internal trench. The outer trench was covered with flax to conceal defenders from the enemy. Commander Hulme issued the order to attack the fort and breach the defences. Chief Nene tried to dissuade him, saying that it would be crazy to attempt such an impossible task.[35]

On 8 May Colonel Hulme ordered three columns to advance, attack the fort and engage the enemy. At the same time he ordered a rocket barrage to be launched. The first rocket exploded in the pa shattering a large stake and unnerving defenders, some of whom wanted to flee. But Heke urged them to wait and test the effect of further salvoes. None caused any damage. The Maori took heart and opened fire on the British. At the same time others under Kawiti's command rushed out of hideout in the nearby bush and threw themselves on the British, attacking them with hatchets attached to long staves. Fortunately, a native ally noticed the clever ambush; otherwise British losses would have been terrible. After some skirmishing the British finally managed to engage the enemy forcing their retreat into the pa. Colonel Hulme found, however, that the pa was impregnable without cannons. He and his troops returned to their ships at Oneroa.[36]

British losses at *Okaihau* were 14 dead and 39 wounded. Enemy losses could not be ascertained. The retreating troops were not attacked, although the enemy could easily have done so. The victors dug graves for the fallen soldiers and summoned a Protestant minister to pray for the dead. Then they chased after the British Maori allies, who beat a fast retreat.

On the campaign, when Captain Sir Edward Home and marines disembarked at Oneroa, they burned down enemy villages, destroyed their canoes and recovered stolen boats.[37] Two hundred soldiers went up the Waikari river and attacked a native *pa*, but the enemy fled at their approach.

Led by their commander, the wounded and some troops returned to Auckland. The rest of the troops occupied the ruins of Kororareka. Auckland settlers had been eagerly awaiting news of their formidable foe's destruction. They were astonished to see wounded troops and soldiers bearing all the signs of defeat and hear that fourteen had fallen in front of Heke's *pa* which had resisted capture; and that the troops were indebted to the enemy for being allowed to escape. With this second defeat, people could hardly control their anger.[38]

Heke sent the governor two letters proposing peace. But their belligerent and patronising tone was found to be antagonising. In one, he wrote: 'If you make peace, you should hold no malice towards your enemy. Caesar, Pontius Pilate, Nabuccodonezar, Pharoah, Nicodemus, Agrippa and Herod were rulers and governors; were they really benefactors of mankind? Did they not kill Jesus Christ?'[39]

Following the arrival of further reinforcements from Sydney, another expediton against Heke set sail and disembarked at Oneroa. On the 23rd it reached *Oheawai* where the enemy were entrenched. Their fortress lay in an open area surrounded by gullies and dense bush-covered hills in the rear. The pa was 74 metres wide and 47 metres long, with salients at every corner. There were three palisades; the two outer ones were close together and the 5-metre high interior palisade was two metres distant from its neighbour. There was a 4-metre deep surrounding ditch between them covered up to a metre by wooden platforms from which crouching Maori could aim their rifles from ground level and fire at the enemy. Inside the pa were bunkers with tunnels and passages which emerged along the palisades. Flax matting covered the exterior fence concealing the defence's strength and structure and number of defenders from the enemy.[40]

The British force comprised 550 infantry and marines, 80 Auckland volunteers and, in addition, 300 native allies; in all, nearly 1000 troops and six field guns and a much larger cannon brought from H.M.S. *Hazard*. There were about 250 enemy armed with muskets in the pa. On 24 June the six cannons began their thunderous fire on the pa from a distance of 200 metres, but with no success, the palisades remaining unbreached. Barrages continued for some days. 'One day, enemy warriors stole from the pa and attacked chief Nene's positions. The sortie was so sudden and unexpected that Colonel *Despard* and other officers were shamed into a humiliating flight, leaving a standard in enemy hands.'[41]

This success cheered the rebels who returned within the stockade and raised the captured flag, under Heke's. Soldiers then positioned the big 32-pounder cannon 90 metres from the *pa* so that it could fire straight at the fence. After twenty-six salvoes Despard, the commanding officer, believed that the palisades were sufficiently breached in two places for him to order the attack. Marlow, however, the sappers' captain, did not share his belief. Meanwhile, the large cannon continued to fire on the *pa* and the commander gave orders for axes, ropes and ladders to be got ready for an attack at three p.m. the next day.[42]

On 1 July at the fixed time 200 soldiers mounted their attack. They found the internal fence intact and tried unsuccessfully to breach it with axes. Within ten minutes two officers and more than half the troops fell under enemy fire. The others were forced to retreat. After their defeat the soldiers retreated to 350 metres from the stockade to spend the night. 'Never,' wrote Thomson, 'had British troops passed a more terrible night. Constantly expecting attack, they huddled together listening to the death rattles of the dying and the moaning of their wounded comrades.'[43]

The British remained a few days, and the opposing sides eyed each other without firing. The day after the assault, E. Williams, an Anglican minister, approached the *pa* to seek to bury the dead, but the Maori warned him off. On 3 July the enemy hoisted a white flag and called out to the British to take away their dead and wounded. According to Thomson they had 36 dead and 66 wounded.[44] Other writers put the figures at 40 dead and 73 wounded. Rev. Taylor mentions that 'in the brief space of time that the assault lasted 120 soldiers were blown into eternity',[45] including Captain Grant and Lieutenant Philpott. Maori losses were inconsequential.

On 9 July, with fresh ammunition for the large cannon, shots were fired on the *pa*. On 11 July a half-caste informed Colonel Despard that the previous evening the enemy had abandoned the *pa*, retreating to *Ikorangi*, fifteen kilometres away. When the soldiers entered the stockade they found ample supplies of potatoes and two field guns used for firing nails and shrapnel. Before retreating, the British burnt the place down and then returned to Kororareka. Colonel Despard was fiercely criticised for assaulting the *pa* before the palisades were completely breached.[46]

Heke's hatred of Europeans, Kawiti's for British native allies and Governor Fitzroy's unsatisfactory peace terms kept hostilities alive. The two chiefs would have preferred a thousand deaths than let the governor have their ancestral lands. In this, they had the sympathy of most Maori. Te Heu Heu, Taupo's paramount chief publicly stated that Heke was in the right and that 'the English were insatiable and set on world conquest.'[47]

After these victories, Heke's reputation among the Maori spread enormously. He was the first war leader to fight against seasoned British troops. He was regarded as the Maoris' liberator and he and his family worthy of their prestige.

4. Meanwhile, in London Parliament was debating the New Zealand situation, undecided which side to take, when news arrived of the uprising in the Bay of Islands, Kororareka's destruction and the troops' defeat. The British government, fearing that the Maori would bury old grievances and unite in revolt to expel the British, immediately dispatched several warships and troops, arms, ammunition and money. Mistrustful also of Captain Fitzroy's ability to govern

the colony, it recalled him and ordered Captain George Grey, then Governor of South Australia, to go to New Zealand and take charge.

Governor Fitzroy was about to recommence hostilities against Heke in October when news reached him of his recall to England and the appointment of his successor. Meanwhile many warships arrived in Auckland, frightening local Maori who immediately began to fortify their *pa* or stockades in readiness for war.[48]

The new governor arrived in Auckland at the beginning of November and straightaway took over the reins of power. From the way he had solved difficult problems in Australia and judging from his writings, the British government considered Captain Grey the most suitable person to untangle the knotty New Zealand situation and deal with the natives. Determined and energetic, he set about investigating the cause of fighting and of Maori discontent. He discovered that the main culprits were Anglican missionaries and other profiteers and landsharks, and he hastened to remedy the situation. He also made it clear that he would never have condoned mistreatment of Maori. A few days later he went to Kororareka where 700 soldiers were at the ready. He informed native allies that the British government would strictly observe the Treaty of Waitangi and on 27 November he sent an ultimatum to Heke and Kawiti for them to decide within three days between war and peace. He then returned to Auckland to await the outcome.

On 29 November, chief Kawiti wrote to the governor: 'I have no intention of relinquishing Kotore's lands, as you have requested, because they are not mine. The land endures while men pass on. Friend, I am not keen on writing but you can reply if you find what I have said acceptable. If you say, Sir, that we must fight, so be it. If you say let hostilities cease, so be it.' Heke's reply was more provocative. He wrote: 'You are a foreigner, we are strangers to each other. We do not understand your thinking, and you do not understand ours. God has given this land to us. It cannot be cut up into strips like whale blubber. Return to your own country which God gave you. God made this land for us; it is not for any stranger or foreign nation to meddle with this sacred country.'[49] Age and virility confronted Grey's demands: They preferred to die as warriors than submit to slavery.

On 12 December Captain Grey summonsed the Legislative Council. He suspended the law allowing individuals to buy land from the Maori by paying a governmental tax of ten centimes an acre. He forbade anyone, under severe penalty, to sell Maori munitions. He ordered an audit of colonial finances, which were found to be far from solvent. Total revenue in 1845 was only 322,475 francs and expenditure had risen to 5,322,475 francs. The British government paid the five million deficit. The colony's total debt, including debentures issued by Fitzroy, amounted to 2,675,000 francs.[50]

5. Meanwhile the enemy and the British prepared for war. The rebels split into two parties; Heke remained at Ikorangi pa while Kawiti fortified Ruapekapeka. On 8 December, troops marched to attack Kawiti. It took them until 31 December to reach the enemy pa defended by 500 Maori. There were 1500 infantry and marines and 450 allies; nearly 2000 combatants in all. They had three 32-pounders, one 18-pounder, two 12-pounders, seven smaller bronze cannons and mortars for firing shrapnel or rockets. On 31 December Kawiti raised his flag from the pa and the British opened fire with all their artillery. There was small skirmishing for several days. On 10 January 1846 batteries opened fire from various distances and continued shelling the whole day without causing significant damage to the palisades. The next day artillery fire was recommenced. Because it was Sunday, the Maori followed their religious teacher's instruction which strictly forbade any work or fighting. They believed the British would do the same. The defenders gathered in a shelter outside the pa to pray and sing hymns. The troops could not see any movement within. Chief Nene and his men stole up to the fence on all fours. Hearing the enemy at morning prayers and singing psalms, they signalled to the soldiers to quietly begin the attack and scale the defences. When some soldiers found their way in, the defenders realised too late their treachery. They grabbed their weapons and tried to retake the pa, but they were attacked from all sides. After a brief struggle they fled to save their lives, leaving the pa in British hands. Their losses were 13 dead and 30 wounded. The troops burnt down the pa, returned to their ships and went on to Kororareka.[51]

After Ruapekapeka's capture, Heke and Kawiti retreated to their inland pa. Safe from pursuit and danger, they allowed their hungry followers, unable to farm during the campaign, to disband and plant potatoes for food. Governor Grey, seeing their willingness to make peace, granted the rebels a general, full pardon and he lifted his martial law edict. The war in the North was over. Heke and Kawiti lived peacefully in their domains until their deaths. Heke died in 1852 at the age of forty-two, and Kawiti died in 1853 aged about eighty.[52]

6. Land disputes which broke out in 1839 were resurrected in the south and fresh blood was needed to expiate injustices suffered by the Maori. During the northern war, native unrest was stirring in Wellington. The bone of contention between the two races was the fertile *Hutt* valley. As has been mentioned previously, Colonel Wakefield claimed he bought the whole area. The Maori denied this and continued farming there to prevent settlers occupying the valley. Governor Fitzroy had paid chief Rauparaha £300 to settle Maori claims. Rauparaha, however, did not give *Rangihaeata,* his brother-in-law, his share. Fitzroy had promised settlers to have them on the land, but Maori had no intention of recognising their ownership, even though they had come to stake their claim.

At the beginning of 1846, seventeen European homes were suddenly sacked by natives. To punish their audacity, Colonel Hulme and 300 soldiers were brought up. On their approach, the Maori retreated to a hill-top stronghold which could not be taken without serious losses. The colonel left 200 men in the area to protect settlers and returned to Wellington to prepare his report on the situation for Governor Grey in Auckland. Grey gathered his available forces of 700 soldiers and cannons, and in February set sail for Wellington. Some chiefs joined the British to fight against their brothers. The 200 soldiers left in Hutt valley had orders not to attack Maori, but to prevent them gathering their crops.[53]

Maori who had withdrawn inland returned to Hutt valley in April and killed an old man and a youth and let it be known that any settler occupying disputed land would meet the same fate. *Rangihaeata*, who was sixty years old, was the driving force behind the revolt. The governor sent 200 men to occupy Porirua and besiege the chief in his pa.

Meanwhile, on 16 May, 50 soldiers stationed in the Hutt Valley were taken by surprise in a dawn raid by 70 natives. They killed six and wounded four before retiring. Success emboldened the enemy and on 16 June they again attacked 40 soldiers, killing two and wounding six. A little later, they killed an Englishman who was farming land they claimed was theirs. European settlers, scattered through the valley, fled in fear to Wellington and the European population was extremely apprehensive.

Throughout the disturbances, Rauparaha maintained his neutrality. In fact he favoured the British, keeping the promise he made two years previously. But settlers loathed him because of the Wairau massacre and did not believe he could be trusted. Governor Grey suspected him of being secretly involved in the revolt, even though he had no proof of treachery. He decided that he could achieve a political coup by arresting the powerful chief.[54]

Without telling Rauparaha that their friendship was over, an hour before dawn on 23 July 1846, Grey and 130 armed men landed at Porirua, surrounded the chief's hut, surprised him in bed asleep, handcuffed him and took him to Wellington. He was held prisoner on H.M.S. *Calliope* in spite of his protestations of innocence. At that time Rauparaha was seventy-seven years old. Army officers remonstrated with Governor Grey over the injustice, considering it worse than Pomare's capture under an armistice flag. Many settlers, however, approved the *coup de main* as a politically astute move. In January 1848 the governor allowed Rauparaha to return home to Otaki.[55]

When Rauparaha reached his village, he went to live with the Anglican missionaries, 'showing what a devout, even saintly Protestant he was.'[56] There he remained till he died. A few days before his death a British settler visited him. At the same time, an Anglican minister came to give Rauparaha the last rites. Rauparaha appeared to be suitably edified and receptive. However, when the minister left, Rauparaha turned to his visitor and said to him: 'What was all that nonsense about? It won't make any difference to my health.'[57] Then he began discussing the Wanganui races. He died on 27 November 1849, more than eighty years old. He died as he had lived, a ferocious cannibal, nominally Protestant but heathen at heart.

Grey had just captured Rauparaha when he ordered an attack on Rangihaeata and his men. On the army's approach, they retreated deep into the bush. The troops followed in pursuit and on 6 August 1846 a skirmish occurred in which the British suffered three dead and eight wounded. Maori had no losses. The army could not use its cannons because of the dense bush and withdrew. The rebels waited a few days for an attack, but then realised the enemy had withdrawn. They needed food, so Rangihaeata allowed them to disband and hostilities ended.

Although Rangihaeata from then on ceased fighting the British, his hatred continued. However, after his brother-in-law Te Rauparaha's death, his loathing for whites lessened and he began to frequent the Anglican church which he belonged to. He died in 1856 at the age of seventy.[58]

Meanwhile British troops withdrew to Porirua, following the August skirmishing. They had taken some prisoners and tried them unjustly as *rebels*. Seven were sentenced to deportation to Tasmania. The eighth, Wareaitu, who had been christened *Martin Luther* in the Anglican church, was sentenced to be hanged and he was summarily executed. Dr Thomson rightly comments that, 'If fairness and justice were respected, the native insurgents could not be described as rebels, because they did not recognise that the British had the right to rule their country. To justify the miscarriage of justice, they claimed that the prisoners were guilty of killing unarmed settlers. But the accusation was not proven in the military court which sentenced them. The native Luther's death is a shameful and dishonourable blot on the military court and Governor Grey. It is very likely that Mr. Grey felt guilty because the incident was never mentioned in his dispatches.'[59] The seven men deported to Tasmania were refused entry by its principled governor who did not see them as *guilty of rebellion*. He freed them to return to their native country.

7. Wellington's troubles were still not over. Wanganui Maori on the island's west coast saw themselves being stripped by settlers of their lands, and rose up against their usurpers. At first they contented themselves with sacking European interlopers' properties, threatening them with worse if they did not quit their land. In December 1846 the governor sent a detachment of 170 troops to quash their demands. Maori saw this measure as the first step towards being forced off their land and they decided to resist their stand-over tactics.

On 16 April 1847 an unfortunate incident occurred which drove natives to revolt. Two Protestant writers provide an impartial account of what happened:

'A sub-lieutenant of Marines asked an old chief to build a hut for him for an agreed price. When the hut was finished, the officer not only refused to pay the agreed price but, taking out his pistol, he threatened to kill him if he kept asking for payment. Brandishing the pistol, unfortunately it went off and the bullet hit the old man's cheek, lodging near his ear. Maori considered this an outrageous, murderous act. They demanded justice, that the culprit be punished, or at least there be an inquiry into the incident. Instead of investigating the unhappy affair, the commander and troops took the officer's side and let him return to barracks with them without giving the furious natives any satisfaction. They closed the gates on them. Their unfair treatment convinced the natives that what had happened to the old chief was no accident.'[60]

Two days later, six young Maori warriors related to the wounded man, in retribution for his spilt blood, according to Maori custom, attacked an English family, killing a woman and four children. Five of the men were captured by natives friendly to the British and brought to the commander. They were sentenced by court martial to be hanged and the sentence was carried out immediately. Only the youngest, who was twelve years old, was spared. After their execution, many native women who had been living with Europeans returned to their tribes and the condemned men's people took up arms to expel the British. Fighting began with a soldier being picked off, and on 19 May 1847 Maori attacked the Wanganui area. As soon as skirmishing began, settlers retreated into the soldiers' garrison. Natives, 300 strong, began to sack a part of the district and for five hours fired on the soldiers holed up behind their defences. From fortifications and a warship troops maintained a steady gunfire, with cannon salvoes and howitzer attacks until late evening, but they were not able to dislodge the natives from the town. During the night, natives sacked houses and slaughtered some cattle. In the morning they took the rest away and abandoned the area, retreating into the bush. The British suffered no casualties because they were behind their defences. Maori had two dead and ten wounded.[61]

The besieged settlers sent an urgent dispatch to Wellington seeking armed protection. The governor immediately sent 500 troops, not including native allies, to Wanganui. Two weeks later rebels again appeared in the area hoping to entice the soldiers out and lead them into an ambush, but they were not successful. On 10 June a strong British detachment was attacked by Maori, but they were forced to withdraw with losses. On 5, 10 and 17 July small rebel raiding parties boldly attacked troops, even up to their ramparts. On 19 July the British raked the enemy forcing their retreat to the edge of the bush where they challenged them to attack. In the exchange total casualties were three killed and ten wounded. On 23 July a small band of natives waving a white flag appeared in front of the British garrison. After a long parley with the Maori allies, they declared they were ready to stop fighting, being satisfied with the number of soldiers killed.

During hostilities, an English settler had been captured and then set free on payment of tobacco and blankets. Soldiers compared the government's treatment of hanging captives to that of Maori savages, who freed them for a ransom. It was evident that the more civilised race was the Maori, not the British. Settlers accused the 500 strong force of cowardice, because when challenged several times by 300 Maori to come out and fight, they hid in their trenches. The troops countered by saying that they were afraid that if they left the trenches they would be ambushed.

On 23 July 1847 hostilities in Wanganui practically ceased, but there was no declaration of peace, because the rebels did not want to lose face by negotiating. The British continued to blockade the Wanganui river preventing natives from obtaining pipes, tobacco, blankets, tea, sugar, etc. Finding it impossible to get clothing and other necessities, they held out as long as they could, but finally sought peace. A settlement was reached on 21 February 1848, with a general pardon issued. Cattle stolen by natives were returned and Governor Grey paid a fair price for Maori land taken by settlers.[62]

The British government recognised the merit of field commanders who took part in the New Zealand campaign. Four were awarded the title of Commander of the Bath. Five captains were promoted to major, excluding commanders in charge at Okaihau and Wanganui who were seen as not deserving promotion. Of the British allied chiefs, Walker Nene was made captain with an annual pension of 2500 francs and the other northern chiefs were given smaller pensions. Te Whero Whero, the Waikato chief, was granted an annual pension of 1250 francs and a fine residence in Auckland and a substantial holding at Mangere. Chief Te Puni of Wellington received a 1250 francs pension. Thomson mentions that, 'Without Maori allies' help, Britain would have been unable to maintain its authority in New Zealand.'[63]

The same year, 1848, a few credulous natives sold the colonial government nearly all the South Island, about 100,000 square kilometres or the equivalent of almost half of Italy, except for a few hectares for their cultivation, for the ridiculous sum of £2000 sterling (50,000 francs), less than six centimes a square kilometre. Once the despicable purchase was made, it was realised that many legitimate native landowners had not been approached or consulted. After their rightful protests, the government promised them trifling monetary compensation, but in fact they received nothing. The government acted similarly in attempting to buy Stewart Island, about 2500 square kilometres, from local natives. When the Maori demanded £6000 sterling, or 60 francs a square kilometre, it decided not to buy it, because it was too expensive.[64] Later it got it for a song. The colonial government acted in just the same way with Maori as the profiteers and landsharks it roundly condemned for exploitation.

8. At length, peace was restored to New Zealand and Sir George Grey, the governor, was made a Knight Commander of the Bath, an order instituted by Queen Victoria in 1848. He pressed the British government not to reduce the army in the colony to less than combat strength. Britain did not want to keep so many soldiers there at such expense. It responded by enlisting 500 pensioned veterans for seven years service, and in 1847 sent them and their families, totalling 2000 people, to New Zealand. They were lodged in settlements around Auckland and the colonial government provided each of them with a four-roomed wooden house and an acre of land, promising every pensioner another five acres at a moderate price, after their seven years service. Officers were given, besides a house, forty acres and the right to another 100 acres under the same terms.[65]

They were given these privileges on condition that they protected settlers against Maori, fought and assisted the militia when required. Many of the soldiers on active service, received their discharge in 1848, but 500 instead of returning home, accepted the same conditions as the pensioners. The government was thus able to recall some of its troops to England without diminishing the colony's forces. Many pensioners remained the rest of their lives in New Zealand. Others sold their holdings and went to live in other colonial settlements. And some, after their seven years' service, left New Zealand. Governor Grey's intention in maintaining a permanent army in New Zealand was to subdue and undermine Maori by intimidation and military force.

9. During the northern war in New Zealand, the *Scottish Company* was set up in Scotland to send *Presbyterian Protestants* to New Zealand and establish a Scottish settlement. The company was founded in 1843 and later expanded. In 1844 members visited the South Island in search of a future homeland for new emigrants. They chose Otago as the most suitable place, buying 400,000 acres (180,000 hectares) from the New Zealand Company.

Every Scottish Company emigrant had the right to a quarter of an acre of town land, ten acres of suburban land and fifty acres in the country, at a standard price of 50 francs an acre. Migrants were to make their selection on the spot, according to availability of land. Of the total amount of three thousand and twelve and a half francs, three-eighths were for emigrants' voyage costs, two-eighths for road construction, one-eighth for religion and education, and two-eighths for land purchase.

In November 1847, the first emigrants from Scotland set sail for Otago, situated on the east coast of the lower part of the South Island. It is surrounded by hills and fertile plains and excellent for farming and wheat growing. The migrants were known as the *Pilgrim Fathers*. They founded the town of *Dunedin* and the nearby *Port Chalmers*. By the end of 1848, 745 Scottish settlers had already landed. Migrants continued to stream into New Zealand until 1885.

10. Shortly after the recommencement of emigration to New Zealand, Wellington and the surrounding area were struck by earthquakes causing inhabitants terror and confusion. From 16 to 19 October 1848 several major tremors occurred, heralded by frightening rumbling and roaring, causing such consternation that people believed they would be swallowed up at any moment. Only three stone or brick buildings were left standing and wooden houses swayed and buckled. There were only three fatalities because after the first minor tremors citizens fled to the hills, bush or to ships in port.

The sea was so rough that distraught residents were not even safe on water. A ship which sailed out to the open sea with sixty-six settlers on board was tossed onto the shore. Fetid sulphur fumes belched from fissures and cracks in the ground. General fasting was ordered and the wooden churches filled with people praying to God for mercy and forgiveness for their far from Christian lives. Damages amounted to more than 400,000 francs. Blobs of pitch, thrown up from the seabed, could be seen floating in Cook Strait and dumped along the coast.

Shock waves were felt as far as fifty kilometres north. The earthquake's centre seems to have been, and probably still is, a subterranean volcano in Cook Strait, near Wellington. Earthquakes in New Zealand are not infrequent, particularly in Wellington and the surrounding area. Major tremors occur, however, every seven to ten years, as verified from experiences over the last fifty years.

11. For several years New Zealand settlers were unhappy with the government's absolute control of public affairs under governors and their executive council. People wanted to be self-governed, that is, to have a general assembly whose members were elected by themselves, as in England. Towards the end of 1846 the British government acceded to their wishes and the new legislation giving near autonomy was to come into effect in January 1848.

New Zealand's *magna carta* was to divide the country into two or more provinces, each of which would be governed by a superintendent, a board and a provincial council. There was also to be a legislative council and general assembly. Leadership was to be in the hands of Sir George Grey, as Governor-General. Legislative Council members were to be selected by the governor and MPs elected by the people. All males over twenty-one, both European and Maori, able to read and write English, had the right to vote. Provincial Councils could legislate for provinces, and the national bodies for all New Zealand, including Maori. An official dispatch of Earl Grey's accompanying the voting rights declaration stated that natives had no legal ownership rights to land they were not occupying, and that this became Crown land.[66]

Governor Grey and other leaders pointed out to the British government that all New Zealand land had legitimate owners, and that although natives did not farm it all, they needed their lands to sustain their way of life. To declare that it was Crown land was in violation of the Treaty of Waitangi and would inevitably cause Maori to revolt. They added that allowing natives to elect MPs was ridiculous because hardly any knew how to read or write English, their literacy being in Maori. Thus it was a misrepresentation to say that colonial law catered also for the Maori when they were not able to participate in electing MPs.

The British government recognised the merit of Sir George Grey's arguments. In March 1848 it suspended the enactment of voting rights for five years, to the chagrin of many settlers who unfairly accused the governor of not wanting self-rule for the colony because of his desire to rule the country as a despot. The truth is he did not favour the new constitution as it was formulated because it was prejudicial to native rights and gave them no real franchise.

12. Official census figures for the New Zealand European population:

1850
22,108 residents, comprising 15,914 in the North Island and 6194 in the South Island.

1851
The population was 26,707, not including 3500 soldiers and their families.

Religions: Protestants, 60 different denominations, 22,673; Catholics, 3574; Jews, 65; those refusing to state their religious belief, 495.

Imports in 1849 were estimated at 6,366,975 francs and exports, 3,241,550 francs.

Colonial revenue in 1850 was: customs duties, 1,090,300 francs, sale of land and title surcharge 213,975. Postal and other charges 178,125; British government subsidy, 1,043,250. Cost of troops paid by Great Britain, 3,277,500. Total revenue: 5,803,150 francs. Total expenditure for the same year: 5,792,125 francs.

Colonial livestock (introduced), figs. for 1851: 2890 horses, 60 mules and donkeys; 34,787 cattle; 233,043 sheep; 12,121 goats; 16,214 pigs. These figures do not include Maori domestic animals.

CHAPTER EIGHT

Protestant and Catholic Missions From 1840 to 1860

SUMMARY. – 1. Governor Grey and Anglican missionaries. – 2. Protestant preaching activity in New Zealand. – 3. Maori Protestant converts and their practice. – 4. Catholic mission in New Zealand. – 5. Differences between Protestant and Catholic missionary education. – 6. Catholic missionary life and activities in New Zealand. – 7. Colonial Catholic education. – 8. Auckland mission's severe trials.

1. From the time of his arrival in New Zealand, Governor Grey, an astute politician, was determined to find out the causes of general Maori discontent. He discovered that the main reason was the unfair usurpation of their land by greedy individuals, whether citizens or ministers, that is, Anglican or Wesleyan missionaries. He immediately sought to remedy the situation. First of all, he removed Rev. Clarke from the position of Maori protector, because he had laid claim to 19,000 acres of Maori land (about 8,000 hectares). He replaced him with a more suitable person. Anglican missionaries saw this wise decision as a vote of no confidence and they began to oppose the governor with every means at their disposal, because they saw control of the country slipping from their fingers.

Sir George Grey was not a man to retreat in the face of adversity. He considered the commission's granting of land to Anglican missionaries, described in the previous chapter, as illegal and unfair to Maori. He strongly recommended them to return to Maori some of their land. The Protestant bishop, Selwyn, an upright and principled man, used all his eloquence to persuade them to meet the governor's rightful request. But neither an appeal to their better nature or to the effect on the London Society's* reputation had any effect in making them relinquish their booty. *Punch*, a London magazine, suggested that a cartoon of Rev. R. Taylor with the caption, *'owner of 50,000 acres'*, should be placed in the London Missionary Society's meeting room.[1]

In June 1846, faced with fierce opposition, the governor sent an official dispatch to the British Colonial Secretary, Hon. W. E. Glandston. In it he wrote, 'Never in my readings or activities have I ever come across a case like this, where a few people sent overseas, funded by devout Christians, to spread the Gospel, have acquired vast amounts of land from ignorant natives whom they

---

* Translator's note: that is, the London Missionary Society.

are meant to spiritually inspire. Although they are missionaries, they have the audacity to attack the person of the governor with violence and venom because he has stood up for the rights of protesting, suffering natives.'[2]

Shortly afterwards, on 25 June the same year, Grey wrote a confidential letter to the colonial secretary, clarifying the situation: 'For the reasons outlined in my official dispatches, I find that the so-called purchases have no validity in the eyes of natives or the majority of settlers. Her Majesty's Government can be assured that these people cannot be confirmed as owners of such large amounts of land without much English bloodshed and considerable expenditure ... Individuals with these property interests form a strong faction. They comprise journalists, Protestant missionaries and their large families, gentlemen occupying important governmental positions who are consequently in touch with all the Government's moves, as well as their relations and friends ... If the Government does not accede to their wishes, it must expect violent, concerted opposition.'[3]

In 1847 the governor accused missionaries of causing Heke's insurrection because of their unjust land claims, and of inciting native rebellion.[4] Ministers were annoyed at having their skulduggery exposed. They enlisted the support of the many exploiters of Maori, who did not give a fig for justice or fairness (as Grey earlier mentioned to his government), against the governor. They then badgered and pestered the British government and their London Missionary Society for justice, protesting their innocence and blamelessness, and declaring that Governor Grey was an out-and-out liar. The matter was brought to the Privy Council. They supported the governor and criticised Anglican missionaries for being venal. In June 1848, the Protestant Missionary Society, notwithstanding its intention of supporting missionaries, reluctantly decided that Archdeacon Henry Williams and the others needed to heed Bishop Selwyn's advice. If they refused, they would be expelled from the society.[5]

In spite of general censure from England, Archdeacon Williams and Rev. George Clarke were determined not to give up an inch of land. A third minister did not wait to be expelled, but voluntarily quit the London Society. Another settled his society entitlements and went into retirement. Others accepted the order and gave up most of their land. In November 1849 the London Society ordered the two disobedient men's eviction and removal from the society. On 25 May 1850, the archdeacon accepted expulsion from the *Paihia* Anglican mission rather than give up any of his ill-gotten land. He set himself up as a *landlord,* or substantial property holder.[6]

W. Williams, Anglican bishop of Waiapu and brother of the renegade minister, went to London to get the society to withdraw its expulsion of the archdeacon, but they refused. However, in 1854, following Bishops Williams' and Selwyn's repeated requests, he was readmitted to his former position, receiving an archdeacon's stipend and 9000 acres wrested from the Maori.[7]

2. In describing the life and labours of Protestant missionaries in New Zealand, objectivity will be maintained by citing only Protestant ministers and other reputable Protestant writers, without comment on our part.

J. D. Lang, a Presbyterian minister, had the opportunity to observe his New Zealand confreres' missionary activities close at hand. In 1839 he wrote several letters, later published, to Lord Durham in London. He commented: 'The Society's ministers in New Zealand were the ringleaders of a large European conspiracy to ruin natives and strip them of their lands.'[8] In 1850 Rev. Fletcher, a colleague of Rev. Walter Lawry, superintendent of the Wesleyan mission, wrote: 'He (Lawry) lends money at exorbitant rates and is presently charging 20 per cent interest. He keeps a watchful eye on the market, buying, selling or pawning to his best advantage.'[9]

Rev. Yate, an Anglican missionary, after writing critically of his missionary colleagues' lack of Christian poverty and self-denial, concluded by saying: 'Some of them are such a disgrace to the Christian sense of self-denial which they preach that they deserve to be ignominiously struck off the London Society's membership list.'[10] If the London Society carried out Rev. Yate's suggestion, we are certain that very few names would remain, and he too would suffer the same fate because he worked both as a minister and butcher. Evidence came to the British Cabinet that he bought pork from Maori for two pence a pound and then sold it to whalers for five pence.

If this is what English ministers and catechists were capable of, what could be expected of their native ministers and catechists who were ordained to work in remote areas? Another reliable Protestant will enlighten us. It should be mentioned that generally Maori do not have any money, and when they get it, it runs through their fingers. 'Native ministers and catechists collected heaps of iron pots, tins, chests, blankets and guns, etc. which they wrung from Maori in payment for marriages, baptisms, burials, etc.'[11]

One might think that Protestant preachers, not having any means of support, needed to *do whatever they could* to scrape together a living for themselves and their families. However, it would be naive to believe that Protestant missionaries were and are without financial support. They are not like Catholic missionaries who work among natives, trusting in Providence, not knowing where their next meal will come from. They won't stir without the inducement of a healthy stipend, knowing it will increase annually. In 1870 Rev. Ward, an Anglican minister, wrote that, 'The London Missionary Society spends 900,000 pounds annually (22,500,000 francs) on its missions.'[12] Mr Terry, another Protestant, admitted that, 'the Society spent 16,000 pounds (or 400,000 francs) each year just on Maori secular and religious education, supporting 8 missionaries and 16 catechists.'[13]

Bishop Selwyn wrote that following an appeal he made for money for his mission, 'he was flooded with mailed donations for several days.'[14] Rev. Turton, a Wesleyan minister, mentioned that 'from 1823 to 1844 the Wesleyan Church spent 80,000 pounds (or two million francs) on its New Zealand mission.'[15]

Some years ago, an old chief speaking to his people said, 'Under no circumstances do I want Protestant ministers in the area. Wherever they set foot, their boots cling to the soil. Nothing is left for us, not even burial grounds for our dead.'

Many missionaries not only stole their land, but disillusioned them with their utterly shameful, disgusting behaviour. Dr Lang wrote, 'I have compiled a dossier of criminal charges which leaves one in no doubt of the culpability of Protestant missionaries living in New Zealand from 1824.'[16] He commented to Lord Durham, 'I am sure, my Lord, that it would be impossible to find any parallel in Protestant missionary history, from the Reformation on, of such ineptitude and moral bankruptcy on the part of its missionaries as my report attests. It truly seems that divine Providence has cast a baleful eye on the Protestant mission in New Zealand and that civil discord and Heaven's wrath have afflicted it up to the present day.'[17]

Rev. Lang justified his damning introduction with examples, mentioning: 'The first head of the New Zealand mission was removed for adultery; the second for drunkenness, and the third in 1836 for an even worse crime ... In short, missionaries' conduct in this regard was the worst ever known in its history of evangelisation and the most shameful for Protestantism.'[18] Referring to 1839, Lang said, 'Glaring abuse is tolerated and practised by *most missionaries*. It is so serious that not even Christ's apostles could repair the damage.'[19] He does not, however, explain the nature of the abuse. Lang continued, 'Mr. White, a Wesleyan missionary at Hokianga had to give up his ministry and leave Hokianga when his immoral behaviour was discovered. This *worthy person* is now a very successful trader.'[20]

'How is it possible,' asked another Protestant writer, 'for greed to be eradicated from the Maori heart when they see the very men sent to preach the Gospel scheming how to get hold of huge amounts of land and indulging in other shameful, despicable vices?'[21] Visiting a Maori village, he asked locals why they did not participate in morning and evening prayers like their Maori catechist, a devout Protestant. They replied, because they could not believe in an adulterer's prayers. These stories do not seem to relate to ordinary events but seem like descriptions of court trials because of their salacious nature!

An honest Protestant trader wrote: 'I respect and esteem churchmen who practise what they preach. I certainly know that no one is without fault. But when someone lets himself give in to the flesh and corrupt nature and feels unable to control his sensual passions, he should at least renounce his sacred ministry and not doubly contaminate his soul and body. Missionary work is discredited by such bad example and gives heathens an opportunity to sneer at our religion.'[22]

In 1867 Rev. Taylor, the frequently cited Anglican minister, mentioned a European Protestant's judgement about Protestant missionaries and their work in New Zealand: 'A European told me that he considered Protestant missionaries were the worst blight to strike the Colony, and that if it were not for them and the London Missionary Society there would never have been disputes and fighting with the Maori. The best thing for New Zealand would be to expel the lot of them.'[23] Rev. Taylor did not mention his reply. Perhaps he thought it better to remain silent, since the criticism also applied to him.

3. It might be said that in spite of Protestant missionaries' weaknesses and failings, the conversion of so many pagans and the salvation of so many souls would compensate for their wrongdoing. Our Divine Saviour replied thus to this excuse: a diseased tree cannot produce good fruit. Many natives became Protestants not out of conviction but simply because of its material benefits. Wilkes, a Protestant, and commander of the American expedition to New Zealand in 1845, wrote: 'Anglican missionaries seem to maintain a distance from the natives and appear stiff and arrogant. Most Protestant natives participate in morning and evening prayers but their actions and attitude belie any real change in custom.'[24]

Another Protestant asserts 'that the majority of so-called native Christians were attracted to conversion solely by the easy life they would enjoy at missions.'[25] Dr Thomson was not afraid to admit that their Christianity was nothing but 'a wretched hotch-potch of Christianity and paganism.'[26]

Their religious teaching left the Maori deeply ignorant of Christianity's fundamental principles, and even of Protestantism. By way of illustration, Rev. Yate mentions a conversation he had with a convert: 'Minister; How would you describe having a new heart? – It would be like yours, full of goodness. – Where does this goodness dwell? – It fills your whole being; it tells me not to work and to rest on the Sabbath, to stay home and not fight. – When did you last pray? – This morning. – What did you pray for? – I prayed: Oh, Jesus Christ, give me a blanket so that I can believe.'[27]

'Converts,' commented another Anglican, 'observe the Sabbath, but they are neither better nor more honest than non-believers.'[28] Bishop Selwyn mentions that in 1845 when he urged a chief to become a Protestant, he replied that 'his reluctance to accept the new religion was due to adherents' terrible example.'[29]

These few illustrations provided by exemplary Protestants are more than sufficient to reveal the calibre of Protestant missionary activity in New Zealand, their conversions and their effect on gullible natives' lives.

Nor need any mention be made of continuous, bitter religious conflict fermented among Maori, throwing the country into chaos. As will be shown later, it caused them to formally reject Christianity.

4. In the decade 1838-1848 the Catholic mission of the vast Western Oceania vicariate made such splendid progress under Monsignor Pompallier's able, energetic leadership that in 1842 some islands were separated from it and another vicariate was established, Central Oceania. In 1847 the New Caledonia islands were also made a vicariate. In New Zealand the number of native and European Catholics increased significantly. Bishop Pompallier could no longer manage his vast vicariate on his own. He presented His Holiness Pope Pius IX a request to create two dioceses in New Zealand to enable Catholicism to expand more quickly in the colony.

The Holy Father received his apostolic vicar's request favourably and issued a decree on 20 June 1848 creating two episcopates in New Zealand. Bishop Pompallier remained in charge of the Auckland diocese which comprised most of the North Island to 39 degrees latitude south. The Wellington diocese covered the rest of the colony.

A devout, zealous French Marist priest, Monsignor Philippe Viard, was appointed as first Bishop of Wellington. He had been Monsignor Pompallier's vicar general. The newly appointed bishop went to Europe for his consecration and to recruit missionaries. He then returned to his bishopric, reaching Wellington on 1 May 1850. He immediately began developing Catholicism within the new diocese, setting up new missions where they were needed and with God's help within a few years he had the consolation of seeing a flourishing European and Maori Christian community, comparable to Auckland's.

5. One might well ask: since Protestant missionaries and ministers were so patently inept, as shown by their own members' and co-religionists' accounts, what briefly explains how they differed and still differ from Catholic missionaries? To enlighten the gentle reader and satisfy his justifiable curiosity, we will refer only to Protestant sources.

Protestant clergy of all denominations become ministers as adults or middle-aged. When, in short, they realise that they cannot enter other well-paid professions they join the Protestant ministry, which provides them with a comfortable, lucrative living. The majority come from occupations such as cobblers, blacksmiths, tailors, shopkeepers, clerks, sailors, soldiers, etc. Their course of Protestant studies at a college or by private tuition lasts about a year, and often only six months. They are then ordained as Gospel ministers. Even less is required to become Protestant *missionaries*. They, usually, have not been able to get generous stipends or have not been accepted as ministers. They first become catechists, as the initial step to later becoming Gospel ministers. Nothing more is required of candidates' personal integrity, morality and piety than for any ordinary Protestant.

This method of recruitment is the cause of all Protestantism's faults. Since its members are cut off from Christ's true Church, it is not God who calls them to be His ministers and missionaries. They thus commission themselves. They have no real training, sense of self-discipline or Christian virtues. With the Bible, their only almanac, tucked under their arm, they set themselves up as teachers and models for their brethren. This describes Protestant missionaries, both present and past, in New Zealand and everywhere else.

Catholic missionaries and priests are completely different. They have a college or seminary education where they receive five years secondary school teaching. If they then believe they have been called to the priesthood, they complete six or seven years philosophical and theological studies. During this period, not only do they receive necessary knowledge but they are introduced to self-discipline, mortification of the flesh, piety and the practice of Christian and priestly virtues. If their progress in the one, true religion is not clearly shown, they are not admitted to holy orders, let alone ordained as priests. The first Catholic priests in New Zealand were educated in this manner. The same method is used presently and will continue for all prospective Catholic priests.

6. Only a few Catholic missionaries went to New Zealand. They had no human support or funds and they were branded as thieves and cut-throats by Protestant preachers. Two qualities, however, lent credence to their cause; their kindliness and saintliness. It is inherent in human nature, whether civilised or not, to revere holiness, purity, kindness and unselfishness even in an enemy. An arrogant man might not follow their example, but still feel compelled to admire them. This is the secret of Catholicism's universal appeal.

Rev. Ward, an Anglican minister, was upset and disturbed by Catholic missionaries' arrival in New Zealand. He wrote: 'We fear that we will lose many souls. We cannot help being upset at Catholic missionaries' efforts to undermine the more authentic faith of our workers … (!). However, we have to admire their missionary zeal, self-sacrifice, self-denial and unstinting efforts.'[30]

Thomson, frequently cited, mentions that Roman Catholic missionaries were not interested in land-dealing (stealing Maori land) because here as elsewhere, they obeyed the sacred precept given to the first missionaries: *'take nothing for the journey, neither bread, nor a haversack, nor money for your purse, nor spare clothes* (St Mark VI.8.)'[31] When Wirimu Tamiana, a famous chief, was asked why he called Catholic priests *heavenly Angels,* he replied: *'Because when they visit our villages they have nothing, so they can't be called worldly.'*[32]

Dr Dieffenbach, a Protestant mentioned previously, adds: 'Catholic priests' humble and unselfish lives and their generally high level of education have earnt them many friends, both European and Maori, and many conversions among the latter.'[33] Heathen Chinese once told Protestant ministers: 'Practise what you preach. Observe the Gospel's teachings yourselves first, and then come and teach us.'[34]

Another Protestant, Dr Thomson, commented on Catholic priests' angelic purity, writing: 'Their celibacy made a remarkable impression on the Maori.'[35] On the other hand natives, living in misery and rags, saw in their midst dandies with gleaming cuffs and their even more elegant ladies, sneering at them and their condition. Protestant missionaries certainly were no witness to Jesus's poverty, humility and sublime purity.

Mr Earle deplored his co-religionist Protestant missionaries' lack of hospitality. Once, he and fellow botanists travelling inland reached a Protestant mission. The missionaries slammed the door in their face. It was Christmas Day, too. Maori, similarly, frequently complained about ministers' rude behaviour and said it was contrary to Christian charity.[36] Rochefort, another English Protestant, writing more recently, mentioned: 'I must admit that Catholic missionaries are generally much more hospitable than Protestant missionaries.'[37] And yet their homes had every conceivable comfort, since they are well paid; while Catholic missionaries lacked even essentials.

Wakefield, an Anglican, said of the zealous Monsignor Pompallier: 'Members of the *Club* (the social elite) and others who had the good fortune to know him spoke very highly of his gentlemanly behaviour and his generosity towards natives.'[38] Terry, another Protestant, mentions: 'Bishop Pompallier is specially suited to head the Catholic mission. He is well-educated and has an attractive personality. He has a serious, expressive demeanour and a dedication and burning enthusiasm for his cause. He has an extraordinary effect on the Maori.'[39]

Catholic missionaries successes among the natives are due firstly to God's grace, and then to their zeal, charity, Christian example and the differences that Maori noticed between Catholic priests and Protestant ministers and between Catholic and Protestant new converts' lives and behaviour. 'We heard with great sorrow,' wrote Father Reignier, a Marist priest, 'on 30 March 1843, that a Protestant Maori war party ambushed an enemy tribe, slaughtered many, dismembered them and ate them. This horrible example of cannibalism cast damage and scorn on their Protestantism and led a great number of Maori to become Catholics.'[40]

Miss Tucker, an Anglican teacher and daughter of a missionary, wrote a book in 1855 in which she depicts Protestant ministers as ardent and zealous as the first apostles. Then, in a far from Christian spirit, she calls Maori 'a barbarous people who should be exterminated rather than converted!' She adds: 'Our missionaries bemoan their ineffective efforts to convert souls.' Continuing her sad tale she says: 'And now, as well as worldliness, there is the peril of *Papism*. This false religion's efforts are relentless.' Who has told you, dear lady, that the Catholic faith is false? Theology gleaned from needlework or spinning? But let the unhappy lady continue: 'Although they (Catholic missionaries) have no permanent effect in areas which have had the benefit of bible teaching for some time, they are often very successful with the gullible and heathens in new areas, causing our missionaries grave concern.'[41]

The worthy Mr Earle, although Protestant, described Catholic missionaries' behaviour among the Maori and European thus: 'I visited many Catholic missions. Their priests live quite differently from Protestant missionaries. They are cheerful and kind to heathen savages and pleasant and hospitable to their European confreres. They win respect from the people they were sent to convert. Although we differ on certain religious beliefs, we must nevertheless acknowledge the success of their mission.'[42]

The oft quoted Presbyterian minister, Dr Lang, wrote, 'I cannot conceal my qualms about Father Pompallier's success.'[43] And Dr. Thomson mentions: 'It is evident that Catholic missionaries have converted natives whom Protestants considered impossible.'[44] Based on letters from New Zealand, a Sydney (Australia) newspaper mentioned, 'Dr Pompallier is reputed to have had considerable success in converting natives in the Hokianga, headquarters of the Wesleyan mission ... Some prominent chiefs have promised His Excellency to join his church.'[45] Another Protestant, Mr Bright, wrote in 1841: 'The Apostolic Vicar seems very popular among the Maori who have met him. He has converted the oldest Bay of Islands chief, with his family and tribe, even though they used to attend Protestant services. Monsignor Pompallier says that he was not sent to be a petty trader, and that he is not a land dealer ... He settled among natives and even before learning Maori he made converts, largely among former Protestants.'[46]

The same author mentioned earlier: 'When I embarked to explore an east coast area, I was surprised to meet a Bay of Islands chief and thirty of his people, including women and children on board the *Moka*. Three times a day during the voyage they raised their rough voices to sing the mass and Catholic hymns. I found a similar situation when I reached Opotiki (Bay of Plenty). Even children playing hummed parts of the mass. Twice daily the church was full of people singing together, although not even a dozen of them would have ever met the Bishop or seen the parish priest.'[47] Mr Angas, vexed at Maori Catholics' exemplary conduct, called New Zealand natives: '*a race of native Jesuits*.'[48] He went on: 'Many Taupo natives are Catholic ...The chief at Motupoi is Roman Catholic and many of his people have embraced *Papism*. At sunset they sing vespers in front of the chief's house.'[49]

In 1854 a Protestant travelling around New Zealand reached a Catholic tribe in Otaki. He wrote: 'They speak very highly of the local priest. The state of the mission bears out what has been said about it, showing sound direction.'[50] From Otaki he went on to a Protestant Maori settlement, stating, 'There was a big difference in standard of dress and personal hygiene, the Otaki natives being far superior.'[51]

7. The apostolic vicar, priests and catechists were not just content with spreading the beneficence of Christian, evangelical virtues and disseminating the goodness of God's law among Maori. They not only taught heathens and Protestants the sound principles of Jesus Christ's true Church, but made prodigious efforts to give new converts and pagans a secular and moral education in extremely difficult circumstances, according to the best, modern European methods.

Monsignor Pompallier and his missionaries established infant and primary schools in all the missions which had a residence and catechists. In 1847 the zealous Bishop published a number of Maori prayer books for converts' and catechists' use. Natives quickly learned to read their own words and consequently memorise prayers and hymns used in the liturgy. In 1849 he ordered an excellent Maori grammar to be printed at Lyons, which was extremely useful for French missionaries to learn Maori.

As though this were not enough, in 1840 he established a flourishing boarding school at Kororareka (Bay of Islands). In 1842 he built another on the *Northshore,* near Auckland, for a large number of Maori children who were given a secondary education because many were to become catechists. Native pupils were provided with food, clothing and lodging and everything they needed in a loving spirit and free of charge. They learned to practise Christianity according to the spirit of the Gospel and from their teachers and spiritual directors' example.

After Kororareka's sacking and the fighting which devastated and practically destroyed the district, the school was closed down. Monsignor Pompallier extended the *Northshore* college to provide more accommodation for Maori children. Shortly afterwards, he founded another Auckland boarding school for European and Maori girls where they were also taught home science to equip them to be good housewives and mothers. A large orphanage for Maori girls was attached to the school. They received free food, clothing, education and every other necessity for their dear, tender souls' moral development and material welfare. The philanthropic, Christian institution was placed in the dedicated care of the excellent Sisters of Mercy who had been asked to come from Ireland. The colonial governor, George Grey, provided subsidies for building schools and caring for Maori children. But most of the costs were met by the mission and individual Catholics' donations. The devoted Sisters later founded convent schools for girls in Auckland, and parish schools elsewhere in the diocese.

Parish schools, orphanages and colleges were run so well and priests, catechists and nuns provided such devoted and effective teaching as to earn settlers' general support and praise, regardless of their religion. Many Protestants sent their girls to the convent rather than their own schools.

Governor Grey frequently visited Catholic colleges and parish schools spread throughout the diocese. He was very impressed and sung their praises even to the British government. In a dispatch to Lord Grey, British colonial secretary, he wrote: 'Roman Catholic schools in this country are run extremely well. They are not only a credit to the Roman Catholic Bishop and his priests but do indeed deserve recognition by the Government.'[52] The Protestant British government turned a deaf ear to the governor's recommendation. It is unfortunately true that gratitude and compensation to Catholics have never been included among Protestant virtues or in Great Britain's egotistical political agenda.

8. In the midst of such wonderful progress for Catholicism, a sad trial was about to beset the flourishing Auckland diocesan missions and its distinguished pastor. About 1848 differences arose between Monsignor Pompallier and his missionary colleagues, members of the Society of Mary, regarding the best way to develop missionary work. The bishop wanted them not to be bound by their society's rule and to devote themselves exclusively to the missions. They, however, maintained that they could not put aside their rule which they did not see as an obstacle to their apostolate, but rather an aid to enhance it. Their superior general supported their view.

It often happens that even the holiest and best intentioned of men, out of their overriding concern for the salvation of souls, do not sufficiently recognise the obligations members of a religious order have as individuals and to the society they belong to, besides their missionary duties. Hence, sometimes differences arise between the heads of the diocese or mission and the religious order supplying missionaries. The former insists they are missionaries first and foremost; the latter asserts that they are firstly members of a religious order and then missionaries. This, essentially, was the cause of conflict between Monsignor Pompallier and the Marist fathers.

The good bishop's request unwittingly undermined the Marist Society and the diocese, even though his intention was the opposite. In fact, members of a religious order or society must scrupulously observe its rules, then cooperate as far as possible in evangelisation. Anyone denying this would not know enough about the intrinsic purpose of the religious life or what constitutes effective missionary work. The religious rule does not hinder missionary work but enhances and strengthens it.

Monsignor Pompallier and the Marist superior general had lengthy discussions but they could not reach an agreement. The society's general then relinquished the Auckland diocese and ordered his members to go to the newly created Wellington diocese which had been assigned to the society by the Holy See. Thus Monsignor Pompallier had to look elsewhere for the missionaries he needed.

It would be impossible to describe the holy bishop's distress in seeing his diocese so quickly stripped of missionaries, and the serious damage this did to schools and other Catholic activities. In attempting to remedy the calamity, he went to Europe to find other missionaries for the Lord's vineyard and he was quite successful. However, their number was insufficient to meet the huge diocese's many and varied needs. He also asked some religious orders for help but met all kinds of obstacles. In 1859 he returned to Europe to get more assistants, and in 1860 Italian Franciscans agreed to support him and to establish a secondary school, which will be described later.

The Marist priests and brothers who in 1849 and 1850 left Auckland for the Wellington diocese, boosted the latter's development considerably in a short period. The *Hutt* mission became the bishop's and several missionaries' temporary headquarters. In 1850 a girls' school was built, housing four religious, and the Nelson mission was also established. The following year, missions were set up at Napier, Pakowai, Wanganui and Otaki. Missionaries also visited Catholics in areas which had no resident priest. The number of European and native Catholics increased daily and the vast mission's educational and civilising effects continued to develop.

CHAPTER NINE

Colony's Material Development From 1851 to 1860

SUMMARY.– 1. New colonists for Canterbury.– 2. Hawkes Bay colony. – 3. New Zealand Company's bankruptcy. – 4. Goldmining in California, Australia and New Zealand. – 5. Colonial constitutional government. – 6. Sir George Grey leaves the colony; Acting-governor and Parliament's first sessions; a new governor. – 7. Maori love of the land. Formation of Native League to prevent land sales. – 8. The Land League causes inter-tribal fighting. – 9. Earthquake. – 10. Maori arms. – 11. Colonial legislature and laws; Provincial Councils. – 12. Colony's material development; education, emigration, agriculture, goldmining. – 13. Colonial statistics, 1859.

1. When in 1847 peace and tranquillity returned to New Zealand, emigration from England recommenced in earnest. While Scottish emigrants obtained land in Otago, intending to create, if possible, an exclusively Presbyterian settlement, at the same time a new society called the *'Canterbury Association'* was formed in England. It was headed by the Archbishop of Dublin and other Archbishops, Bishops and Anglican clergy, and many members of the British aristocracy. The society's main goal was similar to the Scottish Association's: to establish an exclusively Anglican settlement in New Zealand. Canterbury Association emigrants could not settle elsewhere or permit non-Anglicans to join their settlement.

After carefully searching for a suitable location for the so-called Anglican *pilgrims*, or future emigrants, the association's agents chose Port Cooper and surrounding district, on the east coast of the South Island, above the Otago colony. In 1848 the New Zealand Company made available to the Canterbury Society 2,500,000 acres at ten shillings (twelve and a half francs) an acre.

The association's terms stated that every *pilgrim* would pay £3 (75 francs) an acre for district land. Out of this, £1 would be used for religion and education; another went into an emigration fund; ten shillings for local roading costs, and the other ten shillings in payment for New Zealand Company land. In addition, to buy land in the future town would cost £12, or 300 francs, a quarter acre.

Association members bought 20,000 acres and sold it to emigrants at the above-mentioned price. The huge district was called *Canterbury*. The settlement at Port Cooper was called *Lyttelton*. Christchurch, the new town and provincial capital, was established twelve kilometres from the harbour, at the beginning of the plains.

On 16 December 1850, the association's first four ships reached Port Cooper. Among the emigrants were a bishop-elect, ministers and deacons, a lord, two baronets, doctors, lawyers, gentlemen of every rank, numerous workers and farmers. Many of them at the sight of such a desolate place, with no dwellings or conveniences, lamented their fate. The bishop-elect and lord returned forthwith to England. Many clergymen went to other districts in the colony. The remainder were more courageous and determined to succeed and resolved to settle in their chosen land. More emigrant ships followed in the wake of the first and by the end of 1851 there were already 2600 English emigrants in *Christchurch*.

The newly arrived Canterbury settlers were not the usual poor and indigent emigrants. They were better-off and many had sufficient money to cover their initial setting-up costs. Realising how fertile the soil was and having the capital to buy what they needed, they quickly took up agriculture and farming. Within a short time, the Canterbury plains began to fill with sheep and cattle and abound in wheat and other crops. In just three years Canterbury settlers not only reached a level of self-sufficiency but were able to export farm products to other districts.

When they began their settlement they were careful not to sell town or outlying land to non-Anglicans or let them settle in the district. In spite of their extreme vigilance and measures taken in England and in the colony, a well-off English Catholic happened to be among the first emigrants to Canterbury. The association's directors thought he was Anglican. He, like everyone else, was able to buy as much land as he wanted. Later he gave the Catholic Church a fine piece of land in the centre of Christchurch for a church and presbytery. This later became the cathedral and bishopric for the Christchurch diocese. Unfortunately, it has not been possible to discover the identity of Canterbury's first European Catholic and record his generosity for posterity.

Thus Canterbury and Otago soon lost the exclusive religious character intended by their settlements' founders. In fact, the two new centres offered all kinds of emigrants such material advantages that they very soon had to accept settlers of every creed and race in their midst. This is also a reflection of Protestantism itself. No Protestant community can remain committed to one belief for long before several members alter it and a new sect is created. Because Protestantism adheres to the principle of individual interpretation of the Bible, people suit themselves.

Otago and Canterbury settlers realised that they had secured the most fertile plains and arable hill country in New Zealand, offering them a prosperous future. They successfully put their energy into developing farming, agriculture and industry. Ambitious Australian settlers also arrived. They imported herds of sheep and cattle from neighbouring districts and settlements. The two districts' wool became the colony's main source of wealth. Wheat growing started at the same time as grazing. It grew even faster, making the districts the granary of New Zealand and source of its main exports. Even today, the two provinces lead

Colony's Material Development – From 1851 to 1860 151

Christchurch, 1860.

the colony's commercial and industrial development.

Dunedin and Christchurch, the provincial capitals of Otago and Canterbury respectively, are now two elegant, substantial towns, in the English style. They have a flourishing trade and numerous industries. They have access to fine harbours and railways connect them to each other and most other major towns and settlements spread throughout the vast island.

2. While the above-mentioned South Island settlers secured their wellbeing and future prosperity through their industry and farming, something similar was happening on a less publicised, more modest scale in a corner of the North Island's east coast: the settlement of Hawkes Bay. The small settlement developed without the support of any company or association. Its beginnings were quite humble, but deserve mention because of the considerable development which followed.

A few European colonists were searching the North Island for a suitable place for farming and grazing. In 1849 they stumbled upon Hawkes Bay and discovered a broad valley almost 100 square kilometres with a river running through it. Its soil, a combination of alluvial deposits and loam, was extremely fertile. They decided to settle, hoping for prosperity.

The newcomers settled on the shores of the Ahuriri inlet. In 1850 they leased vast areas of land from the strong settlement of hard-working local Maori. They stocked it with herds of sheep and cattle brought from other settlements. And they made considerable profit. During the next two years, other colonists noticed the original settlers doing so well and decided to follow their example and settle at Ahuriri. The number of Europeans grew considerably and in 1855 the government bought nearly the whole valley and adjoining hills from the Maori and sold colonists land at ten shillings (twelve and a half francs) an acre.

In 1851, Monsignor Viard, Bishop of Wellington, established a Catholic mission for Europeans and natives in Hawkes Bay. In 1854, Father Reignier, a Marist priest, bought about 1000 acres in the middle of the valley from the colonial government and built a church and fine school for local natives. Its roll continued to grow until 1862. A Maori uprising linked to the *Hau Hau* political-religious movement then occurred, causing the college's decline. When hostilities between the two races ended, the school was re-opened for Maori and European boys and it still exists. In 1881 the Marist fathers built a spacious dwelling in the college grounds as a retreat and home for their old and infirm members and it too still exists.

In 1855 the colonial government decreed Ahuriri a port of entry where foreign imports could be unloaded, similar to other main New Zealand ports. In the same year plans were drawn up for a new European town. It was to be built near the port and called *Napier*. In 1858 Hawkes Bay district was decreed the seventh province of New Zealand.

Napier settlement, 1873.

3. The English-based New Zealand Company, as described previously, had for ten years played a very active role in exploiting Maori. Although it had a forty-year licence, after only ten years in July1850 it was forced into liquidation. It never recovered because it could not honour its commitments. Its failure and demise were caused by its financial problems.

Between 1840 and 1843 the company's directors hoped to be able to sell their emigrants most of the land that their agent Wakefield claimed to have purchased from the Maori and thus establish a number of European settlements and obtain a considerable amount of disposable capital. But the disputes over land claims which broke out between the two races, the Wairau massacre and ensuing fighting nullified the company's plans and most of their vaunted land remained unsold.

Because of these difficulties the directors needed money and in 1843 obtained permission from the British government to raise a loan of £500,000 (12,500,000 francs) to be repaid from the company's capital and underwritten by its shareholders. When the loan was floated on the market, it was not taken up because the London public had lost faith in the company. To find a temporary remedy, the directors issued debentures for £100,000 (2,500,000 francs), security being the company's New Zealand lands.

This measure also failed to restore the company's financial position. In 1844 the directors approached the British government. The company's funds were exhausted and it could not support the various settlements it had founded in New Zealand without government help. In the next two years, 1846 and 1847, to resolve the problem the government lent the company £236,000 (5,900,000 francs) on condition that if it could not repay the loan by 1850, the company would forego its licence and forfeit all its English and New Zealand property to the government.

By 1850 the Scottish Company of Otago and the Canterbury Association had acquired 400,000 acres and 1,500,000 acres respectively from the New Zealand Company at ten shillings an acre. But they had been able to sell only a fraction of the land and were in no position to pay the company's agreed price of £1,450,000 (31,250,000 francs). The directors had insufficient money to repay the Crown and on 4 July 1850 duly notified the government that in accordance with their agreement the company relinquished its licence and handed over its assets. It thus ceased to exist. The company's accounts were very confused. It claimed it had purchased 30,653,466 acres in New Zealand. In fact, the colonial government bought 28 million acres from the Wairau valley to Otago from the Maori and the New Zealand Company only 2,653,466 acres.[1]

The same year the British government legislated that the £236,000 owing to it by the company was cancelled by transfer of its assets. Company land at the time of transfer (which was 1,073,470 acres) was to be bought by the colonial government from the defunct company's directors at five shillings (six and a quarter francs) an acre. This amounted to £268,370, not including the £100,000 in unredeemed bonds. The British government showed generosity towards the bankrupt company's directors, exonerating them from personal liability, but obliging New Zealand to pay for its generosity.

The unfair concession by the British Parliament to the defunct New Zealand Company caused general indignation, dismay and protest not only in London circles but also throughout New Zealand. Thomson states that, 'A more shameful deal was never perpetrated.'[2] But one should not be surprised. Even Gibbon Wakefield, secret manipulator of all the company's business and scheming, as mentioned earlier, who had gone to New Zealand and been elected an MP, commented in the Auckland General Assembly in 1854: 'The Company's last Directors had *small* minds but large pockets,'[3] which they liked to fill.

Meanwhile, the company directors, fearing that their agreement with the British government might prevent or delay the £268,370 payment, proposed to the New Zealand government that if it paid them an estimated £200,000 (5 million francs) they would forego the balance. The colonial government, forced against its will to follow the British government's commitment, agreed to pay immediately. Not having the necessary funds, it obtained a loan from the mother country's government, and in 1857 it paid the debt. The following year the bankrupt company's directors happily divided up the five million, generously lining their pockets.[4]

4. In 1848 news reached New Zealand of the discovery of gold in California, in the United States of America. A thousand settlers, eager to make easy money, hired ships, loaded them with timber and potatoes, and hastily departed for San Francisco, in California. But disaster struck! As they passed through the tropics the potatoes got soaked and had to be thrown overboard. When they reached their destination, they found there was no need for building timber because it was available locally. Most of the disgusted and disillusioned settlers returned home, some ill and others poorer than when they left.

Three years later, gold was discovered in Australia. No one believed the news at first. But when ship after ship arrived with details of discoveries of enormous gold nuggets and huge deposits of gold just waiting for prospectors, gold fever seized European New Zealanders and caused a considerable exodus to the El Dorado. In just a few months, 1500 colonists and fifty natives left for Australia, and many followed them.

There was no lack of the precious metal. But in the primitive outbacks it was extremely difficult for miners to get basic necessities. The exorbitant prices they had to pay and frequent risk of dying of hunger beside their bulging bags of gold dust forced quite a few to quit. Many, however, remained and several got rich. Others lost the little they had, even though there were very rich pickings. Many of the mines still yield good profits.

With the discovery of mining riches in Australia, many people predicted ruin for the young New Zealand colony because of the amount of emigration. Geologists, however, foresaw a prosperous future, claiming that gold would also be found in New Zealand, given its geological structure and closeness to Australia. On this basis, many went prospecting in mountains and valleys. Finally, in 1852, gold was discovered by Mr Ring in the Coromandel peninsula. Three thousand colonists rushed over but soon realised that there was little to be happy about. There were rich rumours and nothing else. After a few months, the prospectors left because the 300 ounces of gold found, worth 27,000 francs, cost 50,000 francs to extract.

Governor Grey was distressed at the exodus of gold prospecting settlers to Australia. In 1853, following wise advice, he devised a plan to retain settlers, encourage many who left the country to return and even attract Australian colonists to emigrate to New Zealand, by reducing the sale price of government land. Up till then land was sold at a pound an acre. He decreed that henceforth prime land would be sold at ten shillings (twelve and a half francs) an acre, and less attractive lots at five shillings, or six francs, twenty-five centimes. Sir George Grey's aim was to sell the land in sufficiently small blocks to enable anyone who wanted to farm to be able to.

The governor's wise measure was extremely well received by Auckland and Northland settlers but was not welcomed by Wellington, Canterbury and Otago speculators. Mr Grey's decision was a real blessing for the colony. In little more than a year 300,000 acres were sold, as much as was sold in the previous six. Consequently many colonists remained in the country and several capitalists and emigrants came to New Zealand to buy land from the government. The European population, instead of decreasing, grew steadily.

As for the gold prospectors mentioned previously, if they were disappointed not to find gold in Coromandel district in 1852, they were more fortunate in 1869 when rich deposits were discovered in Coromandel settlement. The discovery attracted several thousand prospectors and all kinds of speculators. The township enjoyed wealth and prosperity for some years. Various companies were set up to extract the ore industrially. The leader was the Kapanga Company which spent and still spends considerable money on goldmining. From 1875 to 1887 ore was quite scarce, but in 1888 mining took on a new impetus with the discovery of further deposits.

Coromandel presently has 2800 Europeans scattered in several mining settlements. The district has a strong goldmining character. In 1852 a Catholic mission for Maori and Europeans was founded. In 1870 a beautiful wooden church and presbytery were erected (see photograph opposite page). Later a convent school for infants and girls run by Sisters of Mercy was added. I was in charge of the Mission for more than two years, from 1884-1887. I must needs mention that local Catholics deserve praise, as do the Protestants who always

Catholic church and missionary's house, Coromandel, 1886.

Catholic school, Coromandel, 1886.

treated me with uncommon deference and respect. Many settlers like to say that gold prospectors are the worst kind of riff-raff, but experience has shown me that this is not true. *Miners* are impetuous, hedonistic and spendthrifts. But they are also sincere, well-intentioned and kind, with no trace of hypocrisy.

5. The five years delaying of New Zealand autonomy passed and in 1852 the British government formally approved constitutional rule for the colony. The decree contained the following rules and conditions.

The colony was to be governed by a General Assembly comprising the governor appointed by the Crown, a Legislative Council or senate of ten members (increased in 1857 to twenty) appointed permanently by the British government, and a House of Representatives or MPs of between twenty-four and forty members elected by voters for five years. To qualify as a voter one had to be a British subject, be at least twenty-one years old, own rural land worth £50 minimum or be a leasee paying £10 rent, own a settlement home worth at least £10 or a farmhouse valued at £5 minimum.

The General Assembly had the power to legislate for the entire colony, but always in compliance with British law. The Queen had the right to veto a piece of legislation or law within two years and the governor could reserve certain laws for the Queen's approval. The Maori were obligated to observe colonial laws. But the Crown reserved the right to exempt native areas or settlements from them. Only the Crown had the power to buy land from the Maori. The General Assembly was to vote a civil list of £16,000, of which £7000 was for Maori affairs and the remaining £9000 for the governor's and judiciary's salaries. They also had to regulate tax collection and payment of land bought by the Crown. Revenue sources were under the governor's supervision and any proposal for tax exemption had to be approved by him.

Furthermore, the colony was to be divided into six provinces, later increased to nine: Auckland, Wellington, Hawkes Bay, New Plymouth (Taranaki), Nelson, Marlborough, Canterbury, Westland and Otago. Each province was to have a superintendent, elected by voters. The governor had the right of veto over election results. A province was also to have an assembly, or Provincial Council, of members elected for four years with voting rights in the General Assembly. The council had the authority to legislate for the province, except regarding customs, court matters, coinage, weights and measures, port regulations, marriages, Crown and Maori land, criminal matters and estates. The governor had the right to veto any law within three months. The Crown could establish local councils, subject to the Provincial Council's approval.

New Zealand should be eternally grateful to Sir George Grey for obtaining this liberal constitution from the British government. The present form of colonial government is based on this, except for some later modifications caused by the European population's extraordinary growth. Provinces and provincial councils were abolished in 1876 and replaced by boroughs and local councils. The country is now ruled by a governor appointed by the Queen of England, with a salary of £7000 (175,000 francs) paid by the colony; a Legislative Council or senate comprising forty-five members permanently appointed by the governor, and a House of Representatives of ninety members elected by the people for a five-year term. The governor rules in the Queen's name, but the prime minister runs the colony as in any European country with constitutional rule. Presently every British subject has the right to vote if he is twenty-one and has resided at least six months in the colony and can read and write.

At the beginning of 1853 Governor Grey promulgated the constitution. He defined the six provincial boundaries and set at thirty-seven the number of seats in the colonial Parliament, and recommended the number of provincial councillors for each province. Electoral rolls, which also included 100 Maori names, were prepared without delay. Shortly afterwards general and provincial elections took place.

Sir George Grey, knowing that he would soon be leaving the colony, following his request of the British government, did not summons Parliament, leaving the task to his successor. However, he ordered some revenue be kept for general administration and the rest allocated to the provinces.

6. In December 1852 there was a change of government in London. The new colonial secretary was the dictatorial and arrogant Duke of Newcastle who, Governor Grey realised, was not interested in facts. Grey decided to resign. He obtained temporary leave from the government to return to England, using this opportunity to quit the colony which he had governed very well for eight difficult and stormy years.[5]

News of his departure caused general consternation and distress among Maori and Europeans in the north. They had found him to be energetic and fair, conciliatory in his approach and desiring the good of both races. Only some Protestant ministers, land sharks and many southern settlers were glad to see him go, because he did not pander to their selfish interests. On 31 December 1853 he left New Zealand. When he reached London, some members of Parliament accused him of tampering with the constitution, but the British government successfully defended him and announced to Parliament that the Queen had appointed him Governor of the troublesome Cape of Good Hope Colony.

When Sir George Grey left, Colonel Wynyard of the 58th Regiment took over as acting-governor because he was the most senior commanding officer in the country. He did not have the ability or stamina to govern the colony and acted irresolutely and tentatively. In March 1854, during his governorship, an American ship arrived in the Bay of Islands, introducing German measles. It spread among tribes, killing more than 4000.

On 2 May 1854 he opened the first session of the colonial Parliament in Auckland. Mr Clifford, later Lord Clifford, a Catholic, was elected Speaker. The nature of the Speaker's opening prayer was then discussed. There was a fierce debate because of members' differing beliefs, and in the end the matter was dropped. Discussion followed regarding the necessity for a responsible ministry and the governor's approval was requested. He would not agree without the Crown's consent or the resignation of previously appointed Crown officials.* Ugly and unseemly scenes erupted in the House, signalling open rebellion against the government.

On 17 August Colonel Wynyard sent a notice to the House, suspending Parliament for 15 days. It was not read out and the House continued to sit. The prescribed agenda was ignored, allowing the House to pass various resolutions including not approving essential expenditure and requesting the governor to expel Mr Gibbon Wakefield from his position. Meanwhile a member entered the House with the official gazette containing the notice. A terrible fracas erupted and blows were exchanged. The Speaker then read out the governor's notice and Parliament disbanded. On 31 August the House re-assembled, but was no more successful. It passed a motion of no confidence in the government's councillors, and on 16 September Parliament was dissolved. There were two parties in the House, the *centralists,* which wanted provinces eventually to be abolished, and the *provincial* party, which wanted provinces to have full and complete control of their own affairs.

In July 1855 Acting-Governor Wynyard summoned Parliament for a second session. Very few southern MPs attended because Colonel Wynyard had threatened to dissolve Parliament and did not want the seat of government transferred to Wellington. The House was presented with a letter from the British secretary of state requesting it to make an annual grant of £600 (15,000 francs) to the Anglican Bishop Selwyn. Parliament refused and stated that the colonial government did not want to have an official Church or subsidise any. This is still the case today.

Meanwhile the British government was considering who to appoint as the distant colony's new governor, and chose Colonel Gore Browne, formerly Acting-Governor of the island of St Helena. He was ordered to take up his new position as soon as possible. He reached New Zealand at the end of October 1855. On 6

---

* Translator's note: The reference to a 'responsible ministry' is to the issue of 'responsible government' current in Wynyard's time as acting-governor. Governor Grey had departed leaving it unresolved. Wynyard responded by appointing a 'mixed ministry' of three senior officials remaining from Grey's governorship, and three elected politicians, an alliance which proved unworkable. Eventually in May 1855 Wynyard was instructed by the Colonial Office to introduce responsibility. Sewell was called on to form the first responsible ministry when Parliament met in 1856. (*The Oxford History of New Zealand*, ed. W.H. Oliver & B.R. Williams, OUP, 1981, p. 94)

November Colonel Wynyard stepped down and Browne took over the same day. He suspended and then dissolved Parliament. Regrettably for the colony, the new governor was even more incompetent at governing than Wynyard and he is mainly to blame for the terrible, unjust ten years of fighting which ensued, causing tremendous bloodshed throughout the land.

7. All the fighting and countless disputes between Maori and the British, then and now, were over the purchase and sale of land. Maori have always had a very great attachment to hereditary land or land won by conquest. Even uncultivated or unoccupied lands were and are precious in their eyes. Every hill, mountain, valley, bay; every inch of land has an historical association with their ancestors. If they are forced to lose any land they are greatly distressed, more so than a European noble would be at having to sell up his villas and estates.

There were two values which were paramount to the Maori: women to ensure the tribe's survival and growth, and land for providing food and sustenance. Thus women enjoyed the same status as men, and even higher. Motherhood was sacred and the marriage bed was inviolate, under pain of death. According to Maori law, land was the patrimony and common property of all tribal members, men and women. Even a chief had no greater claim than the least of his subjects. To transfer even a tiny piece of land needed every member of the tribe's consent. If even one person was opposed to it, that was sufficient to prevent or legally nullify the transfer. And if a chief stood in opposition, his word was law.

When the British arrived in New Zealand, they used every means to get hold of native land, as has already been seen. The Maori, unaware of the dismal consequences, sold them huge amounts of land to obtain arms and ammunition, clothing and luxury items. When the British government took over, it replaced the land sharks, giving itself a purchasing monopoly. It acquired vast tracts of native land, paying a few centimes a square mile, and selling it to settlers at fifty francs a hectare. This was done under natives' very eyes.

What then happened? The Maori realised that they were being reduced to penury, deprived of their best lands and that they would end up as serfs, brutalised by idleness, drunkenness and vices introduced by Europeans.

Perspicacious Maori tried to alert their brothers to this dreadful fate, and make them aware of the abyss that lay before them if they did not agree to take the necessary steps to avoid total degradation and ruin. Two serious obstacles stood in the way of a common agreement: the existence of traditional enmity between tribes and secret undermining by the British government. By using bribes it continually sought to foment Maori division and discord and to establish a strong faction serving its purposes. Its policy was completely successful. This division of purpose, sentiment and loyalties among Maori caused consternation in those who sought the real good of their race.[6]

In 1854 while Members were bickering in Parliament, Taranaki Maori were pondering their dismal future. As mentioned earlier, in 1835 the landowners had been enslaved or forced to flee. In 1844 they returned to repossess their land. In 1848 chief Te Rangitake, also known as *William King* (his Anglican baptismal name) returned home from Otaki with 600 tribal members, to settle on the left bank of the Waitara river, sixteen kilometres from the European settlement of New Plymouth. Settlers wanted the fertile area. They were upset at the natives' arrival and tried to persuade them to sell. But the natives replied: 'Money we receive for the land will quickly vanish and you will have our land forever. We do not want to sell our ancestors' lands.'[7]

To prevent Taranaki Maori from selling land to Europeans and ending up without any means of survival, chief Te Rangitake and other chiefs called for a great *runanga* (gathering) of all Maori at Manawapou in Taranaki. It was held about mid-1854. More than a thousand natives attended. The most important chiefs spoke at length about the gathering's purpose, which was to establish a movement to prevent the sale of any more land to the British.

Chiefs deeply concerned about their people's well-being, stability and decency spoke out. Ward, an Anglican minister, provides a summary: 'Land occupied by elders was to be handed down to their children as their sacred and inalienable heritage. Allowing Europeans to occupy their land would lead to the ruin of many maidens and drive young men to the drink. They would get next to nothing by selling land to the Government. And they would fall into the most wretched misery if they allowed the British to settle in their midst.'[8]

Ward then observed, 'It must be admitted that these reasons have validity. It should also be acknowledged, to our shame, that some of the evils sober and thoughtful natives feared have generally accompanied British colonial development. It should come as no surprise then that natives took necessary steps to prevent Europeans opening up more areas for settlement.'[9] Ward, the author of these comments, was normally a strong apologist for everything British and Protestant. It must be said that the civilisation brought to the Maori was rather tainted when they wanted it kept right out of their villages.

After long, serious discussions, the native assembly unanimously passed the following resolutions, binding on all present: '1. No further Maori land will be sold to Europeans without the Confederation's agreement. 2. In Taranaki and Ngatiruanui tribal areas, the *Pakeha* (whites) boundary will be Kai Iwi in the south and a location near New Plymouth in the north. 3. European magistrates will not have jurisdiction in Maori territory and native disputes will be resolved by *runanga* (Maori meetings).'[10] Most who attended were Protestant, either Anglican or Wesleyan. They wanted to give solemn recognition to their decisions and almost, I would say, see God witnessing their pledge. They took a Protestant Bible, buried it and placed a cairn of stones on top.[11] The gathering then dispersed.

Political motives, patriotism and a love of their hereditary lands united all members of the new movement. They believed and still believe that, as long as they did not give up their territorial rights, they would not be British subjects. If they ceded these rights, Maori customs could no longer hold sway because their land would belong to the Queen. They were thus convinced that if their ancestral lands were alienated, their offspring would become a dispossessed, enslaved people whose sole purpose would be to cut wood and carry water for Europeans.[12]

League members immediately set about putting their resolutions into practice (as mentioned by Rev. Thomson). Firstly, they refused to make land available for setting up local Protestant missions and schools. They took the matter even further, repossessing land they had previously given Protestant missions. The missions ceased to exist and natives returned to their earlier paganism.[13]

In November 1856 Te Heu Heu, paramount chief of Taupo, in the central North Island, called for a great assembly of 2000 Maori to devise suitable means for preventing their people's ruin and destruction. Like Taranaki Maori, they passed a resolution not to sell any more land to the British.[14]

Very quickly, the Land League spread its membership to many tribes, with major consequences. In 1854 Poverty Bay natives for 10,000 francs repurchased from a European a block of land which they had sold many years before for next to nothing. In 1857 New Plymouth settlers, realising that Maori did not want sell land, clamoured for the government to annihilate the League and force Maori to sell.[15] This is the kind of fair play exhibited by so-called civilised people!

The irresolute Governor Browne wrote to the British secretary of state, informing him of the settlers' pressurising: 'The settlers really want these lands (fertile North Island land) and are keen to move in and take possession; *recte si possint; si non, quocumque modo* (either peacefully or at any cost). Their determination becomes stronger every day.'[16] This did happen, causing ruin to the Maori and discredit to the government.

8. Cooper, a government agent appointed to buy Taranaki land, shared settlers' eagerness to get fertile country land. He persuaded chief *Rawiri* Waiana, a Land League member, to sell some of his land to the government. Rawiri and twenty-six armed men went to draw up the boundaries of the land he was selling. *Katatore*, one of the league's principal chiefs, and sixty armed warriors went and begged him to stop, saying it was not his land to dispose of. But he took no notice. To show him that he was deadly serious, *Katatore* handed him a gun to defend himself. He told him he would fight to the death rather than renounce his rights. *Rawiri* ignored the warning. Katatore then fired into the air and the ground as a final warning. Rawiri's warriors joined combat. Katatore slew Rawiri as he rushed at him. Five other men were killed and ten wounded. This event happened near New Plymouth in 1854, shortly after the League's establishment.[17]

Settlers campaigned on behalf of the land sellers and relatives and friends of the slain, demanding the government uphold British law and hang Katatore for the massacre. Acting-Governor Wynyard refused to send troops against Katatore. Shortly afterwards, Rawiri's successor, Arama Karaka, attacked Katatore's tribe, killing twelve and wounding sixteen. Widespread fighting broke out and many other tribes became involved. They prepared their defences and made sure they were well-armed. Settlers sided against Katatore, providing Arama Karaka, Ihaia and allies all the arms they needed, inciting the terrible outbreak of war in 1860.

The two warring factions decided not to attack whites. They felt sure they could defend themselves against their bullets but not protect their property, such as horses, oxen, cattle, pigs, farming equipment, homes, etc. Their declaration of not intending to harm Europeans was not believed and in August 1855 450 soldiers with artillery were sent to New Plymouth. Colonel Wynyard wrote to Rangitake, Waitara paramount chief, asking him as a British ally to protect the settlers. He gave his word 'but soon discovered that many of the settlers he was protecting were plotting his downfall so as to get hold of his Waitara lands.'[18] Maori were upset at the soldiers' arrival in Taranaki but they were reassured by the acting-governor's declaration of neutrality. He said he would not seek revenge for Rawiri's death because he had been slain for trying to sell land that was not his.

After several tribal skirmishes in which sixty were killed and 100 wounded, in December 1856 a truce was reached. The aggrieved Arama Karaka died the following year.

Fighting also broke out in Napier, Hawkes Bay, between two Ngati Kaungunu sub-tribes over land sold to the Government and division of the spoils. Chief Moanui said of his rival, 'Te Hapuku has sold the forests; in the future he will have to use the bones of his dead as fuel.' These words caused serious offence and fighting to break out. In August 1857 the two tribes came to blows. Eight were killed and sixteen wounded.

Hapuku's tribe built a fortress on the other's land. Chief Moanui exclaimed that Hapuku would either be killed or have to flee. He besieged their position for several months and frequent skirmishes occurred. The besieged realised they had no chance of success and expected to be wiped out by their enemy. Then, in February 1858, the governor despatched 280 soldiers. Seeing them, the Maori cooled down and with Mr MacLean's help they concluded a fifteen days' truce, during which both sides agreed to let Hapuku with his men and equipment return home. Later the two tribes concluded a permanent truce.

Unrest at Napier was not yet over when hostilities between the rival tribes recurred in Taranaki. Chief Katatore considered that in 1856 his enemies made peace with his tribe but not with him, and he never left his village unarmed. One day, however, he did go unarmed to New Plymouth to seek government protection. While returning, he and a relative were brutally slain by chief Ihaia, Arama Karaka's successor. To revenge their deaths, two men from Ihaia's tribe were killed. Ihaia, fearing for his own life, left the area taking his people with him and set up defences on the right bank of the Waitara river.

Katatore's tribe were furious that he escaped. They burnt down the village, destroyed their wagons, ploughs and farming equipment, slaughtered their pigs and took away their horses. Led by their chief, William King, they went to attack them, declaring that when Ihaia, Nikorima and Pukere were captured, they would be burnt alive. The Taranaki Provincial Superintendent and settlers wrote to Governor Browne asking him to pardon Ihaia, help him against his enemies and force them to sell their land. The governor replied that 'such a course of action would be unjust and politically unwise.'[19]

Ihaia saw that he was on the back foot, and had no chance of successful resistance. He decided that it would be best to concede defeat, abandon his fort and retreat to Mokau, where his tribe still lives. Fighting between the two tribes ceased for the time being. We shall see how the government exploited their division, causing the most devastating war to afflict New Zealand. Ihaia sided with the British against his compatriots, and in 1873 he died from disease and dissipation.[20]

9. While Taranaki Maori were fighting, Wellington settlers were terrified by major earth tremors. At 9.11 p.m. on 23 January 1855, an earthquake occurred similar to the 1848 one. The first quake lasted a minute and a half. It was accompanied by a deafening subterranean rumbling, drowning out the sound of stone houses and brick chimneys crashing down. Fortunately most houses in the town were wooden and consequently only one person died and three were injured. Many houses, however, were struck by falling trees.

Shock waves spread from the north-west to the east. The region suffered continuous tremors for fourteen hours. People fled in terror to the hills. There were many cracks and fissures in the ground, and considerable damage was caused. The terrain in the Wellington area was raised more than sixty centimetres. Huge quantities of dead fish washed up on the shore. After the earthquake, the former low tide mark became the new high tide level. In the Wairau valley in the South Island, there were cracks in the ground several kilometres long, nearly nine metres wide and one and a half metres deep.

As mentioned previously, strong tremors recur in Cook Strait between seven and ten year intervals. The most recent occurred in 1892. They all produced similar results. Investigation has revealed that there is a large volcano under Cook Strait, occasionally erupting molten lava which is carried away by strong currents.

10. In 1845 Governor Grey wisely forbade the sale of arms and ammunition to natives, under severe penalty. He thus hoped to control them and prevent them from fighting. The prohibition was only partly observed because many people engaged in secret arms sales to make money. At the beginning of 1857, Parliament

with the governor's agreement cancelled the prohibition and allowed Europeans to sell, and natives to buy all the arms and ammunition they wanted.

These were the reasons given for this decision: The Maori, as British subjects, should enjoy the same rights as other British subjects. Settlers could freely buy arms, ammunition and powder, so the same principle should apply to natives. The second reason was that, given the country's extensive coastline, it would not be feasible to police it against contraband arms dealing.[21] These reasons might appear valid to the reader, but to us, they were utterly ridiculous. In our opinion, the real reasons were not the ones mentioned. Members of Parliament did not give a fig for Maori rights, but were only interested in making themselves rich and paying off Treasury's 3,000,000 francs deficit.

When the resolution was passed, natives hastened to buy guns and ammunition. In the nine months that the concession lasted, several thousand guns and a huge amount of ammunition were sold to the Maori. 'One Wanganui trader alone sold more than 3000 kilos of powder to local natives. It is impossible to ascertain how much other natives bought.'[22] 'Auckland traders are said to have imported more than 1000 rifles to sell Maori.'[23]

In nine months trading, natives squandered several million, lining greedy traders' pockets. The government was blind to the consequences and let things run their course. When a general outcry arose, in February 1858, the government again decided to prohibit the sale of arms and ammunition to the Maori, but the damage had been done.

11. Maori who seriously considered what was happening in the country realised to their dismay that many of their enemies were now Members of Parliament, intent on their ruin. They saw them violate their voting rights and commit many other injustices to maintain their despotic rule. Because of this, they openly declared that they had no intention of ever recognising Parliament, which they regarded with utter contempt. It should come as no surprise that the unfortunate natives felt they needed to protect themselves against their powerful enemy, the colonial government. To achieve this, they sought assistance and justice from the governor and proposed to him their plan for native rule under a distinguished chief. But Governor Browne took no notice[24] and the Maori deliberated how to take charge of their own affairs.

In December 1856 an assembly of more than 2000 natives was held at Taupo to design a special government for themselves to protect their interests. Most of those who attended were Protestant and members of the Land League. They were familiar with what was going on in Parliament and the laws which the government was planning concerning them, particularly to force them to sell it their land.

After the customary speeches, they came to the main issue, to discuss European conduct towards the Maori and how to overcome their tyranny. Several chiefs spoke, sharply criticising the government, Protestant ministers and settlers' behaviour towards them. Finally, Te Heu Heu, Taupo paramount chief spoke. In a long and bitter tirade, as Ward mentions, he mentioned 'the evils inflicted on Maori by the British, namely, female prostitution, male drunkenness, lack of integrity among chiefs, diseases and universal wretchedness and misery. He concluded by advocating the absolute necessity of expelling all Pakeha* from New Zealand.'[25]

Others, over the remaining eight days of the meeting, expressed their opinions and the following resolutions were passed:

1. To elect a King to govern their people, just as the British had the Queen and Governor.
2. The central part of the North Island, embracing the area from the Hauraki Gulf to the Manukau harbour in the north, to Hawkes Bay and Wanganui in the south to be reserved for Maori occupation and to be the new King's realm.
3. Occupants of the territory would no longer financially support the Queen, sell land to the Government or allow Europeans to build roads therein. Imitating the colonial Parliament, the meeting was called a Maori General Assembly, and was to meet annually. It was also proposed that Te Whero Whero be elected first Maori King. Common agreement could not be reached and the election was deferred, because some members wanted absent tribes' involvement so that the new king would be recognised by all as their legitimate sovereign.

Fervent monarchists tried to convince the meeting to form a united national party. To achieve this, various meetings were held in 1857 and the party gained new members daily. At the beginning of 1857, the great Tauranga chief Wiremu (William) Tamihana Te Waharoa, who was undecided about the creation of a new kingdom, went to Auckland to point out for the last time to Governor Browne wrongs done to Maori, for his correction. The chief enjoyed considerable influence among his people. He was quite conservative but determined, and a government ally. When he reached Auckland he was unable to get an audience from the governor. Following this insult, he quickly returned to Tauranga. In February he circulated a notice throughout the Waikato, declaring his and his Ngatiaua tribe's endorsement of Potatau as Maori King.'[26]

In May the same year, a meeting of 2000 natives was held in the Waikato and was called the second session of the Maori Parliament. 'In it, Mr Ward mentions, Maori strongly complained about settlers and Protestant ministers accusing them of making them lose their lands and independence.'[27] A chief turned to settlers and ministers present. Quoting St Paul's letter to the Corinthians, he said to them, 'Now you have become rich and in possession of your kingdom, to our exclusion. God wished you to rule while we could reign with you.'[28]

* The word *Pakeha* means foreigner. But natives applied it particularly to the British whom they unquestionably mortally loathed; cf., Fr Barsanti, ibid. p. 33 and following.

What he meant was: You have eaten and waxed fat at our expense, and now you are in command. But now we too want to rule by having our own king who will free us from your loathsome command. As good Protestants, they subjectively interpreted the Bible. Poor wretches! Their eyes too late would soon be opened to the truth. Their wrongs were too grievous and practically irremedial and the British government was determined to force their submission or exterminate them.

The Maori realised that the government and settlers were opposed to the creation of a Maori Kingdom. They publicised their position, quoting the Bible to justify their plan, concluding by saying, 'If you disallow this work of God, take your Gospel and go. We cannot see its relevance for us.'[29]

On 2 January 1858, in the presence of 3000 natives from several tribes, Te Whero Whero, a seasoned warrior, pensioned ally of the British government, and paramount chief of Waikato tribes, was proclaimed Maori King. Chief Wiremu Tamihana asked the assembly, 'Do you wish to have this man as your King?' – Yes. – 'Do you wish to grant him full power and dominion?' –Yes. Turning then to the newly elected King, he asked him, 'Do you wish to be our father?' He replied, 'I do'. He took the name of *Potatau the First*. The new sovereign was then acclaimed thrice by the crowd and musket volleys were fired in celebration. The following day he was given a document which read: 'These are the King's rules; the power he is to exercise over men and the land is to protect them from quarrelling, fighting and bloodshed. His power extends over all chiefs and all tribal gatherings. People are to live within their own tribal area and the King is to protect person and property.'

The new monarch was to rule as paramount chief the vast Waikato area, as yet unsettled by the British. Potatau I did not choose Rangiawhia, the largest native settlement, as residence, but the village of Ngaruawahia, where the Waipa enters the Waikato river. A national flag was raised in front of the residence. It displayed a red cross on a white background with the word *Niutireni* (New Zealand) and three stars beneath.

Native surveyors planned a new, substantial township but it remained unbuilt because four years later the British moved in and expelled the natives. Maori also set up a printing press. The press and typesetting cost hundreds of thousands of francs which they paid for themselves. They began to publish a newspaper in Maori which continued for some years. It would probably still exist but for the unjust war which broke out sending the newspaper and press into oblivion.[30]

The kingdom still exists nominally. In 1867 the British government took possession by force of all the best land, relegating the King to poor, hill country in the western Waikato. In 1885 the government encroached even there and is building a railway from Alexandra to New Plymouth in Taranaki, through the Maori kingdom. The Maori king no longer has any real authority over his people.

Right from its inception the new monarchy was practically useless. It did not have the means to make itself effective. It lacked organisation, direction, troops, money and most importantly, it lacked real general support from Maori tribes. Unfortunately, also, the new king was old and decrepit, as well as powerless. He was not up to the task of vigorously heading a national reform movement to tackle the British colossus for Maori independence and freedom. Thus the King movement's constitution was a nonsense. Only because the Maori were ingenuous could they be forgiven for believing that simply making a king would be enough to heal their wounds.

On 25 June 1860, King Potatau I died of old age, not long after his election and his son succeeded him. He first took the name of Potatau and then Tawhiao. He died in 1893 while his would-be-successor, his only son, had died of pneumonia in 1886. Unhappy Maori race! You deserved better treatment and a kinder fate!

11. In 1855 the British government agreed for the colony to have responsible government, which the governor was obliged to consult in all matters except Maori affairs, which were to remain his preserve. A general election of MPs was announced and in April 1856 Parliament was convened in Auckland. It awarded pensions to retired Crown-appointed governor's counsellors and listened to the programme of the new ministry, which lasted only a few days. The same fate befell the second. Finally, on 2 June a seven-member third ministry was formed under Mr Stafford as Prime Minister. He remained in office until 12 July 1861.

Mr C.W. Richmond, Member for New Plymouth, was appointed Minister of Maori Affairs. He made no bones about being totally unsympathetic to Maori rights and privileges. Richmond used every means possible to force natives to lose their lands and he pressured the prime minister, Parliament and the governor to adopt his ideas against the peaceable natives.

During the parliamentary session several laws were presented. The most important were the following: authorisation to borrow 15,000,000 francs from England, comprising 5,000,000 to pay the bankrupt New Zealand Company, 4,500,000 to purchase Maori land, 3,000,000 to pay Treasury's deficit, and 2,500,000 as a reserve fund.[31]

A law was also passed establishing certain places and areas as Crown land for future Maori reserves, so that when they were dispossessed they could be settled there. They were preparing the ground to force natives to divide up their lands, which up till then they owned in common. This would give them the means to make them sell their patrimony. In short, this law was against the natives' land league. Richmond and Taranaki settlers wanted to get hold of the fertile Waitara block and disregard its owners.

British settlers and members of government were obsessed with owning Waitara, as if it was the only New Zealand land available and the government had no land for sale. In fact, however, the government had at its disposal *forty-two million two hundred and forty-four thousand* acres of fine land, distributed throughout the provinces. It had 219,000 acres in the Auckland Province; 25,000 in Taranaki, near Waitara; 3,000,000 in Wellington; 14,000 in Nelson; 9,000,000 in Canterbury and 15,000,000 acres in Otago.[32]

The government paid an average of thirty centimes an acre and sold it to settlers at twelve and a half francs an acre for land in the interior, 125 francs for suburban land, and between 500 and 1200 francs for farmland. From 1840 the colonial government had established an exploitative monopoly over native land sales. Like some new Ahab, it wanted to forcibly gain possession of Waitara, which for the Maori, like poor, wretched Naboth,* was their one precious possession.

The other laws passed in this session regarded: counties, preparing the way for the abolition of provinces; currency regulations; the governor's salary, which was increased from 62,500 francs to 87,500 francs. MPs were also to receive twenty-five francs a day from the government while Parliament was sitting, plus travel and similar expenses.

In 1856 Maori paid taxes of 1,250,000 francs. The government earned in the same year 1,250,000 francs from the little land it sold. And yet it approved only 175,000 francs for Maori education. Even so Stafford wanted to deduct 147,500 francs and allocate it for other purposes. Parliament agreed, but the governor followed sensible advice and refused to sanction such an injustice.

In April 1858 Governor Browne reconvened Parliament, but only sixteen of the thirty-seven members attended. The non-attenders were southern members, many of whom tendered their resignations, saying that Parliament should be situated at a more central place like Nelson or Wellington, rather than Auckland. Many laws of a purely local and administrative nature were passed in the session. Another piece of legislation passed assigned European judges to Maori areas and decreed that Maori were to be tried by jury for crimes committed in their community. The government also tried to give as much weight as possible to the immoral principle of forcing natives to split their land up, contrary to their custom. If any then wanted to sell land, the others would not be able to prevent it and would be forced to see it parcelled out.

Provincial local body administration left a lot to be desired. Superintendents saw themselves as absolute rulers. They swaggered about like despots, motivated by venal self-interest. Provincial councillors, in turn, considered their own interests, promoting their careers and removing rivals. In some provinces things

---

* Translator's note: This biblical reference by Vaggioli is to an incident in 1 Kings 21. King Ahab coveted Naboth's vineyard, planted near his palace. Jezebel, Naboth's wife, bribed two informers to say that Naboth had cursed God and the King. Naboth was found guilty and stoned to death. Ahab had the vineyard but God sent Elijah to tell him that because of the murder his whole family would be wiped out.

reached such a state that honest men with integrity resigned from serving in public office and on provincial councils, leaving less scrupulous men to run affairs. Consequently there were complaints, criticism and inquiries. The government was beset with requests to remedy the situation.[33] But it had enough of its own problems to deal with, let alone sort out provincial matters.

12. Settlers now had their own government and provinces were established. It was time to attend to European children's schooling. Part of the population wanted secular and religious education in the school. Others wanted only secular education. In Otago and Nelson it was decided that the Protestant Bible was to be read out daily in state schools. Local Catholics found this offensive for their children and complained, but with little success. Other provinces adopted fairer measures. There were no special funds for education, so provincial councils taxed families and single adults twelve pence (sixty centimes) a week to cover the cost. Primary schools were built in every district and continued to expand under this system until 1877.

Gold mining in Australia attracted many New Zealand settlers and European migrants. New Zealand had lost its attraction. Governor Grey's land price reduction scheme was not sufficient to remedy the situation. In 1855 the government and provincial leaders devised a clever idea to attract migrants from Europe. The government had more than forty-two million acres available. It had excellent, illustrative maps printed and sent them to its agents in England. They were to offer a scheme to attract people to emigrate to New Zealand's rich and fertile lands, under the following terms: Migrants would pay their own travel expenses and agree to remain in the colony for at least three years. The government or province would give those over 17 forty acres each and those under 17 twenty acres. School teachers would be granted eighty acres.

These inducements attracted many people from England who were keen to own their own land and live from the fruit of their labours. They were not to know, however, where the land was situated. When they arrived in New Zealand, they went to see their land and found that it was miles away from any European settlement, deep in the bush or forest. Moreover, it was covered with ferns, undergrowth and dense forests. The timber could not be sold because of the enormous distance from civilisation. Disheartened, they returned to town. Here they were further disillusioned. They tried to sell their useless land at twelve lire an acre. No one wanted it at that price. Land sharks offered them three or four francs an acre. The poor wretches had to sacrifice their land for such a miserable sum and settle in the district or township to earn a living as labourers.

The scheme continued for a few years but eventually interest in it died. Provinces still wanted migrants and they proposed to pay half their travel costs. Colonial parliamentary records[34] attest that British agents exploited the scheme, profiting enormously. With some modifications this migration system lasted until 1870, when it was replaced by another, which will be described later.

From 1847 to 1860, in the climate of peace between the two races, the number of European emigrants increased constantly. Their presence was visible in many coastal areas, particularly in the fertile plains and valleys. A few years previously, the traveller, naturalist or missionary saw only scrub-covered valleys, knolls, hills, mountain sides and ranges, cloaked in eternal silence, with an occasional native village.

Now, however, the scene was different. Where before there was deathly silence, there was bustling activity. Here could be seen towns in the making with brick and wooden houses and churches. Elsewhere, settlements with more modest homes or cabins appeared like magic in the solitude. Ancient forests were replaced with verdant meadows. Once bush-clad hills were now lush with European grass. Herds of cattle could be seen contentedly grazing. Huge flocks of sheep were happily milling about in vast paddocks, conjuring up a picture of a twinkling white and emerald carpet. Side by side crops were growing and horses and foals neighing, frolicking and prancing on grassy fields in skittish glee.

A closer glance would reveal flocks of poultry feeding near houses and numerous domestic pigs grunting and rooting in the yard. Men about would be building cabins or houses, carting timber or supplies or tilling or sowing. Others would be burning down the bush, fencing, or bathed in sweat cutting down huge trees for building. Some were gathering herds and others would be sitting on their front step quietly smoking a pipe, ruminating on hopes of future prosperity or on misery and failure.

Settlers had the arduous task of starting from scratch, beginning with building a home to rest one's weary limbs. They were faced with the serious difficulty of getting seed and domestic animals from distant countries. It must be admitted that in spite of these and other major obstacles, Anglo-Saxon settlers made incredible material progress in this period. This is borne out by statistics regarding the number of inhabitants, imports, exports and livestock, which will soon be mentioned. And we shall see that settlers, far from slipping back, forged ahead materially, ever increasing their prosperity.

But another source of wealth was to forestall farming development, namely the discovery of gold in tiny grains or small nuggets, hidden in sand and mud, in rivers and valleys. In 1857 gold was discovered at *Golden Bay*, in the Tasman Bay area of Nelson Province. In 1858 gold worth more than three million francs was extracted. Mines continued to yield substantial profits for several years. At the same time gold was also discovered in Otago Province, at the bottom of the South Island. In 1860 a large, rich deposit was found at Tuapeka, about ninety kilometres south-west of Dunedin. In just ten months gold worth nearly thirty-two million francs was mined. News of the discoveries attracted not only New Zealand settlers, but many gold-hunters from Australia, California and other

Colony's Material Development – From 1851 to 1860 173

Dunedin, 1870.

parts of the world. Otago Province's population increased from about 12,000 at the end of 1859 to more than 30,000 inhabitants. Dunedin, which could be described as a small settlement, became within a few months a prosperous, large town and thriving commercial centre. These and later major gold discoveries in Otago Province, Hokitika and elsewhere attracted even more emigrants to the South Island, generating a good standard of living and general prosperity for the whole of New Zealand.

During this period huge coal deposits were also found in Otago, Nelson and Auckland, and later in several other parts of New Zealand. Coal was by far a more important and enduring discovery than gold. It was not long before goldmining ceased yielding significant profits, but the country's extensive coal deposits will continue for centuries to be New Zealand's main mineral export.

13. Between 1800 and 1840 the native population was estimated at approximately 100,000 people, but it was probably not more than 85,000. Fighting, vices and European-introduced diseases greatly decimated the wretched population. In 1858 a census was carried out by Europeans and native assistants. This revealed that were no more than 56,049 natives in all New Zealand, including the Chatham Islands. They were located as follows: North Island: Auckland Province, 38,269; Hawkes Bay, 3749; Taranaki, 3015; Wellington, 7983. In the South Island: Nelson Province, 1120; Canterbury, 638; Otago, 525; Stewart Island, 200; Chatham Islands, 510.

A year later, by the end of 1859, notwithstanding new births, their numbers were reduced by 699 in the North Island where most Maori live. The unfortunate race has declined rapidly since British settlers' arrival and it is now running headlong towards extinction, as illustrated by official statistics included in this volume.

On the other hand, the New Zealand European population through births and migration multiplied every year. The 26,707 recorded in 1851 had by 31 December 1859 increased to 71,593 European inhabitants, not including troops and pensioned soldiers and their families.

Livestock statistics between 1851 and 1858 are as follows: In 1851 there were 2890 horses; 60 mules and donkeys; 34,787 cattle; 233,043 sheep; 12,121 goats; 16,214 pigs. In 1858 there were 14,912 horses; 122 mules and donkeys; 137,204 cattle; 1,523,324 sheep; 11,797 goats; 40,734 pigs. These figures illustrate settlers' astounding progress.

Exports in 1859 were worth about 80 million francs. Wool alone realised more than 7 million francs. Imports that year amounted to more than 120 million. Land sold by the government to Europeans generated 5,590,000 francs. The colonial government's deficit had risen to 21,100,000 francs.[35]

Chapter Ten

Savage Fighting between the Two Races From 1860 to 1864

SUMMARY: 1. Origin of conflict and outbreak of war. – 2. Fighting between the two races in Taranaki. – 3. Governor Browne's departure and Sir George Grey's return as colonial governor. – 4. The Maori king and colonial government. – 5. Grey's Maori policy. – 6. Signs of war. – 7. Merciless fighting in the Waikato and Taranaki. – 8. Maritime disasters. – 9. Fighting in Taranaki. – 10. Fighting in Tauranga. – 11. Prisoners' flight. – 12. New Zealand goldmining; gold prospectors.

1. Bitter fighting was about to break out between the two races and to desolate the North Island between 1860-1870. The devastation, ruin, bloodshed and cost they caused defy description. Who should be blamed for all the fighting and devastation? Settlers and the colonial government were responsible. They had no intention of observing the Treaty of Waitangi and violated native rights.

The Maori, as mentioned elsewhere, suspected that colonists and the government wanted to take their land off them, in spite of the treaty's principles, and reduce them to destitution and slavery. While tribes agreed to sell their land there was a semblance of justice and no complaints, even though the price was unfair. But when they tried to force them to sell against their will, Maori realised that they wanted their ruin and they strongly opposed their unjust demands.

Even though the government had 25,000 acres of unsold land in Taranaki, settlers pestered the governor to help them get their hands on other land for stock, farming, and new migrants. They really wanted the fertile Waitara block where its tribal owners were living peacefully. The governor sent MacLean, his agent, to the area. He persuaded Rawiri, a minor chief, to sell 1200 acres, even though it was not his. This sneaky deal caused fighting to break out among local tribes.

In 1859 Governor Browne went to Taranaki and tried to persuade the paramount chief, Te Rangitake, to allow Waitara to be sold. But he replied: 'These lands will never be given into your hands. We do not want to become like seagulls perching on a rock. When a wave engulfs it, the birds are forced to fly off with nowhere else to land.' From 1844 he repeatedly said: 'This is our decision; we will never part with Waitara.' Chief Rangitake did not want to sell the block because it supported his people. He had other reasons also for not permitting the sale. He had solemnly promised his father on his death-bed never to sell Waitara, and to keep it in trust for the Ngatihawa tribe.

Feeling the pressure to sell, on 25 April 1859 Rangitake wrote to Browne: 'I do not want to allow our bedroom (meaning, the Waitara block) to be sold because this bed belongs to our people ... I must tell you, Governor, that you will never get any of this land, even if it costs me my life.'

Realising that his efforts at persuasion had failed, the governor began to insist that the chief had no rights over the land, that he did not own it, and that Waitara was not his or his tribe's. Rangitake, however, remained firm and resolute, even though he recognised the government's determination to take over. He shrewdly observed: 'The Governor is looking for a way to provoke me into fighting, and offers me the alternative of giving in or being killed, but I will never, ever give in.' In spite of the lies spread about by the government, Rangitake certainly had rights over Waitara as paramount chief, a tribal member and land occupier. This is borne out by the fact that in 1863 Governor Grey recognised his rights by returning his land. Furthermore, Mr Swanson, MP for Newton, in 1881 said in Parliament that the government's claim 'was a blatant attempt to rob Rangitake of his land and the worst injustice ever perpetrated.'[1]

Many Catholic and Protestant missionaries, the intelligentsia and colony's elite, including the Anglican Bishop Selwyn, Judge Sir William Martin, and Monsignor Pompallier protested over the violation of native rights, but in vain. Governor Browne, colluding with the colonial Prime Minister, decided to use brute force to overcome Maori obstinacy, and bear the consequences.

On 25 January 1860 Browne ordered surveyors to peg out the disputed Waitara block. If they met native resistance, military occupation would occur and troops would provide protection. On the same day he decreed martial law throughout the Taranaki province, declaring: 'Since Her Majesty the Queen's forces are compelled to begin hostilities against the natives of Taranaki who *have taken up arms* against Her Majesty's authority, I, as Governor, proclaim and declare martial law throughout the province, to be in force from the issue of this decree throughout the district.'

On 20 February surveyors went to carry out their orders. On their arrival they found a large number of unarmed Maori men, women and children, squatting on the ground. When the surveyors took out their measuring instruments and began to work, three or four *Maori women* approached them. Without a word, one of them took the theodolite and the others the chains, piled them up in a corner and returned to their place. The surveyors kept trying to work, but the women repeated their action. In the end, the surveyors gathered up their gear and returned to New Plymouth.

The same evening the local authorities wrote a letter to chief Rangitake warning him that he had twenty-four hours to seek pardon for his tribe's provocative behaviour towards the surveyors and to promise that he would not prevent surveying being carried out in the future. The chief replied that he had no desire for war, that he liked Europeans but he would not allow his land to be surveyed because he did not want it sold. His conciliatory reply exasperated the government more than ever, and it prepared for action.

On 22 February, as already mentioned, martial law was proclaimed in Taranaki. Several copies of the decree were printed and posted in prominent places throughout the district. Warships with cannons, howitzers, Gatling Guns,* ammunition and soldiers poured in from all directions. Eight hundred and seventy-three well-armed soldiers disembarked and a cavalry corps was also formed. Governor Browne called up as many volunteers as he could and the colonial militia to punish the native *rebels*.

This disgraceful action was taken by a government which called itself civilised! Taranaki Maori were accused of being *rebels* when they had never recognised British rule or ever ceded their independence to the Queen! Where in this is a sense of justice and adherence to upholding the Treaty of Waitangi? But it was a waste of time to mention integrity and justice to Governor Browne and his treacherous counsellors. The British colonists' attitude towards Maori was also extremely degrading and offensive and would cause grim consequences.

2. On 3 March the governor ordered Colonel Gold to occupy the disputed territory, and build defences against the Maori. He obeyed and discovered Rangitake and about 600 warriors occupying a pa not far away. Surveyors, protected by a formidable force, began their work on 13 March. But on the night of the fifteenth, seventy Maori built defences right in the surveyors' path. They removed their pegs and burnt them, escaping the soldiers' detection. The next morning, troops were astounded to see a neatly set up pa which had not existed the previous day.

The colonel was indignant at Maori audacity and ordered cannon and mortar fire on their positions. They replied with gunfire. The bombardment lasted all day. Four Maori and three British troops were wounded. The colonel had cannons drawn up closer to the pa and destroyed the palisades. Fighting continued at Waitara for ten days. There were dead and wounded on both sides and neither side could claim victory. Maori would withdraw from one position and then quickly re-emerge nearby with incredible tenacity and courage, even though their force was less than a third of the British and their native allies.

While this action was taking place, troops were burning down houses and

---

* Translator's note: Vaggioli appears to have allowed himself some licence here. The Gatling Gun, a prototype of the machine gun, would not have been used in this campaign. While according to Windsor Jones, archivist of the New Zealand Army Museum, Waiouru, the British were using the Gatling Gun in the 1860s (pers. comm. 22.3.99), there is no evidence of its use in the Taranaki war. This was confirmed by Kevin Molloy, archivist, National Archives, Wellington (pers. comm. 9.4.99). In making a search of relevant material, he could only locate a reference to the New Zealand government arming the militia and volunteers with Enfield rifles, and receiving shipments of these from the English government. (*AJHR* 1862, A 6 b, p. 6. Memorandum by Mr Fox.)

huts and destroying harvests, food supplies, farming equipment and all native property. The southern Taranaki and eastern Ngatiruanui tribes then took to arms in support of their Waitara brothers. They killed five settlers and threatened the small, relatively unprotected town. Volunteers from other districts and marines from warships came in to defend the town and there were several engagements. The colonel sent reinforcements from Waitara, while he remained shelling Wiremu Tamiana's pa. After a ferocious and tenacious defence, Te Rangitake and his men were forced to retreat, leaving twenty dead in the pa. British casualties were one dead and twenty wounded.

The governor realised that the situation was deteriorating. He begged the Australian governors to send over as many soldiers, heavy artillery, Gatling Guns, round shot and ammunition as they could spare. Four frigates carrying a thousand troops reached the theatre of war in less than a month. Colonel Gold left Waitara and with his forces and reinforcements marched against the southern Taranaki tribe, burning and destroying all native property in his path. He shelled and obliterated Warea *pa*, its natives escaping into the bush. The colonel was vexed at not wiping them out. But he was appeased by the destruction of houses, a watermill, harvests and crops, canoes, ploughs and other farming equipment in every village he passed through, leaving natives in a pitiable condition as winter approached.

Meanwhile nearly 150 Waikato natives went to the aid of their Waitara brothers. They built a *pa* at Puketakawere, a mile from the British camp. The colonel and his troops drew near and on 23 June skirmishing occurred. The following day, a Sunday, the colonel sent over Rev. Whiteley, an Anglican minister, ostensibly to take a service for Maori Protestants, but actually to carefully examine the *pa* and report back its condition and defences.

Gold had under his command 1760 soldiers, not including native allies. On 27 May he ordered Nelson's 350 strong force to attack the *pa*. There was a bombardment and cannon fire to breach the palisades and then the assault began. The troops, however, were driven back by Maori firing from trenches, causing them casualties of thirty dead and thirty-four wounded. Mr Wells, an eyewitness mentioned that, 'The troops' retreat was so precipitous that many dead and wounded were left abandoned on the field. So hasty was the retreat that many of the dead and wounded were left on the field and quantities of ammunition were shot out of the carts into the fern to facilitate the flight.'[2] The following day, the Maori buried the dead soldiers.

After the debacle the colonel immediately sought reinforcements from the governor. He sent 260 soldiers he had available in Auckland and wrote to Australia for fresh troops. Since the campaign was not going well for the British, on 27 July 1860, Major-General Pratt, Commander of the Australian forces, decided to take supreme command of the New Zealand campaign himself. But he too earned no accolades fighting the natives.

On 3 August Pratt and his troops reached Taranaki. He wrote to the government that the army's position was difficult, because Maori made surprise attacks throughout the district and against their defences, striking hard and fleeing before any counter-attack. Browne ordered him to evacuate women and children from Taranaki and ship them to Nelson and to show no mercy to the enemy. Native allies, including Ihaia (Kakatore's murderer), and his warriors, were to be paid like regular troops.

Taranaki district was in a terrible state. There was desolation everywhere. Harvests and crops had been destroyed. Natives carried out harsh reprisals against Europeans. Troops were afraid to engage the enemy. Maori were quite fearless and brazenly set up camp a few hundred metres from New Plymouth. They even dared to set fire to houses being used as barracks in the township without being challenged.

The governor wrote to England requesting more troops and heavier artillery and he ordered General Pratt to annihilate the enemy by surprising them in small groups as they were tilling the soil. That was easier said than done. Pratt told him that it would be impossible to catch them by surprise. Maori noticed the troops' slightest movement. They were on guard everywhere night and day, camped near the bush. If there was any serious danger, unburdened as they were, they deftly escaped into the bush like so many squirrels, moving easily and with incredible speed through dense, tangled vines choking the undergrowth, while pursuing troops were ensnared.

From August 1860 until March the next year there were bitter exchanges all over Taranaki and many lives were lost on both sides. But neither side could claim decisive victory, because the Maori attacked and then retreated, returning to the fray nearby or in another part of the district without respite or rest.

At the beginning of March 1861 Maori took up defences in Te Arei *pa* on the banks of the Waitara river. They were besieged by General Pratt's forces who built three bulwarks to protect themselves against native fire.

Troops dug trenches by day and at night natives slipped past sentries and raided the defences, carrying off tools and equipment. Since the Maori were running out of gunpowder, they decided to seek a truce and negotiate peace terms. The general agreed to an armistice but on the next two days, in spite of the truce, British troops fired on natives. They complained to Colonel Pratt who said that it must have been unintentional. The Maori proposed peace terms which were not accepted. On 16 March hostilities recommenced and lasted until the twentieth. During it, natives collected unexploded shells and mortars around the pa to extract their gunpowder.

Meanwhile a rumour spread that Waikato natives were about to attack Auckland and revenge the deaths of some of their chiefs. General panic seized the inhabitants and the governor recalled troops from Taranaki to protect the town. He also raised a large citizen levy to repel any sudden attack. Shortly after he discovered the rumour was false. On 3 April Browne went to Taranaki to negotiate peace terms with the natives.

There the governor received dispatches from London advising him that within a few days strong reinforcements would reach the colony under General Cameron. On 10 January 1861 he was appointed by the government to command New Zealand forces and replace Major-General Pratt who was ordered to return to his position in Australia.

Peace conditions proposed to Taranaki Maori by the governor clearly showed them that he had no commitment to it. While speaking of making peace, Browne wrote to the British government requesting a further 5000 men to fight Waikato tribes and their Waitara allies. Among his unacceptable conditions was the restitution of property taken by Rangitake.

Rangitake, however, complained that soldiers had burnt down pas, homes, crops, supplies, clothing and even their church; eaten his cattle and sold at public auction the hundred horses he owned. 'If they had respected our property,' he said, 'I would have respected settlers'. If restitution has to be made, it should be made by both sides.' Rev. Ward mentions that it was easy for the government to lay down peace conditions, but difficult to ensure their execution. Natives simply brushed them aside, and tribes between New Plymouth and Wanganui maintained their hostility.[3]

The peace terms were not accepted but because both sides had had enough of arson, destruction and slaughter, there was an unspoken armistice. For the time being cannons and guns ceased their deadly fire. But a strong military force remained at Taranaki and the political climate remained heavy and menacing.

The campaign, from 1 March 1860 to May 1861, cost European and Maori in damages more than 26 million francs. General Cameron told cabinet that he calculated it would cost 10,942,875 francs to maintain 6000 soldiers during 1861 and that if fighting extended to the Waikato annual military expenditure would soar to at least 25 million. This was the profit gained by the colonial government's eagerness to rob Waitara natives of a strip of soil, worth no more than 2500 francs.

3. When some Maori tribes chose their own king, their intention was simply to have an overall ruler to guide them, govern their affairs and be the final adjudicator in disputes over land because they realised that the colonial government was only interested in exploiting, conquering and debasing them. Governor Browne and the government were not worried about it and did not hinder its development. They thought it was a crazy idea and hoped that it would die a natural death, because many tribes were opposed to having their own king.

However, the government noticed that the movement was taking root and that one tribe after another were joining the Land League and accepting the new king as their ruler. They began to fear that all Maori would unite, presenting a real threat to the colony. Because of this, from 1859 the governor viewed the movement unfavourably and tried to suppress it.

Accordingly, Browne invited 250 chiefs to a gathering at Kohimarama, Auckland, for 10 July 1860, to sound out their feelings regarding the new kingdom. Seventy chiefs attended from Northland, Auckland and the bottom of the North Island. None came from the central area. The governor spoke first, followed by senior chiefs, many of whom disapproved of fighting against Rangitake. They urged Browne to make peace. But that was not what he was after. He wanted them to support his cause, as allies in the war he was preparing for against Waikato tribes. He had some success, because, apart from three chiefs, the others declared they did not want to have a bar of King Potatau.

If the governor and his advisors had any brains they would have been absolutely delighted with a Maori King and Council, seeing its enormous advantages to the whole colony and particularly for natives. It would have brought lasting, permanent peace between the two races. Unfortunately, the government, in its blindness, rashly decided on total Maori submission to its unfair demands, or their annihilation.

On 21 May the same year, the governor circulated a notice in Maori to Waikato tribes, accusing them of violating the Treaty of Waitangi by appointing a king, and he ordered their unconditional submission to the Queen, restitution of goods and property stolen during the Taranaki war and reparation to Europeans for damages. In their gathering *(runanga)* on 7 June, Maori advised the governor to 'calm down and listen patiently. They had no warlike intentions; theirs was a war of words not actions.' By appointing a king or supreme chief they meant to ensure that their rights, violated by Europeans, were better protected, in accordance with the Treaty of Waitangi. If there was booty to be returned, whites should take the initiative since they began the unjust war. The natives were quite right and gave the colonial government a lesson in justice.

On 4 June the governor opened Parliament. Maori affairs were widely discussed and the House debated the governor's circular to Waikato tribes, but the majority were against the poor natives. Only one voice was raised to express concern about government policy. Mr Weld, Minister of Maori Affairs, said, 'I would like to mention my deep respect for Te Waharoa (the chief who proposed the concept of kingship to Maori). From his point of view it is a sensible idea, and not at all ridiculous. If we are swept away by emotionalism we will not only destroy the Maori but cause major disruption to colonial development.'[4] His advice was completely ignored.

4. On 20 May 1861, the British government received an official dispatch from Governor Browne in which he wrote: 'European property and settlements in New Zealand have never been in such a vulnerable, dangerous position.' They

realised that the situation had deteriorated seriously because of the colonial government and they decided on an urgent remedy. On 25 May, the Duke of Newcastle informed Mr Browne with diplomatic politeness that the government released him from his position as Governor of New Zealand, appointing him Governor of Tasmania. Sir George Grey was re-appointed, to replace him. He had been governor of another British colony, the Cape of Good Hope.

Everyone was relieved when news of the governor's recall reached New Zealand in September, because most people, both European and Maori, were very fearful of a Waikato war which Browne would certainly have dragged them into if he had remained in charge of the colony. They hoped that his successor, who was familiar to them, would adopt a conciliatory approach.

Sir George Grey soon left the Cape of Good Hope, and on 25 September 1861 he reached Auckland where he was cordially welcomed by Europeans and Maori. Browne conferred at length with him before his departure on 2 October. On 3 October Grey took office. His tactical sense, strong character, commitment to and enthusiasm for fairness and justice manifest in his previous seven-year term as governor, in spite of some mistakes, led people to hope that not only would he maintain the relatively recent semblance of peace, but that he would ensure that it became solid and permanent.

Unfortunately their high hopes were soon to be dashed. Governor Grey was not the same man. His attitude and policy had changed while among the Kaffirs. And we shall see how the British government, after using him as their tool, removed him from the list of governors and diplomats and sent him into retirement.

5. When the governor arrived, Waikato Maori were urged to send a deputation to Grey to congratulate him on his return. At their *runanga* (meeting) a chief got up and said that he had received a letter from Auckland in which he was advised that Sir George Grey just wanted to set a trap for them and that when he was at the Cape of Good Hope he invited Kaffirs to a meeting and took them prisoner. He said it would be better for Grey to visit the Waikato.[5]

Before going, Grey consulted his ministers. They told him that Maori saw the government as nothing more than an out-and-out land agent. They said that the Taranaki war cost England 12,500,000 francs and the colony 4,825,000 francs. Transporting and caring for women and children evacuated to Nelson cost 725,000 francs. European damages now amounted to 8,750,000 francs and Maoris' about 2,000,000. The colony faced a debt of 8,750,000 francs for the cost of the campaign and costs were increasing annually at 2,000,000 francs while the total revenue for the colonial government was only 4,750,000 francs per year.

The governor announced that he would not renew hostilities in Taranaki. He would try to make as many friends as he could among Maori, reducing his number of enemies in case of war. He also proposed a scheme of native rule.

Then, on 4 November 1861, he visited friendly tribes and Walker Nene, their chief, in the Bay of Islands. He was warmly welcomed and feted.

At the beginning of December, the governor, accompanied by Prime Minister Fox, visited Waikato Maori, who were subjects and supporters of King Tawhiao. He was welcomed everywhere with great respect and feasting. It seems that Grey's objectives for his visit were to examine their ideas and attitudes, to reconnoitre the territory and then, if feasible, to destroy the Maori kingdom. Nevertheless, being a wily politician, he did not reveal his intention but, on the contrary, he pretended to be friendly and conciliatory.

In one of the main Waikato Maori meetings, Prime Minister Fox publicly stated that Governor Grey was ready to make seven concessions to Maori, including:

'2. The Governor will not put down the King movement by force, so long as the Queen's subjects are not interfered with. ... 6. The force encamped at Maungatawhiri is not aggressive, but to make roads *(and to restore confidence)*.*
... 7. The Governor will not make roads on Maori land against the will of the owners *(and no mails are to be stopped)*.'⁶ Grey, however, made it clear that he did not approve of them having a king, and that it was not a good thing.

Maori declared that they were satisfied with Fox's promises on behalf of the governor and they believed that a lasting accord and peace between the two races were assured. Unfortunately Mr Grey's underhand politics would soon rudely disillusion them. 'On 26 December he returned to Auckland and immediately ordered troops of the 14th, 40th and 65th Regiments to proceed with road-building to the Waikato river.'⁷ During January 1862 he wrote to the British government that after meeting with and questioning chiefs, and assessing the situation, his conclusion was that Waikato Maori 'showed an entire distrust and want of confidence in the Government.'⁸

The governor's injustice made natives realise that he and his prime minister had deceived and betrayed them, and they decided to resist to the end. Future events would show how damaging the governor's decision was.

6. The governor decided to destroy the Maori kingdom, but being a shrewd strategist he thought he would keep an eye on the natives until his preparations were complete. Then he would pounce and wipe them out easily. Even though he knew that his enemies could never muster more than 2000 warriors he did not consider the 6000 troops he had in the colony sufficient. From 1862 to 1866 he badgered the British government for large reinforcements of troops, cannons, shells, ammunition and frigates for his Waikato campaign. The British government complied with his requests. By June 1863, 5245 troops had been sent from England and by 1 August 1865 there were 10,047. This did not include

---

* Translator's note: Phrases in italics were omitted in Vaggioli's translation of this text.

soldiers who between 1861 and 1862 had come from Australia, nor volunteers and colonial militia, numbering more than 6000 combatants.[9]

Against these 16,000 soldiers Maori could never muster more than 2000 warriors armed with obsolete rifles, hatchets and home-made ammunition. Nevertheless they represented a formidable force. The Maori kingdom after ten years fierce fighting, although stripped of its best lands, remained and still exists today, in spite of the British juggernaut.

Meanwhile, at the beginning of 1862 soldiers following Grey's orders began to construct a road from Drury to Maungatawhiri where 2000 troops were stationed, with the intention of extending it into the Waikato. The government wanted to open up its fertile land to settlers and destroy the Maori kingdom. When troops completed the road to Maungatawhiri, Waikato warriors gathered at Rangiriri to prepare for battle, but King Tawhiao ordered them to wait because, as long as they did not enter Maori territory, there was insufficient reason to engage the British.

At the same time the Duke of Newcastle, who was secretary of state, responded to Grey regarding his request for Britain to pay for the campaign. He said that it was the colony's responsibility. Referring to the so-called native rebellion, he wrote that, 'he wanted it to be acknowledged by all and recognised by Parliament that Maoris were not to be subjugated and that he did not expect the colonists to exact a more thorough allegiance from the Maoris than had hitherto been rendered.'[10]

Natives understood the implications of Grey's demands. They realised that his intention of entering the Waikato would violate their rights and deprive them of their fertile lands. They said that they did not need roads. The tracks they had been using for centuries were all they needed. The Waikato was then, now and must remain theirs and their children's. If they allowed roads to be built, slowly whites would take over their land. They would introduce drunkenness and other vices among local natives, as they had done elsewhere, and they would lose everything. For these reasons, they exclaimed that they would rather die than permit roading. In fact, determination to build roads through native land against their will was a flagrant violation of the Treaty of Waitangi. The British government substantially supported this, when on 24 February 1863 it replied to Grey and the prime minister's dispatches forbidding him to use soldiers for roadbuilding and provoking fighting.

The Protestant Bishop Selwyn was a peace-maker and he tried to lead both parties to a fair and equitable compromise, by suggesting that the Maori king and his council could make laws for Maori to be ratified by the governor, in a similar manner to provincial councils. But the colonial government was not interested, demonstrating its determination to seize the land come what may, against the view of the Duke of Newcastle who substantially agreed with Bishop Selwyn's proposal.[11]

On 1 January 1863 the governor, unaccompanied, entered the Waikato, where natives treated him with considerable courtesy. When chiefs learned that he had suddenly turned up at Taupiri, many went to greet him. Chief Waharoa told him that having a Maori king was beneficial and that under his guidance sound laws could be presented for his ratification, if he was in agreement. He then asked him if he was still opposed to kingship. Grey replied that he was 'committed to its abolition' and he continued: 'I shall not fight him with the sword, but I shall dig around him till he falls of his own accord.'[12] His provocative speech was never forgotten or forgiven by the Maori who now had clear confirmation of their suspicions regarding the governor's intentions.

Soldiers built a barracks at Kohekohe, pretending it was a *court-house*. In response, Maori put up a sign on the Maungatawhiri border which said, 'This is the *pakeha* (British) boundary; the river belongs to the Maori.'

In February 1863, the government paper which was printed in Maori at Te Awamutu in the Waikato, published an inflammatory article on the evils of King Tawhiao's government. The natives were incensed and decided to suppress the newspaper and send Mr Gorst, its editor, packing.

Meanwhile, on 4 March 1863, the governor went on to Taranaki, supposedly on a peace mission. However, he failed to restore the Waitara block to the natives and he put Omata under military occupation on 12 March. Similarly on 4 April he occupied Tataraimaka, seized by colonists during the 1860 campaign. On 4 May Maori warriors ambushed six soldiers and two civilians, killing six. The slaughter opened Grey's eyes to his mistake and on 10 May he announced that he would return Waitara to its rightful owners. At the same time he wrote to England requesting 3000 more men and three Regiments from India.

The governor decided to avenge the slaughter. On 4 June he left Taranaki on board the *Eclipse*. He conferred with General Cameron who had 770 men under his command. Their plan was to attack natives on the Katikora river, attacking them by land and water, and thus catching them in a cross-fire. The troops under the protection of the ship's Armstrong guns forded the river and assaulted the *pa*. In spite of stiff resistance, they took it, killing all who refused to surrender. Those who managed to escape were cut down by shells from the ship. Twenty-eight natives were killed in the battle. The British suffered three dead and eight wounded.

The situation in the Waikato became more and more tense. The few Europeans there, fearing the worst, fled to Auckland. The Maori newspaper *Hikioi*, organ of the Maori King, suspended publication and Auckland settlers spread false rumours, causing the situation to deteriorate daily.

One such rumour was that natives near Auckland were about to rebel and massacre local settlers. As rumours grew, the governor believed it politic to hunt down Waikato Maori near the border so that the invading army would not be closely threatened.

On 9 July 1863 Grey assembled a strong force at Drury and sent magistrates to every Maori settlement (as reported by Major-General Alexander, a participant in the campaign) to order Maori to take an oath of obedience to the Queen and hand over their weapons, or leave their homes and land and quit the territory (of the Maori kingdom) with the *rebels*, and have their goods confiscated. Natives refused to swear allegiance. The great majority crossed the boundary and entered the Waikato while a few hid in the nearby bush.[13] Women and children and an ailing chief who wanted to remain were taken prisoner on Grey's orders.

On 12 July General Cameron's forces invaded Maori territory. Three days later the governor published a notice in English and Maori accusing natives of provoking war. He concluded: 'Those who wage war against Her Majesty, or remain in arms, threatening the lives of her peaceable subjects, must take the consequences of their actions, and they must understand that they will forfeit the right to the possession of their lands guaranteed to them by the Treaty of Waitangi, which lands will be occupied by a population capable of protecting for the future the quiet and unoffending from the violence from which they are now so constantly threatened.' Grey's notice did not disguise the fact that he, not the Maori, committed the violations. His intention to confiscate land was the real basis for the notice.[14]

7. The governor had carefully prepared for the campaign. He had 6542 troops ready for battle gathered in the main European settlements. There were 3100 men under General Cameron's command on the Waikato border, 3000 volunteers at the ready in Auckland and 750 soldiers including seventy-nine troopers in Napier. There were 1200 armed men in Wellington and 873 soldiers in west Wanganui. Besides 719 troops in Taranaki, the settlers were all armed.

In addition to this enormous force the British had several allied tribes from Auckland, Taranaki and Wanganui. Tribes opposing the government encroachment were mostly from the Waikato, Thames, Taupo, Taranaki and Wanganui. The others were either neutral or on the settlers' side.

Naval steamers and a flotilla of gunboats assembled bringing plans to completion. The governor realised that natives would not start hostilities. He then ordered General Cameron, supported by his flotilla, to cross the Maungatawhiri border and invade the Waikato. British troops became aware that they had been ordered into battle not to defend a just colonial cause but as tools in an enormously expensive campaign to exploit Maori and enrich colonial merchants.[15]*

* Translator's note: Vaggioli pungently summarises Rusden's less colourful description: 'It may have been one of the early causes of a general feeling which by degrees spread among Her Majesty's regular forces, that the war was sought, not as a necessary act of justice, but as a means of spoliation, and a stimulant of the expenditure which enriches traders.'

On 12 July 1863 General Cameron and 380 soldiers crossed the frontier, their first action being to destroy thirty enemy canoes. On 15 July, in reprisal, Maori killed two settlers. On 17 July a war party gathered on a hill and after several feints, they engaged the British. They fought tenaciously but were forced to retreat leaving twenty dead on the field. The British had twelve wounded. On the same day, other natives attacked a British escort which they routed, killing four and wounding ten. On 22 July similar exchanges occurred between a convoy's escort and Maori. The same pattern continued for several days.

Meanwhile the colonial government was considering the booty. It decreed as follows:

1. All armed volunteers would receive, besides food, clothing, etc., 2 francs 80 centimes daily pay, and officers would be paid at a higher rate according to rank. 2. A further levy of 5000 volunteers would be raised in Australia and Otago, promising them confiscated land in addition to the same pay. 3. A 1600 kilometre road would be built from Auckland to Taupo through the Waikato, involving 20,000 armed men working in detachments along the route. Construction was to be completed within nine months at a cost of 38 million francs.

The works' total cost was estimated at 100 million francs. It was proposed to finance them by borrowing in London, using confiscated land as collateral. Maori had 2,792,000 acres of arable land in the Waikato and Taranaki. The government planned to put aside a certain amount as a native reservation, for any survivors of the war. The rest was to be divided up as follows: 500,000 acres for Waikato volunteers; 200,000 for Taranaki volunteers. The government would retain two million. This would be sold to settlers for about 75 million francs. In addition, the colonial government wanted the British government to contribute 100 million francs to the campaign. The colony would therefore not lose, but would gain financially from the war and other activities.

On 5 August 1863 conditions regarding donation of land to volunteers and reservists were published in the official *Gazette*. Volunteers were entitled to an allotment of fifty acres of rural land and an acre of town land. Officers would receive more. Settlements would have both allotments and farms for 100 volunteers. To be eligible for this generous allocation, volunteers had to do three years service, and then only local defence duties. It did not take long for colonial government agents to sign up 5000 volunteers in Australia and elsewhere.

Meanwhile fighting was intensifying in the Waikato. On 25 August 1863 twenty-five soldiers were cutting down trees by the roadside. They had stacked their guns under a sentry's watch. A native war party stole up, seized their weapons and began to fire on them. Hearing gunfire, nearby troops ran to the aid of their comrades. After more than an hour's fighting the Maori retreated into the bush.

On 7 September British troops violated the sanctuary of a native cemetery in Papakura, disinterring and committing indignities on corpses, and stealing greenstone adzes buried with them according to Maori custom. While soldiers were committing this barbarous act, a native war party killed Judge Armitage and four settlers as they were transporting soldiers' supplies. In another incident natives surprised one of Cameron's stockades and seized ammunition. Soldiers pursued them into the bush. After an hour's fighting, three troops were killed and five wounded and the natives retreated. On 8 September natives attacked *Razorback* fort, but were forced to retreat, with minor losses on both sides.

On 14 September a Maori war party tried to storm British defences at Pukekohe. Its defenders would have been overwhelmed were it not for the timely arrival of a company of soldiers from the nearby fort, forcing the natives to retreat. The British suffered two dead and five wounded and the Maori six dead. Their number of casualties was not known, because Maori always carried off their wounded, even following a rout. Maori women usually performed this kind deed.

On 23 September a British advance party was attacked by marauding natives, forcing them to retreat. When they had strong reinforcements they set out to punish their attackers, but they had vanished. A few days later General Cameron encamped by the Waikato river. 'One day several large canoes were seen coming down the river from *Meri-meri* with a white flag flying. On being detained at Colonel Austen's post, they were found to contain a large quantity of potatoes and several milch goats, as a present for General Cameron and his soldiers, as the chiefs at *Meri-meri* had heard that the General and his troops were short of provisions, and in obedience to the Scriptural injunction, "If thine enemy hunger, give him meat; if he thirst, give him drink."[16]' Their charity was repaid on 30 September when they were fired on and driven from their pa.

The 400 Waikato Maori retreated from Meri-meri pa to *Rangiriri* on the banks of the river, above their abandoned trenches. General Cameron's 1300 strong force advanced to take the *pa*. On 17 October 1863 General Cameron called for a bombardment and the following day he ordered the attack. The defenders fought like lions from ditches and bulwarks around the pa, repelling their attackers, but they were forced to retreat behind the internal defences of the main redoubt, which stood six metres high. Realising that they could not hold out for long against shelling, grenade attacks and repeated assaults, they decided to evacuate half their force which passed through enemy lines without detection. While they were escaping, a detachment of soldiers attacked the flanking trenches but were repelled with considerable losses. Even though their grenades had a devastating effect, the valiant Maori would not yield an inch.

The British commander decided to try again the next day. In the meantime he had his troops tightly encircle the pa so that the Maori could not escape during the night. Seeing that they had no hope of winning or escaping, the natives surrendered the following day. The 138 men and two women were taken prisoner and sent to Auckland where they were incarcerated in a ship in the port. They left thirty-six dead in the redoubt. The British suffered thirty-nine dead, including a captain, and eighty-nine wounded.

Maori at Ngaruawahia, capital of the Waikato and the King's residence, realised that their defences and flat terrain would not protect them from an army more than 2000 strong, supported not only by cannon and other artillery but by gunboats. On 7 November they evacuated the area, taking King Potatau I's remains with them. British troops took occupation the following day and Cameron transferred his headquarters there.

One Sunday morning, halfway through December, a column of soldiers commanded by Captain Jackson saw smoke rising from the nearby bush. They approached stealthily and found a group of natives absorbed in prayers, singing psalms and hymns. The soldiers fired a volley from only twenty-five metres into the unarmed gathering. Then with raised revolvers they rushed forward to finish the wretches off. The natives were panic-stricken at the surprise attack and fled leaving their dead behind and carrying off their wounded.

While the Waikato was racked with war, Taranaki was no bed of roses either. In September and October there were several engagements between troops and natives. Maori lands were invaded and villages and pas were destroyed throughout the district. In November the situation became more settled and for a few months there was an illusion of tranquillity.

Halfway through October, Parliament convened in Auckland. Domett's ministry fell on 18 October and a new government, no better than its predecessor, was elected under Whittaker. In this session the following legislation was passed:

1. Provinces were permitted to legislate to forcibly take land for building public roads, bridges, etc. This was against native rights according to the Treaty of Waitangi.

2. The government was empowered to borrow 75 million francs to continue the war and cover campaign costs, in accordance with Domett's provisions, cf. above.

3. Denial of civil rights for rebellion. Anyone engaged in civil disobedience was subject to martial law and was to be sentenced by military tribunal and not allowed a civil trial.

4. Finally, the government wanting to confiscate native land, passed a law *'regarding European colonisation in New Zealand'* whereby lands could be seized and given to volunteers or sold, as mentioned above. Governor Grey approved these infamous anti-Maori laws. The session ended on 14 December and it was decided that Parliament would next re-assemble in Wellington.

Waikato natives were not able to match their enemy's superiority in men and weapons and were forced to retreat from one stockade to another, leaving their lands to the victors. Nevertheless, General Cameron was unable to force a decisive battle and he had to consider leaving part of his force to continue fighting in the Waikato while taking the remainder to extend the campaign elsewhere.

Accordingly, Cameron proposed to the colonial government to take Tauranga district on the east coast of the Bay of Plenty. Although most local natives had remained in peace and not been involved in hostilities, the government still approved the general's plan, and the governor ratified it in January 1864. Mr. Rusden quite rightly comments: 'Nevertheless, though the man who looked only from a military point of view might be excused for favouring such a marauding expedition, the Civil Government, charged with equal care of both races, in recommending the expedition, were *worse than pirates,* for pirates have not sworn to do right to those whom they rob.'[17]

In February 1864 British troops recommenced hostilities in Taranaki which continued for some months. They took possession of several stockades abandoned by natives and killed anyone who came into their hands and burnt down all property they came across. In April, being harvest time, Colonel Warre formed flying columns of 100 troopers to destroy harvests and other crops. He wrote to the government that for thirty-two kilometres south of Taranaki there was nothing but wasteland. The same month, one of the detachments under the command of Captain Lloyd ordered to destroy crops was attacked by Maori. They killed the captain and six soldiers, wounded twelve and routed the others. Five of the slain were decapitated and the natives took the heads with them. The fate of Captain Lloyd's skull will be revealed in due course.

At the end of April, a strong Maori force attacked a British defence post in Taranaki, but was driven back with losses. A new phenomenon was noticed on this occasion, when natives stopped in their tracks in the middle of attacking. This was because of the new religion they adopted, after abandoning that of the *treacherous pakeha* (British). It was being used to incite all tribes to fight foreigners and slaughter them or expel them from New Zealand.

At Waitara troops took possession of several *pa* (native forts), burning down villages, destroying harvests and fields, sacking food supplies, and ousting men, women and children from their homes, destroying everything they came across.

On 14 May 1864 at Wanganui, a battle was fought between 300 British allies and 150 rebels, in which the latter suffered forty dead and many wounded while native allies' casualties were twelve dead and thirty wounded.

In the Waikato there was no sign of fighting diminishing. Ngaruawahia Maori retreated in December to the formidable *Paterangi* pa in the Waikato basin. At the beginning of February 1864 it was bombarded by the British without causing damage. Paterangi's supplies were stored at Rangiaohia. General Cameron left 600 men facing the pa so as not to arouse suspicion. On 20 February he took

1100 soldiers to destroy the supplies. At dawn the following day the few natives guarding the Rangiaohia stores were mostly scattered. Others, however, locked themselves in a large building and defended themselves desperately. Troops surrounded it and set it alight. The unfortunate people inside, including many women, were either burnt alive or taken prisoner.

Rusden commented: 'Of what avail was it to preach peace to the Maoris, and tell them to be merciful, when a British force, commanded by a General, and accompanied by a Bishop, burnt women and children in a Maori house? Was it to be wondered that a great grief came upon the Bishop when he heard that a plot was laid by his enemy to take his life?'[18]

Selwyn had been quite popular among the mostly Protestant rebels. But because he accompanied the British army everywhere, they said that he could not be their friend, as he claimed, and live with their enemy. He not only lost their affection, but earned their intense hatred, and there were several attempts on his life. In 1863 Selwyn wrote to colleagues: 'Our work among the natives has become moribund in two senses: the Maori race is dying out *and so is the (Protestant) faith among them.*'

After destroying pastures, harvests and crops throughout the area, Cameron and his troops returned to Te Awamutu with twenty-one women and children as prisoners.

Paterangi's defenders, hearing of the destruction of their supplies and massacre of their dear ones at Rangiaohia, were devastated. They could not believe that the enemy would refuse an invitation to fight to go and attack defenceless women and children, and burn them alive. After the terrible disaster, they gathered their arms and ammunition and evacuated their formidable defences, withdrawing on 22 February to Rangiaohia district.

That day the general attacked a Maori war party near Te Awamutu. Thirty natives were shot dead by British troops using long-range rifles. Natives did not have guns with the same range. British casualties from this and the previous day's battle at Rangiaohia were twenty-eight dead and wounded.

A throng of 300 Maori men and women moving through their desolate countryside, encamped one day at *Orakau*, between Kihikihi and Te Awamutu. In their desperation, they decided to make a final stand and they quickly set about building a *pa*. On 30 March 1864 Brigadier General Carey and 700 men arrived. He ordered two other commanders to attack the pa from the rear and destroy it before its fortifications were completed. The British army encircling the pa was 1650 men strong and was aided by a corps of native allies. Inside the pa there were only 300 Maori, including women. They had no water and very little food, just raw potatoes and marrows.

Heavy artillery commenced firing on the *pa* and continued throughout the day and night, causing no real damage because natives attached large bunches of ferns as gabions to the palisades. When the cannon balls hit them they failed to penetrate. The next day troops launched an assault but were driven back. They tried a second and a third time, but were again repelled with serious losses. Because heavy artillery could not breach the palisades or troops rout the brave band by repeated assaults, the general ordered the pa to be mined and blown up.

Work was begun immediately. Defenders fired at the sappers, causing little damage, because they were shielded. The commander was now certain he would take the redoubt. He requested the Maori to surrender and save their lives. They replied: 'We will fight to the death.' The commander then asked them to at least allow their women to leave the pa. They replied that they would fight alongside their husbands. And indeed they did, men and women fighting like lions.

The garrison grew weary of the continual struggle. They were decimated by grenades, fired on them from every direction, and racked by hunger and thirst. They had not had food for three days, but would not consider giving up or surrendering. On the morning of 2 April the defences were mined and part of the outer palisades blown up. A detachment of soldiers attacked through the breach, but they were driven back in disarray and the natives retreated behind their inner defences. At the same time their flanks were assaulted by other troops, but their returning fire forced them to retreat in ignominy and confusion.

The British commanders conferred to decide on how to annihilate their valiant foe. In the pa, chief Rewi and elders also met. He said that there was no shortage of powder, but hardly any more bullets left. They would need to be kept in reserve. What could they do? They were dying of hunger and thirst, surrounded by relentless enemies, with no escape. There was no choice but to surrender or die. That was not how the Maori saw the situation. None of them would ever surrender. They decided to escape. But how? They had an answer.

The same day at four p.m. the small garrison left the *pa* in a tight group, women and chiefs in the middle, and coolly moved through the soldiers of the 40th Regiment's lines. As they descended the slope, several natives leapt on the enemy and clubbed some of them to death. Soldiers, suddenly finding them on top of them, were so terrified that they let them escape without sounding an alarm. Others realised that Maori were escaping and cried out: to arms, but it was too late. They had just traversed a swamp when they came across British cavalry blocking their way, and soldiers were in hot pursuit. It was here that the natives used their very last ammunition. The chiefs were able to escape but many men and women were killed.[19]

A number of Maori women were in the rear, pursued by a bunch of soldiers. A warrior accompanying them went back, turning every so often, pretending to take aim and fire. In the meantime the women continued to escape. The Maori's bold action kept pursuers at bay. Finally he was shot down. Imagine the soldiers' surprise when they found he had an empty rifle! His brave self-sacrifice saved the lives of many women.

After this *shameful* victory, the British set fire to Orakau pa. Native casualties were about 100 dead and more than fifty wounded. British troops were reported to have suffered sixteen dead and fifty-two wounded.

After such a bruising battle, the colonial government decided not to venture further into the King country, because it was too difficult. It contented itself with the lands it had already confiscated which were the most fertile in the King country, situated as they were in the basins of the Waipa and Waikato rivers, and comprising just over a quarter of the Maori kingdom. Tawhiao was still able to rule from the land he held.

8. As already mentioned, the colonial government decided to confiscate Maori land and force their submission. From 1861 it turned to England for arms, ammunition, troops and warships. Accordingly, for the next five years the British government sent frigate after frigate to New Zealand, but not all of them arrived safely.

One disaster occurred on 7 February 1863 at the mouth of the Manukau harbour, on the west coast, near Auckland. As the magnificent corvette *Orpheus* with its commodore on board was entering the harbour it took the wrong channel and grounded on a reef. Immediately a boat was sent out to its assistance, but as it drew near, the ship sank beneath the waves with all on board. A small steamer was also sent to the scene of the disaster and it rescued as many shipwrecked people as it could. But, in the raging sea, it had to keep clear of the reef and most were drowned. Only seventy were rescued. Commodore Burnett, Commander Burton and 185 officers and men died a miserable death.

In September the previous year, another steamer, *Lord Worsley*, was speeding from Wellington to the Manukau. It went too close to the west coast and ran aground, foundering on the Taranaki shore. It was not, however, a fatal shipwreck because the soldiers and passengers were able to get ashore and rescue their possessions. Local tribes were then at war with the *pakeha*, and wanted to kill the wretches or at least stop them coming ashore. Chief Wiremu Kingi Te Rangitake, who was more humane and kind-hearted, used his authority not only to prevent their massacre but also their suffering any harm. He even salvaged £40,000 (a million francs) which was found on board, conscientiously sending it to colonial government officials.

9. In recompense for his noble deed, chief Rangitake, or Wiremu Kingi, in September 1863 faced a ferocious war with the British which continued through 1864, becoming increasingly violent, as already mentioned.

In October 1863 when hostilities recommenced Taranaki Maori felt an indescribable hatred towards the British for their injustice, pillage and treachery. They decided not to allow Protestant ministers or catechists to move about their territory, because they discovered they were British government spies, or Maori allies or even neutral tribe members, unless they paid a substantial tax. They put up a notice on their border which listed taxes different travellers would have to pay to enter their territory. This unusual document is reprinted to give a better appreciation of their attitude towards the British. It is cited by Rev. Ward, an Anglican minister.[20]

Tolls to be paid by pakeha and their allies

A (Protestant) Missionary minister	1250 Fr.
Mail, i.e., letters and newspapers	7500 "
A Maori British ally	5000 "
A *pakeha* (British) soldier*	12,500 "
A Maori policeman	125 "
A Protestant Maori preacher or minister	1375 "
Subversive letters to tribes will be confiscated, and the bearer will pay	12,500 "

Tolls to be paid by Maori

For things carried on a man's back	10 centimes
For a pig carried in a cart	60 "
For a pig driven	60 "
For oxen, cattle, horses[#]	2 Fr. 50 " (each)
Fine for anyone trying to evade these tolls	125 Fr.

In this way, natives sought to protect themselves against spying and whites' encroachment. Englishmen or government allies wanting to enter their territory had to pay the appropriate tax or be sent back. Couriers carrying letters and anyone else attempting to cross over their boundary were similarly treated.

This system vexed the government enormously. It decided to pursue war against the Maori relentlessly. It would be impossible to describe the year-long course of fighting between the two races. Natives were far fewer than the British but however often they were forced to retreat, they soon returned to the fray. The harm and deplorable loss of life suffered by both sides in their frequent engagements were indescribable. Troops destroyed everything that fell into their hands: harvests, pastures, crops, orchards, huts, supplies, farming equipment, defences and pas. In short, everything was put to the sword or set alight, and soldiers were also responsible for atrocities against the poor savages.

By October 1864 the British succeeded in ousting the natives from the arable Taranaki lands and they had to take refuge on nearby hill tops. They were finally able to achieve the much desired confiscation of the *Waitara* block which precipitated fighting in the first place. The confiscation was the prelude to the total abandonment by nearly all New Zealand Maori of Protestantism. They completely destroyed their missions and expelled ministers, catechists and their

---

* Translator's note: Vaggioli translates Ward's 'policeman' as 'soldato' (soldier).

\# Translator's note: Ward's original statement does not mention 'oxen' ('buoi' in Italian).

families. They were utterly disillusioned with their religion which no longer had credibility. They were convinced that it endorsed injustice and theft of their lands, and that Protestant ministers were nothing but liars. They founded a new religion which they believed would protect them from *pakeha* malevolence.

10. Tauranga Maori in the Bay of Plenty learned that in January 1864 the government was sending a military expedition 'to confiscate their crops, livestock and property' under the pretext that they supported rebels. In fact, in July the previous year the government decided to confiscate their lands, even though they were at peace. Seeing the arrival of troops, warships and artillery, they realised they were after their land at any cost, forcing them to take up arms in defence of their violated property rights. Maori were extremely upset at this manifest injustice and held several meetings to decide the best way to present their case to the government, and what to do in case troops attacked them.

Several chiefs and Patene, native mediator, seeing Maori becoming increasingly agitated, met with Smith, the civil commissioner. He tried to persuade the governor and the prime minister not to commit such a flagrant injustice. Grey responded by 'thanking him for preventing him (Grey) from causing grave harm to many innocent people,' but Cabinet rejected Mr Smith's sage advice. The London *Times* in July 1864 accused the colonial government of New Zealand 'of having shut every door to peace with the Maori, and of involving British troops not in a defensive campaign, but in a war of expansion intended to seize native land by brute force.'

The Maori meetings alarmed Colonel Greer, who commanded 700 troops. He alerted the government, commenting that natives were digging in behind their defences. Another 1000 soldiers were dispatched and two warships, nine cannons, six mortars and other military equipment. Peaceable natives, realising the size of the new expedition sent out to attack them regardless, were outraged. There were many Maori Catholics who exercised considerable influence. In spite of missionary priests' advice to stay put, in their patriotic indignation they joined their brother Maori. Five representative senior chiefs wrote to Colonel Greer, describing how they would conduct war, if they were attacked by troops. The letter went like this:

> Tauranga 28 March 1864. To the Colonel. – Salutations to you. The end of that. Friend, do you give heed to our laws for regulating the fight. 1. If wounded or captured whole, and the butt of the musket or hilt of the sword be turned to me, he will be saved. 2. If any *pakeha,* being a soldier, shall be travelling unarmed and meet me, he will be captured, and handed over to the directors of the land. 3. The soldier who flees, being carried away by his fears, and goes to the house of his priest with his gun (even though carrying arms), he will be saved, I will not go there. 4. The unarmed *pakehas,* women and children will be spared. The end. These are binding laws for Tauranga.

The letter was signed by five Catholic Chiefs.[21]

The letter's measured but determined tone exasperated the government. It ordered Cameron to move his headquarters to Tauranga and attack the *Pukehinahina* stronghold, or *Gate-pa*, where about 200 natives were entrenched.

On 28 April 1864 the general assembled his 1964 strong force in front of the pa. This did not include warriors provided him by his Arawa tribe allies. He drew up three large and three small Armstrong cannons, two howitzers and eight mortars. He then sent Colonel Greer and 700 soldiers behind the pa to prevent Maori escaping. At dawn the following day a torrent of shots and shells was hurled from cannons and mortars against the pa. The defenders were protected by earthworks and reinforced shelters. At 4 p.m. a large breach was made in the palisade and it looked like it was all over for them.

The general ordered 150 marines and another 150 soldiers of the 43rd Infantry Regiment to attack and destroy the enemy. Three hundred men charged the stronghold, cleared the breach and entered the pa unopposed. Maori, hidden in pits and trenches, waited motionless. When the British were all inside they sprang like lions from concealment and raked them with their muskets, causing horrible slaughter. In spite of their commanders' urging them to stand their ground and force the enemy to surrender, the marines and soldiers fled headlong in panic, leaving a pile of corpses behind. Two naval captains as well as Colonel Booth and four other captains fell in the assault. Eighteen officers and ninety-three soldiers were killed or seriously wounded. The British force retreated in confusion and humiliation to 100 metres from the pa, continuing the seige and intending to launch a fresh assault the next day.

After their heroic defence, the Maori realised the impossibility of staying without food and water in the redoubt, which was in ruins and full of corpses. They abandoned it during the night, passing unharmed through enemy pickets. The next day the British occupied the pa and were amazed to find Colonel Booth and some soldiers still alive and not maltreated by the natives. They noticed that the bodies of the dead had not been mutilated or stripped of watches or other personal effects. Quite the opposite happened. Colonel Booth, who was mortally wounded, asked a Maori for some water. Because there was no water in the pa, he took a gourd, left his trench and went to the spring at the foot of the hill where the besiegers were. Exposing himself to the risk of being killed, he carried water to the poor wounded man.[22]

Ward, an Anglican minister, described how Tauranga Maori Catholics conducted themselves as warriors, noting, 'The superior conduct of the natives compared to those of the west coast *(Waikato and Taranaki)** should not be forgotten. Not a dead body was mutilated, nor wounded man ill-treated, nor was anything taken away, although watches, gold rings, money and other valuable

---

* Translator's note: 'Waikato and Taranaki' are added by Vaggioli to Ward's text.

articles were entirely within their reach. The natives suffered about *twenty-five dead and wounded,** many of whom had been long known in the neighbourhood as quiet, inoffensive persons.'[23] The reason for the difference was that Waikato Maori were mostly Protestant or pagan. Tauranga Maori were mostly Catholic: Catholicism is the only religion which exercises a civilising effect on barbarians and savages.

The brave natives, forced to abandon the redoubt, retreated six kilometres away to *Te Rangi*, a hill position. The 600 Maori threw themselves into building defences. But Colonel Greer appeared and attacked them with 1700 soldiers and native allies before their palisades were ready. The defenders hardly had enough time to build dugouts to escape enemy bullets and return their fire before they were attacked on 21 June by the British army. They fought heroically and with incredible determination and coolness but they were outnumbered and had no bayonets or daggers. After desperate hand-to-hand fighting they had to recognise defeat and try to escape.

English writers reported troop casualties as ten dead and forty wounded and Maori as 108 dead, twenty-seven wounded and ten taken prisoner.# Among those slain was Rawiri, the great native warrior chief. Colonel Greer wrote of him, 'Poor Rawiri was a very fine man and he acted towards me in a noble and chivalrous manner.' His death showed how he was repaid!

After the two battles Tauranga Maori fought in open protest against the injustice and flagrant violation of their solemnly ratified rights. Seeing that the government was determined to take their land no matter what, they broke off hostilities to avoid annihilation. The following August they agreed, against their will, for the government to confiscate their long coveted lands. Thus peace was restored to the area.

11. In the war with Waikato tribes, just over 200 natives of both sexes were taken prisoner and in October 1863 they were incarcerated in a ship in the port of Auckland, to await trial. Their health suffered and Governor Grey wanted to free them providing they promised not to fight and to obey the government. Government ministers, however, wanted to have them tried by a military tribunal as *rebels*. But the Maori insurgents, as attested by legal experts in New Zealand and England, as well as reputable writers including General Alexander, one of the commanders in the Waikato campaign, were not rebels at all, for the simple reason that most natives *never recognised* British authority over their country.

---

* Translator's italics: Ward states: 'The insurgents lost about thirty men ...'
# Statistics for both sides' casualties in these and other battles, are British in origin and therefore suspect, because they are biased and inconsistent. Natives did not keep precise records, and therefore it is impossible to know the exact truth. They do however give us an indication of the incredible bravery of the unfortunate savages.

'For my part, commented the distinguished General Alexander, I never considered the Maori as *rebels,* as they had not acknowledged, that is, few of them, the Queen's authority. They fought so as not to be swallowed up by the white settlers. We went to their country and located ourselves in various parts of it'[24] *against their will and we were simply tolerated.* *

Grey and the government could not agree on what to do with the prisoners, so in July 1864 they were sent temporarily to Kawau island in the Hauraki Gulf, forty-five kilometres from Auckland, and three from the mainland. Seeing that there were only a few guards, they planned to escape at the first favourable opportunity. On the night of 10 September, while the guards slept peacefully, they left their huts and climbed into boats they found on the beach, taking with them spades, hatchets and double-barrelled shotguns stolen from the guards. They escaped over to Waikauri, opposite Kawau. Leaving the boats, they took to the hills.

The governor sent food to Omaha, where they were encamped, ordering them to return to their Kawau prison. But they refused, saying that they had no intention of harming anyone, but they would resist with force. Meanwhile local natives provided them with necessary provisions and they began to build a pa to defend themselves in case of attack. The government feared a northern Maori insurrection if force was used against the fugitives, so it tried to win them over with goods, and offered to transport them free of charge to their Waikato homes if they so desired, and to restore them enough confiscated land to support themselves. After several weeks some did return while the others remained with friendly local tribes.

The New Zealand political situation in 1864 was really odd. The European population was more than 160,000 people. There was no insurrection north of Auckland for the government to suppress because the natives remained at peace, causing no trouble. The government had a force of 20,000 men under arms consisting of British troops and colonial militia. It also had several allied tribes in every area, including rebel strongholds. It had conquered and scattered 2000 Maori in Taranaki, the Waikato and Tauranga. Suddenly 200 natives escape from their prison and encamp in the midst of European and native allies, and the governor and the government do not know what to do about the situation! The unarmed fugitives with no equipment built a pa and the government feared a European massacre if it declared war on them. Perhaps the government had a change of heart and was beginning to have a conscience about all the harm its injustices caused the Maori? Nothing of the sort. It saw the horizon darken with the threat of new calamities and disasters and was afraid that northern Maori would rise up against the government in support of the fugitives. Consequently

---

* Translator's italics: The words in italics are an addition by Vaggioli, though the end of the direct quote is accurately acknowledged.

it tried to appease them with everything they wanted. Here can be seen the pragmatism of colonial politics.

12. While the North Island was in the grips of war, devastation and destruction, the South Island was enjoying peace, developing trade and industry, and discovering mineral wealth. Numerous goldmines in Otago and Nelson, described above, continued to yield riches. There was a steady influx of goldminers feverishly searching for gold. Where in 1860 there had been only solitude and sheep quietly grazing, now there were large settlements and instant, bulging townships, a stream of new arrivals swelling the population.

In 1864 new deposits were found in gullies and near the banks of the Hokitika and further along the West Coast. In 1866, other gold deposits were found at Havelock and in nearby Marlborough province on the East Coast, between Canterbury and Nelson. The following year rich gold deposits were found at Thames and in the Coromandel peninsula area, in the Hauraki Gulf, in the North Island. Swarms of miners, adventurers and speculators of every creed and colour, all seeking their fortune, rushed in and the colony's population quadrupled in eight years. In 1859 there were only 71,593 Europeans and in 1868 there were more than 230,000.

Steamships, newspapers and the telegraph carried the electrifying news of the discovery of gold in Australia and California. Countless miners struck their tents, rolled up their blankets, packed their swag and departed full of hope for the El Dorados. Prospectors are like the Bedouin, leading a nomadic life, going from one mine to the next. They are like Jews in their eagerness to get rich. And yet they rarely save anything or settle permanently anywhere. Gold is their obsession. They can't wait to start digging. Often they find more stones than gold, but hope of success spurs them on.

If a newspaper arrives mentioning the discovery of a new mine and a huge, priceless nugget was found, prospectors rush off. Despite their hopes being dashed a thousand times and the advice of those urging caution and to await further information, there is no holding them back. They are only interested in money. But travel costs and mining paraphernalia soak up any profit, and miners generally end up poorer than when they began prospecting.

Chapter Eleven

Continuation and End of the War From 1865 to 1870

Summary. – 1. Origins of a new Maori religion. – 2. Pai marire or Hauhau. – 3. Their political-religious beliefs. – 4. Wellington, the new capital. – 5. Maori supply and manufacture of weapons. – 6. Fighting in Wanganui. – 7. Opotiki and Wakatane massacres. – 8. Culprits' arrest; a new Hauhau prophet-leader. – 9. Prisoners' escape from Wellington. – 10. Fighting and massacres at Gisborne and Napier. – 11. Fighting in Wanganui and Taranaki. – 12. Colonial parliament's activities. – 13. Sir George Grey's recall. – 14. Wanganui and Taranaki fighting and slaughter. – 15. Prisoners' escape from the Chathams. – 16. Fighting the fugitives. – 17. No quarter given. – 18. Continuation and end of fighting. – 19. War's effects on the two races. – 20. 1869 legislation. – 21. Colonial statistics.

1. Nothing pushes a man to commit the worst crimes more than desperation. Overwhelmed by this feeling, reason no longer controls one's actions. He gives way to the primitive instincts he has been harbouring, loses his rationality and acts like a wild beast. If this desperation seizes an entire people or tribe, it leads to a blind fanaticism. Their behaviour becomes really strange and their most brutal passions are unleashed. Without pausing to reflect, they hurtle headlong to their ruin. By 1864 several Maori tribes had fallen victim to this horrible condition.

Up to 1859 the poor savages believed that the colonial and British governments would always respect their legitimate rights, as they had in the past, in spite of a host of cheats and swindlers intent on stealing their lands. But by 1860 they had to alter their view. They were now convinced from experience that the colonial government was against them, enforcing its unjust claims with cannons, and that its intention was to subjugate or crush them. Surprised by this revelation, the Maori conceived an intense loathing for the British and took up arms to defend themselves. But to what effect? Only their destruction.

After four years of fierce fighting Maori insurgents found themselves driven out by force from their quiet settlements. They were desolated to see their churches, villages, pas, huts, food, and everything they possessed burnt down. They were horrified to see their venerated ancestors' remains abused and scattered to the winds. They witnessed many of their dear ones die of hunger, cold and privation, and all were reduced to the most wretched misery. They saw themselves insulted, abused and horribly humiliated by colonial troops and wicked settlers. They realised that the militia were neither God-fearing, moral or had any conscience. They only wanted to get drunk, whore and run riot.

For forty years Protestant ministers had been preaching to them that Protestantism was the religion which epitomised love; that those who joined would be respected, loved and cherished because it was the religion of the Queen and of the great British nation. They were told that if they embraced Protestantism their rights would always be respected and never violated and that they would always enjoy Britain's protection. They would fully participate in the prosperity, wealth and well-being enjoyed by all the vast empire's subjects. Many of the simpletons trusted in these fair promises and embraced Protestantism, at least nominally.

Now, however, surrounded as they were by such misery, they stirred themselves. They were furious and swore to take hideous revenge. The hatred that they had felt for the British for several years grew to boiling point. In 1864 the poor people decided to renounce Protestantism, to return to their former barbaric customs and to drive the British out of New Zealand, seeing them as the cause of all their misfortune. They declared that they were the faithful remnant of God oppressed by the British Pharaoh's yoke.

2. The first indications of a new Maori religion were seen in 1864 in Taranaki. A company of 100 soldiers under the command of Captain Lloyd was destroying a field of rebel maize at Te Ahuahu. Natives attacked them by surprise and killed several, forcing the others to flee. They then decapitated the dead, drank their blood and took the heads away with them. After Captain Lloyd's head was cured to prevent its decomposition, it was taken everywhere they went and they made a show of consulting it regarding the future.

Te Ua (rain) Tuwhakaharo was the inventor and founder of the new sect. He was born and raised in the upper Taranaki area and he was a Tohunga or priest of Maori religion, and a prominent chief in his village. Later he embraced Anglicanism and at his baptism he took the name of Horopapera or Zorobabel. Subsequently, his teachers appointed him to a prominent, expert role as Kai karakia or school teacher, catechist and assistant curate to read the Bible to the congregation and lead prayers in public.

Te Ua assumed responsibility for saving his people from extermination by uniting them in a common religion, freed from Protestantism. He claimed to have had divine revelation and that the archangel Gabriel revealed a new religion to him, and the future destiny of the Maori people. But since these revelations were not sufficient to convince his compatriots, he turned to miracles. He said that he was invested with supernatural powers and he confirmed his mission with amazing feats. He was bound hand and foot with ropes and chains, but tore them off as though they were string. These tricks gained him some converts. Then he claimed that a voice from heaven ordered him to sacrifice his only son and he attacked him with an axe, 'as a sacrifice for his abandoned, desolate and lost people.' The tribe ran to seize and punish the cruel murderer, but, miraculously, they found his son happily alive and unharmed.

His and neighbouring tribes saw this as a sign and were completely won over. From that moment Te Ua was seen as a wonder-worker, and regarded by his followers as Muslims regard Mahomet. He was high priest and prophet, and therefore worthy of their complete veneration and respect. He was a mysterious figure whose words were considered oracles, his gestures inspirational and his dreams as reality.

The new religious phenomenon was called Pai marire and also Hauhau. Its founder concealed the obscure mysteries of the new faith under the mantle of these words which had no clear meaning. The expression 'pai marire' has no precise meaning in Maori. Its adherents seem to have taken it to mean 'good news' and also 'blissful peace'. The most common meaning for the word 'hau' is 'wind' and it seems that its adherents thought 'pai marire' really meant 'divine breath' and that their God was Atua hau, or wind of God.

The fledgling superstition needed specific rites and the great Jewish* high priest and prophet had the archangel Gabriel provide them. He told them to erect a pole as an arcane, symbolic tree. Te Ua planted it in the ground in a prominent position, its tip pointing to the sky, from whence they would acquire knowledge of all languages. All Maori were to gather around it because all religions and the divine breath emanated from the pole's tip. Te Ua, the magician, taught his Maori followers that they were the new people of God, comparing them to Abraham and the patriarchs who without temples or altars rested in their pilgrims' tents in the land of Canaan, waiting to be liberated from their enemies. The revelations, miracles and mysterious happenings which Te Ua claimed to be real were nothing but monstrous distortions of biblical facts, emanating from an unstable mind to prop up his new political-religious purpose.

The first niu or sacred pole was erected by Te Ua in the village of Kaitake in Taranaki in the presence of his first disciples. While the people stood with heads bowed, he began to make strange gestures and utter unintelligible words. He then preached a sermon on the new faith's beauty and virtue. After this, all raised their hands and eyes towards the top of the pole. At the same time they uttered a sound similar to steam under pressure escaping from a valve. Thus they marched two by two several times around the niu, singing appropriate hymns and chants.

The erection of the first niu was seen to inaugurate the new sect publicly and solemnly.

The niu or pole was the most sacred and revered object, occupying prime position in all Pai marire's rituals and ceremonies. Woe betide anyone not treating

---

* 'Tiu' is a corruption of the English word 'Jew'. Since there is no letter J in Maori, instead of Jew they said Tiu, the Maori equivalent. The word also means prophet, priest or sacred person.

it with respect. It was worshipped with great devotion since Jehovah spoke through it and it manifested the divine spirit. People present had to pay homage to it, walking around it three times. On the third time they were to lift their eyes to the top of the pole and raise their right hand to their temple while chanting: 'Praise to Jehovah, the most High, glory, glory, glory, RIRE, RIRE, RIRE, HAU.'

We are convinced that when Te Ua conceived his sacrilegious fantasies, he had no idea of how they would later be adapted by his disciples, chiefly envoys, prophets and high priests: men such as Tahutai, Hepanaia, Wi Parana, Rangitake, Kereopa and Patara, all former Anglicans, and the many other tiu who would later spring up in every tribe. The new sect, encouraged by its envoys, made startling progress and in less than a year was established in every tribe in New Zealand, except at the top of the North Island, traditional enemies of southern tribes. Sacred poles were erected in nearly every village, showing the hold that Pai marire gained over natives' minds and how well it suited them.

3. Anyone wanting to embrace the Pai marire religion had first to renounce the pakehas' (English) God and recognise the Atua (god) of the Maori, not the naked, grotesque Atua of old but adapted, with Christian theological trappings as Atua Hau or Wind of God. Their god was given the Hebrew name, Jehovah, in order to give their theology a biblical foundation and in imitation of the Hebrews whose successors they claimed to be.[1]

Regarding Christian beliefs, they retained only superficial features of the Trinity, linked to their ancient myth of three principal deities collaborating in the creation of man. Regarding sacraments, they kept only a purely ceremonial form of baptism, signifying Hau hau membership. At Opotiki, Tauranga and elsewhere, chief Patara, an envoy, rebaptised all Maori who felt drawn to follow him. They also believed that Te Ua, the great prophet and tiu (Jew), and his emissaries personally witnessed Jehovah ordering them to separate themselves from the Pakeha and dictating to them all Pai marire's articles of faith.[2]

The extent of the sect's superstitious nature is starkly revealed by Father Ottavio Barsanti's summation[3] which he obtained from Father Grange, a missionary at Wakatane in 1865 from statements made by Pai marire followers.

Negative articles
1. There is no such thing as sacred Scripture, because what the British call holy scripture, the Bible, the Gospels and the Word of God are lies.

II. There are no laws given by God to man; because what ministers call divine laws are the laws of the British Parliament.

III. There is no one true religion, because what the Pakeha call Christian religion or the gospel, is an illusion created by ministers to serve their own interests and rob Maori of all their land.

IV. All Pakeha rites and institutions must be abolished, including the sabbath and Christian marriage, because they are simply tricks to beguile Maori.

V. Any communication and relationship with Pakeha is forbidden; because the people of God must not communicate with gentiles (the British), let alone adhere to their preaching.

VI. There is no such thing as 'the end of the world' or 'the last judgement', because they are illusions invented by ministers to intimidate and terrify Maori.

VII. The end of the world and the last judgement are the Pakehas' bullets, guns and cannons.

Positive articles
I. It is good for a man to have more than one wife, because polygamy is necessary to increase the people of God.

II. Maori must return to their former worship, restore Tapu and other ancient religious ceremonies, and not allow Pakeha to desecrate their cemeteries or profane the things they venerate.

III. The end of the world will be signalled when the Pakeha are driven out of New Zealand, exterminated or thrown into the sea. Then the resurrection of all deceased Maori will occur.

IV. They will arise with a loud cry and stand in the presence of Te Ua, the great Maori wonder-worker, as Moses was for the Hebrews.

V. They will stand in Te Ua's presence, in the state they were in when they died, with their infirmities and imperfections. And he will reveal his power to the world, healing the mute, the deaf, the blind and the lame, curing them as he has already cured so many of his followers.

VI. When the Maori rise again, Te Ua's power will be fully revealed. He will reign forever over his people and under his sweet rule they will be one people and one tribe.

VII. No one will be allowed to live with Maori except Hebrews who have the same father, are heirs to the same inheritance and have suffered the same persecution.

VIII. No longer will there be evil, death, distress, poverty, sickness, pain or sorrow because all things will be made new.

IX. Pakeha will be obliterated from the land and the world will be transformed and made beautiful. Jews will join with Maori in this paradise and they will live together blissfully as one family forever.

This is a summary of Pai marire's beliefs, representing a messianic kingdom and a complete return to paganism.

Former Protestant catechists and assistant-ministers became the new political-religious sect's tribal leaders. They spread through the country preaching the new religion, erecting niu or sacred poles everywhere, holding public meetings where they displayed Captain Lloyd's and other slain British enemies' heads as trophies of their heroism, and encouraging others to similar acts of valour. Everywhere they went they exhorted people to exterminate Protestant ministers and the British and they had no compunction about burning Bibles, New Testaments and prayer books or using them as wadding.

These ferocious overtures caused Bishop Williams and other British Protestant ministers to believe the fanatics would massacre them, and they fled to Auckland or Wellington, not waiting to be ordered to leave. The many Maori Protestant ministers stayed with their tribes, all converting to the new Pai marire sect. The Anglican diocese of Auckland had six Maori missionaries. They all renounced Protestantism and became Hauhau or Pai marire members. On the other hand, Catholic missionaries living among the Maori were never harmed by sect members because they were not British but French or Italian. In February 1865 Fathers Grange and Boibieux's stations were right in the heart of the Pai marire movement.[4]

Rev. Ward, an Anglican minister, explains why Protestant ministers and Catholic priests were treated differently: 'Pai marire followers condemned the London Missionary Society as a political organisation whose main objective was to gain possession of their land for colonisation, and its missionaries were regarded as Government spies.'[5] The fanaticism engendered by the sect would send its savage horde on a more than five-year orgy of destruction, bloodshed and slaughter of Maori and the hated British.

4. While Pai marire was preparing for its massive struggle with its enemy, on 24 November 1864 Parliament opened in Auckland. Prime Minister Whitaker's ministry fell the same day and was replaced by Mr Weld's, which was not much better. In the session, southern members proposed that another town needed to be chosen as capital and seat of government, because Auckland was not central enough. After a brief debate Wellington, near Cook Strait, was proclaimed the colony's new capital, even though Auckland had a greater population than Wellington.

This greatly annoyed and upset Auckland settlers because by losing the seat of government, Auckland would greatly diminish in influence, population and trade. But complaining achieved nothing. To foil the move, Auckland sought to have the North Island declared an independent colony, separate from the South Island. But the proposal completely failed. While Auckland was most distressed to lose its supremacy, Wellington was very happy to house Parliament and its host of employees.

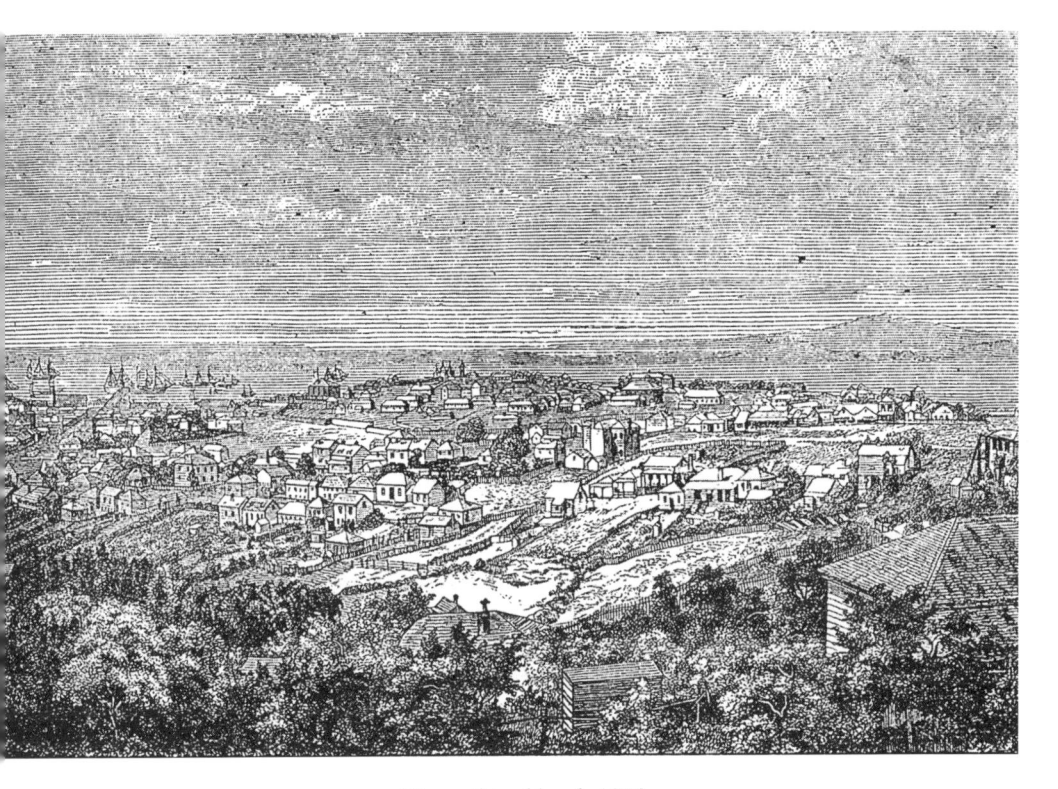

View of Auckland, 1870.

At the beginning of 1865 the furniture, papers and other equipment of the various departments and ministries were being transported from Auckland to Wellington. A steamship carrying official documents hit a reef near Taranaki. Many precious papers were lost and those that were salvaged were badly water damaged. The cost of transporting cargo and government employees rose to more than two million francs. This did not include the not inconsiderable cost of erecting public buildings and government offices.

When Parliament realised that London financiers would not lend it the 75 million voted the previous year at five per cent annual interest, it authorised the government to offer six per cent. Since Treasury was in dire financial straits, it sanctioned, in anticipation of the loan, an issue of bonds redeemable within three years for 18,750,000 francs at eight per cent annual interest. Customs taxes on imports were increased, bringing in 3,750,000 francs to help defray expenses. Maintaining 20,000 troops was enormously expensive, so it was decided to send the 10,000 British troops back to England, keeping only colonial troops and as many Maori allies as possible. Parliament authorised the government to expropriate settlers' and native land for public use, giving them fair compensation. Before closing the session, on 17 December 1864 Governor Grey proclaimed that all land occupied by British troops as well as Maori land in the Auckland district would be confiscated.

5. Maori warriors were either armed with spears, hatchets and other outmoded weapons, or old muskets and small stocks of ammunition to press home their campaign against the unwarranted British invasion. They were very concerned about their lack of weaponry and had no hope of getting further supplies from European friends since the governor had forbidden the sale of munitions to Maori rebels under pain of death.

Sometimes they succeeded in capturing a military convoy carrying ammunition. They also collected enemy shot which fell around their defences and retrieved unexploded shells and mortars within their fortifications, from which they extracted the powder. These measures still did not provide them with all the ammunition they needed for fierce, long-term campaigning.

Faced with this dearth, industrious natives began manufacturing their own powder from abundant supplies of sulphur, saltpetre and coal. The Ngati-ruanui and other King country tribes were very active and successful in this industry even though their powder was inferior to the British. For shot, they bought as much lead as they could and they moulded their own bullets. They made extra ammunition from bits of copper coins, nail heads, and European children's marbles bought from shopkeepers. They also shaped wooden pellets and used round stones from riverbeds and streams. They made do with phosphorus matchheads for caps, encasing them in cobblers' brass eyelets and for wadding they used sheets of paper from Bibles and New Testaments which Protestant ministers had left them over the years.

6. The colonial government was still intent on grabbing land. It began its war in 1860 to steal Waitara in Taranaki. It then carried the campaign into the Waikato, confiscating land after driving the natives out. Afterwards, it attacked nonbelligerent Tauranga natives, beating them and taking their land. After their surrender in 1864, it decided to carry hostilities to Wanganui to gain possession of the Waitotara block which it claimed to have purchased. This was untrue because the supposed seller never owned it.[6]

The government decided to confiscate this fertile area and build roads through it. In January 1865, General Cameron was ordered to carry this out and remove the natives. On 21 January, very shortly after his arrival, the general wrote to the governor: 'The more I think about this business (the occupation of the Waitotara block), the more I am convinced that we have done wrong to bring war to an area which has been so peaceful,' and he tried to persuade Grey to cancel the unjust campaign, but in vain.[7]

The general spread out his soldiers in various pickets thirty kilometres from Wanganui. Maori rebels suddenly made random attacks, forcing their retreat and causing major casualties. Maori lost twelve men. Shortly afterwards, fanatical Pai marire attacked tribes allied to the British, but neither side suffered casualties.

To counter Pai marire's fanaticism, Cameron sought reinforcements of 2000 troops, and an even greater number if he was required to build a road from Wanganui to Taranaki, necessitating an occupation of the whole district. Meanwhile he called up troops from Wellington and Taranaki and on 5 February he occupied the Waitotara block. Natives killed a settler and a volunteer engaged in sacking one of their villages. On 14 March the general and his soldiers attacked a Hauhau band near Patea and pursued them, inflicting heavy casualties.

Since General Cameron viewed the colonial government's claims as unjust and his views received a hostile reception, in February he proffered the British Minister of War his resignation as commander-in-chief of the troops in New Zealand, and asked to be recalled. In June he received permission to return to England and he was knighted.

Governor Grey returned to campaigning and he took over command. With 400 Maori allies and 700 infantrymen and cavalry he swooped on a village. He captured fifty natives with their weapons and two barrels of powder. On 21 July he bombarded Weraroa pa at Waitotara, putting to flight the few natives defending it. Meanwhile Pai marire and Hauhau bands tried to take the British redoubt at Pikiriki, but after a three-day siege they had to give up.

On 2 September 1865 Sir George Grey publicised the confiscation of a great part of the Ngatiawa and Ngatiruanui tribes' territory. Thus the garden of Eden, as the area was known, became greedy settlers' prey. The same day the governor brazenly proclaimed peace between the two races. He announced that 'the war begun at Oakura (in 1860) was now over. Rebellious tribes had been sufficiently punished; their troops were defeated and enough of their land was confiscated to dissuade them from taking up arms again.' He declared an end to fighting, and pardoned them their offences, except for those who killed innocent, law-abiding citizens.'[8] This was just a mockery and a ruse to cover up his own disgraceful behaviour.

7. In January 1865, Wanganui Pai marire, seeing that the government intended fighting them, sent followers to the Bay of Plenty to make converts. Colonel Greer, commander of Tauranga district, requested his Maori allies to capture the emissaries and bring them to him. On 8 February Arawa warriors succeeded in capturing fifty and they were imprisoned. Learning of his envoys' capture, the great prophet, Te Ua, sent out others led by two of his colleagues, Patara and Kereopa. They gained a great following among Taupo, Rotorua, Tauranga, Whakatane and Opotiki tribes, both Protestant and Catholic, attracted by the

idea of national independence. Shortly after Hauhau fanatics arrived at Opotiki a horrible incident occurred involving the unfortunate Charles Silvius Volkner, an Anglican minister.

Volkner was a German who as a Lutheran minister accompanied compatriots in founding a settlement at Puhoi, north-east of Auckland. Seeing that it offered no chance of advancement, he became an Anglican and was ordained a minister in 1859 by Bishop Williams, who appointed him to Opotiki. In 1860, at the beginning of the war between the two races, he made an arrangement with the colonial government to pass on to them information about the Maori concerning their meetings, plans and their decisions. The natives found out and they began to regard him like all other Protestant ministers, as government agents or spies.[9]

As fighting became more bitter, natives suspected Volkner even more. When they were certain that there was a secret correspondence between him and the government, they decided to kill him at the first opportunity. Maori allies of the British and his friends advised him of the decision, but he trusted in the government's protection and took no notice. 'Even Catholic missionaries told him that it would be better for him to remain in Auckland because his life was in danger at Opotiki. But he saw them as simply jealous, and paid no heed.'[10]

On 26 February 1865, Volkner and Samuel Grace, Taupo's Anglican minister, left Auckland for Opotiki on board the schooner *Eclipse*, captained by Samuel Levy, a Jew. On 1 March they reached Opotiki. Captain Levy's brother was a local shopkeeper and as a Jew he was respected by Pai marire. As soon as they arrived he hastened to warn them to flee because the previous evening it had been decided to kill any ministers, soldiers and British settlers who dared to venture there. Meanwhile Pai marire members took over the ship, tied up the two ministers and took the passengers and crew (including the captain) prisoner. They were brought ashore to be sentenced according to the laws of the new Canaan. Realising that Captain Levy was Jewish, they assured him that he had nothing to fear, that the Atua Hau protected all the sons of the people of God and they immediately set him free. The others were locked up in a hut guarded by a band of armed natives.[11]

The Hauhau held several meetings into the night. At two p.m. the following day they led the unfortunate Volkner from the hut without telling him where they were taking him. But very soon he realised that he was going to be hanged. Captain Levy who was an eye-witness of the gruesome tragedy said that Maori tied a rope to the highest branch of a willow tree about 180 metres from the Anglican church. Volkner was taken to it and stripped of his clothes apart from his shirt and underclothes. He was then barbarously hanged in the sight of about 800 natives, most of whom were Protestant. After an hour he was taken down and carried into the church. They laid him on the floor and stripped off the skin and flesh around his neck and cut off his head.

Then Maori filed up in two rows to drink the blood dripping from the victim.

Women competed for it. The ferocious Kereopa gouged out his eyes with his fingers and ate them. The flesh from Volkner's neck was fed to the dogs but when they hungrily bayed for more they tossed them his body. After it was savaged, the corpse was thrown into a toilet. Only eight days later was Levy able to get permission to bury his mortal remains. Volkner's head was preserved according to Maori custom and 'displayed from the pulpit of the church where he so often preached.'[12]

A Protestant New Zealand newspaper commented on the crime:[13] 'We need to acknowledge a significant difference between Volkner's death and the martyrdom of Catholic missionaries. Pagans have often persecuted and martyred the true preachers of Christ's Gospel before even experiencing missionaries' behaviour and the benevolent effects of their calling. It is unheard of for such cruel treatment to be meted out when they experience the value and excellence of their sacred ministry. But this has not been the case in New Zealand. Scarcely had Protestant missionaries arrived as unfamiliar Europeans than natives welcomed and greeted them. But after discussions with them, joining the church, witnessing their behaviour and the effects and purpose of their preaching, they then armed themselves with hatred against the missionaries.'

To clarify this issue, mention must be made of a document conveniently ignored by English writers wanting Catholics to be blamed for causing Volkner's death. Opotiki Hauhau sent it to Governor Grey and it was read out in Parliament. It is accurately reproduced here:

Opotiki; land of Canaan, 6 March 1865.
To the office of the Governor, Auckland.

Friends! This is addressed to you. Mr Volkner, minister, is dead. He was hanged according to the laws of the new Canaan, in the same way that the British parliament orders the guilty to be hanged. The minister, Mr Grace, has been captured and is being held prisoner according to our laws which have been established in the same way as the British parliament which decrees that the guilty be imprisoned.

Friends! Do not ask why they have been so punished. They themselves were the prime cause, as representatives of the Church which exercises deceit over our land.

The same Church said that they were sent here by God. But we now know that they were sent by that scheming organisation, the Church of England. Second, the origin of these sins lies in the first crime committed by the Governor at Rangiriri, when women were cruelly killed. Third, consider Rangiaowhia where women were shot down. Where is the Governor's respect for the law?

We now know that these laws come from the oppressive authority of the British Parliament. We wonder how the Governor is not ashamed of so many laws issued in his name which debase us.

You continue to tell us to hand over our powder and guns to you. But do you not treat us like dogs? Do you really want us to hand over our weapons because you fear we will shoot you? Have you thought how possible is it to kill with wooden swords?

Friends! Our country is aware of your actions. Pay heed! Arrest Maori and we will arrest Pakeha. Hang Maori, and we will hang Pakeha. Hand over Hori Tupaea and his men to us and we will hand over Mr Grace. But if you keep Hori Tupaea,[14] we will keep Mr Grace.

If you pay favourable attention to our words, talk to the Jew.[15] He will bring your reply to us, and we will then hand over Mr Grace to you.

Confederation of Ngatiawa, Wakatane, Ariwera and Taranaki.

Meanwhile Grace continued to be held prisoner. Captain Levy made many ransom offers to the Maori, even promising them 25,000 francs, but they refused, saying that they would agree to free him only if the government handed over Hori Tupaea. While the Hauhau awaited a reply to their letter, on 15 March the naval steamer *Eclipse* with the commodore and Bishop Selwyn on board reached Opotiki. They had gone to Waiapu to rescue Bishop Williams and his ministers from the Maori. Levy went on board and informed Selwyn of the present situation and that he had not been able to ransom Grace.

The Maori, observing the steamer's arrival, quickly gathered to decide what to do. Captain Levy returned to the village. He saw that the warriors guarding the hut where Grace and the native crew were imprisoned were some way off. He opened the door and let the minister out. Some women noticed their escape and gave the alarm. Armed men chased after them but they were too late because with a favourable wind and tide Grace and his companions were able to escape in a skiff to the steamer before the Maori could fire on them. Thus Grace was saved from being killed.

When he reached Auckland, he wrote to the papers thanking the authorities, the Anglican community and his friends for their urgent haste in delivering him from the Hauhau. He thanked everyone except Levy, who risked his own life to save him. Being a British bigot he did not want to recognise that he owed his life to a Jew. Grace's ingratitude towards Captain Levy caused more indignation among Auckland inhabitants than Maori cruelty towards Volkner. His fellow Anglicans in the North did not want him as their minister, saying that mere mention of his name would cause local Maori to rise up.[16]

On 22 April Governor Grey issued a public notice in both languages condemning the Pai marire or Hauhau religion, murders, cannibalism and their treatment of the heads of the slain as being repugnant to human decency. He sought the support of sympathetic European and Maori to condemn the barbaric acts. His edict, instead of intimidating the Hauhau, riled them even more, inciting them to redouble their efforts. In fact, shortly after its issue, a massacre at

Wakatane, near Opotiki, was carried out.

In May Commodore Fremantle and his troops went to Opotiki to capture or exterminate Volkner's murderers. He tried unsuccessfully to surprise a bunch of natives. After a few skirmishes, the Maori withdrew. A marine, disguised as a Maori, surprised and captured a native involved in the minister's death, but he freed himself and escaped, even though soldiers fired after him. On 24 May Captain Fremantle met with the Tiu and prophet Patara, hoping to take him by surprise. But he came with several of his warriors and was prepared for any eventuality. He approached the commodore with a whip under his arm and two pistols hidden in his pockets. After a brief meeting in which he declared that he had no part in Volkner's death, he and his men left. The British did not dare attack him.

At the beginning of July, the schooner *Kate* left Auckland for Maketu and Wakatane. Captain Pringle, a Mr Robinson, Ned, a sailor, and Campbell, a half-caste were on board. They waited some days at Maketu for a favourable wind. While they were there the steamer *Rangatira* arrived from Auckland with a quick-witted half-caste young man. Finding that the schooner was about to sail for Wakatane he embarked on her. His name was James Fulloon. Maori called him 'British Parliament' to indicate that he was an agent of the colonial government.

James Fulloon was born at Wakatane. His father was English and his mother Maori. He was Anglican, very intelligent and twenty-two years old at the time. At the beginning of the war he was appointed as an army interpreter and he accompanied General Cameron on his Waikato campaign. After Volkner's murder, Fulloon was the government's main agent on the frigate *Eclipse* which pursued his murderers along the East Coast. When his plans for capturing them were unsuccessful, some newspapers tried to discredit him. To retrieve his honour he decided to go to Wakatane and gather a government force to fight the prophet Kereopa and his followers. He pretended to have a great love of the Maori, while actually seeking their destruction. But his secret agenda was known to the natives.[17]

On the evening of 21 July the ship reached Wakatane. The following morning White, the trader and his half-caste son went on board to inspect his cargo. At the same time, some Hauhau approached the ship and asked how many people were on board and who they were. Fulloon who was on the bridge asked them if they had come to kill him and he brandished a revolver at them. Seeing that Fulloon was on they returned forthwith to shore. The great Tiu Horomora (Solomon) was waiting. When he heard their news he held a meeting with other chiefs and they decided to kill them, take their goods, and burn the ship.

Chief Te Hemara and twelve armed warriors boarded the *Kate* and without a word they shot down Captain Pringle, Robinson and Ned, who were on the bridge. They then shot at Fulloon who was with White in the cabin, wounding him in the arm. White leapt from cover and cried out in terror at the sight of the bodies, 'Are you going to kill me, too?' They replied, 'Pai marire! We shot at you three times without hitting you. Atua Hau has spared you, do not be afraid; you are under his protection.' Thus White, his young son and Campbell, the half-caste sailor, were not harmed. The wounded Fulloon was then axed to death.

8. After troops spent four fruitless months trying to capture Volkner's murderers, the government requested Maori allies' aid. Three East Coast tribes under the command of their chiefs Ropata, Mokena, and Henare, were provided with arms and ammunition. In June 1865, accompanied by colonial troops, they invaded the huge area occupied by Pai marire and for the next five months they ran amuck, killing, massacring, raiding, pillaging and torching all the pas, villages and foodstores which fell into their hands. Throughout this period there was fierce fighting and both parties suffered many casualties. But the government side, with all the means it had at its disposal, including a greater number of combatants, won out, and took a large number of prisoners.

After the Wakatane massacre, the government had an ally tribe transported from Wanganui to Opotiki to arrest Volkner's murderers who were still at large and confiscate their land. Five hundred thousand acres were seized. After several exchanges the allies took Opotiki and some forts. But the Hauhau evaded capture. At the same time the friendly Arawa tribe took up arms against the Wakatane Hauhau. In initial engagements they were driven back with major losses. After they received reinforcements of troops, cannon and mortars, on 17 October the Arawa succeeded in taking about fifty prisoners, many of whom were involved in the Opotiki and Wakatane massacres, but the prophet Kereopa and a number of his followers were able to escape. A further seventeen of the twenty-three men involved in Volkner's murder were captured in the bush near Opotiki.

While troops and Maori allies ravaged the East Coast, fanatical Hauhau killed several settlers and friendly Maori at Wanganui, on the West Coast. Kercti, a native constable, bearing Governor Grey's declaration of peace, suffered this fate. He was seized and shot. Similarly, Broughton, an army interpreter, and another European were slain and mutilated by ferocious savages. Grey offered a reward of 25,000 francs for the murderers' arrest. But no one dared take it up.

In October, a military tribunal at Opotiki condemned thirty-two Maori to death for their part in the Opotiki and Wakatane murders. But Sir George Grey had the case transferred to a civil court in Auckland and in February 1866 some were sentenced to death and others to several years' imprisonment.

The extremely severe penalties inflicted on the poor fanatics seem to have intimidated the great prophet Te Ua, founder of Pai marire. Fearing the same fate and lured by the governor's seductive promises, he surrendered and went to Wellington where he recanted his errors and adopted the government's side. His followers were indignant and called him the government's lackey. Shortly afterwards they met to discuss Te Ua's betrayal. Taikomako, one of Maoridom's finest representatives, attended the meeting. He was gifted as an orator, highly respected as an important Taranaki chief and for his valour as a warrior. After chief Rewi, advisor and right-hand man of the Maori king, Taikomako was the highest placed Maori in New Zealand. Members at the gathering unanimously proclaimed Taikomako, already famous for his involvement and generous sacrifices on behalf of Pai marire, as a worthy successor to the traitor, Te Ua. He accepted the position of great prophet and all members of the new sect followed him.

9. The fifty prisoners taken at Wanganui during the 1865 campaign, as already mentioned, were sent to Wellington and incarcerated in a ship anchored in Wellington harbour, about two kilometres from shore and guarded by European soldiers. After six months' confinement, they were fed up with their harsh, isolated conditions and they plotted their escape. On the night of 6 January a violent gale struck, whipping up the sea, and a cannon hatch was blown open. One after another they escaped through it, plunging into the sea. They swam through the surf, and all safely reached the shore. They travelled through bush and over mountain ranges and after some days' journey through thick forests they reached home, happy to have regained their freedom. Because of the storm's fury, the guards on the bridge were unaware of the prisoners' escape until the following day. They were astounded at their daring, risking their lives to escape. They immediately notified the government of what had happened, and a party was dispatched to recapture the fugitives, but they were already safe in the bush.

10. The Anglican Bishop W. Williams who had gone to New Zealand in 1822 to devote himself to looking after the Maori became instead a wealthy millionaire at the poor savages' expense. In January 1865, on his return to Waiapu, Hauhauism's stronghold, his flock turned on him and wanted to get rid of him. At the beginning of February a warship rushed to his rescue. Otherwise he would have been done for. Two months later he went to Poverty Bay, where he had land and his family were based, sure of his safety. But he was wrong.

After killing Volkner at Opotiki, Kereopa and his courageous, loyal followers went south, taking Volkner's head, visiting many tribes, gaining a wide following, and erecting many niu. They continued their proselytising journey, reaching Poverty Bay. Kereopa made a great number of converts among Protestant Maori of the huge district. They immediately considered getting rid of Bishop Williams and his coterie, as had happened to Volkner.

What harm had Williams done to become his former flock's target? He had usurped their land. He was English and they believed he was a spy. People could only go to communion who paid him two and a half shillings (3.15 francs) each time. If they did not pay, they were not allowed. He allowed his Maori maidservants and devout native women converts to live in sin. It is no surprise then that natives had ill-feeling towards him. Having embraced the new Hauhau faith, they decided to kill him, or at least expel him from their territory.[18]

Williams had an inkling of their intention. At night, before armed natives could surprise him, he abandoned his home and property at Waerenga-a-hika and embarked with his family for Napier. He remained there until his death in 1878. When the Maori turned up, they were upset that he had fled. After ransacking the mission they burnt it down, completely destroying the compound and surrounding area. It has remained in this condition up till the present.

While the Anglican mission was in flames, in November 1865 colonial troops and native allies reached Gisborne, eight kilometres away, intent on hunting down the Hauhau. MacLean, the government agent, went to Waerenga-a-hika which Hauhau had fortified, warning them to hand over their guns or they would be attacked. The troops dug in around the pa and there was minor skirmishing. On Sunday morning about a hundred defenders came out of the pa. They approached the troops' picket line carrying a white flag, intending to surrender or parley. But when they drew near they were fired on by the British. Fifty were killed and many were wounded. They then took the pa, capturing those inside and burning it down. Such a violation of people's rights brands the soldierly rabble who called themselves civilised. No one was punished for the atrocity. Unfortunately, similar and even worse acts happened elsewhere. On this occasion troops took 200 prisoners, including chief Te Kooti who was on their side, because they suspected him of colluding with the enemy. Major Fraser deported the unfortunate people to the Chatham Islands, 600 kilometres from New Zealand.

In January 1866 the colonial militia and 500 allies under the command of Major Fraser and chief Ropata and others, attacked rebels at Wairoa, between Gisborne and Napier. After several exchanges they engaged in fierce combat. The Hauhau came off worse. They either fell on the battle field or fled into the bush. After the fighting a military tribunal sentenced four prisoners to be shot simply because they had fought against the government. 'This,' said Rusden, 'was how they fought for the Queen!'[19]

Hauhau superstition reached even Hawkes Bay and an armed band of natives decided to attack Napier settlers. But colonial troops and Maori allies surrounded their village at night, and in the morning, after an hour's fighting, most of them surrendered. Others who tried to escape were pursued, shot and killed. Attackers suffered sixteen dead and wounded and Pai marire fifty-six. More than seventy were taken prisoner. The wounded were treated at Napier hospital, and once healed, they were sent by Colonel Whitmore with the other prisoners to the Chatham Islands.

11. Hostilities again broke out in the east when the brutal General Chute recommenced his Wanganui campaign against the Hauhau. He had 700 soldiers and 300 natives under his command. He had no intention of giving any quarter. On 4 January 1866 he took and burnt down Putahi pa where he took only one prisoner, who was soon executed. Colonel Weare captured one of the rebels who had escaped into the bush. He was brought back to camp. 'On 11 January before dawn, General Chute broke camp and ordered the native prisoner to be executed without trial.'[20] The officer carried out the command against his will. The callous general continued his swathe of destruction. He attacked and took Otepawa pa, killing twenty-nine Hauhau. Army casualties were twelve dead, including a colonel and twenty wounded.

The victorious general proceeded then towards Taranaki, burning, destroying and looting horses, cattle, sheep and whatever fell into the hands of his army, many of whom were often drunk. In fact, the soldiery seemed more like a bunch of savages, cursing everything and everybody, including their commanders. On their approach, the natives hid in the bush and the soldiers went on to New Plymouth.

The general continued raiding from there. He forced a non-partisan chief and his followers to be placed unarmed in front of his troops when he attacked a relative, chief Matekatea. He had crops and orchards destroyed, villages and pas burnt down and herds looted. On 6 February after destroying another redoubt, he returned to New Plymouth and then went on to Wellington. His barbaric deeds only served to increase rebel numbers and to make natives more hostile than ever. Mr Parris, government agent, sought by conciliatory gestures to bring Pai marire to parley. However, Colonel MacDonell who succeeded Chute as commander-in-chief was no better than him and wanted to make peace by wiping the natives out. When the weather improved he began his campaign.

He ordered certain chiefs to come to him. When they did not obey he declared that this was an act of rebellion and he prepared to punish them in a suitably harsh way. While Pokaikai village was settled and its inhabitants sleeping, late at night on 1 August 1866 the colonel and his men attacked. He put them to flight, bayoneting men and women they surprised. One soldier who could not remove an earring from the chief's wife, cut her ear off to get it![21]

On 2 September, after further raids and sorties, Colonel McDonell prepared for an engagement with the enemy. He built trenches for protection. The Hauhau fired sporadically on the workers, and they also surprised a supplies convoy, putting its escort to flight and making off with the booty. On 6 October the colonel attacked Pungarehu village. Its defenders fired from their hut windows, but soldiers clambered onto the roofs, uncovering them and firing down on the wretches. A great number of natives perished, either being shot or burnt alive as the village was torched. Only nine prisoners were taken.[22]

Shortly afterwards the army was attacked in the bush and MacDonell and his men retreated. They then resumed marauding, advancing towards Popoia pa. He and his troops were again attacked. MacDonell was wounded, the army retreated and Colonel Rook took over command. When MacDonell recovered, on 5 November he attempted to take a fort but without success. His splendid military prowess was about to be eclipsed by Titokowaru, as will soon be revealed.

12. For seven years the South Island's numerous gold mines attracted a huge number of soldiers of fortune as speculators of every nationality. They gradually infiltrated every level of society, including Parliament and government office, and they had a disastrous effect on the country. Rusden mentions: 'The influx of people seeking only wealth, most of whom were intent on personal gain and self-interest, swamped the settler element of Parliament's first sessions. The South Island was not only home for unscrupulous types and villains whose deeds alarmed the whole country, but sent men to Parliament whose aim was power and for whom ends and means were identical. And they were soon to become a majority in Parliament.'[23]

Because of these elements, Parliament neglected the country's real interests, preoccupying itself with trifles, intrigue and self-interest. In June 1866 when it reopened, Prime Minister Stafford mentioned the British government's decision to recall its troops, leaving only three infantry and one artillery battalion temporarily. They were to be paid for by the colony and they were not to be engaged in protecting confiscated land or to be stationed in remote areas. Shortly afterwards they, too, left the colony. Stafford also mentioned that 3,256,000 acres had been confiscated in the three provinces of Auckland, Taranaki and Wellington. The most important legislation approved in the session was permission given to Wellington to raise a loan of 625,000 francs.

In July 1867 Parliament held its annual session. It was decided to have four Maori representatives in Parliament. A debt of 175 million was approved and provincial debts would be taken over by the colonial government. On 27 August Governor Grey received official notice from London of his recall as governor, and of the appointment of his successor. The announcement caused much displeasure in Parliament; there was protestation against the British government's decision, and threat of separating from the mother country and putting themselves under the protection of the United States of America. But this was stupid, silly nonsense, or rather, spontaneous childish prattling. On 9 July 1868 the new governor, Sir George Bowen, convened Parliament in Wellington. Four Rangatira (chiefs) participated, elected to the House of Representatives by native allies of the government. They represented north, east, west and southern Maori. Since they could not speak English, an interpreter explained proceedings and they were given written translations of important matters. But what influence could four members have over fifty? Later another native was made a member of the Legislative Council.

13. From 1866 the British government was unhappy with Governor Grey for not requesting an inquiry into the shooting of the native prisoner ordered by General Chute, as already mentioned. In June 1867, following a complaint by Grey that General Chute did not keep him informed of his military movements, the Secretary of State, the Duke of Buckingham, replied that he was unhappy about the disputes and that in a short time he would know the name of his successor and when he would arrive in New Zealand. In fact, on 27 August he received notification of his recall and arrival date of the new governor.

Sir George Grey offered his humble services to Her Majesty, the Queen, but he was not granted a further appointment, nor thanked. Nevertheless he had rendered important service for many years for his government in various colonies. Such treatment was not at all typical of the British government. It must be recognised that there was greater rancour between the British government and Grey than is revealed to us in their correspondence. I have been told by several settlers well informed about the country's affairs that Grey received this treatment because of a certain incident. Disaffected as he was, one day he spoke disparagingly of the Queen to some friends and it was reported back to Her Majesty. She was so angry with him that she wanted nothing more to do with him. I know Sir George Grey personally and I would not pay too much heed to the rumour. He had a more serious fault, namely, his unfair treatment of the Maori.

He should not have allowed himself to be dominated by his ministers, whose aims were to exploit and annihilate the natives. If he had listened to Sir William Martin, Mons. Pompallier, Selwyn, Chief Waharoa and other men of integrity, he would have been able to restore peace to the country after his arrival in 1861, which was everyone's hope. Instead, he allowed his ministers to rob the natives, bringing a terrible war on the colony, with its associated effects of murder and material and moral ruin. The heavens cried out for revenge for the barbarous slaughter of so many innocent victims. In His infinite justice, God used the British government to unseat and strip the man who was the main instrument, if not the cause, of so many calamities.

Grey's career as governor ended in January 1868. On 19 October the same year, he went to England to seek justice. After living there for quite a while he returned to New Zealand to reside on his Kawau Island property, in the Hauraki Gulf. He then became a Member of Parliament, continuing to represent Auckland in the colonial Parliament.

As mentioned above, Sir George Grey was replaced by Sir George Bowen, Governor of Queensland, Australia, and he arrived with his family in Wellington at the end of January 1868. He took up residence in the capital in a newly built Government House. His official duties began on 5 February. In spite of his good intentions, he allowed governmental ministers to have a free hand in running the country.

He saw that the temporary peace of 1867 was followed the next year by a new and fiercer struggle. Accordingly, in January 1869 he sent the British government a petition drawn up in Auckland, seeking the repression of the constitution 'as the only remedy for the colonial government's evident inability to restore order. A similar petition was sent to London by South Island settlers.' But they did not get what they wanted. Fearing a general Maori revolt, Bowen asked Britain to leave him the regiment still stationed in New Zealand. It was agreed, and he began to enter into negotiations with Tawhiao, the Maori King.

14. Pai marire attacked everywhere. Driven into the bush, they always returned to the fray with inflexible tenacity. On 23 May 1867 at Opotiki they attacked four settlers, killing two. The others managed to reach the colonial army a few kilometres away. Troops rushed to punish the murderers. But they had disappeared. They fought for several months against local rebels, but with little success. On the west coast the situation became even worse.

Hauhau between Wanganui and Taranaki had never given in, and they waited to be attacked by Pakeha. Some of Judge Booth's horses were stolen. He ordered Colonel MacDonell to arrest three chiefs on suspicion of theft. When he could not catch them he took another chief hostage. Booth accompanied the troops and they seized other chiefs. When they realised they were innocent, they were freed. Booth's unjust action greatly offended the chiefs who responded in June 1868 by killing a settler. Chief Titokowaru, great prophet of the new faith, who had been non-belligerent, put himself at the head of his followers to oust the British from their land.

Until July the natives had generally been on the defensive, but they then decided to change their tactics and attacked military fortifications defended by volunteers, national guardsmen and Maori allies under a Captain's command. Although repulsed, the attack was disastrous for the defenders. The Captain, a sergeant, some other officers and a good number of soldiers were killed or wounded. The survivors, hoping for reinforcements and even more, to save their lives, fought like lions against the Maori who returned to the fray. When Major Von Tempsky arrived with reinforcements, the natives retreated and thus the few remaining in their trenches were saved. Colonel MacDonell returned to Wanganui, pursuing the war with even more determination and further minor battles were fought up till September.

On 7 September the colonial army suffered another major defeat at Ngutu-o-te-manu, near Patea. When troops commanded by Colonel MacDonell attacked Titokowaru's pa, not only were they driven back, but they were put to rout and pursued by the victors. They were forced to retreat behind the Waihi redoubt. In this engagement, Major Von Tempsky, two captains, two lieutenants, several other officers and many soldiers and native allies including chief Hori Te Anawa, a renowned warrior, perished. Many of their bodies were cooked and eaten by the victors. Rev. Father Ronald, a Catholic priest at Wanganui, accompanied troops on this and other occasions. He often risked his life bringing the last rites to the dying and assisting the wounded.

News of the disaster caused general panic in the colony, particularly in Wanganui and New Plymouth. They were afraid of a general Maori revolt. Native allies, disheartened by the defeat, returned to their settlements in Wanganui. The government wanted to dismiss MacDonell for his defeat, but was dissuaded. MacDonell, however, resigned his command of colonial forces and the vacant position was given to Colonel Whitmore who quickly went to the scene of action. He arrived towards the end of September and tried in vain to dislodge the valiant Titokowaru from his position. He then thought it prudent to vacate the Waihi redoubt, which was too close to the enemy, and retreat with his troops to Patea and await fresh reinforcements.

Colonel Whitmore called up four companies of the Wanganui militia but they refused the summons for fear that rebels would attack Wanganui. Maori allies offered 300 men. Were it not for them, Titokowaru would have been absolute, undisturbed ruler of the entire coast and district. When the colonel received major reinforcements from other parts of the colony, he moved to engage the enemy and found them well fortified at Moturoa. On 7 November 1868 he attacked the pa, but he was forced back with serious losses of officers and troops, among whom was Major Hunter. He had to pull back. The following day the 300 native allies, disenchanted with another reversal, decided to return to their villages.

Shortly afterwards, the fiery victor, Titokowaru, dispatched two of his men with a white flag to take a letter to the colonel, telling him that the Pakeha should return to England and leave their home, New Zealand, to the Maori. Whitmore, in violation of human rights and the conduct of war, took the two messengers prisoner,[24] and prepared to reconquer. While he was getting ready for a second attack on the pa, he received bad news. Prisoners had escaped from the Chathams and were spreading death and destruction in Poverty Bay. The news upset his military strategy for Moturoa. He took some troops and sailed to Poverty Bay, leaving the rest to continue the campaign against Titokowaru and his allies. In three months, those left at Patea succeeded only in slaughtering some women and children who left the pa to bring in pigs for food.[25]

To recruit a sizeable army, the government increased the militia and native allies' pay, giving each person, besides their mess money, 5 francs a day. Constables were to be given 6.25, guides and outriders 10 francs a day. In addition, the government promised a reward of 25,000 francs to the person who handed over Titokowaru dead or alive, and £125 for every rebel captured.[26] These bribes not only encouraged excesses, but were contrary to the rules of war. But the New Zealand government of the day did not appear to be bound by any laws.

In January 1869, Colonel Whitmore returned to Wanganui with fresh troops and pursued native rebels. On 3 February, Titokowaru and his warriors retreated into the forest reaches without giving battle and were followed by the colonel and his men. An enemy ambush caught some soldiers by surprise as they were fishing. About a dozen were killed and the others were put to flight. On 13 February a band of Taranaki natives pounced on the British fort at White Cliffs, massacring its few occupants, namely sub-Lieutenant Gascoigne, his wife and three young children, two British soldiers and J. Whiteley, a Wesleyan minister who in 1860 had been ordered by the commander to spy on the rebel pa at Waitara and report back to the colonel. Meanwhile Whitmore and his allies vigorously pursued the campaign against the rebels. They chased them through the bush, but they succeeded in escaping into the mountainous area of Taranaki. Some, though, were captured and sent as prisoners to Otago in the South Island.

Maori allies continued to pursue Titokowaru and his men for some months, but without any real success, because the enemy escaped into the inland mountain ranges of the island. Towards the end of July peace was restored to the Taranaki district and Colonel Whitmore returned to the east coast to punish Te Kooti and his native allies, where we will soon conduct the gentle reader and appraise him of events.

15. The rebels, whether hiding in the bush, locked in prison or deported to remote places, were determined not to enter any pact. The 200 men deported to the isolated Chatham Islands in January 1866 (who were later joined by their wives and children in voluntary exile) were confined illegally, without even the semblance of a trial. They had merely been told that they would be released within two years.[27] The wretches waited patiently for two years even though the guards treated them badly.[28] The time elapsed, and still they were not freed. They then decided to escape from the islands. Among them was a certain Te Kooti, unjustly accused of treason and condemned like the others without trial to deportation. He decided to take revenge and avenge the wrongs done to him and to lead a revolt. He hatched an escape plan and waited for the right time to carry it out.

At the end of June 1868, the colonial government sent the eighty-two ton *Rifleman* to the Chathams with provisions for the guards, soldiers and prisoners. The prisoners took advantage of its presence to execute their plan. On the day after the ship's arrival, when the captain was ashore, the prisoners rose up and attacked the homes of the few Europeans and guards. They seized their arms and ammunition but did not kill the guards, apart from one who tried to resist with force. He was axed to death. The others were tied up, so they could cause no harm, and the rebels took their weapons. They did not use violence against anyone else, even though they could have massacred all the Europeans on the island.

The prisoners were now masters. They took the captain's skiff which was anchored just offshore and they went on board the ship. They ordered the sailors into the hold, threatening them with death if they resisted; and they obeyed. The 163 men, sixty-four women and seventy-one native children then embarked. Only three Maori men and one woman wanted to stay. Before leaving the island they destroyed the only boat in the harbour so that no one could follow them or carry news of what had happened to New Zealand.

On 4 July they set sail for their homeland. Once at sea, they let the sailors out of the hold and told them that their lives would be spared on condition that they steered the ship straight for Poverty Bay where they wanted to land. They had no choice but to obey.

Te Kooti took command and he was ready for any emergency. A well-armed native stood guard on the bridge night and day. Another with a rifle and sabre stood besides the helmsman making sure he stayed on course. Sailors were not allowed to cook food for fear that they would set fire to the ship. When the wind was against them, an old native was thrown into the sea in propitiation to their god. Finally, on 10 July towards evening, the ship dropped anchor at Whareongaonga, nine kilometres south of Poverty Bay. The sailors were kept in the hold while the women, children and some Maori men disembarked during the night. The next day, early in the morning, natives took some of the provisions ashore and returned on board with two barrels of drinking water for the sailors, telling them that they were free to go where they pleased. They sailed to Wellington and described what had happened. The news caused a deep shock throughout the colony. The savages' brazen bid for freedom showed their ability and courage in adversity.

16. Poverty Bay settlers received news of the Chathams' fugitives arrival on 12 July. There was panic and consternation in Turanga, or Gisborne, as it is now known. Major Biggs, commander of the colonial forces in Poverty Bay telegraphed the news to the government and sought military reinforcements. He quickly assembled fifty volunteers and fifty-three native allies and he went after the fugitives, ordering them to surrender their weapons and give themselves up. Te Kooti replied that he had no intention of doing either. He requested him to let them take peaceful possession of their land, saying that he had not harmed Europeans and that his intention was to enter the Waikato and engage in a campaign against Tawhiao, the Maori King. He proceeded to withdraw inland, far from any Pakeha settlements. Major Biggs thought it would be prudent not to provoke or attack for fear of coming off worse.

The government telegraphed Colonel Whitmore, recalling him from Taranaki to Poverty Bay and immediately sent reinforcements, including the warship *Rosario* with troops to help Biggs in his campaign against the fugitives. Major Biggs and his force and Major Westrup, commander of a cavalry corps comprising sixty-six Europeans and twenty-two Maori, assembled as many militia and Maori allies as they could. They then went in pursuit of the enemy and found them in a stronghold near Paparatu, about fifty kilometres from Gisborne.

The army was then divided into two corps commanded by Biggs and Westrup and they set about taking up position to dominate the trail, but Te Kooti did not let them complete their plan. He and his men suddenly pounced on the cavalry corps and routed them, occupying their camp and seizing their supplies and many horses. The other detachment suffered the same fate. Both events occurred on 20 July 1868. British casualties were light, namely, one dead and seven wounded, because as soon as they were attacked they fled.

Their defeat influenced many local natives, who up till then supported neither Hauhau nor Pakeha, to join the victors' side and many government allies from that day refused to fight the rebels. If Te Kooti had taken advantage of his victory and given chase there would been a wholesale slaughter and he could have overrun the barracks and taken over Gisborne. But he was satisfied with beating them. He encamped in the same area for what was left of winter and to prepare for future hostilities.

After a brief rest, he struck camp and took the women and children to safety. Traversing sixteen kilometres of dense and mountainous forest, he reached the banks of the Hangaroa river on 24 July. There he encountered a corps of armed soldiers from Napier, under the command of Major Richardson, who were pursuing him. The two parties engaged each other but after three hours' intense fighting Te Kooti succeeded in putting the attackers to flight, inflicting serious losses on their Maori allies. He and his people then continued their planned journey.

Meanwhile the government called up the colonial militia to boost the number of troops and on 1 August Colonel Whitmore and a detachment of Taranaki soldiers reached Gisborne. With further reinforcements, including a mounted constabulary corps, the commander left immediately and desperately sought to surround Te Kooti and his followers. On 8 August the colonel's whole force caught up with the enemy and engaged them in battle, but after a brief exchange the British were driven back by Te Kooti with considerable casualties, including Captain Carr. The humiliated army returned to Gisborne for fresh supplies. Te Kooti showed his prowess as a commander in this campaign. Although he had only about 200 warriors he always kept a small number of his veterans in reserve to press the advantage at the right moment. He did not permit firing unless it was necessary and then at close range. He was the first to attack and directed his men personally. An officer who fought against him said he had no equal in this kind of fighting.

Having repulsed Colonel Whitmore and his superior forces, he and his people rested and then resumed their march. In a month they were about 160 kilometres from the coast. The women and children were left in a mountain stronghold in the interior. He considered then that the time had come to avenge the wrongs Pakeha had done them. Like a bloodthirsty tiger he returned stealthily with a small band of Hauhau whose leader and prophet he was. They paused on the hilly reaches of Poverty Bay, calculating the right time to carry out their intended massacre in the western district.

17. News that Te Kooti and his armed men were in nearby hills quickly spread among settlers scattered in the valley. Several withdrew in fright to Gisborne for security against raiding. Many, however, believing they were safe, remained in their homes. The militia stationed to defend them either did not believe the enemy was close, or were sure they would not dare attack Europeans. Instead of remaining on guard, they took no precautions. Whatever they believed, a small number of volunteers were inside their homes scattered in the valley, and the others were quartered in Gisborne.

On the night of 9-10 November 1868, while everyone in the bay was sleeping peacefully, Te Kooti and his guerillas were on the watch. They came down stealthily from the hills and the leader divided his force into small bands, ordering them to enter homes of Europeans and government allies in the vicinity and wipe out as many as they could find. His order was carried out, and in a few hours more than fifty European men, women and children were killed, including Major Biggs, Captain Wilson and a good number of allies. People who heard the attackers' first shots got up and ran for help to Major Westrup who was nearby. He quickly gathered some men and collected the barefoot, half-naked fugitives, some with babes clinging to them, and accompanied them to Mahia Peninsula, south of the bay. After two days' strenuous walking they reached the beach and embarked on a schooner, arriving safely in Napier. A few other Europeans who managed to escape and others not discovered by Hauhau sought refuge in the troops' quarters in Gisborne.

Te Kooti cut many Poverty Bay Maori allies' throats, but some he spared. He invited the survivors to join him and many agreed. He then withdrew a short distance from the scene of slaughter. Refugees carried calamitous news of the catastrophe. Gisborne citizens were overwhelmed with fear of a further attack and sought safety in boats in the harbour. Many sailed for Napier. The rest joined the militia and native allies and dug in behind the barracks and fortifications, waiting for help.

News of the massacre was sent by telegraph causing horror and terror throughout the colony. Many clamoured for savage revenge to be taken against the Hauhau. Thirty volunteers and 440 Maori allies set out from Napier and Gisborne to attack the enemy. They caught up with them and engaged in battle. During the combat, Te Kooti sent some of his men to intercept supplies and they succeeded in getting crates of ammunition and as many provisions as they could carry off. The army retreated and faced being surrounded by Hauhau when Ropata, their bold Maori ally, arrived from Wairoa. He took command and attacked the enemy at Makaretu. After a grim battle the Hauhau were forced to retreat, leaving behind thirty-six dead and wounded. 'Some of the wounded were barbarously killed in cold blood by the victors.'[29]

To encourage Maori allies to exterminate Hauhau, the colonial government first promised a reward of 25,000 francs and then of 125,000 francs to whoever captured or killed Te Kooti, and smaller amounts for other rebels. Halfway through December 1868, Ropata and the troops succeeded in preventing Pai marire from carrying out killing raids in Poverty Bay. In various clashes Te Kooti lost many warriors and was himself wounded. He retreated to the hills and fortified Ngatapa.

Colonel Whitmore returned to Gisborne with forty-two constabulary, 200 volunteers, and joining forces with Ropata's 230 warriors he set out to besiege the enemy. They reached Ngatapa pa and began their siege on 31 December, immediately starting a bombardment. The defenders replied with rifle fire. Shelling continued until 5 January 1869 and they also tried to mine the pa.

Te Kooti made several sorties but was forced to retreat every time. He mourned the loss of several warriors and during the siege the British army suffered many fatalities, including Captain Brown, and quite a few were wounded, including Captain Capel. Te Kooti had run out of food and water and realised that he could no longer hold out against such a superior force. On 5 January he decided to abandon the pa. During the night he and his followers let themselves down the cliff with ropes and escaped into the bush. They succeeded in getting away because the enemy thought there was no way of escaping them.

Up till then the British force was confident it had the Hauhau and Te Kooti, their leader, in the bag. They were furious at the escape when the next day they took possession of an empty pa. Ropata's savage horde and other allied chiefs and many militiamen went in hot pursuit of the starved, exhausted fugitives. In a short time they reached a group and captured them. The other group with Te Kooti found safety in the dense bush. Meanwhile Ropata implacably requested to deal with prisoners in his own way. 'J.C. Richmond, a Crown minister, and Colonel Whitmore, commander-in-chief, proffered no opposition to his request.'[30] By their reprehensible behaviour they virtually sanctioned it.

The prisoners were brought back to Ngatapa pa. At Ropata's orders, they were barbarously slaughtered. Lieutenant Gudgeon[31] was an eye-witness and described the scene: 'Those who surrendered were taken to Ropata. After a few questions, he ordered them to be shot.

'The execution method was simple: They were taken to the edge of the cliff (from where they escaped), stripped and shot. Their bodies tumbled into the ravine below. Their bones remain there to this day.' It should also be mentioned that 442 troops, their officers and Colonel Whitmore, their commander, stood by impassively watching the horrible slaughter which lasted some hours![32]

Following the bombardment of Ngatapa pa and fugitives' massacre, 130 of Te Kooti's followers were killed, including women. Colonel Whitmore then left Ropata, allied chiefs and a few militia to pursue the fleeing Te Kooti. He and the rest of his troops left for Taranaki to deal with Titokowaru, chief and prophet, as mentioned previously.

18. Although an exhausted Te Kooti had been put to rout, lost half his warriors and had run out of ammunition and provisions, he did not give in. He continued his struggle with even greater determination. At the beginning of 1869 he made a surprise attack on a Wakatane tribe friendly to the British and on local settlers in the Bay of Plenty. They had to flee to Tauranga and Opotiki for military protection. He took a pa, destroyed a village and killed all who resisted. But owing to a lack of supplies, his forces diminished considerably and he had to retreat with the few he still had to the mountain climes of his Uriwera allies. Major Mair and his troops, reinforced with 200 warriors of the friendly Arawa tribe, followed in pursuit. But he was soon forced to abandon the chase because Te Kooti's refuge was too remote and inaccessible. He also risked having his retreat cut off.

The bold and shrewd Te Kooti was perched on top of Ahikereru from where he could easily raid into the Rotorua district near the centre of the island, the Bay of Plenty to the north-east, Hawkes Bay or Wairoa to the south, according to his whim. Being short of ammunition, on 11 April he and his warriors surprised a British allied tribe at Mohaka, nearly sixty kilometres north of Napier. They killed 100 natives and seven Europeans and destroyed their homes, carrying off barrels of powder and a number of rifles. He then attacked and besieged another native fort for two days. But when 400 British troops appeared he retreated with his Mohaka booty.

When uneasy peace was established in Taranaki, Colonel Whitmore, most of his colonial troops and native allies set off to pursue Te Kooti. To have a greater chance of success he divided his forces into three separate armed corps, one under his command, a second under Colonel Herrick and the third commanded by Colonel Saint John. The strong expedition crossed into Uriwera territory, the fugitives' refuge. They could not entice the rebels to battle, however, because when troops approached their defence posts, after light skirmishes, they abandoned them and retreated further into the interior. Hemmed in on every side, eventually Te Kooti found refuge in a place where he could not be reached. From there he could make inland or coastal raids.

The thing that affected the ferocious leader more was not bitter fighting but harsh wintry conditions which from the end of April 1869 began to take their toll. His lightly clad guerillas suffered terribly in the ranges, in the midst of snow and frost. A worse worry was their great shortage of food. They were forced to eat fern roots to avoid starvation. Government allies subsequently refused to pursue the rebels in such harsh conditions, saying that they had no intention of dying from exhaustion or exposure in gorges or on mountain ridges. Anyone else, in similar circumstances, would have stopped fighting, waiting for better weather. But that would have seemed like cowardice to Te Kooti, and unworthy of a warrior.

Like a starving tiger he watched from his lair, waiting for the right time to maul the European army. Since they could not come to grips with him in the forest, they planned to block him off and prevent him finding refuge in the King Country. They occupied all the exits to Opotiki, Wakatane, Tauranga, Rotorua and Taupo. What a waste of effort! Te Kooti could not care less. He laughed at all their measures. From his mountain retreat he watched Colonel Saint John leave Galatea fort and with a strong military escort head towards Lake Taupo to guard the pass. He and his men stealthily followed them at a discreet distance. When they made their first stop at Opepe they fell on the escort, annihilating them. Only three managed to escape back to Galatea fort. The rest were slaughtered. However Te Kooti was disappointed not to have killed the colonel because he and four soldiers left Opepe before Te Kooti and his warriors arrived. Still he succeeded in capturing all the escort's arms and ammunition.

After this success he struck out boldly again, exterminating twenty native government allies in a village he came across in his march to set up camp in the mountains near Taupo. This terrified Europeans and natives. His intention was to choose the time to visit King Tawhiao and persuade him to adopt his cause of expelling the British from the country. The colonial government feared that the Maori King would join Te Kooti and they tried to block off his entry to the King Country from Taupo. But they were not successful. 'The Government was mortified that two savages (Titokowaru and Te Kooti), unjustly compelled to take up arms to defend themselves, had been able with a few enthusiastic, raw recruits to beat the colonial forces of 2000 Europeans and 1000 Maori allies.'[33]

Prime Minister Stafford was responsible for the conduct of the war. While he pursued the conflict with Te Kooti, he also sought to come to terms with the Maori King, not because he intended to remedy wrongs done to the natives. Rather, he was aware that he no longer had 10,000 British troops and was burdened with debt. He realised that it would be impossible to sustain a campaign if King Tawhiao took Te Kooti's side. The government persuaded Rapihana, a Waikato chief, to go to Governor Bowen for preliminary peace discussions. Their conversation went as follows:

The governor asked him: Will Tawhiao come and visit the Queen's son, the Duke of Edinburgh when he arrives in New Zealand? – Rapihana: I doubt it. – Governor: Do you have a message from the King or the Waikato people? What has brought you? – Rapihana: I bring this message from the Maori: 1. The sword must be sheathed. 2. Leasing Maori land must stop. 3. Sale of Maori land must stop. 4. Gold-prospecting on Maori land must stop. – Governor: The sword has been sheathed; but I must punish Te Kooti and Titokowaru. I desire peace with Tawhiao who is a good man. He did not address the other points at all. Bowen then wrote to the King saying that he would be delighted to present his friend, Tawhiao, to the Duke if he decided to come, but the Maori King did not reply.

Mr Firth, representing the government, went to Orohiri to negotiate peace with Tawhiao, but he was allowed to speak only to chiefs who were members of the King's council. Firth asked chief Te Araha: What are your peace conditions? Te Araha replied:

Restoration of confiscated Waikato lands, European withdrawal, and reinstatement of the former boundary. The emissary replied that the King's authority would not be recognised in certain areas. Tamati Ngapora's response was: It does not matter to us whether you agree or not. What matters is what we want (a king). Firth continued: But the murders cannot go unpunished. The chief replied: What you call murders we do not regard as such. Our custom, when war is declared, is to kill any enemy we come across, unless they approach under sign of peace. Another chief added: General Cameron told us to send our women and children to Rangiohia where they would be safe. And then he went there and massacred them and some were burnt alive in huts. You do not mention these facts, because you wish to conceal your crimes. When Maori commit the tiniest wrong, you make sure everyone knows, but no one stands up to criticise your crimes.[34] After a lengthy discussion, no agreement was reached, and nor could Tawhiao be persuaded to visit Queen Victoria's son.

At the end of April 1869, the Maori King called for a great runanga (meeting) and more than 3500 natives took part. He declared that he did not approve of chiefs Titokowaru and Te Kooti's uprising, that he did not support them and he had no intention of aiding them. His intention was universal peace. When the colonial government heard of Tawhiao's decisions, it breathed a sigh of relief, because it realised that there would not be a renewal of hostilities. Mr MacLean, in recognition of the Maori King's peaceful intentions, awarded him an annual pension of 15,000 francs, similar to that of his father Potatau I. But he could not be persuaded to accept a piece of land near Auckland which his father was gifted but had given up.

Returning to Te Kooti, after his massacre of Colonel Saint John's escort, he was able to reach the mountain area near Taupo. In May he set off to obtain King Tawhiao's support, but he would not receive him and he was told to return from whence he had come. The ferocious warrior returned to Taupo. Shortly afterwards he was attacked by a Napier tribe which was beaten, losing many men and more than 100 horses.

Meanwhile the colonial government relieved Colonel Whitmore of his command and sent Colonel MacDonell to Taupo to fight the rebels. He had 440 native allies and 110 soldiers under him. Te Kooti attacked with 250 warriors.

He fought desperately but was defeated and forced to withdraw, suffering casualties. His wounded were slaughtered at MacDonell's command.[35]

On 3 October 1869 Colonel MacDonell and his troops attacked Te Kooti in his fortified base. After a bloody battle and serious losses, he was forced to escape into the bush. He then trekked into the upper Wanganui, territory of the Maori King. He was certain that the troops would not bother them for fear of provoking a war with the strong Waikato tribes. Although he was opposed by King Country, Wanganui and Taupo tribes as well as by the colonial army, Te Kooti feared no one. Surrounded by enemies, in December he raided a Wanganui tribe's village. He and his men were pursued but fled with the speed of lightning, to re-appear menacing Cambridge in the Waikato's small military garrison. Soon afterwards they escaped into the bush. Hunted down on every side by his enemies, Te Kooti asked to be left in peace, declaring that he would never attack anyone again. But MacDonell would not listen, feeling certain he would now capture him.

On 24 January 1870 Te Kooti's force engaged 800 colonial troops and suffered major losses. He retreated to his mountain hideaway in the Uriweras, his favourite haunt. For five months the 800-strong force pursued him relentlessly. But when the government saw they were having no success, it ordered them to leave it to the allies to capture Te Kooti. The colonists had shown how inept they were. In fact, official records[36] show that a good many of the colonial constabulary were of poor calibre. From July 1869 to June 1870, of the 1400 European soldiers 330 had to be dismissed from service for drunkenness, 263 for dereliction of their duties and thirty-eight for insubordination. Such an army would hardly cause the desperate Te Kooti and his veterans to fret.

Thus Te Kooti's capture was entrusted to native allies. The government made Ropata a major-general. With 400 of his men and the assistance of three other chiefs and their people, on 1 March 1870 he set off to track down and capture his formidable foe, and earn the government's reward of 125,000 francs for the person who took him dead or alive. It would be impossible to describe how grimly they fought against the fugitive and his few remaining followers. There were several clashes in which many were killed on both sides, but Te Kooti always got away. In this campaign, however, the ferocious Ropata, on Mr MacLean's orders, was more humane towards his prisoners, not cutting their throats, his usual practice. In June that year he and two other chiefs went to Wellington to each receive from the governor a sword sent to them by Queen Victoria in recognition of their special services to the government and to the entire colony for fighting against their fellow Maori.

Meanwhile, the previous February the last battalion of the British army left the colony for home. In July, on their return from Wellington, the three chiefs took up fighting against Te Kooti and his Hauhau supporters with fresh vigour. The campaign continued for more than eighteen months, until the end of 1871, but still they could not get their hands on Te Kooti and the coveted 125,000 francs promised as reward. Tired of continuous fighting, in August 1871 Te Kooti withdrew into the King Country, where he lived peacefully for many years. We will have occasion to refer to him again later. The prophet Kereopa, who had ordered Volkner's execution at Opotiki, was one of Te Kooti's loyal supporters. He was hiding in the depths of the Uriweras when some of his former fellow warriors betrayed him, leading Ropata and his men to his hideout, where in November he was arrested. He was taken to Napier, tried and condemned to death. On 5 January 1872 he was hanged. Thus ended the war which had raged between the two races.

19. Casting a brief glance at the lengthy war described in the last two chapters, and comparing forces and the means the two warring parties had at their disposal, it is evident that, considered from a purely military point of view, the campaign brought no glory on the Anglo-colonial army and clearly showed that the tactics, daring and valour of the Maori were far superior to their opposing forces.

By 1868 the native New Zealand population was 38,517. Twelve major tribes, with a population of 18,214 were totally on the colonial government's side. More than half the members of ten other tribes favoured the government. There were thus 28,000 Maori allies, of whom about a quarter took up arms on its behalf against their hostile compatriots. The rebels were all members of three tribes with a population of 2900. They were supported by some members of ten other tribes. Including them, the total was less than 10,000 men, women and children. In the war against the troops only between 2000 and 2500 warriors took part, and there were never more than 600 in any one battle.[37]

When the colonial army was mobilised, it was 20,000 strong. More than half comprised British troops and the remainder were constabulary, veteran soldiers, Australian volunteers, enlisted colonial mounted militia and many native allies. The formidable force was generously provided with all it needed for a long campaign against the native rebels. It had several steamers at its disposal and a flotilla of river boats to press home the attack. There was no shortage of cannons, mortars and other artillery, shells and long-range rifles. They had tents, blankets and other essential camping equipment, as well as generous supplies and provisions. The 20,000-strong force opposed about 2000 native warriors scattered throughout the country. Their military equipment was pitiful. Because of their lack of firearms, half of them used spears, axes and adzes. Their guns were old and accurate only at short-range and generally inadequate. They had no side-arms, for example, revolvers, cannons or grenades, at all. They had no good quality gunpowder, having to make do with what they made themselves. Instead of lead shot they had to resort to using nails, cut-up copper coins and bits of metal. The inadequately equipped force was also poorly clad, exposed to the elements, and frequently without food and water.

In spite of native rebels' huge inferiority, the formidable European forces' victories were so slight that they should be recognised as humiliations and almost defeats. The government was determined its army would overwhelm the indomitable Maori, but it failed. It used all its power to destroy the King movement and was not successful. It had to come to terms with King Tawhiao and gave him a generous pension. It used all its resources to arrest just one man, Te Kooti, and send him to the gallows. Not only was it not successful but later it pardoned him and ended up making him a government agent in dealing with Maori. The end result of so much bloodshed was the confiscation of more than two million acres, some of which was given to volunteers, some to Maori allies and some returned to rebels to entice them to make peace. One hundred and thirty-seven thousand acres of the remainder were sold between 1868 and 1872. So much military equipment and so many bloody battles made a mountain out of a mole hill, and loaded the colony with debt.

Who was responsible for these calamities and the 200 million francs debt? Parata, a Maori Member of Parliament, in an address to his European colleagues in July 1872[38] made it quite clear: 'Unfair conditions were imposed on the Maori, he said, contrary to the treaty of Waitangi ... The aggression they (natives) suffered came from those responsible for protecting them. If British subjects had acted more humanely to other subjects of the Queen, the deplorable deeds which occurred in New Zealand would never have happened. ... There would have been no warfare if the promises made to the Maori were put into practice.'[39] None of the honourable Members, including the guilty, questioned the truth of the Hon. Parata's speech. They swallowed the bitter pill in silence, without, however, admitting their guilt and promising to make amends.

The long war was not disastrous in itself for the Maori, so much as its consequences. About 2500 European and native allies were killed and the native rebels lost about 2000 men, women and children. It can be stated with certainty, however, that about 10,000 Maori perished in the next decade from hunger, privation, destitution and exposure, against which they had no defences.

20. On 1 June 1869, Governor Bowen opened the colonial Parliament in Wellington. For some time Julius Vogel, a Jewish MP, was trying to win power by launching the country on a grandiose public works programme. He was preparing the ground for Prime Minister Stafford's fall. He did, in fact, lose the confidence of the House and his government fell. Soon afterwards a coalition government was formed by Fox and Vogel, who for the next two years enjoyed the confidence of a Parliamentary majority. Several laws were passed by Parliament, the following deserving mention.

A New Zealand University College was established, affiliated with an English University, teaching the same subjects, particularly arts. Examination scripts would be sent to the English University for awarding masters' and doctors' degrees. Provincial schools were abolished and primary and secondary schools were established for all children, provided by the government, at the colony's expense. Education was to be under state control. Religion was not to be taught in schools, and if parents wanted religious instruction for their children, it had to be provided outside school hours.

Since the European population had greatly increased through gold prospectors' immigration, the number of Members of Parliament was increased from forty-five to seventy-four, including four Maori members. The Minister of Finance proposed a loan of 175 million to increase immigration to the colony and for state railways, telegraph and similar works. Parliament approved a loan of 125 million. Parliament, which in 1866 had been elected for a five-year term, dissolved itself in 1870 and at the beginning of 1871 new elections were to be called. Accordingly, at the end of 1870, Governor Bowen announced the dissolution of Parliament and a general election.

21. In 1858 census figures for the native population were 56,049. In 1867, nine years later, it was only 38,517. It is true that some Maori were not registered because they hid in the bush and could not be located by census officers. But there would not have been more than a thousand in this category. Thus in nine years, the native population had decreased by about 17,000 people. By 1870 it was believed that there were no more than 35,000. And numbers were seen to be decreasing rapidly.

On the other hand, the European population continued increasing through immigration. In 1859, there were 71,593 inhabitants. Numbers increased to 248,400 by 1870, not including 6000 pensioned soldiers living in New Zealand. There were 36,000 Catholics. Migrants were scattered throughout the country. In the North Island there were 94,975 Europeans. The provincial capitals had the following populations: Auckland and environs, 20,431; New Plymouth (Taranaki) 1837; Napier, 2179 and Wellington 7908. In the Thames mining area near Auckland, there were 5800 Europeans. The rest were scattered in small settlements and villages.

The South Island had 153,425 Europeans. Town populations were: Nelson 5534; Hokitika 3572; Greymouth 2121; Christchurch 7931; Lyttelton 2551; Timaru 1418; Oamaru 1657; Dunedin 14,857; Port Chalmers 1406 and Invercargill 1960. The rest of the population were in rural areas and numerous remote gold fields throughout the South Island.

It was estimated that in 1870 colonial imports amounted to 115,975,400 francs and exports, 120,568,900 francs, consisting almost entirely of wool and gold, the former worth about forty-seven million and the latter fifty million. Colonial taxes through customs duties, post and telegraph charges, the sale of land, etc., amounted to 32,605,875. Total expenditure was 37,500,000. In 1870 the national debt was 188,905,405 francs, a figure which was soon to be increased dramatically.[40]

In this decade, livestock increased considerably. The 1871 census gives the following information: horses 81,028; mules and donkeys 397; cattle 436,592; sheep 9,700,629; goats 12,434; pigs 151,460; poultry of various kinds 873,174.

If New Zealand's moral development had kept apace with the colony's material development, it would have been the most fortunate country in the world. But there was no such momentum. In fact, there was a regression through the introduction of an anti-Christian, selfish and Jewish-masonic spirit into the colony.

Chapter Twelve

Colonial Religion From 1861 to 1879

Summary. – 1. Evaluation of Protestant sects and Anglicanism in New Zealand. –2. Mass Maori renunciation of Christianity. – 3. Franciscan missionaries in Auckland diocese. – 4. Missionary Aletag's death; accusations against Catholic missionaries, especially Rev. Garavel. – 5. Maori Catholics' indifference and apostasy. – 6. Monsignor Pompallier's resignation from Auckland diocese; his death. – 7. Dunedin diocese's establishment. – 8. Auckland's new bishop. – 9. Franciscan fathers quit Auckland. – 10. Monsignor Viard's death. – 11. State of Wellington diocese, 1875. – 12. Comparison of Maori and European church membership, 1879.

1. The more than sixty Protestant denominations transplanted from the Old World and the New to New Zealand by numerous British colonists and emigrants, except for two, had very few native disciples or members. Their sphere of activity was almost entirely restricted to European settlers. The Anglican and Wesleyan denominations were the only ones up to 1860 to have a significantly Maori following. Besides the vast number of ministers and preachers available to settlers throughout the country, natives had many catechists and ministers who assisted their European masters in maintaining and spreading the errors of the Protestant reformation.

Wesleyan and Presbyterianism together with the countless other Protestant denominations, except Anglicanism, are purely lay religious bodies, with no hierarchy. They are totally and fundamentally democratic and completely controlled by their members, who boast about having the power and authority to appoint pastors and preach the Gospel. The sects need no backing or special organisation to be set up. They only require members for their maintenance and development. They are like any commercial enterprise which needs only people to invest capital and take out shares to guarantee its survival. Although religious bodies, they have a lay character. People select ministers and preachers, and the congregation controls everything. It chooses pastors or dismisses them at will and anyone may become a pastor if the congregation agrees. Denomination members can believe what they want and choose their own expression. Their religion involves simply observance of the sabbath, which means going to church and reading a passage from the Bible, singing psalms or hymns, listening to the minister or a church member's sermon or some young lady's twittering.

But this description does not apply to the Anglican church. It had the largest number of members among settlers and Maori in the colony. And although it had many European and native ministers it was stymied by a lack of organisation. Anglicanism owed its origin to the blind lust of an English king, and its development to Elizabeth, his unhappy, illegitimate daughter. It modelled its structure on the Catholic church, but in spiritual and temporal matters it was entirely dependent on the state. It adhered to it and in turn was supported by it. It received generous government funding from the wealth stolen from the Catholic church and suppressed religious orders in order to pay its bishops, archdeacons, canons and ministers. The Anglican church in New Zealand, however, did not receive similar support and patronage from the colonial government and struggled to maintain its position.

While the London Missionary Society provided enormous funds for its bishops, archdeacons and clergy in the colony, they did not consider they had sufficient to meet their needs. The London Society also resented sending them so much, to the detriment of its other missions in pagan and Christian countries throughout the world. It is common knowledge that money was used to convert unfortunate Catholics, encouraging them to attend the Anglican church. This is why the Missionary Society required Anglican colonists to contribute, at least in part, to the cost of supporting their clergy, when the colonial government would not give them official recognition and thus provide salaries and stipends.

The Anglican Bishop Selwyn tried every possible means to have Anglicanism recognised as the official church of New Zealand. He had private meetings with the colony's most influential and prominent Anglicans and with MPs, members of the Legislative Council and Crown ministers, trying to convince them of the value and necessity of this measure for the good of the church. He cited the great support the church afforded it in the past and pledged its future support if the colony, in imitation of the British government, would recognise Anglicanism as the official church. But all the schemes and ruses of Selwyn and his clergy failed completely. In 1855 an MP loyal to Selwyn presented his proposal for the necessity of an official church in New Zealand. Parliament unanimously and unequivocally declared its opposition to giving official recognition to any church, desiring to give all denominations the same protection without any inclusion of material support.

This defeat did not cause Selwyn to lose heart. He turned to London where he sought the help of many influential people in his homeland, trusting that they could obtain what he could not achieve in the colony. He also addressed the directors of London missionary societies and several prominent citizens, asking them to pressure the British government to request the New Zealand government, as an initial measure, to award him an annual grant as primate of the colony. If this was granted, the more important official recognition of his church would follow. That same year, the British secretary of state wrote to Governor Browne regarding the desirability and necessity of granting Selwyn as primate £600

(15,000 francs), as a suitable recognition of Britain's prestige. The governor presented the proposal to Parliament, which formally refused any grant to Selwyn or his clergy, declaring again their refusal, as for other colonies, to have an official church in New Zealand.

This failure caused the Anglican church to remain for several years without any substantial organisation. When it did achieve this, it took a democratic form similar to those of other Protestant denominations, subject to their members' dictates and demands. In England, the church has the government's financial support and is constituted through its bishops, archdeacons, canons and other dignitaries and clergy to guide its members. In New Zealand, since Anglican colonists provide most support for their hierarchy and clergy they wanted to have a free hand in their control. Nor did they then nor have they now any trust in their ministers.

To compensate for his lack of government funding, Selwyn obtained as many grants of land as he could from the government. He gained considerable sums of money from London groups and many aristocratic friends through his zealous promotion of the church. He was thus able to purchase many other pieces of land from the colonial government very cheaply and lay the foundation of future prosperity for the Anglican church in New Zealand. This was partly achieved through the fact that with the passage of time the value of land grew considerably. Rent through leasing met the required grant and upkeep of clergy and parishes.

In May 1857 Doctor Selwyn held the first synod in Auckland. Those taking part were Selwyn as Bishop of New Zealand and president of the assembly, the Anglican Bishop of Christchurch, five archdeacons, two ministers and seven members of the laity. They discussed the most suitable form of organisational structure. After the synod Selwyn travelled to England to petition the Queen for governmental recognition of the church in New Zealand. But he was told that that lay in the hands of the colonial government and he would have to address his request to them.

This was not what the head of the Anglican church in the colony wanted to hear. However his mission was not entirely fruitless. Besides collecting considerable sums of money for his church, in 1858 he secured recognition of the Anglican mission in New Zealand as an ecclesiastical province with four bishoprics in Auckland, Wellington, Christchurch and Dunedin, together with a Maori bishopric earlier established on the east coast. Selwyn was made primate. On his return to the colony, he asked Parliament to allow him, his clergy and laity the right to own property on behalf of the church. The government agreed to permit the various denominations' leaders to act as trustees of church land, akin to a participative business enterprise.

2. When the unjust 1860 war between Europeans and natives broke out, the fanatical political-religious Hauhau or Pai marire sect was soon established. It

quickly spread like a flood to most North Island tribes and villages. Natives reacted to it as if seized by demonic fury in their hatred of the British, their mortal enemies. They renounced Protestantism *en masse*, throwing themselves wholeheartedly into the new superstitious movement. The Bible and other Christian books were burnt or used for gun wadding in their long struggle against England.

With the creation of the new sect, a mixture of distorted biblical ideas and old pagan beliefs, Maori did no more than follow the teachings of Protestantism, their adopted religion, which allows free interpretation and individual choice in religious matters. They thus interpreted the Bible ministers had given them in their own way, just as had happened in England and elsewhere. Freedom of conscience was seen as the right of European Protestants to embrace or invent a religion which best suited them and still remain British subjects. This idea was also prevalent among Maori, who believed that they were entitled to create a religion which suited them. Maori, in short, simply followed Queen Elizabeth's Protestantism and declared their religious independence of the hated Pakeha.

Not only Protestant native rebels and supporters of the Maori Kingdom, but also government and colonists' allies adopted the new religion, including many Catholics. The new religion spread like wild fire among tribes both friendly towards and opposed to the British. With dizzying speed, it swept up teachers, catechists, preachers and native ministers, both Anglican and Wesleyan, who readily converted to the new sect. To remove any sign of Christianity, they renounced Christian names and took traditional native ones instead. There were many government Maori allies in the Hauraki Gulf, near Auckland. They were devout Protestants, whom Selwyn called his favourites, because he had devoted himself to their education. However, as soon as they heard about the new sect, they embraced Pai marire.

In 1864 when the Hauhau sect was adopted by tribes, Protestant missionaries and their families had to flee to Auckland, abandoning their possessions, homes, churches and parishioners to escape harm and a terrible death. Volkner, the Opotiki minister, did not listen to Catholic priests' friendly warning and was consequently barbarously hanged, as already mentioned. Grace, an Anglican minister, would have suffered the same fate if a Jew, well regarded by natives, had not rescued him from them. Williams, the Bishop of Waiapu, left his Maori diocese and rebel flock in a hurry to flee to Auckland because Kereopa had decided to strangle him and his clergy, as was mentioned in *Waka*, a native newspaper. In 1864 the same Bishop Selwyn, once admired and esteemed by all Maori, was shot at by Waikato natives because he was chaplain to the British troops fighting the Waikato campaign.[1] Thus the fanatical fury of the new Hauhau sect suddenly destroyed the Protestant missions.

On 26 December 1865 Bishop Selwyn wrote in distress to Rev. Coleridge. Protestant ministers, especially those who boast about their missionary spirit should ponder his words: 'Oh! How things have changed. Instead of the nations of believers who greeted me as their father, they are like a flock that has scattered, abandoning its shepherd. Presently, Maori regard us with suspicion and scorn.' He continued, 'The Hauhau superstition is simply an expression of belief completely opposing anything British to do with clergy and anything similar. ... This is the result of (Anglican ministers) pursuing other things than what really counts, that is, the kingdom of God and Divine justice. The Queen, the law and religion have been cast aside in the pursuit of one thing only, acquiring land.'[2]

In 1865 Dr Selwyn held a provincial synod in Christchurch. He voiced his grave concern about the Anglican church's failure among the Maori. 'All our native followers,' he said, 'have melted away. Our advice has not been heeded. Natives have decided to abandon their enemies' religion and create their own.' Selwyn, as primate and president of the Anglican synod, was one of the most learned and intelligent members of the English clergy. He knew full well that a lay person or a woman, even if she were Queen, should not be head of the church. He did not want to be put in the ridiculous position of having a woman appointing and licensing bishops. In agreement with members of the synod and the other three bishops, a petition was drawn up and sent to Queen Victoria in which the four prelates asked to be freed of their obligation to obtain her letters of authorisation and that they be recognised as able to elect and consecrate bishops in conformity with the synod's decisions, without referral to anyone else.[3]

Their proposal may have appeared to have merit in the eyes of the world, but it was still a long way from the teaching of the Gospel, the evidence of history, and eighteen centuries of solid and consistent religious experience. The Queen's council interpreted scripture in their own way, like the New Zealand Anglican synod, and refused their request. That was the end of the matter.

In 1866 Bishop Selwyn returned to England and the following year he attended an Anglican bishops' conference. He was later promoted by the Queen to the bishopric of Lichfield. Realising that he could no longer be effective among the Maori, he accepted the new position and returned to New Zealand in 1868 to farewell his friends. The Protestant synod of New Zealand formally thanked him and asked him to find a bishop to replace him and have the appointment ratified by the Queen.

3. Before the native situation deteriorated to such a degree, Mons. Pompallier, aware of his shortage of priests for both European and Maori Catholics, returned to Europe in 1859 in search of workers for the Lord's vineyard. He endeavoured to find new missionaries for his diocese and he had the good fortune and consolation to be able to start on his return journey on 4 September 1860 with twenty-four priests, including a small band of dedicated and devout Franciscan

monks. On 30 December the same year they reached Auckland, to the great delight of local Catholics who prepared a formal and enthusiastic reception for their esteemed pastor and new missionaries.

The first Franciscans who went to New Zealand comprised three priests and three lay brothers. According to the agreement between Monsignor Pompallier and the Father General of the Seraphic Order in Rome, the monks were to have a convent and a boarding school and substantial property for secondary education. They were also to work in parishes designated by the bishop. The Auckland convent and boarding school were to be built and paid for by the mission. It was to serve as the order's mother house, which monks after working in the missions could use as a retreat, in the spirit of their founder. It would also provide local Catholics with a cradle of learning and education. Theirs was a wise plan, worthy of the Franciscan Order. It would benefit children, provide spiritual care, promote learning and redound to the glory of Catholicism in that far distant land.

The Franciscans arrived at the same time as the Bishop. They were soon faced with two enormous difficulties. The bitter fighting which had broken out between the two races was expanding into frightening proportions. People were in fear and trembling about the future. As well as this, the mission's finances were in a parlous state. The situation instead of improving worsened, whether because of the fighting Catholics contributed less or because of diocesan administrators' inability to manage its scarce funds.

In order to devote himself more to the salvation of souls and tend to the spiritual needs of his vast mission, Mons. Pompallier approved qualified men to manage the mission's financial affairs, boarding schools, other schools and charitable institutions with care and caution. But whether due to a shortage of funds, their ineptitude or an over-reliance on their subordinates, they made conditions worse to such a degree that within a few years the diocese was burdened with a debt of more than 180,000 francs and had no means of paying it. To decrease the liability a large amount of suburban land in Ponsonby had to be sold off. This had been bought some years earlier by the bishop to support the mission. In these straitened circumstances, Mons. Pompallier unfortunately had to tell the Franciscan priests that he would not be able to keep his agreement of building them a convent. He asked them to wait until the situation improved and they agreed.

Meanwhile the Franciscans were assigned Parnell parish, an Auckland suburb, by Mons. Pompallier to serve as their mother house and home of their superior. The bishop also assigned them the northern area of the diocese, embracing four main districts of stations: Kororareka and Wangaroa on the east coast, and Mongonui and the Hokianga on the west coast, excluding the Puhoi mission, north-east of Auckland, which had been a German settlement for thirteen years and included 250 Catholics. They had a priest of their own nationality providing spiritual direction.

Shortly afterwards, a further five Franciscan priests left Europe to come to the aid of their distant confreres. The eight missionaries then began to devote themselves to the care of the Lord's vineyard, notwithstanding the countless difficulties the devil put in their way to prevent them carrying out their holy work of saving souls. A further obstacle soon to be experienced was the war between Maori and the British. Not only the warring parties but the whole country was absorbed in the conflict. And then the crazed, fanatical Hauhau burst on the scene.

When the natives' new political-religious sect sprang up, the Franciscans opposed it implacably, in their efforts to save native faithful from this flood of fanaticism. None of them abandoned their posts, and all remained steadfast at the breach, protecting Maori Catholics from the madmen's snares and lies. But they were only partially successful. Catholics living among Protestant Maori who had embraced the new Hauhau superstition were often forced to follow their example, particularly because they were nearly all related and were afraid of becoming their enemies if they refused. To win them over, Protestant converts to Hauhauism claimed that when the British were expelled or exterminated, Catholic missionaries would also disappear and they would then be left without shepherds or teachers. They thus succeeded in persuading some Catholics to change over to the Hauhau sect.

Notwithstanding the trials and tribulations Christianity suffered, the Franciscan fathers managed to keep a good number of their native flock strong in their faith. Their statistics show that in 1874, the year they left the country, the missions entrusted to them had the following numbers of native Catholics: Kororareka, 50; Wangaroa, 60; Hokianga, more than 500, and Mongonui, 60. In 1868 the Franciscans were also given the new Thames mission in the Coromandel peninsula where a great number of Europeans, including many Catholics, had gone in search of recently discovered gold. Two Franciscan priests laboured untiringly for the good of the people. Their zeal, charity and devotion to others are still remembered by miners today.

4. In 1863 a serious misfortune occurred which affected the Auckland mission and the Opotiki station in the Bay of Plenty particularly. Father Aletag, a zealous, devout German Catholic missionary, who had been parish priest of the huge area for fourteen years, was drowned. He was a dedicated man who founded a large, flourishing congregation who loved and revered him as a father. His blameless, exemplary conduct as well as his devotion to the Maori earned him the name of beloved Father of his children. He led a very difficult life, frequently having to visit the many tribes in his area which had a strong Catholic following to say mass and attend to their other religious needs. On 23 December 1863 Fr Aletag was returning home on horseback to Opotiki after one of his visits. As he was crossing the river leading into Opotiki harbour, he was swept away in the

racing current and drowned. The unfortunate accident deeply upset all the local people. Maori mourned his death for eight days and erected a monument in the Catholic cemetery. His grave is visited and revered even today.[4]

Monsignor Pompallier sent Rev. Joseph Garavel, a Frenchman, to take over Aletag's place in the Opotiki mission. He followed in his predecessor's footsteps, discharging his duties well. Garavel was loved and respected by the district's many Catholics and did much good, while the devil made use of fanatical Protestants to bring confusion and desolation, destroying not only the Catholic but also the Protestant mission, as shall soon be mentioned.

When fighting broke out in the Waikato in 1864, fanning natives' mortal hatred of the British – particularly Protestant preachers, soldiers and colonial government officials – many Protestant ministers and bigots blamed foreigners for inciting hatred and rebellion among the natives against England, wishing to damage the Catholic mission and its priests. Among the 'foreigners' were Bishop Pompallier and many Catholic missionaries. In 1864, in order to refute the wicked calumnies, Mons. Pompallier published many copies of the letters he wrote at various times to chiefs and Catholic catechists, in which he recommended peace to them as the finest gift that can come to us from Heaven, and he deplored warfare as the worst evil to afflict humanity. The prelate exhorted them to submit to the government's laws and make peace, because resistance would only destroy them. Later Mons. Pompallier had the letters printed in a small volume, to make clear to the government and settlers his views on the matter, previously circulated among his people.

The bishop summoned Father Garavel and gave him copies of his letters, requesting him to visit the Waikato, Tauranga and Taupo tribes, where resistance to the government and the British was particularly strong. He was to distribute them to Catholic tribes, convince them of their truth and urge them to follow their pastor's wise recommendations, which were for their own good. Father Garavel faithfully carried out this sensitive task, first visiting rebel territory in the Waikato, hoping to persuade them to make peace. He then went to Taupo for the same purpose. A Maori Protestant gave him a letter which he had received from chief Wiremu Tamiana, a fellow Protestant, asking him to take it to an Anglican chief at Opotiki to whom it was addressed. Without knowing the letter's contents, the good priest agreed, there being no postal service in the area. He then went to Tauranga and when he completed his task there he returned to his Opotiki mission. He quickly gave the chief his intended letter.

Rev. Garavel knew the paramount chief Tamiana very well, including his influence as a chief, his level of education and intelligence. Although he was the Maori king's right-hand man and counsellor, the missionary also knew that he was respected by all, including the British, for his peace-loving ideas and for always seeking the best for both races. He was aware that he had good relations with the colonial government to which he made several wise recommendations to redress the wrongs done to Maori and to come to a firm and lasting pact. Garavel also knew that Tamiana was the strongest force for peace among the Maori king's followers and supporters. He could never have dreamed that the paramount chief would depart from the principles he always professed.

When the Opotiki chief received Tamiana's letter he read it to his people. He was urged to adopt the Maori king's patriotic cause and to stop vacillating between King Tawhiao and the Queen of England. Tamiana's entreaty produced no real effect on the majority of the tribe, who continued to remain indecisive. The fact that Father Garavel took the letter to the Opotiki chief quickly came to Volkner's notice at Opotiki. He wrote to Governor Grey that Garavel and other Catholic priests were assisting rebels and from the enemy camp had taken the rebel Tamiana's letter inciting rebellion to Opotiki tribes. Garavel was accused of stirring up local natives against the British by urging them to take the Maori king's side.

The gullible governor believed Volkner's false accusations and ordered Mons. Pompallier to summon Rev. Garavel to Auckland to account, in the presence of the bishop, for his activities in the Waikato, Taupo and elsewhere and to answer the accusations made against him. The missionary and his bishop had no difficulty in proving that the accusations were false. Garavel asserted that he had acted as a messenger carrying the letter of a Maori not involved in the campaign and that he was entirely ignorant of its contents. He believed it was non-inflammatory because Tamiana's ideas and statements had always been to promote peace. He demonstrated to Grey that the mission to local tribes entrusted to him by his venerable superior was a mission of peace, not war, and that he had impressed on all natives, whether Catholic or non-Catholic, the need to obey the law and the colonial government, for the protection of their rights.

The governor said that he was satisfied with the explanation and the evidence provided to justify the missionary's behaviour. But, not wanting to upset settlers, he asked Mon. Pompallier not to send Father Garavel back to Opotiki until after the end of the Waikato campaign, which he hoped would be over in a few months. They agreed that Rev. Garavel would go temporarily to the North Shore or another European parish according to the bishop's pleasure. Father Garavel sensed that Grey still doubted his innocence and asked the bishop if he could go to Sydney (Australia) for a few months to recuperate. He agreed and he left on a mail steamer for Australia.

Meanwhile Taranaki Hauhau were sending prophets and tiu (Jews) all over the North Island to gain converts to their fanatical political-religious movement. Two of them, Kereopa and Patara and many followers went to Opotiki in January 1865. There they preached about the new religion, Pai marire's glories and successes. In his first sermon, Kereopa made a significant statement: 'Up till now we have laboured under a grave error. Protestant missionaries have stolen our land, our money and our life-blood through the lies they have preached to us.' A Maori asked Patara why they had come from Taranaki to Opotiki. He replied: 'To bring back the heads of all the ministers, soldiers and the British and place them at Te Ua's [the great prophet and founder of the sect] feet.'[5]

When the fanatical emissaries had converted the people to their religion they then prepared to carry out the plan they devised in Taranaki: the murder of ministers, soldiers and any British settlers who fell into their hands. Volkner, the Anglican minister, returned with Grace to Opotiki. His flock, who had converted to the new religion, made him their first victim by hanging him from a willow tree and drinking his blood, as has been described elsewhere.

After this terrible deed, understandable in a savage people and provoked by all the wrongs the British did to them, some Anglican ministers, especially Archdeacon Hadfield, vilified the Catholic church and its priests, writing to colonial and London newspapers that Roman Catholic missionaries were to blame for Volkner's tragic fate. They singled out Garavel, saying that in his journeys he incited natives against Volkner. The wicked lie caught on among Protestants, ever willing to believe anything bad about Catholics. Governor Grey knew well that the accusations were unfounded, but instead of refuting them as one would expect of a person of integrity, he remained silent. Nor did he meet with the ministers to take them to task. It was useless to expect fair play from Protestants in New Zealand. The missionaries of the Church of Rome were accorded no rights, and were treated on the same level as Maori rebels, and thus could be lied against with impunity.

Some Members of Parliament believed the lies spread about Father Garavel and other Catholic missionaries by the brazen Hadfield and his cohort. Since Grey had made no statement to the House regarding the outcome of his inquiry, they asked the prime minister in his official capacity for detailed information. Mr Frederick Weld, then prime minister and colonial secretary, mercifully honest, officially requested Mons. Pompallier to give a full written account regarding the matter to satisfy their justifiable concerns. In a courteous and lengthy reply prepared for Parliament, the bishop clearly demonstrated that Father Garavel played no part whatsoever, directly or indirectly, in Volkner's murder. He also enclosed a copy of the letters he had written at various times to many tribes. When Parliament received Mons. Pompallier's detailed report, they declared they were fully satisfied and recognised that comments made about Garavel and other Catholic priests were without foundation.

In describing Volkner's murder, he drew attention to the real reasons for the barbarous crime, citing the official documents the murderers sent to the government in Auckland. It was not motivated by religious hatred but hatred of land grabbers, hatred of traitors to the Maori people, and hatred of British settlers' arrogance. Nor should chief Wiremu Tamiana be blamed as the indirect cause of Volkner's death. He was not a Hauhau fanatic. Not only did he disapprove of murders and slaughter, but of fighting altogether. He constantly sought the good of both races and peace and harmony between them, like Bishop Selwyn, Sir William Martin, chief colonial judge, Mons. Pompallier, the Catholic clergy and many other honourable and upright citizens of the colony.

Even though it was evident that the accusations against Father Garavel and other Catholic priests were false, English historians are either silent on the matter or choose to support the mendacious Hadfield by taking it as a fact that Catholic missionaries played a part in Volkner's death. They pass over any evidence to the contrary, especially the murderers' official letter to the government explaining the reasons for and motives behind the crime. Rusden is one of these traducers of truth, and yet he boasted of writing his history from official documents! How poorly has History been treated! In the hands of unscrupulous writers, it becomes a conspiracy against the truth, intended to cover up Protestant ministers' infamies and the shameful deeds of the church which appointed them. Instead of being punished as he deserved, Archdeacon Hadfield was shortly afterwards made Bishop of Wellington, where we understand he continues to enjoy his well-earned position!

5. The campaigns which the government pursued against the Maori were not only materially disastrous for natives, but caused infinite harm morally, physically, psychologically and spiritually not only to the government's native enemies but also to their allies, including a good number of Catholics. They noticed the militia and settlers' crude behaviour (in whose company they were forced to live for long periods while on campaign). Seeing their lack of respect for religion and their free and easy lifestyle, they were considerably scandalised and gained a very jaundiced impression of their religion.

Maori are a straightforward but thoughtful people. Observing the behaviour of a good many of the militia and colonists, they concluded that Protestant missionaries had deceived them, giving them to believe that everyone, whether Maori or European, had to practise religion. Many of them wrongly concluded that religion was meant only for the natives and not the Pakeha, since they did not bother practising it. They reasoned that if Pakeha could call themselves Christian and not observe Christian teachings, why could they not do the same? Rusden, who did not wish to draw his compatriots and fellow Protestants to this delicate subject, made only one very pertinent comment: 'From the Waikato campaign and afterwards, even native allies became lax in their religious practice and their dissolute behaviour increased the more they associated with European riff-raff.'[6]

What was the consequence of natives' harmful contact with godless and loose-living whites? Maori enemies of the government abandoned Christianity because it was their hated adversaries' religion. They renounced Christian baptism and their Christian names, and received Maori baptism and adopted ancestral names. For example, King Potatau II changed his name from Matuataera to Tawhiao. Religious books, the Bible, New Testament, etc., were burnt even before the advent of the new Hauhau sect. Friendly Maori abandoned Christianity because they observed that a great number of soldiers and colonists among whom they lived did not bother about religion or morality, and gave free rein to their base instincts. They abandoned their belief and gave themselves over to excesses and indolent living like Europeans.

The creation of Te Ua's new fanatical political-religious sect as a substitute for British religion should therefore cause no surprise. No wonder that in such an hysterical climate, Pai marire's absurdities made capital among every tribe and that the new Maori sectarians used all their ingenuity and energy to restore and modernise the superstitious worship of Atua Hau, God of the Wind. Why should not the colourful Hauhau sect make inroads when the ground was already prepared in the people's simple, patriotic minds? They saw themselves surrounded by bitter enemies, who called themselves Christians and were intent on stripping them of their possessions, and even of the means of survival.

If Hauhau fanaticism instantly brought down Protestantism, it also caused major damage to Catholic missions and the survival of Catholicism among them. Catholic missionaries, unlike Protestant preachers, were neither hunted down nor hated, because they were not English and did not take part in exploiting natives. But it is also true that tribes which converted *en masse* to Protestantism used every means to force native Catholics to adopt the new sect. They wanted them to believe that Atua Hau, God of the Wind, would finally free them from the yoke and tyranny of the British, and restore to them their former independence. Their Catholic kin and neighbours who did not want to adopt the new religion were threatened with severe reprisals. To avoid internal tribal conflict or war with their neighbours, many Catholics allowed themselves to be persuaded to embrace, if not voluntarily, at least out of human necessity, the fanatical Hauhau sect.

Catholic missionaries, who lived among them, demonstrated Pai marire's stupidity and refuted the spurious reasons given to support it. It was claimed that belonging to the Hauhau was a gesture of true patriotism and political wisdom, because it would bring about salvation and independence from their tyrannical exploiters. Priests' arguments and proofs had no effect on the great majority of native Catholics. The revolutionary current stirred their patriotic fervour and caught them up in the new religion's national political movement. In their obtuseness, they allowed the good of the country to prevail over any other consideration and the majority of Catholics blindly followed Hauhauism's errors. Later, however, they realised that it would not benefit the country but cause its harm, and they were distressed, but the damage was done.

The missionary priest at Rotorua, Father Boibieux, had a flourishing congregation. But in May 1865 he left his post because Maori advised him that he was no longer welcome. He realised that they no longer wanted to practise the faith and that it was useless to remain, so he decided to go to Auckland. He had hardly gone before Hauhau agents sowed their errors among local tribes, and most Maori rushed to embrace the fanatical sect, except for a few Catholics still in 1884 loyal to their faith. They, with good reason, can take pride in the fact that they never submitted to Hauhauism and its Atua.

Rev. Fr Grange, a missionary at Wakatane in the Bay of Plenty, was looking after Catholics in the Opotiki area, which had been without a priest because of Father Garavel's recall to Auckland, as mentioned previously. In June 1865, he wrote to his Taranaki missionary confrere that from the previous February Maori Protestants had gone over to Hauhauism and had hanged their former minister shortly after his return. They also coerced Catholics into the new religion. He mentioned that in spite of everyone's efforts there were only about twenty loyal Catholics left. Referring to other tribes, which included a good number of Catholics, he presumed they had all become Hauhau.

The good missionary ended his letter by saying that the Catholic tribes of Kopeopeo, Nazaret and Wakatane were still steadfast in the faith, even though Protestant tribal members had embraced the new superstition and were putting pressure on Catholics to follow their example. Unfortunately, two months later they too were persuaded to adopt Hauhauism. Father Grange found himself almost without any followers and the tribes of the huge area were at war with the government because of their massacres. He realised that it would be useless to remain among people, most of whom had given up the true faith. At the end of August he left Wakatane for Auckland, to wait for things to improve and fighting between the two races to end.

By 1870 Hauhauism had lost its fanatical energy. The great majority of Maori adopted the attitude of many colonists, becoming indifferent to religion, and they remain so. By 1870 Hauhau fanaticism was crushed by the government's forces. Many of its former Catholic followers were now chastened and contrite and asked for the missionaries to return, saying that they joined the Hauhau not from conviction but out of fear of being killed by the rogues. The hand of God, however, punished them for their cowardice in abandoning the faith, because there were no missionaries available to meet their request.

Priests who had been with the natives in the central North Island had to abandon their missions in 1865 because of Maori desertion of the faith. On reaching Auckland, they were sent by the pastor of the diocese to tend to European colonists' needs. New missions were created, reflecting the increased number of priests now available. It was a fitting punishment for Maori ungratefulness for God's goodness!

However, God did not allow even the guilty to be completely abandoned. Two missionary priests were assigned to visit the few remaining faithful Maori in the central North Island regularly. They were to receive back into the fold those who were truly repentant and to counsel those who had gone astray to reconsider. From 1874 to 1885 there was only one priest to minister to Maori Catholics of the Auckland diocese scattered in the bush and remote areas. Those who lived near local colonists were looked after by the missionary assigned to Europeans.

6. The considerable material devastation and moral decline in New Zealand severely affected and distressed Mons. Pompallier, who was suffering ill health. Worn out by his thirty years of missionary work and the burden of his responsibilities, he humbly beseeched His Holiness Pope Pius XI of holy memory to be freed from his office, so that he could return home and prepare himself for death which he foresaw approaching. The Pope recognised the validity of the worthy prelate's request and in 1869 gave him permission to return to Europe.

Monsignor sadly bade farewell to the dear children of his diocese who were deeply upset at his departure, fearing they would never see him again in this world, since he was close to death. He left New Zealand, embarking on a French steamer for France. Once there he journeyed to Rome to report on his diocese to Christ's Vicar. After a brief stay in the Holy City, he returned to his homeland where on 20 December 1870 he died a holy death. His Holiness had hoped that, after a brief period of convalescence in France, the good bishop would recover his health and be able to return to work in the mission he founded and had tended with such care and devotion. When he heard that far from getting better he was rapidly approaching death, on 23 June 1870 the Pope appointed the Most Rev. Thomas Croke, an Irishman, to succeed him.

7. Rome, ever mindful of its flock's spiritual well-being, not only gave the Auckland diocese a new pastor, but had already considered creating another diocese in the lower part of the South Island, to facilitate the development of Catholicism among the many Europeans flocking to the country. Early colonisation of the district, and later, Province of Otago has already been described. The few Europeans settled there from 1848 devoted themselves for the next ten years to agriculture and grazing. From 1859, with the discovery of substantial gold deposits in rivers, valleys and gorges, prospectors rushed in droves to Otago from all over the world, particularly from Australia, California and England. From 1860 numerous sailing ships and steamers arrived daily at Port Chalmers, full of emigrants seeking their fortune.

Mons. Viard, Bishop of Wellington, had the huge Otago Province in his diocese. As soon as he was aware that there were Catholics in the mostly Presbyterian population, he appointed a priest to visit them from time to time and bring them the consolations and comforts of religion. Due to the discovery of gold, the number of European Catholics arriving was increasing daily. In 1861 the bishop sent Father Moreau to live in Otago to tend to the spiritual needs of the faithful in the huge district. He made Dunedin his base and from there he travelled periodically to the gold-mining areas where there were Catholics. But what could one priest achieve in the midst of so many people scattered over a more than 30,000 square kilometre area, with the Catholic population increasing constantly? Nevertheless, he stretched himself to the limit and tried to be everywhere at once to meet the needs. Realising the impossibility of his task, he turned to his bishop, telling him it was vital to have more priests.

The prelate recognised the urgency of his request but could not immediately take action because of his lack of missionaries. Only in 1864 did he have the consolation of being able to send two other Marist priests, Fathers Aime Martin and Rolland. Dunedin now had a parish church and missionary home, a school for Catholic children and a convent for Sisters of Our Lady of the Mission. They also opened another convent school and a boarding school for girls. The three devoted missionaries worked conscientiously for the good of souls. Aided by goldminers' donations they were soon able to build churches and homes for the missionaries in the main provincial goldmining areas of Tuapeka, Nanukira Junction, Kawaru Junction, Dunstan, Fox Diggings, Quinstawn and Inverkargil where there were numerous Catholics. Shortly afterwards, Mons. Viard sent other priests there. European migration, however, was continuing, and more missionaries were requested for the various settlements springing up as if by magic. But there were none available and several populated areas remained some years without a resident priest.

The Bishop of Wellington was responsible for a huge diocese which he needed to visit and provide with priests, which were in short supply. He believed it was opportune to create another diocese in New Zealand. Writing to his superior general in Lyons, requesting more priests, he explained the appropriateness of dividing his diocese in two. He was quite old and unable comfortably to make lengthy journeys to his flock scattered through eight huge provinces. The division would also lead to the growth and advancement of Catholicism in the region. He made a similar submission to the Holy See, for its wise consideration.

His Holiness, Pope Pius IX, the Marist Superior General and the Sacred Congregation of Propaganda Fide approved Mons. Viard's sensible observations and recommendations. It was decided to create a new diocese in New Zealand in the lower half of the South Island.

The Marist Order was already responsible for several other vast missions, besides Wellington. It was not able to administer the new diocese and suggested to the Sacred Congregation of Propaganda Fide to entrust it to secular clergy or another religious order of congregation. His Holiness Pius IX approved its being given to Irish clergy to manage.

In 1869 His Holiness decreed the erection of the new diocese of Dunedin, its boundaries being contained within the areas of Otago, Southland, Stewart Island and neighbouring islands. On 3 December Pius IX appointed Monsignor Patrick Moran, an Irishman, born in 1823, as the diocese's first bishop. From

1856 he had been Bishop and Vicar Apostolic of the British colony of the Cape of Good Hope in South Africa.

The new pastor hastened to take up his new appointment. He arrived by the middle of 1870 and was welcomed with great rejoicing by the clergy and Catholic population of Dunedin. Right from the outset he had major difficulties to overcome. He still needed to recruit Irish priests for the various mission stations, and promote the development of Catholicism including the construction of a cathedral, bishop's residence, several other churches and schools. With his enthusiasm and devotion to his flock, he succeeded in time to overcome every obstacle and establish a solid base for diocesan growth.

Not long after Mons. Moran's arrival in Dunedin, the Marist Fathers stationed in the diocese returned to their Wellington headquarters, leaving in their stead the Irish priests the prelate brought with him, and others were soon to follow. Later, also, the French sisters of Our Lady of the Mission left for their Wellington convent. They were replaced by Irish Dominican nuns. By 1874 Dunedin diocese had more than 10,000 Catholics and twelve flourishing parish schools attended by 900 boys and girls. There were eight priests and another four were expected from Ireland by the end of the year. Dunedin had a Dominican convent with ten nuns who ran a successful girls' boarding school for the diocese and a convent school for town girls. There were also twenty churches and chapels throughout the diocese.[7]

8. While Catholicism was steadily developing in Dunedin, Catholics in the Auckland diocese were busy preparing for the arrival in 1871 of their eagerly expected new Pastor, Mons. Croke. When he reached Auckland he was greeted with great celebration by the clergy and Catholic laity of the town, most of whom were Irish. He immediately set about organising the diocese's spiritual and material affairs with great devotion and zeal. He was new to colonial life and used to the orderliness of his noble Ireland. Croke was not happy with New Zealand settlers' free and easy lifestyle and expressed his dissatisfaction with the sorry state the mission was in. There was much restoration and building to be done. A considerable amount of painstaking effort was needed to bring things back on an even keel because of the disastrous effects of the terrible warfare, Hauhau fanaticism, a lack of clergy and the material means for development. Nevertheless, Mons. Croke threw himself into the task.

Shortly after his arrival in Auckland, the prelate sent a brief report on the diocese to the Cardinal Prefect of Propaganda. The following statistics are tabled:[8] By 1871 the Auckland diocese had eleven mission stations with church, residence, school and parish priest for European settlers and any Maori who wanted to use them. There were also twenty other stations visited periodically by one or more missionaries, or their assistants. There were only sixteen priests of Italian, French and Irish nationality. There were twenty-eight Sisters of Mercy who ran parish schools, a girls' secondary boarding school and an orphanage for European and Maori children, partly subsidised by the colonial government. The schools were a real asset and were admirably run by the good sisters. The North Shore boarding school for Maori and European boys had to close for lack of funds. The diocese was short of parish schools because of a lack of priests and school teachers.

Mons. Croke did not know the number of Maori Catholics since he did not have statistical information. There were about 300 in the Franciscans' Northland missions. Elsewhere it was estimated there were about a thousand. Because the prelate did not have sufficient missionaries to spare any for natives, he had Father James MacDonald visit the Maori throughout the diocese to maintain them in the faith which in spite of all the upheavals they had preserved. The good Father MacDonald toiled away as vicar general for the Maori, until his death in 1885.

The holy Irish priest earned the admiration of all by his self-sacrifice, dressing in the simplest clothes when he visited tribes and adopting their way of living. Without complaining, he suffered hunger, other privations and all kinds of hardship for the good of their souls. Often, after a long and arduous journey through forests and mountains he would arrive at a kainga (village) in the evening, tired and exhausted, hoping to find natives there and a place to rest and he would find the village deserted. He was forced to lie down on the bare ground, without having had anything to eat all day. On other occasions, gnawed by hunger, he would have to eat raw cabbage. Only God knew all the tribulations he suffered and now he will rightly be enjoying glorious immortality with the Lord to whose services he dedicated his whole life.

9. As if there were not sufficient disasters affecting the Auckland diocese, in 1874 a further one occurred; the Franciscan Fathers' abandonment of the diocese. Their withdrawal was caused by a repetition of what happened to the Marist Fathers in 1848 under Mons. Pompallier's leadership, when they left for the Wellington diocese. From 1860 eight Franciscan priests and three lay brothers worked in the diocese for the well-being of the faithful under the guidance and direction of their religious superior, as agreed in Rome between the Order's General and Mons. Pompallier.

The dedicated Franciscan Fathers for twelve years suffered all kinds of difficulty and hardship with heroic courage and self-denial, without getting their convent or boarding school at Parnell promised them by the diocese, because of lack of funds. In 1872 they approached Mons. Croke explaining to him the agreement made by the now deceased Pompallier and asked him to honour it. The prelate replied that he would think it over. Later he told them that he had no intention of recognising them as a separate body and part of the Franciscan Order. He saw them as simply priests together with the secular missionaries, under obedience to the diocesan bishop. He would treat each of them according to what was in the best interests of the diocese and the faithful entrusted to his care. He considered he had no obligation to negotiate with religious superiors.

Mons. Croke believed he had made the right decision and he did not realise that it would be harmful to the diocese and the faithful. Members of religious orders would not and could not agree to his demands because they would be contravening their vows and canon law. The Franciscan Fathers told him that Mons. Pompallier's agreement guaranteed their rights and privileges as Religious and that the contract applied equally to his successors. They said that as members of a religious order they were accountable to their own superiors and that they would rather abandon the diocese and sacrifice everything than betray their religious vows.

They had lengthy discussions trying to convince the prelate that his request was untenable, without success. The Franciscan General then recommended to his New Zealand members to go to other missions, namely Australia, China and Egypt. In 1874 the good Fathers and brothers left Auckland, except for Father Mahoney, an Irishman who was persuaded by the bishop to get his superior general's permission to remain in the diocese.[9] Words cannot describe Catholics' grief on their departure. Mons. Croke also was bitterly upset, and the diocese lost a band of dedicated, learned missionaries which it desperately needed.

Shortly after the Franciscans' departure, the Auckland diocese became vacant because on 23 June 1875 His Holiness Pius IX promoted Mons. Croke to Archbishop of Cashel in Ireland. When he was in Rome he reported to the Holy Father on the state of his distant diocese. From Rome he departed for his new archdiocese where he continues to work zealously on behalf of his compatriots and his unhappy, oppressed country. Until 1879 the vacant diocese was entrusted to the solicitous care of the Very Rev. Father Fines (later created a Domestic Prelate by His Holiness Leo XIII) firstly as vicar general and later as administrator. He deserved great praise and commendation for his prudent management of the diocese, succeeding in restoring its financial position and improving its administration, earning general approval not only in New Zealand but also in Rome.

10. Meanwhile, the Wellington diocese was also struck by a grave, sad event. Mons. Viard, bishop for twenty-four years, suddenly died. Worn out by constant toil rather than the effects of age, after a brief illness which he endured with Christian resignation and courage, on 2 June 1872 he expired in the arms of the Lord. Faithful missionaries and their religious confreres greatly mourned his loss. The Catholic laity felt similarly, since he was loved and revered as a father by all. There was general mourning in Wellington, clear proof of people's admiration and esteem for his intellectual gifts and kindness. Solemn funeral rites were carried out in the beautiful church of St Mary built by him in the centre of town. His mortal remains were buried in the church.[10]

Wellington, colonial capital, 1872.

Wellington diocese did not have to wait long for a pastor. On 8 February 1874, His Holiness Pius IX appointed the Very Rev. Francis Maria Redwood, an English Marist, as the important diocese's new bishop. He was born in Birmingham, England, on 8 April 1839 of a well-to-do family who brought him as a child to New Zealand. Under his parent's watchful eye he was raised in fear of God and an atmosphere of piety. They kept him well away from the corrosive influence of colonial society and bad company. While very young, Redwood showed he had a priestly calling to the Marist Order, whose salutary example he had constantly before him.

He mentioned this to his confessor and spiritual director, and to the venerable Mons. Viard. They encouraged him to follow his vocation, promising him all their support to achieve his goal. He was very happy with his spiritual directors' encouragement and told his parents of his decision to enter the Society of Mary and dedicate himself to the service of God and people. His loving parents were devout and God-fearing. Unlike many misguided parents learning of such an event, they did not oppose their young son Francis's wishes. They told him that they were pleased for him to be free to follow his divine vocation.

Redwood then eagerly began to study Latin, and to become familiar with the Latin, English and French classics under the expert tuition of Father Gavin, a missionary in the delightful Nelson settlement. In a short time he made such rapid progress that Monsignor Viard decided to send him to France to complete

Catholic cathedral, Wellington, 1875.

his novitiate and education. When he completed his training as a novice, his superiors sent him to study philosophy and theology and other relevant subjects. He distinguished himself by gaining the highest marks, demonstrating his high intelligence, logical mind, and other gifts as well as his kindness and piety. The superiors of the society were aware of his considerable abilities and very shortly after his ordination as a priest he was assigned important roles in the congregation's houses.

While Father Redwood was assiduously carrying out his duties, God made manifest that his light shine with greater brightness for the good of the Society of Mary and the Catholic Church in the distant land of New Zealand. As mentioned earlier, on 8 February Pius IX appointed him Bishop of Wellington to replace the lamented Mons. Viard and on 17 March 1874 he was consecrated bishop by Cardinal Manning in London. Towards the end of the same year the prelate, accompanied by a band of fresh missionaries, departed for his new diocese. He received a festive welcome from the town's missionaries and laity, who were thrilled at the arrival of their new father and pastor. They were pleased to throw off mourning and welcome the new bishop sent them by the Pope.

11. Monsignor Redwood very soon began to devote his energy to Catholicism's development in the vast diocese. He found ready support and cooperation from his priests and laity. The report he sent on 10 October 1875[11] to the Congregation of Propaganda shows proof of the Wellington diocese's steady progress. The following is statistical information from the report:

By 1 March 1874 the European population of the Welllington diocese was 146,950 of whom 19,528 were Catholic. By 31 December of the same year, mostly due to immigration, the population had risen to 170,431 of whom 22,000 were Catholic. 'At the present time (October 1875), added the Prelate, the population has increased to 180,000 of whom there are 23,000 Catholics.' There were then about nine or ten thousand Maori or natives in the diocese, including about nine hundred practising Catholics. That year the prelate had thirty-one priests helping in the mission, of whom only three were members of the Society of Mary. The rest were secular clergy. There were also five other Marist Fathers who, worn out by fatigue and old age were retired, no longer being able to work in the Lord's vineyard.

The diocese was divided into twenty-four districts, excluding Wellington's urban parishes, which occupied considerable areas. Each district had a priest's residence, and from two to four sub-districts which the priest visited regularly, including Sundays to say mass and administer the sacraments.

Wellington cathedral could hold between 800 and 1000 worshippers. There were also fifty-six churches and chapels in the diocese, able to hold between 150 and 700 people. Two churches were built with stone; the others of wood, for economic reasons and safety because of the country's frequent earthquakes.

Twenty-two churches, including the cathedral, were not completely finished inside. Seven others were being constructed or nearly completed, and three had just been started. The good bishop added that there was an urgent need to build another eight as soon as possible to accommodate the growing population. The average cost of constructing a small wooden church was 15,000 francs.

The diocese had thirty-four schools; five of which were under the care of the Sisters of Mercy's two convents, and three Houses of the Sisters of Our Lady of the Mission. Besides parish schools, they also ran girls' boarding and secondary schools. Other schools were run by lay male and female teachers. Catholic parents did not send their children to state schools because they were secular and anti-Catholic.

12. Official statistics for Maori religious affiliation are not available. Accordingly, only approximate figures can be given. In 1859 of the natives in New Zealand, 18,000 were still pagan; about 13,000 were Anglican Protestants, 6000 Wesleyans and 14,000 Catholic of whom one northern tribe alone had 5000 members. Of these 33,000 Christians, a good many, particularly Protestants, were only nominally and superficially Christian, taking part in prayers, but they still led pagan, immoral lives. When in 1864 the new Hauhau sect was established, the majority of these baptised Christians embraced it, as already mentioned. By 1870 Maori Protestants were reduced to about 4000 nearly all uneducated, nominal members. There were not even a hundred practising members. There were, however, 3500 Maori Catholics, of whom only 2000 could be described as committed members.

From 1870 the religious condition of Maori was much the same as for Protestants. Bad habits and drunkenness learnt by living in contact with the militia and colonial idlers reached every tribe whether pagan or Christian, causing infinite harm. King Tawhiao himself became a drunkard. In addition to these evils should be added their crass ignorance in religious matters, inveterate sloth and a nomadic, vagrant life followed by many. It is no wonder that these factors soon disposed the wretches to religious fantasies. They were also surrounded by many Protestant denominations, including the weird Mormon religion, so that even those who meant well, were unable to discern the truth. Indifference to religion was and still is a very significant factor among European settlers, who are members of so many Protestant denominations in New Zealand. For most of them, religion consists simply of honouring the Sabbath, that is, going to church and singing hymns and psalms. Most of the New Testament is disregarded and considered to be rubbish.

Fortunately, by 1875, most Catholics, especially Irish emigrants, were committed to their faith. Although indigent and poorly educated, they generally remain Catholic wherever they happen to be, in spite of the many ways used to encourage them to abandon their ancestors' faith. Nevertheless, the free and easy colonial lifestyle and contact with Protestants exercise a damaging effect on Catholics, making them prone to lapse. However, all Catholics, whether of Anglo-Saxon or Irish origin, always feel the need of religious sustenance for themselves and their children. All, without exception, receive the priest with great affection and respect, eager to retain him in their midst.

CHAPTER THIRTEEN

Migration, Public Works and Debts From 1871 to 1880

SUMMARY. – 1. Colonial legislation. – 2. Julius Vogel's achievements. – 3. Post and telegraph. – 4. Free passage. – 5. Continuous damaging effects of migration. – 6. A more suitable plan for Catholic migration. – 7. Parliament buildings. Colonial railways. – 8. New governors. – 9. National defence. – 10. Abolition of provinces and creation of counties. – 11. Acquisition of Maori lands. – 12. Slave trading in the Pacific. – 13. Masonic or secular state education. – 14. Effects of anti-Christian education in New Zealand and Europe. – 15. Colonial statistics.

1. We are pleased to begin this chapter noting the suspension of hostilities between the two races and the prospect of a long, enduring peace. This was not achieved, however, by the colonial government's recognition of its wrongs and injustices towards the Maori and a willingness to set things right. Quite the opposite; it continued its policy of tyranny and exploitation, making all kinds of fine promises, with no intention of keeping them.

From 1856 to 1866 the great majority of politicians, that is, MPs, members of the Legislative Council and government ministers in New Zealand, were essentially pragmatic, self-interested and prejudiced towards Maori. During this decade there were eight successive ministries bidding for power to benefit their supporters. None of them cared a fig about the Maori. The natives became so fed up with the intolerable injustices they suffered that they decided to rebel. Parliament and the government authorised ministers to use force to annihilate them, where possible, as has already been mentioned.

From 1862 to 1872 the huge number of gold prospectors and soldiers-of-fortune had a virtual monopoly of electing members of Parliament, apart from the four Maori seats. They were keen to elect people like themselves, out to get rich at any cost. 'Thousands of the same men,' commented Rusden, 'who contributed to Government corruption in Victoria, Australia, are now doing the same thing in New Zealand.'[1] Money is their god, and the only thing they care about. A war of extermination against the Maori was good as far as they were concerned, so that they could get their land. However, this had not been achieved in ten years fighting and its continuation would serve no one. Because of the enormous financial harm the colony had suffered, the new legislators had to change their policy.

The majority of MPs and members of the Legislative Council realised the stupidity of hoping for advancement and wealth through brute force. They recognised that the past war, besides involving the sacrifice of so many lives, cost England 100 million* and the colony seventy-five, to no one's benefit. Much harm had been done and both sides were sick of bloodshed. In 1869, Parliament decided to change tactics, without abandoning its underlying intentions, and earnestly seek peace between the two races so that it could concentrate on promoting colonial stability and progress. Accordingly, Prime Minister Stafford was removed from office by colleagues, and Fox replaced him with Vogel as Minister of Finance and Donald MacLean as Minister of Maori Affairs. But Vogel was really in charge.

Freemasonry withers and destroys everything it touches. It is a diabolical secret society founded for the destruction of Christianity. It had for some time been established in New Zealand after being transported from England, its natural home. In the colony it made rapid progress and its members had the majority of the best-paid, most influential positions. Their god was the golden calf. Senior masons were provincial councillors, militia leaders, government officials, MPs, members of the Legislative Council and ministers dictating their new society's laws, mirroring their benign bequest to the Maori.

The new government formed in 1869 was composed mostly from their ranks. It had abandoned any notion of continuing to fight Maori. It turned its thoughts instead to making New Zealand the greatest, most flourishing, wealthiest and most envied colony in the world, with a stamp of modernity. A freemason was needed to initiate the ambitious project, clever enough to hoodwink the majority while serving his own interests. This was exactly the new colonial minister, Julius Vogel's, intention.

2. Julius Vogel was a German adventurer. Before 1860 he ran a struggling shop in a small Australian mining settlement. Once he heard of the discovery of gold in Otago, in 1860 he, like many others, rushed over in search of wealth. When he arrived in the new country he realised that the real path to fame, fortune and position in provinces and parliament was through journalism. A typical Jew, he was plausible, cunning and educated. When he arrived in Dunedin he abandoned his former occupation as a trader and studied journalism. He soon gained a good position on the Otago Provincial Council and in 1861 he was elected to represent Dunedin in Parliament.[2]

In his first eight years as an MP Vogel lay low, observing everything that happened, quietly analysing events and mapping his and the country's destiny. His policy, as for most of his colleagues, was based on personal advantage. Up till 1869 he gave his full support to provincialism, because it suited him. He then became a centralist and in 1877 he had provinces abolished because they stood in the way of his plans. He was not responsible for war with the Maori and did not want to quarrel with them. His aims were all directed towards

*Translator's note: Presumably francs.

getting money and spending it.

In 1869, Mr Vogel became Minister of Finance, Post and Telegraph and Customs. Describing the country's financial state to the House, he said, 'What is the outcome of eight years of war? A number of dead on both sides; the loss of land by Maori, and considerable loss of money and property by us. Are we so blind that we cannot see that the country's financial ruin would provide the rebels' victory? We have seized native land worth about 10 million francs. However, the war has cost more than 95 million, not including compensation for damages done to settlers' property which is not yet known.'[3] Vogel was certainly right. He hastened to end hostilities and to seek peace, without providing the poor natives justice.

In 1870, before Parliament's closure, Vogel proposed to contract a debt of 150 million francs for the colony's defence, public and community works. He argued the necessity of having between 2400 and 2600 kilometres of national railways. The network he planned could be paid for by the sale of 2,500,000 acres and obtaining a loan of 187,500,000 francs. Another 25,000,000 would be required to carry out the other proposals he considered necessary. He showed, at least on paper, that in ten years the increase in colonial income would cover the costs and that the British government would be willing to loan 25 million francs for public works. Members of both Houses were dazzled by the prospect of universal prosperity promised by the minister of finance. They sanctioned the speculator's extravagant proposals without a murmur and he pronounced himself extremely satisfied with Parliament's compliance.

As soon as Parliament's session was ended, Vogel departed for England to raise funds for the works he planned. He passed through America and made a contract with a shipping company to carry mail from New Zealand to San Francisco in California. Colleagues helped him obtain tax exemption from the American government for wool and flax brought into the country. In England he pressured the British government for postal regulations and to enter into a defence pact. He also concluded contracts for railway construction and large scale emigration from the United Kingdom and northern Europe. He was successful in floating 30 million francs of colonial shares at 5 per cent interest and sold them at 95.82, collecting 29,052,375 francs. In spite of an exaggerated picture of New Zealand's wealth, in 1872 colonial revenue was 2,075,000 francs less than the previous year.[4]

But this did not bother Vogel. He accrued debts for the colony and he thought only of his own advantage. This can be seen from colonial records and official documents, and from statements made in Parliament. From the end of 1869 to the beginning of 1872, Vogel's travel expenses, paid for by the government, were 95,525 francs. Just for a trip to Australia in spring, 1872, he spent 14,125 francs at the country's expense. 'The New Zealand donkey,' said Rusden, 'was saddled with the cost.'[5] But even more extravagant spending was to come. In

October 1876, when Vogel had been removed from office, the Commission for Public Expenditure reported to the House that 'besides his salary and travel expenses, Vogel spent 75,000 francs and a further 165,000 francs on his trips to England in 1869 and 1871, without government authorisation or permission.'[6] He used government funds to support newspapers and journals to back his projects. 'Vogel lavishly bestowed special, personal favours which he justified to Parliament saying, that as a former journalist himself, he knew that it was an acceptable practice to many newspaper owners. And he awarded plum positions to MPs to win their support.'[7]

Nearly every year Vogel badgered Parliament to agree to contract more debts and feed their own greed. In 1875 he sold Rothschilds the colony's new loan of 100 million, giving the Jewish bankers two per cent profit. For 100 million francs the colony got only 91,950,000. In recognition of his financial acumen, Queen Victoria knighted Vogel as a member of the Order of St Michael and St George! What a debasement of the honours system! In 1874 Vogel declared in Parliament 'that 37,500,000 francs needed to be diverted from the purpose for which it was borrowed, to appease the provinces.'[8] To arrange covering the colonial debt through the London Stock Exchange, it appears that Vogel demanded £18,000 or 450,000 francs.[9]

Although in 1876 he was removed from office as minister of finance, servile government ministers appointed Sir Julius Vogel as their agent general in London without requesting him to account for the public funds he diverted without authority. By 1880 Parliament realised that Vogel was pursuing his own interests rather than the colony's. His ambition was to become a British Member of Parliament. He still demanded not only a fat salary but generous fees for services rendered. Fed up with his behaviour, they dismissed him as colonial agent general.[10] When his hopes of entering the British Parliament were dashed, he returned to New Zealand to further his career, and he came close to being prime minister more than once. In his twilight years he retired to London, weary after all his years of hardships!

By 1870 New Zealand's national debt was not yet 189 million.* Thanks to Vogel, by 1877 it had risen to 525 million. In 1877 colonial revenue was 17,500,000 francs less than expenditure. Parliament approved a further loan of 62,500,000 francs and in 1879 another of 125 million francs. The South Seas colony followed this direction under the magnetic sway of Sir Julius Vogel, vilified as a national swindler by the people of Auckland in 1886.

3. New Zealand had acquired an international reputation as a country of inexhaustible wealth and infinite resources. Egged on by Vogel's ambition to make the colony a great nation, its leaders readily launched the country into a

---

*Translator's note: Presumably francs.

huge sea of debt in order to build railways, roads, bridges, ports, develop a post and telegraph network, bring emigrants from the old world, introduce a state education system and carry out other similar projects. The government did not have the funds for these undertakings and added new debts to the old, seeking major loans on the London market. In 1870 New Zealand's national debt was a little less than 189 million francs. In less than nine years it contracted further debts of 575 million. With these huge funds, the colony began to execute Vogel's plan. Undertaking governmental projects were the major activities between 1870 and 1880 and will be described in some detail, illustrated by official statistics.

The first project was to develop a post and telegraph service. A postal service was introduced about 1860, when New Zealand issued its own stamps, similar to Britain's. Initially, the service existed only in towns and provincial centres. Later it was set up in European towns, villages and settlements which had roading, in both the North and South Islands. As well, a weekly mail steamer served towns. A fortnightly service was also set up with Australia, which became a weekly service in 1872. By 1862 there was a monthly service to Europe via Australia and Suez. In 1872 another monthly service from New Zealand to San Francisco was established. It was connected by rail to New York and thence by sea to England. Of the two services, the latter provides a faster service to England.

The San Francisco Company selected to transport European luggage did not fulfil its contract and in 1876 Australia and New Zealand hired another company to carry mail via America. The colony paid 700,000 francs a year for the service and 500,000 for the Suez route. In 1884 the Union Company, which for some time had provided the coastal Australian mail service, was also awarded the contract to carry mail to San Francisco. It continues up to the present to have a monopoly of the sea postal service. In the same year, 1884, another monthly postal service was created, via Cape Horn and Rio de Janeiro to London. But colonists did not find it very useful as the service was irregular and not really needed. By 1880 colonial expenditure on its postal system rose to 3,533,950 francs and revenue was 3,757,900 francs, resulting in a net profit of 223,950 francs.

Postal services were quickly followed by a telegraph network. By 1862 towns in both islands were able to communicate by telegraph. In 1866 an underwater cable was laid in Cook Strait connecting the whole country to Wellington, the capital. In 1875 work began on laying an underwater cable between Australia and New Zealand, separated by more than 1600 kilometres of sea. On 20 February the following year, telegraphic communication was opened between the antipodean colony and England. From then, even the tiniest European settlement had a post and telegraph service. By 1880 the New Zealand telegraph network was little less than 6000 kilometres, and every year new post offices are being opened. In 1885 inland settlements were connected by telegraph, while towns could boast of telephone services. Up to the present, however, costs exceed revenue, and there is a justifiable fear that they will never make a profit.

4. Once 25 million francs was approved to bring farm workers and labourers into New Zealand from Europe, Vogel and his colleagues got the scheme moving. The government's aim through immigration was to sell land for farming and thus make money to increase the colony's population.

The scheme's conditions were: 1. Emigrants to New Zealand would be given free passage by the government. 2. On arrival, families would be allocated twenty acres, with the option of buying them within two years at 25 francs an acre. 3. They would receive paid employment as roadbuilders to enable them to make a living, until their land could support them.

The New Zealand government established three kinds of emigration agents under the overall direction of Vogel and its agent general in London, Dr Featherstone: those appointed by the government, and others appointed by the agent general for the United Kingdom and Northern Europe. Several agents, including Protestant ministers, were sent from New Zealand to England, to encourage as many people as possible to migrate. Besides having all their travel costs reimbursed, they received an annual commission of between 6250 and 7500 francs. Some received even more. A further 120 representatives were appointed throughout England by the agent general. They were to recruit emigrants under the following conditions: 1. All their travel costs to find emigrants would be reimbursed by the colony. 2. They would receive 12.5 francs for every married man and marriageable woman they recruited for migration. 3. For all other migrants, they would receive 6.25 francs. 4. They were to explain to migrants that their food and travel costs would be paid for by the colony. Local trading companies were chosen as emigration agents for Germany, Denmark, Sweden and Norway, with the agreement that they would receive 25 francs for every emigrant they recruited for New Zealand.[11]

Imagine the far-fetched stories the band of self-interested agents spread about New Zealand's beauty and prosperity. They described it as a land flowing with milk and honey, unbelievably rich, abundant in gold and ripe for the picking. For nearly a decade Northern Europe was bombarded with such excessive claims about the great colony and people's minds were dazzled with the prospect of unheard-of wealth and wonders in the antipodean paradise.

Many migrants were credulous country folk eager for a better life. They allowed themselves to be deceived by venal agents' nonsense. Others came because they could not make a living in their own country. A great number of them, however, were the dregs of English and German society. They were out of work, idlers, prostitutes, criminals and people who did not want to do an honest day's work. The colony was meant to wax rich and prosper with their ilk.

By 1873 the colonial government realised that of the 40,000 emigrants who had arrived up till then, very few were or wanted to be farmers. In order to recruit a better class of person, it decided to give every married man or family member, besides their free passage, thirty acres for a home. But even this measure failed to create farming communities, because arable and accessible land in the districts had already been taken by government employees or their friends, and migrants had to accept what was left over, or land hundreds of kilometres from habitation.

Several migration agents, especially in Germany, far from being satisfied with their fat fees from the colonial government, heartlessly used ruses and tricks to inveigle money from emigrants themselves. They asked some of them for a fee for obtaining their free passage from the agent general. They gave others to understand that they themselves had to pay half the cost of their passage. Still others were requested to pay a quarter of the costs. The wretches often had no means of support and they gave the little they had, begging them to be content with that, as it was all they had. Exhibiting great compassion, the agents pocketed the money and promised to obtain their passage to New Zealand without any further cost. This is no exaggeration. 'On 24 November 1873 in Parliament, Vogel publicly accused the same agents of corruption.'[12] And in Parliament various MPs also denounced them not so much for their mistreatment of emigrants, as for their devouring of huge amounts of money at New Zealand's expense.[13]

The 25 million set aside for emigration was soon gobbled up by all who could greedily dip their hands into the colonial purse. To gain more migrants, New Zealand had to go further into debt. From 1870 to 1880, the colony spent nearly 80 million francs on emigration. This enormous expenditure brought in 101,096 immigrants, whose nationalities are as follows: English, 51,400; Irish, 25,311; Scots, 16,825; Germans, 3038; Danes, 1955; Norwegians, 703. Other nationalities selected in England and Germany: Italians, 312; French, 284; other nationalities, 582.

5. There are two kinds of emigration: temporary and permanent. Many emigrants belong to the first category, leaving their family in their home country and returning later. They will not be discussed here. Permanent emigrants are those who leave their home country forever, seeking an adoptive motherland to improve their circumstances. Permanent emigration is of two kinds: collective and random, and there is a vast difference between them. Collective emigration describes a group of people having the same objective, to settle in a new homeland and build settlements similar to the ones left behind in their native country. This kind of migration rarely occurs, but in our opinion is the one to be recommended. Random emigration occurs when people in dribs and drabs, and with no common goal, go to one town, settlement or another, and mix with the locals seeking work and their fortune. This is practically the only kind of migration which occurs these days.

Much has been written and discussed about the best way to organise permanent emigration from the Old World to the New, and many economists and scholars have written papers and treatises on the subject. There is no doubting their good intentions to solve the difficult problem. In our opinion, their proposals are often good in theory but impractical. Emigrants' travel arrangements are given considerable attention and agents ensure that there will be assistance and work for them in New Zealand before their departure. But this is paltry compared to what needs to be done after their emigration.

When they reach the New World, migrants still need economic and moral protection. Economic protection consists in checking employers offering them work, to ensure that migrants get fair play and are not exploited. Moral protection consists in seeing that Catholic emigrants stay strong in practising the faith of their fathers, live good Christian lives and avoid the attractions of vice. If support and moral guidance are not available, Protestants, libertines and rogues who infest the world will divert them from the path of righteousness and destroy them soul and body. Moral and economic protection cannot be exercised on single migrants. Since they have no fixed abode, but wander from district to district to make a living, there is nothing to hold them to one place. Practically speaking, they are homeless and deprived of a homeland.

Furthermore, left to their own devices, with reasonable wages at their disposal, once they have provided for their daily necessities they use the rest of their money for personal pleasure and slowly start down the road to ruin. Catholic migrants often settle among people with different customs and religion. They have no fixed abode to help them feel settled. They spend their daily wages with no thought for the future. There is no one to guide their stumbling footsteps. Many, if they do not completely abandon their faith, lose interest in it and become loose-living. Hence, random migration is doomed to fail. In our opinion, there is no practical, effective remedy for these evils because it is impossible to guide people who are scattered and frequently change their abode.

This is generally the complaint made by Catholic missionaries in the New World and in British colonies concerning Latin migrants, because after devoutly practising their faith in the first months, slowly they become neglectful. In the end, a good many stop going to church. It is thus evident that random emigration, as presently practised, is considerably spiritually and materially damaging to the majority of migrants.

6. Three elements, not included in present migration schemes, are needed to make emigration worthwhile and effective: 1. ensuring that migrants can own the land they work. 2. being settled in a fixed location, previously selected. 3. staying in the same area and not moving about. These are the characteristics of collective emigration, whereby a given group of migrants travel together and take possession of a new area in a distant colony.

To enable migrants to have a sense of security and permanence, it is not enough to have work. They need land. Workers, especially the many farmers who migrate, feel very attached to land. If they emigrate it is an indication that either they do not own any land or the little they have is insufficient to support their family. When a migrant eventually owns his own home and plot of land to support himself and his family, he becomes emotionally attached and committed to it. As he rests up in his old age, having secured a future for his children, he enjoys saving, nurturing a sense of security, family unity and decency. He is a man who feels settled, devoted to his family and attached to his new chosen home.

Owning land naturally incorporates the other two requisites of collective emigration: settling in a determined area and having a fixed abode. This gives practical protection to individuals and families as well as meeting their moral, material and economic needs. It is equally important for them to have priests of their own nationality attending to their well-being. Thus migrants of the same nationality and settled in the same area retain their language, habits and customs and they can feel as though they have not left their own country.

It could be said that this all sounds fine, but how can collective emigration be put into practice? The emigrant does not have the means to buy land. If he did, he would buy land in his own country and he would not consider migrating.

It is very true that in general migrants do not have the means to buy property. However, in our opinion, our plan is the only one feasible. In the New World, in numerous colonies, in Asia and in South Africa, there are still huge areas of arable land in healthy climes which are totally or nearly uninhabited. Some of these empty areas have been abandoned for lack of manpower to farm them. They can easily be obtained from their respective governments for nothing or a token amount, providing planned and permanent colonisation is established. Governments would stand to be practically advantaged from agricultural produce and an increased farming and industrial population.

In our view, there would be two ways of making the plan work. The first would be for prominent members of the Catholic laity to establish an emigration company, with sufficient capital to operate it. The company would appoint able, responsible people to find arable, healthy areas in the New World or elsewhere. Huge tracts of low-cost land would be needed for emigrants. The company would give migrants the means to build adequate housing. They would have to pay back the cost of the house and land at low interest within ten years, starting from the third year of emigration. Travel costs and farming equipment would be the onus of migrants. After completing their payment by the end of ten years or earlier, the company would give legal title to the head of the family or single adult. If married, he would not be able to mortgage or sell the property without his wife's consent, or place any impediment upon the property. It would be bequeathed to his children and their offspring, to prevent usurers and cheats breaking up the family unit.

The second scheme, which does not have any commercial basis, seems more feasible. A Catholic emigration society would be established, supported by donations enabling it to carry out its philanthropic mission. The society's managers would be bishops and distinguished members of the Catholic laity. Bishops who were residents of the New World and colonial territories would officially represent the society overseas (outside Europe). They would send reports to the central directorate regarding suitable places for colonisation with respect to climate, soil, communication and links between centres. Once a decision was made, bishops would negotiate with governments and landowners a minimum price for land to be reserved for migrants, building requirements, method of land purchase and paying back construction costs, so that migrants would not suffer financially. As guarantee of payment, the state or colony would maintain right of ownership of land and property until payment was settled. Migrants who met the requirements would be given legal title to their property. People who failed to make payments would pay an annual rent until full payment was made.

Prospective emigrants would need to meet the following conditions: 1. Families wishing to migrate would need the society board's approval. 2. Emigrants would have to pay travel expenses, including food, and the society would determine date of departure and means of transport. 3. Heads of families would have the right to twenty hectares. Single males not attached to their family would be excluded. Adult family members would have the right to ten hectares, should they later leave their family. 4. Legal title would not be given until full payment was made for house and land. 5. For the first two or three years emigrants would not be required to make payments. In the following eight or ten years they would pay the government the price agreed for their land and home in so many annual amounts. 6. Colonists' legal titles given when full payment was made would stipulate that neither the land, house, chattels or farming equipment could be mortgaged or encumbered. A husband could not sell without his wife's agreement and in the case of the parents' death, the property would be kept for the children subject to the same conditions, until the youngest child had grown up. 7. If a colonist did not pay the agreed price he would forfeit his right to the property and be obliged to leave his farm, or pay an annual fee until he met it. 8. In every district, land would be reserved for the construction and future endowment of churches, convents, schools and charitable organisations which could initially be set up provisionally until they were fully equipped.

In our view this would be the most practical scheme for organising permanent migration and to ensure that migrants fulfilled religious, moral and social requirements. It might be argued that governments approached to accept emigrants might not be interested. On the contrary, we are convinced that they would be very pleased to have honest, law-abiding, hard-working farmers in their countries instead of dissolute, idle migrants. Governments would welcome the scheme and support it fully, knowing that it would be as much to their advantage and suited to their needs as to the emigrants. The United States, Canada, Australia and nearly all Anglo-Saxon colonies have had for some time a homestead scheme for workers and farmers similar to our proposal.

7. The New Zealand government not only recklessly launched into promoting emigration, as already mentioned, but also embarked on costly public works. In 1870 Parliament approved a debt of 125 million francs and in the following years approved further debts amounting to 325 million. The 125 voted in 1870 was to be spent as follows: 50 million for railway works; 25 million for emigration; another 25 million for colonial defence; 10 million for roading, bridges, etc; 6,500,000 for drainage and providing water for gold-mining; and the remaining 8,500,000 to buy Maori land and extend the telegraph network and for other minor works.

Road and bridge construction and establishing communication links between districts were quickly undertaken throughout the colony. When the ten million was spent, more money was borrowed so that work could continue. One of the public works deserving mention is Parliament Buildings in Wellington (see next page). Three large buildings were joined to form a spacious four-storey edifice. It has no artistic merit to attract a foreigner's eye. But it does have the distinction of being entirely wooden, including the roof and exterior walls. Apart from housing MPs and the Legislative Council, most of the other offices are for government officials and various ministries. It is the largest wooden building in the world and was built of impermanent material because of the frequent earthquakes which occur in the country.

State railways were begun in 1872 and construction continued feverishly over the following years. Because the colony is currently facing major financial difficulties, it has decided to slow down the railway construction programme. Julius Vogel was the principal instigator of large-scale public works, promoting them like a despotic godfather and his ministerial colleagues let him have free rein. When in 1870 he went to England he immediately made contracts with Jewish and Freemason bankers and entrepreneurs to provide capital for colonial railway construction, and he committed the colony to meet annual interest payments of five per cent. It is somewhat droll that it was not until 1872 that it became known that the railways contracts signed in London in 1870 were for 100 million francs, even though Parliament had authorised only 50 million.[14]

Contractors not only sent engines, tracks and other mechanical equipment from England, but also wooden coaches and 5000 construction workers. In four years, up to the end of 1875, more than 870 kilometres of track were laid. By 1880 there were more than 2000 kilometres, laid at a cost of 290 million. Two thirds of track were in the South Island and a third in the North Island. After 1880 colonists' enthusiasm for railways greatly diminished, and money was spent only on completing vital lines. By 1887 there were 2732 kilometres of

Parliament buildings, built entirely of wood, Wellington.

track and the colony had spent just under 400 million on them.

If the government had kept to Parliament's decision in 1870, New Zealand would have been far less in debt and perhaps enjoying considerable profit. Parliament that year gave approval for just two railway lines; one between Auckland and Wellington, and the other from Nelson to Bluff at the bottom of the South Island, totalling 1200 kilometres of track. But the people in charge changed the plan and had lines and tracks built through their and their cronies' vast holdings, to greatly increase the value of their properties.

Colonial railway carriages are very basic and there are only first and second class, which are less comfortable than second and third class in Europe. Fares are much higher than in Europe. Nothing has been spent on guards, protective railing or barriers along routes. And they still do not pay their way. According to official information, New Zealand railways, taking consideration of maintenance and service costs, are only able to pay two and a half per cent of the annual interest bill and the government has to pay the other half to meet the five per cent annual interest for the original debt.

From 1880 many colonists recommended that the colonial government sell the railways to a private company. But what company would want them, considering the likelihood of losing money? The government sails along, saying that when the network is completed, things will improve. In our view, that is wishful thinking and any improvement is unlikely for many years to come.

8. While government ministers vigorously pursued their grandiose public works schemes, burdening the colony with enormous debt, at the beginning of 1873 the British government transferred Bowen to be Governor of Victoria, an Australian colony, informing him that he would be replaced by Sir James Ferguson, then Governor of South Australia. But Bowen remained in New Zealand until the beginning of June. In the meantime, the colony was governed by the country's chief justice, Sir George Arney, as acting-governor. He held office for three months, until the arrival in Wellington of Sir James Ferguson, on 14 June 1873. He, however, governed for only a short period, announcing his resignation the following year and leaving New Zealand in November. On 3 December 1874, he was replaced by Lord Normanby.

At the beginning of 1875 Auckland citizens elected the well-known Sir George Grey as provincial superintendent. Shortly afterwards he was also elected to Parliament. He quickly realised that positive results could not be achieved in Parliament, because members were motivated and consumed by *auri sacra fames*. Sir George Grey was an erudite man, a distinguished speaker and a gracious gentleman. He was also very popular because he was universally acknowledged to be one of the few not implicated in Maori land exploitation or embezzlement of public funds. In Parliament he tried to repair the harm he had done as governor to the natives between 1861 and 1867, but his efforts were fruitless in obtaining even a modicum of justice for them. And many of his fellow MPs often betrayed him, selling themselves to the opposition.

After governing New Zealand for five years, on 21 February 1879 Lord Normanby was sent by the British government to govern the colony of South Australia. He was replaced by Sir Hercules Robinson. Until his arrival, New Zealand was governed by the colony's chief justice, James Prendergast, as acting-governor. He was a bitter enemy of the Maori. 'His contemptuous scorn for the treaty of Waitangi and for the rights of Maori, who were British subjects, was clearly demonstrated by him when Government compensation for Maori heads was discussed.'[15] He had the gall to write that the Maori had no right to be treated humanely. And this man was the colony's chief judge! Justice had fallen into such disreputable hands!

Governor Sir Hercules Robinson reached New Zealand on 27 March 1879 and took up office the same day. In July that year he opened Parliament. He did not, however, remain long in the country. On 18 September 1880 the British government sent him to govern the Cape of Good Hope in South Africa. Sir Arthur Gordon, former Governor of Fiji in the Pacific Ocean, succeeded him.

9. Among public works approved by Parliament in 1872 was included colonial defence, aping the great European powers. They voted a loan of twenty-five million in order to put the country in an adequate state of defence, not against the Maori, but against attack from a foreign naval power, in case England was involved in fighting another country. But New Zealand's defence was, and is, a considerable problem, given the vast extent of its coastline. It would need not twenty-five but hundreds of millions which they did not have, to secure it. Parliament decided, therefore, first of all to reorganise the colonial army by reducing its size and changing its structure, leaving the rest to later. The twenty-five million was raised and then spent without achieving the desired defence goal. In 1871 the colonial army had 15,554 soldiers of whom 4263 were militia men or pensioned soldiers, 6568 volunteers, 723 constable and 4000 native allies. By 1880 the army was reduced to 1481 constables and 7200 volunteers, totalling 8681 armed men.

For many years New Zealand had two voluntary army corps, because like the mother country it does not have compulsory military service. The first is the constabulary. Up till 1882 constables were divided into two groups: police and reservists. Both followed the same rules and regulations. Police were used to maintain law and order in towns and country districts. Reservists were to build public roads and were quartered in areas where there was fear of Maori conflict. In emergencies they acted as constables. The most able and promising constables join the secret police and are called detectives. By 1880 there were 1841 constables. From 1882, constables were reduced to one body, to maintain law and order in the colony. In 1887 the force was 502 strong.

Soldiers enlist voluntarily for not less than five years, after which they can renew their contract or leave the service. Their number is not fixed and varies according to the colony's needs. The government provides arms, ammunition and lodging even for married men, and from their pay they have to provide for their own food and uniform. Daily pay rates, varying according to the length of service, are between eight and eleven francs. In 1880 it cost more than seven million francs to maintain 1481 constables.

The volunteer corps uses various arms including field guns and naval cannon and incorporated cavalry units. They remain in their own district and take part in military manoeuvres from time to time. The government provides them with uniform, arms and ammunition. They wear their uniforms only on manoeuvres and when they are called up to defend the country or go to war. They remain in civilian clothes the rest of the time and go about their normal routine in their locality. Their strength varies between six and eight thousand. They receive no pay except when called up for defence. However, the government allocates two to three hundred thousand francs a year for volunteers. By 1887 the volunteer corps numbered 8029.

Colonial defence works were not begun until 1882, when there was a sudden fear of a Russian invasion if Russia went to war with England in Asia, particularly Afghanistan. The colonial government decided to build forts and batteries at the entrances of the four main ports, to protect Auckland, Wellington, Christchurch and Dunedin from enemy attack. The Auckland and Wellington forts were provided with electricity, to illuminate the area and detect ships entering the harbours. They also had supplies of mines and torpedoes to prevent enemy shipping getting through. A special army corps, the permanent militia, was formed to guard the forts and protect the colony. This body comprises artillerymen, engineers and naval personnel to service torpedoes. By 1887 there were 350 soldiers assigned to fort duties. They receive the same pay as constables.

10. Earlier we described how in 1853 New Zealand was divided into provinces, and their power extended to provide district legislation, under the governor's supervision. Superintendents and provincial councillors legislated, imposed taxes, approved borrowing and governed provinces as they saw fit. After 1860 the kind of people promoted to government and provincial councils were self-serving, fellow masons and their colleagues. Consequently Parliament was full of freemasons, fortune-seekers and speculators of every kind. Provincial councils were no better served. The majority of members were money-hungry bigots, bestowing their munificence on friends and colleagues, similar to the way Napoleon distributed other countries' crowns to his relatives. In spite of these abuses, the provincial ruling class preferred this kind of government, since it preserved their lucrative positions. Many of them were Members of Parliament as well as provincial councillors or superintendents.

Prime Minister Vogel had committed the country to a programme of public works, involving debts. To facilitate borrowing in London he needed to offer creditors land as guarantee. Government land was insufficient, so he turned his eye to provincial land and property. He decided to abolish provinces to make provincial holdings the government's. He made no mention of this plan before 1875 because he knew that the vast majority in Parliament would be opposed to their abolition. Vogel won members and superintendents' silence by giving them a huge, irresistible bribe of 37,500,000 francs previously designated by Parliament for railways. In 1875 he was thus able to obtain the abolition of the North Island provinces and the following year the South Island's, promising to replace them with improved local government by means of substantial funding through proposed district committees and borough councils.[16] If this was not blatant government corruption, what was? One should not be surprised, however. Sectarians are like Cerberus, insatiable in their greed.

Provinces were abolished and New Zealand was divided into sixty-two districts called counties, each having the right to send a member to Parliament, except for towns which could elect a member for every 10,000 inhabitants. By 1879 there were eighty-four colonial MPs, and four Maori members, as before. Each town and borough had a local body office dealing with local affairs and every county had a council and roading committee locally elected to deal with county and district matters. They had the power to impose taxes on business and trade, industry and property and to use the revenue to construct and maintain public roading and carry out other public works. The government agreed to subsidise half their costs. Local bodies were also allowed to borrow for public works, but the government would not act as guarantor.

The government now had all provincial land holdings and left local bodies and counties to impose taxes and tariffs for road works and communication links between the various districts, and for local works. Parliament's promised substantial subsidies to counties were reduced in practice to a government contribution of about a third of the costs, or approximately five million a year for the sixty-two counties. At present, excluding town roading and a few main transport routes through fertile lands and plains, other roading is scarce and inadequate. It will be many years before New Zealand has good district roading. It must be acknowledged, however, that counties are constantly trying to improve roading according to their limited financial resources.

11. The poor Maori race had to use its land to pay the cost of enriching the colonial government and a good many settlers. There has been earlier mention of exploitation from 1818 to 1840, and the government's exploitation from 1840 to 1860. As though this was not enough, a further period of exploitation was to follow. In 1862 the government renounced its pre-emption to buy Maori land, and allowed colonists to join in. Thus natives, besides having the rapacious

government at their throats, had to contend with a host of individual thieves robbing them with impunity.

It would be discreet to draw a veil over civilised Britons' abominable behaviour in New Zealand, stripping Maori of their land, but this would be a betrayal of truth and events. Nevertheless, only the briefest information will be given and the gentle reader who wishes to pursue the matter is referred to Parliamentary records.

Sir George Grey's 1865 proclamation, authorising the incautious and unjust confiscation of Maori land, stated 'All those who have remained and continue to remain our friends will retain full possession and enjoyment of their lands.' But these were empty words. Many such friends found themselves stripped of their patrimony. They complained and the government promised to see justice done, but nothing happened. On the contrary, they have continued to suffer further harm and depredation up to the present. Taiaroa, a Maori member, replying to a member in the House in 1876 said, 'I would rather be dead than be a living witness to the miseries and distress my people suffer because of the deceit and empty promises of lying Europeans. You have a saying, practise what you preach, but neither I nor my people have felt any benefit from Europeans.'[17] No member could contradict him, but it did not help Taiaroa obtain justice.

That same year Sir Donald MacLean, Minister of Maori Affairs, smugly announced to Parliament that, 'a fifth of the North Island (6,284,250 acres) had been bought by the Government for about eleven million francs.' Taking into account agents' fees of 80 centimes an acre and surveying fees, natives would have got less than 80 centimes a hectare for such a huge amount of land. How did they get the land? Karaitiana Takamoana, a native member, has the answer. In Parliament, in the same minister's presence, he stated: 'He (MacLean) bought vast amounts of Maori land for himself. He obtained his position (as Minister of Maori Affairs) through graft and corruption and he got hold of so much land through illegal, unfair sales.' Swanson, another member, addressing his colleagues in Parliament in 1881 said, 'I feel ashamed of the greed shown to get hold of land the natives still hold. And you talk to me about equal rights! Maori have been taxed, stripped and robbed enough.'

About 1850, on the outskirts of Dunedin, land was set aside as a native reserve. A few years later Otago Province took it over and leased it. For many years Maori demanded its restitution or fair compensation for it, to no avail. The natives went to court. The court connived with the government and ruled against the legitimate owners, hoping they would not have the money to pursue the matter further. But the Maori taxed their people and raised 25 thousand francs to appeal to the British Court. Otago Province was afraid of being sharply rebuked and negotiated a settlement. The natives were persuaded to accept 125 thousand francs, even though the land had been valued at nearly three million francs.

While the government and provinces robbed poor natives with impunity, many colonists did a lot worse. They first destroyed their physical health and mental well-being to make it easier to steal their land. In 1876, a member, Mr Travers explained to the House 'how a Napier chief was stripped of all his lands, worth ten million francs, by giving him raw spirits and a small handcart. When he was completely drunk, he was made to sign the deed of sale for his lands.' A colleague of Travers, Captain Russell, replied, 'You seem astonished. Console yourself that Napier swindlers don't rob natives as much as the Government does.' And Captain Fraser mentioned a little earlier that 'Europeans would never have got their 48,000 acres from the Maori, if they had not made them drunk first.'

Using similar means and tricks, many members and colonists, mostly long-standing masons, freely helped themselves to Maori land. And no one tried to put a stop to all their wrong-doing. Another fraud committed related to payment of land surveying fees. Maori were urged to have their land surveyed to be able to sell it, and being gullible they agreed. When it was done, the surveyor would request his fee. Because they could not pay they were summonsed and convicted. Their property was then sold by public auction and the creditor got possession of the land.

In 1873 in the House, Dr Pollen, a member and government agent, said that, 'he knew natives who had 30,000 acres surveyed. They were not able to pay the fee calculated at between 3700 and 5,000 francs for 30,000 acres (14,000 hectares). Their lands were sold at public auction to pay the surveyor. The Maori did not receive a penny and became dispossessed.'

Speaking before him, another member, Sheehan said 'that he could testify that on many occasions Maori land had only met surveying costs and nothing more,' and he continued, 'I can tell you that a certain chief had a vast area of his lands surveyed. The cost was actually 625 francs but the surveyor was allowed to charge 3,000 francs, and the vast estate is to be sold at auction to pay his bill.' There is no doubt that the scoundrel obtained the man's property for that amount. If this was not outrageous, what was?

12. The Anglo-Saxon race claims to be the supreme exemplar of civilisation and makes out that it is full of compassion for suffering humanity throughout the world. It constantly rails against the barbarity, real or imagined, of other peoples and nations. In practice, in its own domain it is no better than them. It is not concerned with the good of humanity, but its own advantage. In protesting about wrongs done by others, it seeks to conceal its own. Noble Ireland's children have been forced to scatter throughout the world. Australia's aboriginals have been practically exterminated. New Zealand Maori, denied justice, have been despicably robbed. They and so many other peoples subject to England confirm through their bloody history what we have described. It is laudable to plead on

behalf of suffering humanity, but the British are hypocrites because they do not practise compassion as rulers. They have no right to speak of inhumanity when they treat their own subjects and fellow men unjustly. They have no right to advise others and turn a deaf ear to just demands for fairness and justice. The following sad example will illustrate that a certain nation's humanity is nothing more than self-interest and refined barbarity.

In the latter half of 1871 news reached New Zealand that on the island of Nukapu in the Pacific, Patteson, an Anglican bishop and two native companions were barbarically murdered by islanders. Hearing of the atrocity, New Zealand, Australia and England were angered and hastened to seek revenge. What did investigations reveal? Why did Patteson meet such a grim fate? Information is found in New Zealand parliamentary records and in its petition to Queen Victoria. It asserted that Dr Patteson's death was due to the infamous slave trading carried out there, which was a disgrace to the British. They begged her to take appropriate measures 'to redress the wrongs done to the islanders, and redeem the good name of her subjects.'[18] It had been known for some time that British merchants were slave trading in the Pacific, but a discreet silence was maintained. It was too lucrative, like importing opium from British India into China! Patteson's death was needed to momentarily bring to people's attention the infamous trafficking.

Many years before, the British established vast sugar cane plantations in Queensland and other tropical areas of Australia. Planters were not happy about paying high costs for European labour. To reduce expenses they decided to bring in cheap Pacific Island labour to work their plantations. This was the origin of the trade in Pacific Islanders. Several British ships scoured the South Pacific. Sometimes they flew the British flag and sometimes another to better conceal their crimes. Poor Kanaks (natives) were either enticed on board or taken by force by the pirates. Some natives agreed to work in plantations for three months. The rogues changed the contract to read three years. When the ships were loaded their human cargo was taken to Australia. Traders were paid handsomely by plantation owners who treated their workers like slaves.

Once Kanaks realised what was going on, they refused to go anywhere near the wicked traders or go on board. The traders then used even more infamous ways to carry out their operation. When ships reached an island, natives were enticed to approach to barter for food. The wretches paddled out but did not go on board.

When a large number had come out the slavers suddenly threw heavy weights into their canoes, sinking them immediately. Fearing drowning, the poor natives had no option but to allow themselves to be taken on board. Those who tried to swim away were shot dead. If the haul, as they called it, was insufficient, they went to another part of the island and did the same thing. The wretches on board were treated worse than animals. If they dared to resist, they were killed without mercy. Ships loaded with this merchandise went to Australia and elsewhere and sold their cargo to plantation owners.[19]

Following the general outcry over Dr Patteson's murder, the British government passed a law prohibiting such trading and ordered Australia's Commodore Starling to suppress the abominable trafficking which had grown to alarming proportions. But these stern measures were ineffectual because they were not accompanied by the means to make them work, namely, confiscation of ships and gallows for the culprits. Colonial governments did not care to intervene, the British government was too far away, and colonial officials closed a blind eye. Thus the iniquitous trade continues, if more secretively. We have met some of these civilised English traders who have described their activities between 1877 and 1884. They are meant to be proud examples of British civilisation!

13. Masonry had its origins in the London ghetto at the beginning of the last century and was intended to eradicate Christianity wherever possible. It was transplanted to New Zealand in 1859. It began by destroying the little sense of social responsibility that existed in the country up to 1860. After a number of upheavals, Parliament became dominated by adventurers and opportunists, the majority of whom blindly obeyed the secretive sect. Masonic leaders continued on their ruinous course, plunging the country into enormous debt in order to enrich themselves and their members by undertaking hugely expensive public works. Many of these served private interests, fuelled by graft and corruption. As if this were not enough, masons wished to crown their efforts by gifting New Zealand with their wholly anti-Christian and atheistic education system, in order to rob the youth of the country of faith and morality. Sycophantic MPs and members of the Legislative Council, many of whom were masonic members or sympathisers, imitating masonic European governments, sanctioned this grotesque evil. Sir Julius Vogel must be given credit for this further insult to parents' sacred rights and duties, for it was he who manipulated his colonial parliamentary disciples.

When colonisation began in New Zealand, children's education (except Maori children, who were taught by missionaries and catechists to read, write and count) was not under state control, because the number of European children was very small and they were scattered throughout the country. From 1843 Catholic missionaries began teaching children and soon afterwards nuns came to the colony, offering teaching to European and native children. The number of migrants and children began to grow and from 1846 many private schools sprang up. From 1850 local schools and then district schools were founded. Nelson set up the first one in 1855. From 1865 to 1868 secondary and trade schools were established in provincial main towns, that is, Dunedin, Christchurch, Nelson, Wellington and Auckland.

In areas where provinces did not subsidise schools, boroughs determined that parents send their children to local or private schools. Every adult in the district had to pay sixty-three centimes a week for local schooling. Those who sent their children to private schools paid the tax to their teachers and not to the borough, which was a sensible arrangement. People were therefore free to send their children to the school of their choice, either public or private. In both cases they had to pay towards teachers' costs and school maintenance.

Since colonists had to pay for their children's education, they were not keen on local and district schools, which were recognised as hot beds of corruption. They preferred to send them to private schools, where they received a better scholastic and moral education. Catholic schools were pre-eminent, particularly those run by brothers and nuns. Many Protestants patronised them. This education system continued until 1877. The colonial masonic government then made private schools fend for themselves and took over responsibility for providing free colonial schooling. In 1869 Parliament sanctioned the establishment of a university, which was later approved by the British government. In 1875 the Queen granted the University of New Zealand the privilege of conferring degrees which would be recognised throughout the Empire.

Secret orders were sent by the chief masons in London to their New Zealand confreres to adapt to the times and follow the example of anti-Christian European governments. Arrogant, cocksure local masons immediately wanted to endow the country with their education system. State education, as it was known, excluded God, religion and Christian morality. Masons' real but undisclosed aims were first, to corrupt childrens' minds and hearts, encouraging laxity and immorality; and second, to provide plum administrative positions to many of their colleagues, friends and associates.

In 1873 Vogel and his subordinates succeeded in having their new education bill introduced to Parliament. In spite of many Catholics' and Protestant members' opposition, they succeeded in having it approved by the House. The more perspicacious Legislative Council, however, rejected it. Masons were not disconcerted by this rebuff and began to prepare their ground better. They had a number of masonic members appointed by the governor and in 1877 they again presented their state education bill to Parliament. Several members, appreciating the new system's evils, proposed that private schools be subsidised and placed on an equal footing with government schools. But because this proposal was contrary to masons' aims, it was rejected.

Dr Grace, a Catholic member, proposed that at least the taxes Catholics would have to pay with the passing of the new education bill, be devolved as a private school subsidy because Catholics could not, in conscience, accept state education. He very clearly argued that it would be a flagrant miscarriage of justice if Catholics were forced by paying taxes to provide an education system that in their view was pernicious. Dr Grace represented Catholicism and true

Christianity in protesting vehemently against the unfairness of the Education Bill, by which Catholics particularly would be forced not only to pay for their own schools but also for the State's, from which, in conscience, they had to deny themselves access. Parliament and the Legislative Council were now full of anti-clerical masons and paid no heed to the wrongs and injustices that would arise for Catholics. They approved the unfair bill which provided for a 'Free, secular and compulsory education.'

State education was free; that is, it was available to all, free of charge. This was nothing more than a sham, because contributors had to fund it. It was secular, that is, liberal and atheistic. It was also compulsory, because parents who did not send their children to either state or private schools would be fined or suffer some other penalty. The bill's title smacked not a little of tyranny. Those gentlemen, who saw themselves as the country's fathers and saviours, were not really concerned if people were tyrannised.

The curriculum's description began, 'In state schools it is strictly forbidden to teach religion of any kind.' It is impossible to impart knowledge without any mention of religion. In any field of learning one must needs encounter God, the Supreme Being, Creator of all things, and his attributes. Not to teach religion is to deny God and his manifestations. Thus it is false to provide education without including religion. But anti-clerical masonic parliamentarians boasted of man's link to apes and other beasts.

Thus, their education system is in perfect harmony with their evil intentions. Good, devout Protestants and Catholics sought justice, but their appeals and protests achieved nothing. The pestilential, anti-Christian education system continued and continues to be colonial masons' and most Parliamentarians' prize possession.

Scarcely was the new education bill approved than schools were rapidly built everywhere: in towns, suburbs, settlements and in the country. Teachers, all eminently qualified, appeared from nowhere, eager to feather their nests. Soon the pot of gold was empty and the colony was on the brink of ruin. Masons at every level cried out that the state education system, the greatest triumph of human progress, should be saved at all cost. It was preserved by increased taxation and borrowing millions more.

In every former province, there is an education board, comprising many members including inspectors, nearly all creatures of masonry. They have complete control of all matters regarding local schooling and teaching. Every county in turn has an education committee supervising local education. Official state education statistics for 1880, or three years after approval of the system, are as follows: State schools, 836 attended by 64,407 children; 958 male teachers, 1142 female teachers; education costs, ten million francs. Private schools, mostly Catholic; in 1879 there were 257 attended by 10,236 children.

14. The lamentable effects of this education system are evident to every settler. They can be summarised under four main points:

1. Some young people leaving school, especially secondary school, intend to become state school teachers. If they are not irreligious or atheistic, they are certainly uninterested in religion. It could not be otherwise because that is the example their teachers have set them.

2. It is often the case that when males and females mix together in the same school, familiarity between the sexes develops. This encourages bad habits and loose behaviour. Impressionable youths find themselves lured into temptation before they even know it. Some poor children as a result end up in reformatories, several of which exist in New Zealand.

3. Without religion in schools, young people become arrogant and insubordinate. Fed a diet of geography, biased modern history, natural history, physics and botany, their ingenuous minds are filled with grandiose and starry ideas and they become incredibly conceited. These blinded youths consider themselves superior and no longer listen to their parents or friends. They are convinced that they know more than anyone else and are free to do what they want.

4. When their schooling is over, youths in general do not want to work as farmers or in a trade, considering such work beneath them. They aspire to clerical or government employment, or to become primary or secondary school teachers. Few, however, succeed in finding such employment. Thus nearly all those left behind become lazy layabouts, a constant public nuisance and bother to honest citizens, women and the elderly. People in towns and suburbs complain about them as they are always getting into mischief. A special word, larrikins, has been coined to describe them. There are complaints in newspapers about them and every one is fed up but the government, well aware of the problem, remains silent.

If girls do not get up to the same mischief as boys, as described above, they become irresponsible in their own way, showing a surliness and unwillingness to do domestic duties and chores appropriate to their sex. How can they become mothers when they think of nothing but pleasure and appearances? The unhappy state of New Zealand education forces us to conclude that either the education system needs to be changed radically or the colony will become a hotbed of disbelievers and hedonists.

New Zealand's state education has been created by the same anti-clerical forces which have controlled many European states, including poor Italy. The same disastrous effects are felt in New Zealand as elsewhere; the false values of anti-Christian education at a local and national level. The infamous Jewish-masonic clique arrogantly lauds its control, determined to destroy the wonderful benefits of eighteen centuries of European Christian civilisation. It wants to eradicate the contribution to culture of religion, morality, modesty and especially Catholicism which recognises Christ as God. It has sworn an implacable, eternal hatred for it, intending to restore to the world a reign of falsehood, slavery and paganism. It would re-instate Satan, the Devil himself, as leader and guide of a future pagan society.

In decadent European society, masons gain new ground every day over impressionable, abandoned youth. Vice is triumphant and spreads everywhere. Virtue is outlawed, scorned and mocked. Catholicism is despised, derided, cursed and assailed shamelessly. Jesus who saved the world from its abominations and degradations is reviled and reduced to the level of Socrates! The present generation, given a modern education, grows up arrogant, rebellious and dissolute. The majority think only of luxury, soft living, entertainment, thrills and pleasure. Most worship the golden calf and what money can buy, because everything can be bought, including one's conscience. If people do not wake up from this profound lethargy and shake off the oppressive yoke of masonry, society will soon revert to loathsome paganism and anarchy, and the world will be reduced to ruin. One does not need to be a prophet or be particularly keen-sighted. A grain of common sense would reveal to even the most dim-witted the deplorable consequences of masons' atheistic, libertine education system. As you sow, so shall you reap.

15. According to the 1868 census the native population of New Zealand was 38,517 people. Later that figure was found to be wrong because the census was not completed owing to fierce fighting between Maori and European settlers. Fleeing Maori hid in dense remote forests and were neither searched for or discovered by natives carrying out the census. When peace was restored in 1872, Maori fugitives returned to their villages and a census could be carried out with greater accuracy.

In fact, the 1874 natives' census showed that in spite of the many deaths through the ten years fighting, starvation and privation, the population was still 46,016.

The native population, instead of growing, is declining steadily. In the 1881 census there were no more than 44,099. In seven years there was a decline of 1917 people. It is obvious from these figures that the Maori race is destined to disappear altogether, sooner or later. The rapid decline is due to three evils introduced by the British into the country, namely, drunkenness, immorality and excessive smoking, hastening Maoris' death.

On 3 April 1881 the New Zealand European population was 489,702. Of these, 192,776 were living in the North Island, 296,684 in the South Island and 242 in the Chathams. Included in these figures are 2044 half-castes or Pakeha-

Maori. They were children of European fathers and Maori mothers. Statistics for religious affiliation are: Protestants, comprising some seventy different denominations, 385,662. The main seven denominations comprised: Anglicans or Episcopalians, 200,816, Presbyterians, 113,038, Methodists, 39,544, Baptists, 11,476, Independents, 6699, Lutherans, 5793, Mormons, 271, other dissident sects, 8025. According to the same official census there were 67,039 Catholics. There were also seven Muslims, 1536 Jews, and 5004 Chinese pagans. The official census recorded that there were 13,978 free-thinkers, 7357 who did not belong to a religious denomination, 7847 who made no declaration of religion, and 272 professed non-believers or atheists. The last four categories can be grouped together as an expression of materialism and free-thinking. They number 30,454.* This is what Protestantism and masonry produce.

Colonial revenue in 1879 was 78,372,625 francs and expenditure was 96,125,900. In 1880 imports into New Zealand were valued at 154,050,275 francs and exports 158,817,300 francs. The colony's debt was 750 million francs.

In 1880 European livestock in New Zealand was as follows: horses, 137,768; cattle, 578,430; sheep, 13,069,338; pigs, 207,337.

---

* Translator's note: Actually, 29,454.

Chapter Fourteen

Exploitation of Natives From 1881 to 1893

SUMMARY. – 1. Injustices against Maori. – 2. Prophet Te Whiti. – 3. Prophet's and followers' capture. – 4. Te Whiti's triumph; Government's humiliation. – 5. Peace negotiations between government and King Tawhiao. – 6. Monsignor Steins, Bishop of Auckland. The Benedictine Fathers in New Zealand. – 7. New governors; governors and the people. – 8. Unsuccessful Maori appeal to Queen of England. – 9. Monsignor Luck, Bishop of Auckland. Destruction of St Benedict's church. Monsignor Fines' death. – 10. Te Kooti's fate; Te Whiti's re-imprisonment. – 11. Australasian ecclesiastic congress. Christchurch diocese. – 12. Colonial statistics. – 13. Catholic Maori mission. – 14. Evaluation of European religious practice. – 15. Catholic diocesan statistics. – 16. Evaluation of Maori religion and morality. – 17. Material progress and seeds of moral decline; fears for the future.

1. 'This period of our history will be seen by our children as a sorry testimony of the strong trampling on the rights of the weak' lamented Hutchinson, an MP, in Parliament in 1882, and he was supported by colleagues.[1] His comment was an accurate summary of the history of Maori and European interaction in New Zealand. His pitiable cry, however, had no effect on making the great majority of settlers and the government re-examine their sense of humanity and justice towards the Maori. Colonists were as keen as ever for the natives to disappear off the face of the earth or be blown into kingdom come. Then they could take all their lands, or at least get their hands on their farmland, and leave the Maori miserable, degraded and landless. From 1865 the government fully supported settlers' ambitions, as has been illustrated already, and will be further revealed in this chapter.

In spite of ten years' ferocious fighting, the Maori had not been exterminated. Nor were they dying off as quickly as anticipated. Colonists complained that native land was still indivisible and held in common by the tribe, making its removal a lengthy and difficult process. Captain Fraser, however, commented that 'Communal ownership was a very good thing, because without such a land ownership system Europeans long ago would have swallowed up all Maori land.'[2]

The legal fraternity had no qualms about joining with settlers in their rapaciousness and greed, sucking Maoris dry in the Native Land Courts. In 1882 in Parliament, Ngatata, a Maori MP, commented about this scourge, 'The Government made a grave mistake in admitting lawyers to Native Land Courts. As soon as they were admitted, Maori were skinned by them. Maori were a lot better off when they were not involved; and I hope the Government will find a way to close the Courts' doors in these robbers faces. They pour into every session no matter how remote to get rich at the natives' expense.'[3]

But the colonial government, partly encouraged by greedy settlers, was contemplating an even worse example of exploitation. For some time it had had its eye on the fertile plains of Waimate in Taranaki and was intent on getting them at any cost. The problem was it had to deal with natives determined to die rather than be unjustly stripped of their land. When Governor Grey in 1865 proclaimed the confiscation of Taranaki land, he specifically excluded 'all the property of allies and non-belligerent natives.' And he further promised 'restitution of their property to those who had taken part in the insurrection, or that they be given land in the same area, if they surrendered within a reasonable period.' The government, however, promised settlers they could keep land confiscated in southern Taranaki, between Waitara and Waingongoro river. When the war ended in 1869, European and native allies returned to settle. When some rebels, who had surrendered following the proclamation's promises, went to reoccupy their land, settlers shot the men down, and arrested and deported their wives.

Regarding northern Taranaki, the Waimate and Parihaka plains, opposite Cape Taranaki, between the Waingongoro and Stoney rivers, the colonial government through MacLean, Minister of Maori Affairs, renounced any confiscation, reserving the area for the Maori. It not only allowed natives, whether friendly or rebels who had surrendered, including chief Titokowaru, to reoccupy their lands, but strongly urged them to do so, saying that they would suffer no harm.[4] Natives accepted this declaration. They settled on the plains and also welcomed their compatriots who had been forcibly expelled from southern Taranaki. To illustrate the fact that natives were reinstated in full possession of their lands between 1872 and 1875 MacLean, the government minister, bought 186,000 acres in the area from the Ngatiruanui tribe.[5]

For ten years the government kept its promises to natives, letting them enjoy their land in peace. However, in 1877 it needed money and remembered that the 1865 proclamation of confiscation had not been officially revoked. Without discussing the matter with the Maori or reserving any land for their survival, it ordered all the fertile land to be surveyed and sold. Surveying began immediately, but natives opposed it peacefully. They demanded the observance of the proclamation's conditions and the government's promises to them. Atkinson's government fell shortly afterwards and it was succeeded by Sir George Grey's. He knew that the government's claims were unjust and suspended the surveying and sale of land, assuring the natives that he would keep the promises made earlier by MacLean. But the following year Grey and Sheehan lost power and were replaced by Messrs Hall and Bryce. They immediately ordered the surveying to be continued, for roads to be built and all land confiscated. Maori were extremely distressed at this manifest injustice and sought Te Whiti's advice. He told them to remain calm, not to arm themselves, but to bear insults stoically and then they would come to no harm. They carefully followed the prophet's counsel.

2. Te Whiti, known as the oracle of Parihaka, has played a great part in modern New Zealand history and is presently the settlers' most formidable enemy. It is, therefore, relevant to give a summary of his life and achievements. He was born about 1839, son of a minor chief who was also one of Taranaki's first Wesleyan catechists. He grew up in the shadow of Protestantism and learned much of the Bible by heart. He had regular features, was thickset and muscular, with a clear and powerful voice which could be heard all over his village. He was gifted with intelligence, eloquence and uncommon insight. He did not participate in the wars which devastated the country between 1860 and 1865, but he could not prevent most of his people throwing themselves into the struggle.

When in 1864 the Hauhau movement began he was one of the great prophet Te Ua's first disciples. When a new uprising in Taranaki occurred led by Titokowaru, Te Ua's successor, Te Whiti, who aspired to the same position, dissuaded his people from taking part. In 1869 Titokowaru was defeated by colonial troops and lost his aura of invincibility. Consequently the mantle of great prophet passed to Te Whiti. From then on his influence continued to spread throughout the district. He began to preach to the people who hastened to listen to his prophecies. He did not preach Hauhau doctrine but a curious mixture of mysticism he had concocted. For him, all religions are nonsense. Only his teaching represents the truth. He is a free-thinker and it is not clear whether he admits to God's existence. He is shrewd; never stating clearly what he thinks about religion. He is calm in the face of danger, sarcastic and quick-witted. He gives a convincing semblance of being inspired, declaring that he is the saviour of his people and ready to die for them. He jealously guards the prestige he has acquired and his followers believe him utterly, seeing him as an oracle.

Colonists describe him as stupid and crazy, but they are wrong. Te Whiti never showed himself in this light, especially when he peeled away European hypocrisy. He is far from crazy. In fact, he is so politically astute that he can outwit the whites. The following is an extract from one of his speeches at a public meeting attended also by Europeans: 'When I mention land, surveying, farmers, fields and other insignificant matters, reporters' pencils move with the speed of lightning (to record everything I say); but when I speak about spiritual matters they say that I am a raving lunatic! They are so keen on money that it seems that they are only interested in what will help them to get rich. Traders who get rich by using false weights and tawdry merchandise and other tricks to strip and rob their victims, men who steal Maori land and amass herds of sheep and cattle, people who extract the last penny from widows and orphans, enriching themselves, are considered decent and respectable. They pass by the humble seeker of truth without heeding or acknowledging him; etc.'

The shrewd, intelligent Te Whiti, noticed the incalculable moral and physical damage being caused to natives by Europeans plying them with alcohol, bribing them to get their land. He observed the idleness, drunkenness and other vices which were harming his people. He decided to establish defences to prevent their destruction. Using his considerable prestige, he assembled a great number of local Maori, forbidding them to use alcohol or to bring it in to Parihaka. He spoke strongly against his people being seduced by Pakeha money. He urged them to work, farm, build and be pacifist. The great majority of his listeners faithfully obeyed him. Drunkenness and accepting bribes which encouraged vice were abandoned. Soon the Waimate plains abounded in wheat, maize, potatoes and all kinds of vegetables, as well as large numbers of domestic animals. Order, comfort and peace reigned in the villages. Such was the man and the people the colonial government wished to plunder.

In April 1879, government agent Mackey* went to Te Whiti to talk him into agreeing with the government's wishes. The prophet told him, 'In accordance with MacLean and Parris, I ceded to the Government all the land between Waitotara and Waingongoro, and no more.' He asked the agent if he was authorised by the government to leave him and his people at least part of the land they still possessed. Mackey replied that he had no such authority. Te Whiti then said, 'By the way my lands are being surveyed I take it that you intend to strip me of everything and leave me naked.' The government paid no heed to his protests and despoliation continued.

Being unable to obtain justice, the prophet ordered his people to plough their fields to demonstrate their rights and prevent the surveying. But ploughmen were arrested by the constabulary. By the end of July 1879, when ploughing ceased, 180 Maori were imprisoned in New Plymouth and Wellington, where they languished for two years without trial. The government, aware of its arbitrary, unjust actions, feared that a judge would free them for not having committed a crime. It had Parliament pass iniquitous laws, allowing Taranaki Maori to be arrested simply on suspicion and held indefinitely without being charged or tried.

Natives had acted perfectly legally. It was the government which was unjust. Governor Gordon, writing to the British secretary of state, commented, 'In my opinion, the Maori are substantially in the right. Their actions have served simply to demonstrate their peaceful insistence on their right of occupation.'[6] But the prime minister and settlers did not share his point of view. They were furious at

---

* Translator's note: James Mackay (1831-1912), as McLean's agent, pursued a policy of alienating as much Maori land as possible. He was an official for whom 'the Treaty of Waitangi was a closed book'. (*New Zealand Dictionary of Biography*, 1990, p. 253.)

Te Whiti, prophet, Parihaka, 1880.

the natives' audacity, and threatened to annihilate them. They requested troops be levied to wipe out the innocent people. Bryce sent in 800 constables, hoping to provoke the Maori to take up arms, giving them a reason to massacre them. Te Whiti, however, urged his followers to have forbearance and to suffer insults and injustices peaceably, assuring them that they would win out and that if they took up arms, they were doomed. They followed their prophet's suggestions and were saved. Te Whiti demonstrated that he was more politically astute than any New Zealand politician, by not allowing his followers to break the law.

In the meantime, the government began surveying and road-building in

Waimate and Parihaka. When road construction reached cultivated land, the fences were pulled down and the roads were continued across natives' sown fields. They then repaired the fences to protect crops from animals, especially pigs, but they were arrested and the fences were pulled down again by constables. Other natives repaired the gaps and they in turn were arrested and the repairs demolished. The same thing happened about fifty times and 316 natives were seized and sent to prisons in the South Island, without trial. Eventually Maori closed the gaps with fencing wire and the government allowed it to remain to protect crops.

At that time the government had 800 constables on the scene and knew that at Parihaka there was only a handful of defenceless men with no guns or ammunition and that they were unsupported by the Maori King. Its intention was to use its overwhelming power to force the Maori to resist and then massacre them. But the natives obeyed Te Whiti, who told them not to resist and to endure the unjust provocation. Bryce and his associates were thus thwarted in their hopes. They still persisted, however, thinking that they would force the natives to resist by arresting the prophet himself and putting him in irons. They could not believe that his followers would stand by and let him be taken prisoner.

3. Governor Gordon was not the kind of man who would allow government ministers to commit such an awful deed. But they patiently bided their time. On 13 September 1880 the governor-general left for Fiji. In his absence, Judge Prendergast, a bitter enemy of the Maori, was acting as acting-governor. The government used him to carry out an unwarranted attack on Parihaka. They began by spreading false rumours about Te Whiti's supposedly war-mongering speeches and natives' arming, as if a revolt was imminent. A great number of volunteers enlisted throughout the country and 2000 men were sent to Parihaka. In Fiji Governor Gordon received newspapers and correspondence from his private secretary, revealing the New Zealand government's manipulation of the situation to provoke fighting. He cancelled his visit to other islands, and on 8 October he set sail for Wellington. At the same time a steamship left Fiji for Sydney (Australia). From there Gordon's impending arrival in Wellington was telegraphed.

When the unexpected news arrived on the morning of 19 October, the government set things in motion. At eight o'clock that evening, Prendergast summoned the cabinet and a proclamation was prepared for Te Whiti and his followers. They were ordered to obey the government or be treated as rebels and be attacked. The same evening many copies of the proclamation were printed and it appeared as a supplement in the official gazette. Before dawn Bryce left for Taranaki, taking several copies of the manifesto. For his part in the illegal action, Prendergast was knighted by the British government on 30 October. Meanwhile, at ten p.m. on 19 October the warship *Emerald,* which was carrying the governor, anchored in the port of Wellington, while Prendergast was meeting with his ministers. The governor did not go ashore until the next morning. As soon as he landed he asked Prime Minister Hall for an explanation of the secretive dealings. He promised a full explanation but nothing came of it. Gordon believed that Prendergast's proclamation was unjustifiable, but not wanting to get into conflict with the government, he let the ministers concerned bear responsibility for their actions.

By the end of October, there were 2500 troops with cannons and howitzers assembled around Parihaka. The natives had finished sowing crops and fencing. On 31 October Te Whiti addressed his people, saying: 'Salvation lies in your courage, peacefulness and forbearance. Follow my teachings or you are lost. Stay at Parihaka and none of you will perish. Should you fight, you will die. The Pakeha are nothing but thieves. I do not intend arguing with them. Our Saviour did not die. He was crucified for the sins of the world; He is God, and I also will be deified. I will sacrifice myself for the sake of peace. I am here to be taken ...'

Bryce had a large cannon brought up in front of the settlement and Maori levelled the road so that enemy cavalry and infantry could easily enter the village. On 5 November, all the natives, numbering about 2000 men, women and children gathered in their open meeting area. Te Whiti and Tohu, his spokesman, counsellor and aide, exhorted the people to stoically endure insults and intimidation. At eight Bryce, riding a white charger and accompanied by a swarm of soldiers, rode up to the assembly. He requested Te Whiti to give his reply to Prendergast's ultimatum. Te Whiti pretended he did not understand. Major Tuke then read out for all to hear the measures that would be taken against rebels. Bryce approached the prophet and ordered him to accompany him. Te Whiti stood still and Bryce then ordered both Te Whiti and Tohu to be arrested. The prophet offered no resistance and with dignity allowed himself to be led away with Tohu. He was followed by his wife. As he departed, Te Whiti said to his people: 'Be of good cheer, and keep your spirits up,' and they remained seated and impassive. The prisoners were put in a wagon and taken to Pungarehu fort and thence to New Plymouth.

Bryce ordered the natives to vacate Parihaka, but they took no notice. At the same time all the huts in the village and district were searched and some old guns, hatchets and axes were found and confiscated. Constables also stole a precious heirloom and £2. Since the natives would not leave, Bryce had several huts destroyed, including the one in which medicine was kept. The natives still would not leave and so he ordered their arrest. Throughout the whole area 2200 people were imprisoned, including Titokowaru, although he had nothing to do with Te Whiti's tribe.

On 12 November Te Whiti, Tohu and the other prisoners were charged with inciting rebellion in the district and for disobeying orders. They were sentenced to imprisonment and to appear, in due course, for trial in the supreme court. In December while the innocent men were in prison, Bryce ordered the destruction of their harvests and crops, and troops carried it out. The supreme court was to sit in New Plymouth in May 1882. Two weeks before the trial the government ordered the prophet and Tohu to be transferred to Christchurch prison. The other prisoners were summoned to appear in court for sentence. The government realising that Judge Gillis considered them innocent and that he would therefore have freed them, ordered the attorney general to request the judge not to proceed with the trial. He then freed them to return home.

The government was now unable to proceed with Te Whiti and Tohu's trial because they were innocent, but it did not want to set them free like the others. So it passed a special law. On 18 May 1882 when Gordon opened Parliament he mentioned: 'A bill will be presented to you permitting Te Whiti and Tohu not to be formally tried and preventing their return to Parihaka for the time being.'[7] Several honest members protested vehemently against the injustice and the government's shameful actions at Parihaka. Dr Lautour spoke out with biting sarcasm: 'The government at Parihaka hypocritically pretended it was carrying out the law, while it was in fact violating it. It read out an ultimatum to rebels, when it was itself the rebel.'[8] The complaints and protests of a few men, however, had no effect. Most members supported injustice and sanctioned whatever the government wanted.

4. Te Whiti had said that he was willing to sacrifice his life for his people. Shrewd as he was, he did not want to lose his influence over his Taranaki people. He kept his promise, demonstrating his willingness to go to prison, and even to die if his enemies were thus determined. During his two years' imprisonment he showed no sign of being upset at his unjust treatment. He maintained a dignified, sombre and taciturn demeanour. He presented himself as the would-be saviour of the Maori race. Imprisonment, rather than lowering his prestige, served to enhance it. He was regarded not only as a great prophet but as a glorious martyr for his people.

Here was a man who could keep an entire people pacifist when forced to endure provocation and injustice. There was no one to compare to him in Maori history. Te Whiti rendered the colonial government's plans useless. In prison he became a hero to the Maori while his enemies regarded him rather as a serious embarrassment; they wanted him released and liberated as soon as possible. The government, defeated and bewildered, sent Te Whiti and Tohu home and they also gave them and others back their land at Parihaka.

Te Whiti's release and his return to his people in 1883 was a personal triumph. Through all the native villages he passed, he was greeted with festivity, singing and dancing, and he was accompanied triumphantly from village to village to Parihaka. The reception he received overwhelmed him with delight and made him famous. He is now known as the great oracle of Parihaka. After its reversal the government tried to befriend Te Whiti but he continued to reject any gestures of conciliation by the British. However, he maintained peace in the district and he is still Taranaki's great prophet. Local people have richly rewarded him, ensuring his comfort. They have made it possible for him to build two fine houses in which he receives frequent visitors. He has had the village which was half destroyed by the government rebuilt on a better site. It is surrounded by fertile, cropped fields. Te Whiti continues to hold well attended monthly gatherings where he makes obscure speeches, redolent with symbolism and difficult to interpret. Occasionally he makes a pointed, threatening speech against the Pakeha. The government gets frightened and threatens him with arrest again. I believe the government is wrong in being so preoccupied with Te Whiti's every word and gesture. This only serves to make him more important and popular.

It is strange that this man who is so gifted with ability and intelligence and who has such a good grasp of the various forms of Protestantism and Catholicism continues to cling to his religious misconceptions. I believe that the reason for this anomaly is the pride and ambition which dominate him, preventing him from recognising the truth of the Catholic Church, which he has often said would be the only religion invented by man to survive on earth.

5. While Te Whiti was languishing in prison in Christchurch, Tawhiao, the Maori King, was being feted by Auckland settlers. For more than ten years he had resisted overtures of peace and friendship offered him by the colonial government. In the interview he had in 1874 with MacLean, Minister of Maori Affairs, Tawhiao made it clear that to come to an agreement, Europeans would first of all have to return to him the confiscated Waikato lands. MacLean replied that it was impossible and presented the government's peace terms, namely, 1. he would be allowed to exercise authority over his kingdom, 2. he would be free to appoint a council from his chiefs to maintain law and order, 3. the Government would support his authority, 4. a house would be built for him at Kawhia and he would be granted pieces of confiscated Waikato land. But Tawhiao, in spite of the enticing offers, bluntly refused. In 1878 Sir George Grey made similar promises, but the Maori King rejected them.

From 1860 King Tawhiao had never left the confines of his kingdom. In 1879, however, he decided to visit European settlements in the Waikato. The news was telegraphed everywhere. Accompanied by many chiefs and 600 armed warriors, he crossed his border. When he reached Alexandra, settlers greeted him with great deference, and he was feted with receptions, speeches and public luncheons in which the Queen, King Tawhiao and the royal family were toasted. From Alexandra the King's procession proceeded to Kihikihi, Cambridge and Ngaruawahia, where he was similarly treated. Settlers hoped that he would also visit Auckland, but when he reached Mercer, the boundary of his former domain, he decided not to travel on, and he returned home with his followers.

In January 1882, Tawhiao decided to visit Auckland with some of his senior officials, and preparations were made for a formal reception. When the train reached the station, the mayor, a government minister and other government officials welcomed him enthusiastically. Escorted by several coaches, the royal traveller was taken to the town hall and was cheered by a crowd along the route. A great banquet was held in his honour, and he was shown the marvels of the town and suburbs. These receptions were held not to honour the Maori King, but to further the government and settlers' interests. They feted Tawhiao to entice him to open up the rest of his kingdom to Europeans, to get land, build roads and railways, and finally to destroy the Maori kingdom and its king. But the veteran Maori remained very wary and in speeches he spoke only of peace between the two races.

Prime Minister Hall travelled from Wellington to Auckland to negotiate with the Maori King. He told him what the government and the settlers wanted and concluded saying that there could be only one authority in New Zealand, the Queen's. Being a shrewd politician, Tawhiao told him that he would get his reply in the general tribal runanga which would be held in March. During the assembly the king was drunk. Chief Te Wheoro read out the king's message to the tribes. He declared that in the Maori kingdom surveying, leasing and selling land, building roads and railways would continue to remain forbidden until an agreement was reached by both parties.

The natives were in the right, supported by the Treaty of Waitangi's solemn promises, but the government and colonists based their demands on force, and this necessarily would prevail over justice. In fact in 1886 the Maori kingdom was violated by the government. They used force of arms to continue the railway from Te Awamutu through Tawhiao's territory. Although the natives put up a determined but non-violent resistance to the infringement of their rights, they were ignored, and they were then constrained to turn to violence. At present, work is being carried out to continue the railway and to link it to Taranaki. Colonists are occupying land along the line, forcing Maori to continue retreating further into unproductive, mountainous areas. The line begun in Auckland could easily be linked up with Taranaki, by extending it from Oinemutu, near Taupo. But they wanted to occupy the little that was left of King Country farmland, and insisted on building the line through there. The government's intention is to own everything. And it will not stop until it has achieved its goal, leaving the natives totally dispossessed.

6. From 1875 the Auckland diocese had been deprived of a pastor. Finally a replacement was provided. On 25 April 1879 His Holiness, Pope Leo XIII appointed Monsignor Steins as Bishop of Auckland. He was a Dutch Jesuit, who previously was Archbishop of Calcutta in India. The worthy prelate was

known for his zeal, prudence, learning and piety. He had served the archdiocese of Calcutta for more than thirty-five years. Exhausted by his labours and in poor health, when he was more than sixty-eight years old he sought and obtained permission to retire to France to convalesce. After two years' rest and fresh air, the good bishop regained his health to some degree and the Holy Father determined he was to rule the Auckland diocese, if just for a short period.

Monsignor Steins was an expert on missionary work. He saw the necessity for the diocese to be in the care of a religious order. Accordingly, he turned to his superior general. But he was informed that the society could not assume responsibility for the diocese, since it had so many others to look after. He then petitioned other religious orders, but was equally unsuccessful. Finally he succeeded in getting the Ramsgate Benedictine Fathers of the Cassino-Subiaco congregation to go to Auckland. They were to assess the situation and then decide after two years whether they would accept the mission. Steins at the end of two years would retire and the Holy See would appoint a new bishop for Auckland. An agreement was reached between the Sacred Congregation of Propaganda, the Superiors of the Benedictine Order and Mons. Steins. Accompanied by three Benedictine Fathers and two brothers, he departed for New Zealand towards the end of October and arrived safely in Auckland on 22 December 1879. They were welcomed with great rejoicing by local Catholics.

The new bishop found that the diocese was served by only fourteen priests. The flock was large indeed but there were few shepherds. He immediately entrusted the Newton mission in town and Gisborne in Poverty Bay to the Benedictine Fathers. In the first half of 1880 another four priests and two brothers arrived to join their confreres. The bishop assigned them three more missions: Coromandel, the Waikato and Waipa. Later more Benedictines came to labour in the Lord's vineyard and everywhere their work was blessed.

Meanwhile parishioners in Newton, realising that their small church was completely inadequate for more than 2000 people, proposed to the Benedictines and Mons. Steins to build a majestic gothic church capable of seating more than 2000. The Fathers welcomed their proposal with joy, and the cautious prelate also praised the zeal of the faithful. He suggested, however, that they build a more modest church, so as not to incur too much debt. They were insistent on the original plan. He would not permit them to go ahead unless they could secure at least half the building costs through offerings and voluntary subscriptions. He would then agree to the building of a three-naved church, postponing the construction of the sanctuary and annexes. Sensible people suggested building a simple brick church, but most voted for a gothic wooden structure designed by Mahoney, an architect (cf. next page), without considering fire risk or cost. A committee was established to collect offerings and subscriptions. Lectures were given, and concerts and fairs held to fund raise. In two years 100,000 francs were collected. In June 1881 the foundation stone was laid for the new

St Benedicts Catholic church, Newton, burnt down in 1886.

church, which was dedicated to St Benedict, the renowned founder of western monasticism. Soon afterwards, construction began. Instead of building one section, they decided to complete the whole building, except for the left tower. By May 1882 the exterior was completed and the very fine church was solemnly blessed by His Excellency Monsignor Redwood, Bishop of Wellington. The wooden building and surrounding land cost 236,000 francs. But there was still a debt of 137,000 francs due to be paid within the next few years.

Monsignor Steins was a very dedicated bishop. Immediately after his arrival in his new episcopate, he began with speed and zeal to organise the spiritual and temporal affairs of the diocese, with the assistance of his missionaries, and particularly Monsignor Fines, his vicar general. Unfortunately, his indifferent health began to further deteriorate and he decided to return to Europe to prepare for his death. He celebrated the Easter of 1881 in Auckland, and then departed for Sydney. When he arrived he became critically ill and went to stay with his Jesuit confreres. After a few months of intense suffering, he died at the age of seventy-two years. News of his death reached New Zealand and caused the whole Catholic population to mourn the death of the bishop who had been their father and pastor for such a brief period.

7. The governor, Sir Arthur Gordon, did not share the same view as the prime minister regarding the means used against Parihaka Maori and the prophet, Te Whiti. And he was even more displeased that the prime minister had waited for his temporary absence from the colony to carry out his evil plan, described above. He had no hesitation in making it known that he did not share Hall and Bryce's views, even though they had the support of Parliament and most of the settlers. Sir Arthur declared that if as governor he had approved the government's actions which were sanctioned by Prendergast, he did not approve of them personally. Seeing that the new elections of 1882 favoured Prime Minister Hall and his policy, the governor left the colony early the same year. Shortly afterwards he tendered the Queen his resignation as governor, and it was accepted.

With Gordon's departure, the government of the colony rested temporarily in the hands of the notorious Prendergast. In 1883 the British government appointed Sir William Drumond Jervois as Governor of New Zealand. He was a timid man who was inclined to leave the people in charge of the colony to get on with it. He was governor from January 1884 until January 1889. In March that year he left the country and was succeeded by Lord Onslow, who reached New Zealand on 22 April 1889. The new governor was a high-ranking mason. Fellow masons held banquets in their lodges and made congratulatory speeches, encouraging his patronage of their cause in New Zealand. What a sad state of affairs for the colony!

We have not mentioned the frequent changes of government because there was little difference between them. The British government appoints governors who preside over the colony, but they do not in fact rule. The government is responsible for running the country. Every British subject over the age of twenty-one who has lived in the colony for six months has the right to vote in local and central elections, whether he is rich or poor, a fraudulent bankrupt, a drunkard, a rake, or an ex-convict. All this is of little account. Even women lately have been given the vote. In New Zealand there are no major political differences. The parties in the colonial Parliament are not very distinct, and are called 'conservative' and 'liberal'. Their members, however, change opinion readily and sell themselves to the highest bidder for their own benefit. Hence the frequent changes of government.

Another misfortune for New Zealand is that because the South Island is more populated than the North Island it has a greater number of representatives in Parliament. Hence South Island members, being the majority, nearly always get what they want at the expense of their northern neighbours. Thus the South Island has twice the amount of railways, main roads, port installations, etc. This partisan spirit became so exaggerated that in 1884, 1888 and again later, it was proposed that the seat of government be transferred from Wellington to Christchurch in the South Island. I believe that this will not occur. If it did happen, it is almost certain that two independent colonies would be established, one being the North Island and the other the South.

Meanwhile self-interest dominates colonial politics and the masons pull the strings. Instead of developing the economy, politicians want millions to spend recklessly. The government borrows money to pay the interest on its debts and never succeeds in balancing the books. In 1880 the colony was near bankrupt and only managed to save itself by using 50 million it had reserved for public works. In 1882 it borrowed another 75 million, and thus it continues to progress on the back of other people's money. Ministers and members make long-winded, ineffectual speeches in the House. The history of Parliamentary democracy world-wide is more or less that of talking about public and personal welfare and doing nothing.

Most of the population are either workers or traders and are only interested in making lots of money. They are keen on huge expenditure on public works, so as to have a share of the profits. When there is much money about and they are enjoying good incomes, they are very happy and they are not worried about the burden of taxation. But if public works decrease, there is a general outcry and people clamour for work. If no one pays attention, they threaten to topple the rulers from their seats, and then the government considers how to placate them. Regarding politics, colonists are generally in favour of constitutional monarchy and very few would support a republic, because they know that if they shook off the yoke, England would no longer give money to its greedy offspring.

Great Britain, aware of the Australian colonies' republican aspirations, has bestowed its affection on New Zealand, hoping to keep it submissive and able to be used in the future. The colony takes advantage of its mother's indulgence to extract millions from her. When England tries to curb its extravagances and tells it to be reasonable and not throw money away, the colony sulks until England doles out millions more pocket money. Thus every three or four years New Zealand repeats its entreaties and petitions and they are granted. How long will the game go on for? It is hard to predict. I believe it will continue as long as England rules the waves. When things change, New Zealand could well hear, 'Look after yourself! I cannot help you!' Then the spendthrift colony, overburdened with debt, will be in real trouble.

8. When the Maori realised that they could not achieve justice, in 1877 they sent a petition signed by more than a thousand natives to Parliament, in which they requested compensation for wrongs done to them. They requested natives not be forced to sell their lands, that vendors of alcohol in their villages be severely

punished, and they threatened that if their just requests were not heeded, they would ask the Queen to send an impartial commissioner to the colony to examine the validity of their grievances. The poor natives' petition and complaints were totally ignored by Parliament and the government.

The Maori therefore decided to appeal directly to Queen Victoria in the hope of securing a more favourable response. In 1882 chief Parore and senior members of the Ngapuhi tribe, which had always been loyal to the British, went to England personally to present a memorial to the sovereign. They were not able to obtain the desired audience. On 8 July they were permitted only to present their petition to Lord Kimberley, colonial secretary. The Maori memorial outlined the contents of the Treaty of Waitangi and then described the numerous unjust wars and thefts which followed, as described in this work. It continued: 'The desire to confiscate Maori land and to trample on the Treaty of Waitangi were the reasons which drove Pakeha to these injustices. As this was happening the people were in unspeakable distress, suffering and sorrow. While the Maori kept to the Treaty of Waitangi as the basis for seeking justice from you, Your Majesty, the Pakeha maintained that the Treaty was worthless and should be cancelled. We do not believe that what has been said to us came from Your Royal authority, and our conclusion is that such acts were not authorised by you, O Queen, whose kindness to Maori is manifestly known ... In 1881 the colonial government devised a new plan to rekindle war. Soldiers were sent to Parihaka to arrest innocent people and send them to prison, steal their property and possessions, destroy their crops, demolish their homes and commit other acts of injustice. We have examined the Treaty of Waitangi to find justification for the Government's unjust acts but we found none. We beg you, O Mother and Queen, not to allow further harm to befall your Maori children, and that you will establish a British Royal Commission to repeal the evil laws made against the natives in violation of the Treaty of Waitangi.'[9]

Lord Kimberley was totally biased in favour of those who were exploiting natives, and he considered the Treaty of Waitangi to be a worthless document, not worthy of consideration. He replied to the Maori delegation: 'It is not the Colonial Secretary's role to advise the Queen on local matters such as these. The Queen should be advised by colonial ministers and not by him.' What a despicable statement! He described as a 'local matter' the observance of a solemn treaty concluded between England and the Maori! England was the power which formally dealt with the natives at Waitangi, not the colony. It was thus the strict duty of the British government to observe and make the colonial government observe the treaty. But the colonial secretary would not have a bar of it.

When King Tawhiao learnt of Ngapuhi chiefs' lack of success in presenting their petition, he hoped he would have more success by going to London himself. In 1884 he went, accompanied by some of his chiefs. He outlined the wrongs and injustices Maori had suffered. But his pleading achieved nothing. Humiliated and disheartened at seeing hopes for justice for his people dashed, he hastened to return home, and he informed his people that in future they would have to look to their own resources to remedy the injustices caused by Pakeha.

Disenchanted Maori resolved from then on to act autonomously. They now use every means available to prevent the colonial government from completely stripping them of everything. The government has passed laws by which natives wishing to sell land must sell it to the government at the government's price. Even as this history is being compiled, I have learnt that Taranaki and Northern Wanganui Maori, followers of the prophet Te Whiti, held a runanga at Parakino in January 1892 to find appropriate means to legally resist the government's unjust demands and not be obligated to acquiesce. They decided to resist the government and its agents, and not to listen to them when they came to negotiate land purchases. The unfortunate Maori certainly have to use their wits to save themselves from the grip of the devouring serpent. However, they will never succeed in freeing themselves from its tenacious coils, and will eventually perish forever, overcome by its brutal force.

9. Although the Benedictine Fathers had been in New Zealand for two years, they still could not accept responsibility for the whole diocese because they did not have sufficient priests available, owing to a lack of vocations in England. They decided to remain, however, and to work in the missions and areas assigned to them. When the Holy See learnt of Monsignor Steins' unfortunate death, in 1882 it hastened to appoint as successor Father Dom John Edmond Luck, a Ramsgate (England) Benedictine of the Cassino-Subiaco Congregation, as were his confreres in New Zealand.

He was born in London on 18 March 1840 of a very devout, respectable family. He studied literature at St Edmond's College, Westminster, and philosophy at St Sulpice Seminary in Paris. He realised he had a vocation to the monastic life. On 13 November 1860 he and Augustine Francis, his younger brother, received the Benedictine habit at the mother house of Subiaco in Italy. He was professed on 17 November the following year. He studied theology and canon law at the Gregorian University, Rome. Having obtained his doctorate, he was ordained a priest on 23 September 1865.

As a humble religious, he sought to hide his rare intellectual and moral gifts. But God who loves to exalt the humble, had greater plans for him in the service of His Church. Auckland needed a new bishop. The Sacred Congregation of Propaganda and his religious superiors who were very well aware of Father Luck's zeal and holiness, proposed his appointment to the difficult position. On 13 July His Holiness Pope Leo XIII issued a papal brief announcing his appointment as Bishop of Auckland. He was consecrated by his Eminence Cardinal Manning in St Augustine's church, Ramsgate, on 13 August the same year. Shortly afterwards the new prelate, accompanied by some monks, left for

Catholic cathedral, Auckland, 1885.

New Zealand and arrived in Auckland at the end of October. He was welcomed with great joy by the missionaries and Catholics of the town.

Immediately after his arrival the new prelate put all his energy into promoting the development of charitable works in the diocese. It would take too long to enumerate his achievements. When he discovered that his cathedral was too small for the needs of the faithful, even though there was a lack of funds, work was begun immediately to enlarge it. It was altered to a traditional cruciform stone building, with a brick central nave and belfry. The extension cost less than 100,000 francs. He had the pleasure of consecrating the new cathedral on 15 March 1885. During the extension works on the cathedral, Monsignor Luck returned to Europe to recruit more workers for the Maori mission which had languished for so many years. He had the good fortune to find willing support for his work with the St Joseph congregation of Mill Hill in London, which accepted to take responsibility for bringing the Gospel to the natives of his diocese.

Shortly after the bishop's return to his mission a great disaster struck St Benedict's church in Newton. On the morning of 11 December 1886 the large wooden building was totally destroyed by fire, together with the Benedictine

Fathers' presbytery and seven nearby houses. The fire started in a house 100 metres from the church. Wind from the north-east blew sparks on to the roof of the church, which immediately became engulfed in flames. Within seventeen minutes it was completely destroyed to the foundations. Only a few sacred vessels could be saved. The huge building was insured for 125,000 francs. The insurance firm kept 80,000 it was owed and handed over the 45,000 to the trustees of the destroyed building. The Catholics of the diocese were most upset, especially Newton parishioners. But they did not lose heart and immediately they began to raise money to build a new church. This time, heeding good advice, they decided to build it in brick. On 16 October 1887 Monsignor Luck laid the foundation stone of the new church of St Benedict. For the time being the main church was to be without a sanctuary or side chapels. It was solemnly opened and consecrated towards the end of 1888. Within a short period it is hoped that further construction will begin.

Meanwhile the good bishop and Auckland Catholics suffered another serious blow with the death of Monsignor Fines who died in Parnell where he was stationed on 16 June 1887 at the age of sixty-six. Some years before his death, realising that the colonial government would persist in denying justice to Catholic parents regarding their children's education, he bequeathed his entire, substantial estate of 250,000 francs for this good purpose. Auckland Catholics owe him eternal gratitude and recognition. The name of such a generous benefactor will ever be revered.

Shortly before the unfortunate events described above occurred, an even worse disaster terrorised the inhabitants of New Zealand. On 10 June 1886 about one a.m. terrifying rumblings were heard and the central North Island was shaken by repeated earthquakes within an 800 kilometre radius. The first shocks caused many people to believe that an enemy invasion had occurred, and they were firing heavy artillery, or that a shipwrecked warship was signalling distress. They soon realised, however, that nothing like that had happened. An underground eruption had occurred in Lake Rotomahana. Mount Tarawera suddenly blew up, spewing huge amounts of fire, lava and ash more than ten kilometres, burying the village of Te Ariki and its hundred natives, and destroying Wairoa village and killing four Europeans and six Maori. The others barely managed to escape.[10]

In the midst of these misfortunes, Monsignor Luck redoubled his efforts. After the extensions to the cathedral, he began in 1888 to build a presbytery for the cathedral's priests. Their earlier habitation was a decrepit and unhealthy wooden building built in 1841. In 1889 the worthy prelate started construction of a substantial, handsome bishop's residence, which the diocese lacked. He wanted these buildings made out of solid, durable material. In 1890 he returned to Europe in search of more priests and financial assistance to pay for the debts incurred for building. He was so successful that he was able to settle them all.[11]

10. The notorious Te Kooti, whose bloodcurdling exploits have been described elsewhere, retreated into the King Country in 1871. He remained quietly hidden until 1883 because a sum of 125,000 francs had been placed on his head for whoever took him dead or alive. He was polygamous and an influential prophet of the barbaric Hauhau cult. He retained a good many Maori admirers and his name was on everyone's lips. People still feared his rage and fury. After his bloody campaigns, he lived in retirement and idleness in his village, and gave himself over to drunkenness and other vices, like many of his colleagues. However his hatred of the Pakeha and their religion did not die. The colonial government was afraid that the ferocious warrior would champion Te Whiti and other Taranaki natives' cause. With his considerable influence a new war of extermination of Pakeha could start. It sought to court him with enducements to yoke him to its wagon. In 1883 the government granted him a full pardon and a fine piece of land in the Waikato and complete freedom to settle where he chose.

The government's reprehensible weakness towards Te Kooti caused great indignation throughout the colony, but it let them jump up and down without taking any notice. The truculent Maori accepted the favourable terms offered and, escorted by more than 200 warriors, he travelled in triumph through most of the North Island. He visited a great number of tribes, who received him with considerable honour. Everywhere he exploited and abused traditional Maori hospitality, fattening himself and his companions at the expense of poor tribes to whom he promised a good deal with no intention of keeping his word. The government went even further, not only gifting Te Kooti a 600 acre tract of land on the banks of Port Ohiwa, near Opotiki, where he settled, but also making him government agent to the Uriwera tribes. At the beginning of 1893 he was sent a dispatch, officially thanking him for persuading Uriwera natives not to oppose surveying of their land. To achieve its goal of robbing natives of their land, the government was not concerned about degrading itself and using a man like Te Kooti as their instrument.

Shortly before he died, the savage, in one of his most rabid speeches, said to his followers: 'Now my axe is broken! I go to hand it to my Deliverer! Take heed. There is another axe which for eighteen centuries has been hacking the forest of humanity; the axe of Catholicism! Beware! It has felled the greatest trees, the kauri, rimu, kaikatea. Now there are only thin saplings left. Be on your guard! When I go, this axe will strike down everything.'[12] Let us hope that Te Kooti's words will soon come to pass. He spent his last years in drunkenness and debauchery. Te Kooti died in April 1893 and his fanatical followers predicted his resurrection. The fact is that he will rise like everyone else on the day of judgement.

Meanwhile Taranaki Maori continued their pacifist, legal opposition to unjust usurpation of their land. In 1886 the government, not wanting to be beaten, had recourse to its old stratagem of imprisoning Te Whiti as the main instigator of native rebellion to make them realise that force would prevail over justice. Te Whiti allowed himself to be captured and put in prison without resistance. Later he was set free and in the eyes of his credulous disciples he acquired even greater esteem and prestige, being seen as a man who sacrifices himself for the good of his people. A few years later he was again arrested, but since they could find no pretext for charging him, they had to send him back home. Te Whiti is the only Maori who has found a valid way, in so far as it is possible for the powerless, to defend the rights of the weak against the strong. But let there be no illusion. The struggle is unequal. The Maori in the end will have to succumb.

11. God's Church is ever youthful and robust. In the midst of raging storms which assail it from all sides, it fearlessly pursues its divine destiny as assigned to it by Christ, in spite of the Devil's fury, Protestant plotting and the iniquitous goals of a decadent society which would want its death and destruction. In less than a century the Church began to sow, through trial and tribulation, its first divine seeds in the arid lands of Australia. In less than fifty years numerous priests and missionaries intent on spreading the kingdom of God witnessed abundant harvests throughout the land. As the numbers of faithful increased, the Supreme Pontiff, who surveys all the Church's activities, suggested to the bishops of those distant lands, to hold a solemn congress to deliberate if the time was ripe to establish their own Catholic hierarchy, as in Europe, to promote Catholicism.

On 5 November 1885 a national congress of Australian bishops was held in which two archbishops and sixteen bishops of Australia, New Zealand and Tasmania participated. It was presided over by His Eminence Cardinal Moran, Archbishop of Sydney, as special representative of His Holiness Pope Leo XIII. The congress lasted twenty-five days. It proposed to the Pope to establish a Catholic hierarchy, with parishes and resident parish priests in every Australian state and the erection of four new dioceses, three vicariates, and an apostolic prefecture, and to elevate the dioceses of Adelaide, Brisbane and Hobart in Australia to the rank of archbishoprics. It was also proposed to make Christchurch a diocese, and to create an archbishopric.

Other measures were proposed relating to the management of dioceses and parishes, the promotion of the faith, Catholic societies and sodalities, mixed marriage and Catholic children's education, extolling the faithful to persevere in urging their respective colonial governments to respect their rights regarding their children's education. The congress's recommendations were immediately sent to Rome where they were examined, discussed and finally approved in May 1887 by the Holy Father Pope Leo XIII. He issued a Brief on 5 May the same year, creating Christchurch a diocese. In another Brief on 13 of the same month, he elevated the Wellington diocese to a metropolitan diocese and its worthy bishop to the rank of archbishop. The three other dioceses were accorded suffragan status.

Part of the Christchurch diocese in the South Island, because it was so extensive, was attached to the Wellington diocese. Its present southern boundary is the same as the Dunedin diocese's. Its northern boundary starts at the Conway River in the east and continues along the Clarence River up to Mt Franklin and from there descends from Mt Spencer to Lake Chartodel. It then follows the Grey valley and continues along the left bank of the river to Greymouth in the west. The diocese also includes the Chatham Islands, which lie about 600 kilometres east of New Zealand.

On 13 May 1887 Father John Grimes of the Society of Mary was appointed by papal Brief as the first bishop of the new diocese. He was a man of considerable ability, learning and piety. The new bishop was born in Westminster, England, on 11 February 1842. He studied in England, France and Ireland. He taught literature for a few years in the College of Dundalk, in Ireland. He was then appointed Superior of Jefferson College, Louisiana, in the United States of America. From there he went as Superior to the Marist novitiate at Painton in Devonshire, England. While he occupied this important position he was made bishop. Monsignor Grimes was consecrated Bishop of Christchurch on 26 July 1887 in London by His Eminence Cardinal Manning and towards the end of the same year he reached his new post accompanied by a large number of Marist priests. He received an enthusiastic welcome from the faithful of the diocese, particularly the people of Christchurch. We join in wishing him a long and happy episcopate promoting the good of his people and the glory of the Catholic Church.

During the Australian congress, Wellington's intrepid Marist priests, encouraged by their venerable bishop, worked hard for the building of a large, magnificent college in the colony's capital. Their aim was to provide a secondary school for Catholic boys throughout New Zealand which could also serve eventually as a seminary which young men called to the priesthood could enter. In 1886 the building was solemnly blessed and officially opened and within a short period a chosen number of boys entered the haven of learning and Christian piety. About a dozen able Marist fathers also taught secondary and technical school and matriculation subjects. By 1889 St Patrick's College already had eighty pupils and in 1893 it had 130, the majority being boarders. There is promise of further development.

12. The following figures are taken from the New Zealand census of March 1886: Maori population 41,627. The unfortunate native population according to the 1881 census was 44,099. Thus in five years it had declined by 2472. Their population is still decreasing. By 1886 the number of colonists was 578,482.

Official statistics published by the government and taken from its census figures provide the following information regarding colonist's religious affiliation: Protestants, comprising seventy-five denominations 447,113; Roman Catholics 80,715; Jews 1559; pagans (Chinese) 4472; atheists, free-thinkers and others who refused to declare their affiliation 44,623. This category of people uninterested in religion or disbelievers had risen in eight years by 11,533, and was an indication that agnosticism in the colony was making rapid progress. In 1888 the European population was 607,380 and at present, in 1893 it is estimated to have risen to 650,000 people.

Imports in 1886 were valued at 168,975,325 francs and exports reached 166,719,775 francs. Colonial revenue was still lower than annual expenditure and the colonial government had to resort to raising loans to make up the difference. In 1885 colonial revenue was 102,429,900 francs and expenditure increased to 106,072,525 francs. The colony's public debt, which in 1842 was less than 500,000 francs, in 1845 had risen to 21,100,000 francs. In 1867 it was 100,765,000 francs. In 1870 it exceeded 188 million francs. In 1881 it had reached 750 million and in 1885 it was 894,760,550 francs. At present, in 1893, it has touched the enormous figure of a thousand million francs. Combined with the debts of counties, boroughs and private individuals which add on another thousand million francs, there would be a debt of 3075 francs per individual (the population being calculated by us at 650,000 in 1893).

European livestock in 1886: horses 187,382; cattle 853,358; sheep 16,564,596; goats 10,220; pigs 277,901. Maori livestock figures were: sheep 112,850; cattle 42,103; pigs 92,091.

13. In 1878 the Bishop of Wellington decided to revive the Maori mission in his diocese. He sent the natives Father Soulas to recommence the work of spreading the Gospel to the poor people, a work which had been suspended throughout the long war and because of Hauhau fanaticism. In 1882 Monsignor Redwood sent out other Marist missionaries and, later, sisters to teach children. Very soon their work produced pleasing results, leading one to be strongly optimistic. Maori who have not been subjected to debauchery and drunkenness show a keen interest in Catholicism and a complete indifference to Protestant sects, in spite of enticements and big promises many preachers make to them.

By 1893 native missions of the Wellington diocese had six Marist missionaries and a lay brother, and fifteen sisters to teach Maori children in three vast areas. They contained eleven churches and chapels, and a further two under construction. There were two primary schools and a boarding school for Maori girls. Out of a native population of 6627 in the diocese, according to the census figures of 1886 they already had 1600 baptised and the hope of a still richer harvest. On the east coast of Wairarapa and at Te Pakipoki the good missionaries were assisted by Sisters of Our Lady of the Missions, who already had a boarding school at Napier in which they accepted daughters of native chiefs to give them a higher education. However the diocese lacked secondary schools for chiefs' sons and for training catechists. But Archbishop Redwood is zealously working to meet this need.

A similar revival is occurring in the Auckland diocese. From 1874 there had been only Rev. James MacDonald to look after natives' welfare. In 1883 Monsignor Luck obtained missionaries from the London-based Mill Hill Society. They took charge of evangelising the Maori and reviving the old missions. In 1887 the society sent two missionary priests who immediately began working at Maketu in the Bay of Plenty. Shortly afterwards, another two missionaries arrived to help their confreres. At present (in 1893) there are four Mill Hill missionaries in the Auckland diocese, tending to four vast areas: Matata in the Bay of Plenty, Hokianga in the far North, Taupo and Oinemutu in the central North Island. There are thirty-nine churches and chapels for natives. The number of Catholic Maori is 5000 out of a native population of 35,000 natives.* There are many conversions, and one hopes that within a few years the number of Catholics will treble, since the poor Maori show themselves to be extremely interested in the Catholic faith.

14. The condition of religion for both Protestants and Catholics in New Zealand is, in my opinion, far from satisfactory and threatens to get worse in the future. Mr Cholomondeley wrote of his co-religionists in 1864: 'The truth of the matter is that British colonists are not religious. And the least religious among them are those who belonged to the Anglican church when they lived in England.' Elsewhere he wrote: 'If our Anglican church retains its present state of indifference, Anglican children will become either Roman Catholic, atheists or agnostics.'[13] The observation made about Protestant settlers in 1864 still applies today, with this difference: few become Catholic. The majority join the ranks of free-thinkers and disbelievers of every hue. Many Protestants become freemasons, abandoning the little belief they had, and have no interest in religion.

Masonry is in full control in New Zealand. Many Protestant ministers are members and the Orange and Oddfellows Societies are aligned with it. Even the tiniest settlement has one or more masonic lodges, which exercise a monopoly over elections. All important and well-paid positions are under their control and non-members are excluded from office. Masons take no notice of the law, justice or any sense of fairness. I have irrefutable proof of this from colonists' experience. Two examples will suffice. Recently, a postmaster-general and chief mason

---

*Translator's note: At the beginning of Section 12, Vaggioli refers to a native population of '41,627' (March 1886 census). He notes its decline in five years (1881 census) by 2472; he probably used this last figure to anticipate that by 1893 the Maori population would have declined by a further 6000.

embezzled funds and was discovered. An inquiry was held. By way of punishment he received an annual pension for life of 500 francs. If he were not a freemason, he would have been sent to gaol. A Protestant friend of mine applied for the position of chief gardener of an agricultural society. He was the most suitable applicant but he was told that to have the position he had to become a mason. He refused to compromise his freedom to the loathsome organisation. Consequently, a totally unsuitable person, who was a mason, got the position. Thus no Catholic or Protestant can occupy any important position unless he becomes a member of the evil sect.

Masonry is intent on eradicating religion, morality and decency from society. Its adherents become immoral and dissolute. They turn away from religion and become materialists and atheists. It has introduced secular education to the colony and elsewhere, thus gaining a ready source of young recruits to carry out its foul intentions. This organisation denies justice to Catholics and devout Protestants who want their children to have a moral, Christian education. Masonry is an implacable enemy of Christ and his Church, of honest, decent government and Christian morality. Its aim is to restore Satan's iniquitous rule and to plunge the world into its former barbarity. If people throughout the world want to avoid ruin and desolation they need to open their eyes while there is time to the danger that threatens them. The detestable sect which is driving society into chaos and complete ruin must be annihilated.

In 1893 there were 88,500 European Catholics in New Zealand. Although they are much more loyal in practising their faith than Protestants, many leave a lot to be desired. It appears that about a third of adult Catholics do not practise their faith, although many of them attend church on Sundays. This indifference can be attributed to four factors:

1. Mixed marriages between Catholics and Protestants, wisely disapproved of by the Catholic Church. The frequency of such unions within the Anglo-Saxon race causes the gravest harm to the faith of the Catholic spouse, and even more to their children because frequently they become indifferent to religion and eventually abandon their faith. Bishops do everything they can to prevent such marriages, but with little success. It has been proven, that because of mixed marriages, the Catholic Church in America, in little more than a century, has lost eight million adherents, offspring of these marriages.

2. Secular state schools, to which many Catholics send their children. In these schools, there is no mention of God, religion or Christian morality. They scorn religion and children grow up having absorbed pernicious doctrines and slogans. Carnal desires and pleasure-seeking flourish, throwing them into debauchery and vice and eventually they abandon their religion.

3. Tepid Catholics in close contact with Protestants are infected by their apa-

thy. This association also kindles in them a strong desire for wealth and material pleasures, driving them to abandon religious obligations and turn away from spiritual pursuits.

4. Finally, the sheer physical distance separating many Catholics from a church, making it impossible for them to attend functions and religious instruction regularly.

15. Summary of the present state of the Catholic Church in New Zealand: Archdiocese of Wellington. Archbishop Monsignor Francis Maria Redwood. Parishes 21, smaller stations visited regularly by missionaries 62. European Catholic population 24,000, Maori 1600. Churches 62, chapels 15 and priests 40. There are 26 primary schools and several girls' secondary schools, a technical school, St Patrick's secondary school, described above and four orphanages. Marist Fathers 40 and Marist Brothers 22. Religious orders (nuns): Sisters of Mercy, Sisters of the Missions, Nazarenes, Josephites, Good Shepherd nuns and Tertiaries of St Mary.

Diocese of Auckland. European Catholic population 20,000, Maori Catholics 5000. Quasi-parish stations 21 and minor centres visited by missionaries 54, and 4 Maori stations.

Churches for Europeans 53, for natives 39; priests 29. Primary schools 25 attended by 1850 children; a technical school, a girls' orphanage accommodating 80, three convents for girls and a hospital for the elderly and infirm run by Sisters of the Poor. Religious Orders: Benedictines 10 of whom three are lay brothers; Marist Brothers 5, Mill Hill Fathers 4, Sisters of Mercy 58, Josephites 12, Sisters of the Missions 18, Little Sisters of the Poor 6.

The Diocese of Christchurch has 21,000 European Catholics with 18 parishes and 37 outlying centres; churches and chapels 51. Bishop of the Diocese, Monsignor John Grimes, a Marist. Priests 32 of whom 20 are Marists and English Benedictine and 11 secular priests. Primary schools for boys and girls, four each. Mixed schools, roll of 2937, one reformatory. Religious Orders: Marists 20; Marist Brothers 11; Sisters of Mercy 42, Sacred Heart nuns 19, Good Shepherd nuns 15, Josephites 15, Sisters of the Missions 55.

The Diocese of Dunedin has 25,000 European Catholics with 15 quasi-parish stations and 59 outlying centres. There are 36 churches. Bishop of the Diocese Monsignor Patrick Moran*. Priests 21. Catholic schools 20, roll of 720 boys and 915 girls. Religious Orders: Jesuits 2, Christian Brothers 5, Dominican nuns 70 in four convents, Sisters of Mercy 4.

16. If New Zealand settlers are far from models of virtue and propriety, modern

---

* Died 22 May 1895.

Maori are even less so. They are less barbarous but no better than their ancestors, and have learned vices from Europeans, not virtues. There are three main vices which control the natives: idleness, drunkenness and debauchery. In the old days they had to work the whole year to gather the necessities of life. Now, with the introduction of vegetables and cereals, families need only work ten or fifteen days, for example, to gather sufficient potatoes to last them for the year. They pass the rest of their time in gossip, laziness and loitering. It is well known that idleness breeds many other vices. There are very few sober Maori these days. They spend the little money that comes their way in grog shops. But let us allow Rev. Taylor, an Anglican minister and champion of his compatriots to speak on this subject.

'(European) Christians' double standard has become a stumbling block for natives. When Chief Te Hapuku, an inveterate drunkard, was threatened with imprisonment if he continued drinking, he replied to the constable that it was not fair to arrest him because the law was made for ordinary mortals not for Rangatira (nobles) such as himself. To back up his assertion he mentioned the names of several magistrates and judges who were addicted to alcohol and were not arrested.'[14] Later, referring to Maori allies who assisted British troops against rebels, he said, 'They received rum rations and acquired a great love of grog. Now they swear and curse like British troops. They are seen frequenting pubs and many are completely dissolute.'[15] Abuse of alcohol causes the Maori moral degradation and shortens their lives. If the government is really concerned about natives' welfare it would prohibit alcohol being sold, under severe penalty. This, however, would lead to the closure of many pubs throughout the country because publicans would have no one to sell their toxic beverages to. The government would not want to damage this very important industry from which it draws its highest customs dues. It would rather let the natives go to the devil!

Bad habits, introduced into New Zealand by Europeans, have put down deep roots for the two reasons mentioned above and they cause infinite harm. Native youths love entertainment and amusements and easily allow themselves to be seduced by false hopes and promises. Degenerate Europeans, of whom there are many, insinuate themselves into their lives to their utter ruin. What is worse, colonial laws protect the very people who do such harm. We will not expose their vile practices, but if this is supposed to be the civilisation which is meant to benefit the Maori, it would have been better for them to have remained in their former state of barbarity and ingenuousness. Mr Cholomondeley succinctly describes the consequences of this degradation: 'New Zealand Maori are dying off. Their young people are miserable and sickly and children are extremely malnourished.'[16]

17. New Zealand, driven by the Anglo-Saxon race's enterprising spirit and the powerful injection of Britain's millions, has made extremely rapid material

progress in half a century of colonisation. Its founding 2000 colonists have increased to more than 650,000 settlers. Its commerce has increased a hundredfold. Livestock of all kinds are a great source of its prosperity. Main roads between districts multiply daily. A network of railways is in place. The entire country is connected by telegraph and the colony is linked to the outside world. There are large towns, populous suburbs and numerous settlements throughout the country. Forests have given way to fields and farms. The whole country has a European atmosphere, with the appearance of European settlements, farms, factories and businesses of all kinds. There is hustle and bustle everywhere. Steamers and sailing ships of every shape and size regularly visit New Zealand. Only the Maori are in decline. Aware that they cannot survive under the onslaught of colonists' invasion, they prepare themselves for death with a distressing fatalistic resignation.

Will New Zealand's material progress continue? I think not. It carries with it the seed of destruction. In fact, expenditure still exceeds income and instead of debts diminishing, they only increase. The considerable progress has been made with others' millions, and the money has to be repaid. When that time comes the colony's illusory greatness will probably disappear like mist. If New Zealand's material progress has been great, its citizens' moral and religious development has been minimal, for the reasons described above.

Governments and people do not wish to recognise that without God, without religion and without Christian morality, it is impossible for a decent society to survive for long. They do not want to acknowledge that by dispensing with Christ and his teaching they are digging a chasm under their feet. Rulers and people, you would do well to remember that God is not mocked. If governments and people do not humbly turn to God, the day will come when their eyes will be opened to their wrong-doings. But it will be too late, because if God is scorned and despised He will turn thrones and crowns to chaff. A world infected with such corruption will become one vast cemetery in the midst of which the grim reaper will reign. Pointing his finger at any terrified survivors on the barren earth, he will exclaim: Here lie the crawling maggots who chose to ignore God!

Notes

INTRODUCTION

1. Vaggioli, Felice Dom, 'Le Avventure di un Refrattario Descritte da lui stesso' *(A Deserter's Adventures)*, unpublished manuscript, 5 volumes, Praglia archive, 1908-1910.
2. Vaggioli, Felice, 'New Zealand correspondence', unpublished, file 5, 4, 1, Library Santa Maria della Castagna, Genoa.
3. Mostardi, Faustino, in *I Monasteri Italiani della Congregazione Sublacense (1843-1972)*, Saggi storici nel primo centenario della congregazione, Parma, 1972, p. 419.
4. Vaggioli, 'Le Avventure di un Refrattario Descritte da lui stesso', Book 4, p. 476, unpublished ms., 1910.
5. Vaggioli, ibid., Book 5, p. 30.
6. Ibid., p. 60.
7. 'In the old language', according to Hemi Waikato Tainui Taupiri Whareherehere, 'ta waho' has the significance of representing 'a bubble in the water', indicating a spirit and thus acknowledging Vaggioli's wairua and spiritual nature, rather than the more customary modern meaning of 'outsider'.
8. Interviewed 30 September 1998.
9. Vaggioli, ibid., Book 5, p. 91.
10. Ibid., p. 110.
11. Ibid., p. 110.
12. Ibid., p. 123.
13. Ibid., p. 176.
14. Ibid., p. 186.
15. Ibid., p. 187.
16. Ibid., p. 201.
17. Ibid., p. 215.
18. Mostardi, Faustino, op. cit., p. 427.
19. Vaggioli, *Storia della Nuova Zelanda E Dei Suoi Abitatori*, vol. 1, Parma, 1891, preface, pp. 1-2.
20. Ibid. p. 3.
21. Vaggioli, 'Le Avventure di un Refrattario Descritte da lui stesso', op. cit., Book 4, p. 75.
22. Ibid.
23. Ibid.
24. Ibid., p. 213.
25. Ibid., p. 254.
26. Vaggioli, *Storia della Nuova Zelanda E Dei Suoi Abitatori*, vol. 1, p. 254.
27. Ibid.
28. Ibid., p. 255.
29. Ibid., p. 255.

30 Carpenese, Dom Callisto, O.S.B., interviewed Praglia Monastery, Padova, 12.4.1996.
31 Bussoni, Dom Anselmo, O.S.B., interviewed Monastery of San Giovanni Evangelista, Parma, 26.4.1996.
32 Simmons, E. R., *In Cruce Salus, A History of the Diocese of Auckland (1848-1980)*. Catholic Publications Centre, Auckland, 1982, note 1, p. 139.
33 Simmons, ibid., note 9, p. 155.
34 Riseborough, Hazel, 'Saviours and Savages, An Italian View of the Nineteenth Century Maori World', unpublished essay, Massey University, 1983, p. 34.
35 Riseborough, ibid., p. 97.
36 Riseborough, ibid., p. 157.
37 Vaggioli, letter to Rev. Teodoro Cappelli, Gisborne, 4 Nov. 1881, Library Santa Maria della Castagna, Genoa.
38 Vaggioli, 'Le Avventure di un Refrattario Descritte da lui stesso', op. cit., Book 4, p. 426.
39 Vaggioli, *Storia della Nuova Zelanda E Dei Suoi Abitatori,* vol. 1, op. cit., p. 179.
40 Ibid., p. 181.
41 Vaggioli, l'Australasia Britannica, Rivista Internazionale di scienze sociali e discipline ausiliarie, Roma 1899, p. 4.
42 Ibid., p. 5.
43 Hughes, Robert, *The Fatal Shore,* Collins/Harvill, 1987.
44 Vaggioli, *Storia della Nuova Zelanda E Dei Suoi Abitatori,* vol. 2, op. cit., p. 528.

Visitors to Nineteenth-Century Aotearoa/New Zealand

1 Alison Moses, 'The Contribution of Anthony Trollope to Colonial Formation. Analysis of Trollope's travel guide *Australia and New Zealand,* published 1873', BA Hons Long Essay, Otago, 1973.
2 Mark Twain, *Mark Twain in Australia and New Zealand,* Penguin facsimile, Ringwood, Victoria, 1973.
3 George F. Angas, *Savage Life and Scenes in Australia and New Zealand: Being an Artist's Impressions Of Countries And Peoples At The Antipodes*, 1847, Smith, Elder and Co., London, 1847. Augustus Earle, *A Narrative of Nine Months' Residence in New Zealand, in 1827*; together with a journal of a residence in Tristan da Cunha, an island situtated between South America and the Cape of Good Hope, Longman, Rees, Orme, Brown, Green, and Longman, London, 1832. E.H. McCormick (ed.), OUP, Auckland, 1966.
4 See John Stenhouse, 'The Battle between Science and Religion over Evolution in Nineteenth Century New Zealand', PhD, Massey University, 1985, pp. 10-12.
5 Ernst Dieffenbach, *Travels in New Zealand,* 2 Vols, London, 1843.
6 See Michael King, *The Collector. Andreas Reischek:A Biography,* Hodder and Stoughton, Auckland, 1981.
7 Henry Demarest Lloyd, *Newest England: Notes of a Democratic Traveller in New Zealand, with some Australian Comparisons,* Doubleday and Co., New York, 1902.
8 Charles Dilke, *The British Empire,* Chatto and Windus, London, 1899; Michael Davitt, *Life and Progress in Australasia,* Methuen, London, 1908.
9 *Constance Astley's Trip to New Zealand, 1897-1898,* ed. Jill de Fresne, Victoria

University Press, Wellington, 1997. This intrepid woman traveller very nearly met the Maori King, Mahuta, at Huntly (pp. 136-137). She certainly developed a more favourable impression of Maori once she met them personally than she did learning about them from prejudiced settlers.

10 See David Hamer, 'Newest America?', in Malcolm McKinnon (ed.), *The American Connection: Essays from the Stout Centre Conference*, Allen and Unwin/Port Nicholson Press, Wellington, 1988, pp. 12-24.

11 See Grant Phillipson, '"The Thirteenth Apostle": Bishop Selwyn and the Transplantation of Anglicanism to New Zealand, 1841-1868', PhD, University of Otago, 1993; Octavius Hadfield, *One of England's Little Wars: a letter to the Right Hon. Secretary of State for the Colonies*, William and Norgate the Duke of Newcastle, London, 1861; A.T. Yarwood, *Samuel Marsden*, OUP, Melbourne, 1968; Lila Hamilton, 'Christianity Among the Maoris. The Maoris and the Church Missionary Society', PhD, University of Otago, 1970; Kerry Howe, '"The Bishop Alien": Selwyn and the New Zealand Wars of the 1860s' in Warren Limbrick (ed.), *Bishop Selwyn in New Zealand, 1841-1848*, Dunmore Press, Palmerston North, 1983, pp. 94-120; J.M.R. Owens, *Prophets in the Wilderness: The Wesleyan Mission in New Zealand, 1819-1827*, AUP/OUP, Auckland, 1974; Jane Thomson, 'Some reasons for the Failure of the Roman Catholic Mission to the Maoris, 1838-1860', *NZJH*, III, 2 (Oct. 1969), pp. 166-74, and Michael King, *God's Farthest Outpost: A History of Catholics in New Zealand*, Penguin, Auckland, 1997, pp. 31-61.

12 J.F.H. Wohlers, *Memories of the life of J.F.H. Wohlers of Ruapuke, New Zealand, An Autobiography*, translated by John Houghton, Otago Daily Times, Witness and Newspaper Company Ltd. Dunedin, 1895, pp. 103, 113 and 102.

13 See Paul Clark, *'Hauhau': the Pai Marire Search for Maori Identity*, AUP/OUP, Auckland, 1975; Bronwyn Elsmore, *Mana from Heaven: A Century of Maori Prophets in New Zealand*, Moana Press, Tauranga, 1989; Ann Parsonson, 'The Pursuit of Mana' in W.H. Oliver and B.R. Williams (eds) *The Oxford History of New Zealand*, OUP, Wellington, 1981, pp. 159-161; Judith Binney, *Redemption Songs: A Biography of Te Kooti Arikirangi Te Turuki*, Bridget Williams Books/Auckland University Press, Auckland, 1995; Hazel Riseborough, *Days of Darkness, Taranaki, 1878-1884*, Allen and Unwin/Historical Branch, Wellington, 1989.

14 Jessie Munro, *The Story of Suzanne Aubert*, Bridget Williams Books/AUP, Auckland, 1996.

15 Darwin, from the *Voyage of the Beagle*, quoted in Stenhouse, 'The Battle between Science and Religion ...', op. cit., pp. 10-12.

16 Ernst Dieffenbach, *New Zealand and its Native Population*, Aborigines Protection Society, London, 1841, Hocken Pamphlet Collection, 58/1; and *Travels in New Zealand*, Vol ii, London, 1843, pp. 1-8, 36-41, 70-71, 111-114, 139-141.

17 Edward Shortland, *The Southern Districts of New Zealand, with passing notes on the customs of the Aborigines*, Longman, Brown, Green and Longmans, London, 1851.

18 Charles W. Dilke, *The British Empire*, Chatto and Windus, London, 1899, p. 87.

19 Geoffrey Blainey (ed.), Charles Dilke, *Greater Britain: Travellers' Tales of Early Australia and New Zealand. Charles Dilke visits her new lands, 1866 and 1867*, Methuen Haynes, Melbourne, 1985, pp. 75-77.

20 Ibid., pp. 71 and 75.

21 Ibid., p. 77.

22 Augustus Earle, *Nine Months Residence in New Zealand*, pp. 8-14, 39-57, 123 and

254; and George F. Angas, *Savage Life and Scenes*, pp. 303-314.
[23] Earle, op. cit., p. 257 and Angas, op. cit., p. 339.
[24] Andre Siegfried, *Democracy in New Zealand*, translated by E.V. Burns, with an introduction by David Hamer, Victoria University Press with Price Milburn, Wellington, 1982. First published in French 1904, and English 1914, pp. 1-12.
[25] Henry Demarest Lloyd, op. cit., pp. 2-7. Frank Parsons, who relied heavily on Lloyd for information, presented a more romantic portrayal of Maori both in his text and accompanying line drawings, but had no doubt that they had been well beaten by 'the Anglo-Saxon brotherhood'. See *The Story of New Zealand*, C.F. Taylor Equity Series, Philadelphia, 1904, pp. 1-46.
[26] David Hamer (ed.), *The Webbs in New Zealand in 1898*, Price Milburn, Wellington, 1974, p. 55. Although the Webbs spent two days in Rotorua they made no comment on Maori.
[27] A. Moses, 'Anthony Trollope in New Zealand', pp. 41-45.
[28] Michael Davitt, *Life and Progress in Australasia*, Methuen and Co., London, 1898, pp. 344 and 383.
[29] Mark Twain, *Mark Twain in Australia and New Zealand*, pp. 321-22.
[30] Ibid., p. 318.
[31] G.W. Rusden, *History of New Zealand*, Vol. 3, Melbourne, 1889, p. 229; and *Tragedies in New Zealand in 1868 and 1881, discussed in England in 1886 and 1887*, London, 1888.
[32] Sygurd Wisniowski, *Tikera, or, Children of the Queen of Oceania*. Translated by Jerzy Podstolski, edited by Dennis McEldowney, Auckland University Press/OUP, 1972, p. 22
[33] Ibid., p. 272.
[34] P.J. Gibbons, 'Non Fiction' in Terry Sturm (ed.), *The Oxford History of New Zealand Literature in English*, OUP, Auckland, 1991, pp. 52-68.
[35] Jessie Munro, *The Story of Suzanne Aubert*, AUP/BWB, 1996, p. 19.
[36] On de las Casas and his *Historia Apologetica*, De Bry's paintings and their part in constructing the 'black legend', see Charles Gibson, 'Spanish exploitation of Indians in Central Mexico' and J.H. Elliot, 'The Impact of America on Europe Was Complex and Uncertain' both in Lewis Hanke (ed.), *History of Latin American Civilization. Sources and Interpretations. Volume I: The Colonial Experience*, 2nd edn. Little Brown and Co., Boston, 1973, pp. 151-57 and 41-52.
[37] James Belich, *I Shall Not Die: Titokowaru's War. New Zealand 1868-1869*, Allen and Unwin/Port Nicholson Press, Wellington, 1989, p. 293.

Chapter One

[1] *New Zealand, the Britain of the South*, by Charles Hursthouse, ch. II, p. 7. London, 1861.
[2] See also *The Little History of New Zealand*, by E. M. Bourke. Chapter IV, p. 9. Melbourne, 1882.
[3] *Te Ika a Maui*, by Rev. Richard Taylor, conclusion, p. 706. London, 1870. *The Story of New Zealand*, by Arthur Thomson M.D., vol. 1, part II, ch. 1, p. 229. London, 1859.
[4] *Toki* is Maori for Captain Cook.
[5] Op.cit., p. 231.

6. Op.cit.
7. Idem, ibid., p. 238.
8. Abbe Rochon, *Voyages*. Paris, 1791.
9. This subject is discussed in vol. I, par. 2, ch. 14, no. 2, and ch. 20, no. 10 [*Storia della Nuova Zelanda E Dei Suoi Abitatori*].
10. See Dr Thomson, ibid., pp. 236, 237 and 238, who refers to local native sources.

Chapter Two

1. Thomson, ibid., ch. III, p. 289.
2. Mss. Reports. Native Secretary's Office. Auckland.
3. Parl. Papers, 1838. – Mr Enderby.
4. Thomson, ibid., pp. 298, 301.
5. Parl. Papers, 1838. – Mr Nicholas's evidence.
6. Regarding whale hunting, see *Storia della Nuova Zelanda E Dei Suoi Abitatori*, vol. I, par. I, ch. VI, par. 2, p. 137 and following.
7. Evidence before the House of Lords, London, 1838.
8. *Life among the Maoris of New Zealand*, by Rev. Robert Ward, ch. VII, p. 157. London, 1872.
9. *New Zealand*, by J.L. Nicholas.
10. Rev. W. Yate, *Evidence before the House of Lords*, 1838.
11. Rev. W. Yate, *Evidence before the House of Lords*, 1838.
12. *Proceedings of Church Missionary Society*, vol. V – Dr Thomson, ibid., vol. 1. p. 253.
13. *The British Colonisation of New Zealand*, published by the New Zealand Association, p. 167. London, 1837.
14. Library of Useful Knowledge.
15. Dr Thomson, ibid., p. 253.
16. Dr Thomson, ibid.
17. *New Zealand in 1839*, by Rev. J.D. Lang D.D., p. 30.
18. Act. 4, George IV, ch. 97.
19. Rev. Richard Taylor, *Te Ika a Maui*, p. 587. London, 1870.
20. *A Little History of New Zealand*, by E.M. Bourke, ch. XI, p. 23. Melbourne, 1882.
21. *New Zealand*, by J.L. Nicholas, vol. II, ch. VII, p. 193.
22. *The Fathers of the London Missionary Society*, vol. II, p. 598.
23. Balmes, *Protestantism and Catholicism*, vol. I, ch. II, p. 57. Parma, 1850.
24. Idem, ibid., ch. I, p. 27.
25. Cobbett, *History of the English Reformation*, Eighth letter.
26. Idem, ibid., Seventh letter.
27. Cochloeus, *Luther's Life and Writings*, 1523, p. 64.
28. Walch, *Luther's Works*, in German.
29. Richelieu, *Treatise for converting people separated from the Church*, Book II, ch.10.
30. Calvin, *Commentary on Peter's Second Epistle*, ch. 2, verse 2, Weislinger.
31. Baldwin, *Reply to Calvin and Beza*, p. 81. Cologne, 1564.
32. Froment, 'Amazing Events in Geneva, recently converted to the Gospel', mss, ch. 16.
33. Cobbett, ibid., Letters 1 and 16.
34. Father Ottavio Barsanti M.O., *I Protestanti tra i selvaggi della Nuova Zelanda*, p. 261. Turin, 1868.
35. Idem, ibid., p. 262. He states that this is mentioned in Dr Lang's fourth letter to Lord Durham.

Chapter Three

[1] Thomson, ibid., p. 257.
[2] Thomson, ibid., p. 254.
[3] Wakefield, *Adventures in New Zealand*.
[4] C. Hursthouse, *New Zealand*, ch. II, p. 15. London, 1861.
[5] Taylor, ibid., ch. XXX, pp. 510-511.
[6] Dr Arthur S. Thomson, *History of New Zealand*, vol. I, p. 255. London, 1859.
[7] Dr Arthur S. Thomson, ibid.
[8] Dr Thomson, ibid.
[9] Rev. Taylor, ibid., pp. 511-512.
[10] Rev. Taylor, ibid., p. 512.
[11] Idem, ibid., pp. 512-513. – Rev. R. Ward, *Life among the Maoris*, ch. V, p. 126. 1872.
[12] Taylor, ibid., p. 513.
[13] Rev. Ward, ibid. – Rev. Taylor, ibid., p. 513.
[14] Taylor, ibid.
[15] Idem, ibid.
[16] Taylor, ibid., p. 513. Thomson, ibid., p. 255.
[17] Taylor, ibid., p. 514.
[18] Idem, ibid.
[19] Thomson, ibid., pp. 256. – Hochstetter, *New Zealand*, p. 315. – Taylor, ibid., p. 514.
[20] Thomson, ibid., vol. I, p. 256.
[21] Taylor, ibid., p. 514.
[22] Ferdinand Hochstetter, *New Zealand*, ch. II, p. 242.
[23] Thomson, ibid., p. 256.
[24] Taylor, ibid., pp. 514, 515.
[25] Hursthouse, ibid., p. 17 and other Protestant writers.
[26] Wakefield, ibid.
[27] Taylor, ibid., p. 515.
[28] Taylor, ibid. – Thomson, ibid., p. 256. – Hursthouse, ibid., p. 18.
[29] Taylor, ibid., p. 516 – Thomson, ibid., pp. 256-257.
[30] Idem, ibid., pp. 516-517. Idem, ibid., p. 257.
[31] Thomson, ibid., p. 258.
[32] Pakeha Maori, *Old New Zealand*, p. 94.
[33] Idem, ibid.
[34] E.M. Bourke, *A Little History of New Zealand*, ch. X, p. 22. Melbourne, 1882.
[35] Thomson, ibid., p. 258.
[36] Thomson, ibid., p. 259.
[37] J. Busby, *Authentic information relative to New Zealand*. 1832. – Bourke, ibid., p. 22.
[38] Thomson, ibid.
[39] Rev. Yate, Parliamentary Papers, 1838. – Thomson, ibid., p. 263.
[40] H.R. Fox Bourne, *The Story of our Colonies*, ch. XXVI, p. 330. London, 1869.
[41] Rev. R. Taylor, *Te Ika a Maui*, ch. XVIII, p. 324. London, 1870.
[42] Idem, ibid.
[43] Thomson, ibid., p. 263.
[44] See *Governor's Gazette*, Sydney, 16 April 1831.
[45] Description of the Expedition. – Thomson, ibid., p. 264.
[46] Thomson, ibid., p. 269 – Taylor, ibid., ch. XXXVIII, p. 707. – Bourke, ibid., ch.

XII, p. 25.
47 Thomson, ibid., p. 267.
48 Thomson, ibid., p. 268.
49 Idem, ibid., vol.II, p. 31.
50 Idem, ibid.
51 Thomson, ibid.
52 Byrne, *Twelve Years Wandering*, etc. vol. I, p. 48.
53 Dr John D. Lang, *New Zealand in 1839*, p. 34.
54 Idem, ibid.
55 E.G. Wakefield, *Adventures in New Zealand*, vol. II, ch. XIV, p. 334.
56 Rev. W. Yate, *Account of New Zealand*, ch. IV, p. 168, 2nd edition.
57 Parliamentary Papers – Mr Earp's evidence, vol. VII, p. 156.
58 J.C. Bidwell, *Rambles in New Zealand*, p. 86.
59 Dr Lang, ibid., p. 33.
60 Father Barsanti, ibid., part V, ch. I, p. 171.

Chapter Four

1   Thomson, ibid., p. 259.
2   Thomson, ibid., p. 280.
3   *Missionary Register,* 1828. Cf. Thomson, ibid., p. 281.
4   Taylor, ibid., p. 527.
5   Taylor, ibid., p. 528.
6   Taylor, ibid.
7   Taylor, ibid., pp. 528-529. – Thomson, ibid., p. 260.
8   Idem, ibid.
9   Taylor, ibid., p. 529.
10 Thomson, ibid., p. 264. – Taylor, ibid., p. 530.
11 Idem, ibid. Taylor, ibid.
12 Thomson, ibid., p. 265. – Taylor, pp. 530-531.
13 Idem, ibid. – Taylor, ibid., p. 531.
14 Thomson, ibid. – Taylor, ibid.
15 Idem, ibid.
16 Taylor, ibid., p. 532.
17 Thomson, ibid., p. 266.
18 G.W. Rusden, *History of New Zealand,* vol. I, pp.164, 166 and 167. London, 1883.
19 Taylor, ibid., p. 532.
20 Taylor, ibid., p. 533.
21 Thomson, ibid., pp. 260, 261.
22 Idem, ibid., p. 261.
23 Thomson, ibid., p. 260, 261.
24 Idem, ibid., p. 261.
25 Thomson, ibid. – British Parliamentary Records, 1838, No. 122.
26 Thomson, ibid.
27 Thomson, ibid., p. 292.
28 Idem, ibid.
29 Shortland, *Southern Settlements*.
30 Thomson, ibid., p. 293. – Bourke, ibid., ch. IX, p. 20.

31 Thomson, ibid., p. 293.
32 Thomson, ibid., pp. 293, 296.
33 Idem, ibid., p. 294.
34 Wakefield, *Adventures in New Zealand.*
35 Shortland, *Southern Districts of New Zealand.*
36 Parl. Records, London, 1851. Captain Stokes' Report.
37 Thomson, ibid., p. 295.
38 Idem, ibid., p. 296.
39 Thomson, ibid.
40 Thomson, ibid., p. 299.
41 Thomson, ibid., p. 299.
42 Idem, ibid.
43 Idem, ibid., pp. 299 and 301.
44 Thomson, ibid., p. 300.
45 Idem, ibid.
46 Thomson, ibid., p. 269.
47 Thomson, ibid., p. 270.
48 Thomson, ibid. – *British Parliamentary Records,* 1838.
49 Bourke, ibid., p. 25.
50 Thomson, ibid.
51 *Parliamentary Records*, London, 1840.
52 Thomson, ibid., p. 271.
53 Resident's Brief, *Parliamentary Records*, 1840.
54 Thomson, ibid., p. 272.
55 Letter of Lord Aberdeen, *Parl. Records*, 1840. – A. Kennedy, *New Zealand*, ch. II, p. 71.
56 Thomson, ibid., p. 272.
57 G.W. Rusden, *History of New Zealand*, vol. I, p. 171. London, 1883.
58 Idem, ibid., p. 175.
59 Thomson, ibid., p. 273.
60 Idem, ibid., pp. 273-274.
61 *Parl. Records,* London, 1835. No. 585. Marshall's Account.
62 *Parl. Records,* London, 1838. – Thomson, ibid., p. 268.
63 *British Parliamentary Records*, 1838. – Thomson, ibid.

CHAPTER FIVE

1 Cf. 4th Letter of Dr Lang to Lord Durham. – *Br. Parl. Records*,1838. – Rev. Taylor, *The past and present of New Zealand*, etc., in Appendix. – Thomson, ibid., pp. 275, 276. – Rev. Ottavio Barsanti, ibid., pp. 261 & 262. – Bourke, ibid., pp. 26-27; and other authors.
2 *Br. Parl. Records*, 1838.
3 Summary of a document in the archives of the Colonial Government of New Zealand. – Cf. also Thomson, ibid., pp. 276-277.
4 Rev. Barsanti, *I Protestanti tra i selvaggi della Nuova Zelanda*, p. 262. Turin,1868; and Thomson, ibid., p. 278.
5 Thomson, ibid., p. 279.
6 Thomson, ibid., p. 284.

7. Bourke, ibid., ch. XII, p. 25.
8. Thomson, ibid., pp. 284 and 285.
9. Ch. Hursthouse, *New Zealand*, etc., ch. II, pp. 21 and 22. London, 1861, 2nd ed.
10. Hursthouse, ibid.
11. Thomson, ibid. p. 285.
12. R. Ward, *Life Among the Maoris*, etc., ch. VII, p. 168. London, 1872.
13. Thomson, ibid., p. 285.
14. Bourke, ibid.
15. Cf. Dr Lang, *New Zealand in 1839*, p. 30.
16. Thomson, ibid., p. 286.
17. Thomson, ibid.
18. *Southern Cross* newspaper, Auckland, 1855.
19. Thomson, ibid., p. 283.
20. Thomson, ibid., p. 288.
21. From records in Propaganda's Archives, Rome, 'New Zealand', vol. 1.
22. Ibid.
23. Thomson, ibid., p. 279.
24. Idem, ibid., pp. 279-280.
25. *British Parl. Records*, 1838.
26. Cf. *Adventures in New Zealand*, etc.
27. E. Dieffenbach, *Travels in New Zealand*, vol. 1, ch. XXVII, p. 407.
28. Rev. A. Strachan, *Life of the Rev. S. Leigh*, ch.XV, p. 439. London, 1853.
29. Cf. Bright, *A History of New Zealand*, etc.
30. Cf. Letter of Father Servant dated Hokianga 22 May 1838, published in the *Annals of Propaganda Fide*, January 1839.
31. Idem, ibid.
32. *Annals of Propaganda Fide*, etc., January Volume 1839, p.145 and following.
33. *Annals of Propaganda Fide*, etc., ibid.
34. Idem, ibid.
35. *Annals of Propaganda Fide*, January 1839 volume.
36. Idem, ibid.
37. *Annals of Propaganda Fide*, etc., ibid.
38. Documents from Propaganda Archives, Oceania, vol. I, p. 364.
39. Cf. *Annals of Propaganda*, etc., vol. 12, July 1840, p. 406.
40. *Annals*, etc., vol. XIII, Jan.1841 file, p. 38.
41. Idem, vol. XII, July file, 1840.
42. This information is taken from Propaganda archival documents, Oceania, vol.I, pp. 516-517-560.
43. Thomson, ibid., p. 313.
44. G.W. Rusden, *History of New Zealand*, vol. 1, p. 191. London, 1883.
45. *Parl. Records*, 1840. Letter of Lord Durham. – Thomson, ibid., vol. II, pp. 5-6.
46. Thomson, ibid., vol. II, p. 6. – Mirror of Parliament, 1838.
47. Rusden, ibid., p. 185. – Thomson, ibid., p. 7.
48. Thomson, ibid., p. 8.
49. *British Parliamentary Record,* 1840
50. Orders given to Captain Hobson, 14 August 1839.
51. Bourke, ibid., p. 28. – Rusden, ibid., p. 136. – Thomson, ibid., p. 12.
52. Thomson, ibid., p. 14.

53. Thomson, ibid., p. 15.
54. Thomson, ibid., p. 16 – Rusden, ibid., p. 204.

Chapter Six

1. Thomson, ibid., vol. II, pp. 17 and 18. – Rusden, ibid.
2. Thomson, ibid., p. 18. – Rusden, ibid., p. 214.
3. Op. cit.
4. Rusden, ibid., pp. 213 and 214.
5. Thomson, ibid., p. 18.
6. Rusden, ibid., p. 214. – Rev. R. Ward, *Life among the Maoris*, etc., ch. VII, p. 174.
7. Thomson, ibid., p. 19.
8. Rusden, ibid., p. 215.
9. Thomson, ibid., pp. 20-21.
10. Thomson, ibid., vol. II, p. 21. London, 1859.
11. Thomson, ibid.
12. G.W. Rusden, ibid., vol. I, p. 219.
13. Thomson, ibid., p. 22
14. Hursthouse, *New Zealand*, ch. II, p. 28. London, 1861.
15. Cf. *Parliamentary Records*, 1844.
16. Rev. Ward, *Life among the Maoris*, ch. VII, p. 179.
17. Thomson, op. cit.
18. Terry, *New Zealand, its Adventures*, etc., part I, ch. I.
19. Rusden, ibid., p. 221.
20. Dr Thomson, ibid.
21. Swainson, *New Zealand and its colonisation*.
22. Fr. O. Barsanti, *I Protestanti tra i selvaggi della Nuova Zelanda*, pp. 42-43. Turin, 1868.
23. Thomson, ibid., p. 25.
24. Dr F. Von Hochstetter, *New Zealand*, ch. VI, pp. 124-125. Stuttgart, 1867.
25. Thomson, ibid., p. 24.
26. Thomson, ibid., p. 25.
27. E.M. Bourke, ibid., p. 29.
28. Rusden, ibid., p. 243.
29. Rusden, ibid., p. 244.
30. Thomson, ibid., p. 37.
31. Thomson, ibid., p. 41.
32. Thomson, ibid., p. 44.
33. Thomson, ibid., pp. 46, 47 and 48.
34. Thomson, ibid., p. 50.
35. Hursthouse, ibid., ch. XIX, p. 483.
36. Rusden, ibid., pp. 327-328.
37. C. Hursthouse, ibid., p. 39 and p. 492, Appendix.
38. Rusden, ibid., pp. 330-331.
39. H.R. Fox Bourne, *The Story of our Colonies*, p. 350.
40. Thomson, ibid., p. 79.
41. Thomson, ibid., p. 84.
42. A. Kennedy, *New Zealand*, ch. 4, p. 99.
43. New Zealand Government *Gazette*, October 1844.

44 Thomson, ibid., p. 32.
45 See *British Parliamentary Records* 1844.
46 Fr. Barsanti, ibid., p. 252.
47 Fr. Coignet, *Maori Tales*, ch. III, 1894. – Fr. Barsanti, ibid. – *Sydney Morning Herald*.
48 Idem.
49 Rev. John Dumnor Lang, ibid., p. 34.
50 Fr. Barsanti, ibid., pp. 262-263.
51 Thomson, ibid., vol. II, p. 155.
52 Fr. O. Barsanti, ibid., p. 253.
53 Fr. Barsanti, ibid.
54 Rusden, ibid., p. 274.
55 Thomson, ibid., p. 64. – Hursthouse, ibid., etc., etc.
56 Figures are taken from official Government statistics.
57 Thomson, ibid., p. 67.
58 Kennedy, ibid., p. 98.

Chapter Seven

1 Thomson, ibid., p. 95.
2 C. Hursthouse, *New Zealand*, etc., ch. II, p. 43. London, 1861.
3 C. Hursthouse, ibid., p. 42.
4 Thomson, vol. I, p. 324. – *Parliamentary Records,* London, 1850.
5 Idem, vol. II, p. 96.
6 Thomson, ibid., p. 97. – Rusden, ibid., vol. I, p. 387.
7 Thomson, ibid., p. 98. – Rusden, ibid., p. 388. – Taylor, ibid., p. 545.
8 Thomson, ibid.
9 Thomson, ibid., p. 99.
10 Idem, ibid., p. 100.
11 Cf. *Parliamentary Records* 1844. –Thomson, ibid. – Rusden, ibid., p. 393.
12 Rusden, ibid., p. 389.
13 Thomson, ibid., p. 101.
14 Idem, ibid.
15 Idem, ibid., p. 103.
16 Rev. R. Taylor, ibid., p. 546.
17 Letter of Father Walter MacDonald, Mons. Pompallier's Secretary, 2 Feb. 1860; cf. *Records of Propaganda Fide*, vol. 32. p. 310, July 1860 file.
18 Taylor, ibid., p. 547.
19 Thomson, ibid., p. 102.
20 Idem, ibid., p. 103.
21 Thomson, ibid.,
22 Taylor, ibid., p. 548. – Thomson, ibid., p. 104.
23 H.F. MacKillop, *Recollections of 12 months service in New Zealand,* p. 36.
24 Col. Mundy, *Australasian Colonies*, vol. II, p. 179.
25 Letter of Father W. MacDonald, op. cit., p. 311.
26 Letter of Father W. MacDonald, ibid.
27 Thomson, ibid., pp. 104-105.
28 Thomson, ibid., p. 106.
29 Idem, ibid., pp. 106-107.

30 Letter of Fr. W. MacDonald, op. cit. Cf. also Records, Prop. Fide, op.cit., pp. 311-312-313.
31 Fr. W. MacDonald, ibid.
32 Thomson, ibid., p. 107.
33 Cf. *British Parliamentary Records* 1845. – Thomson, ibid., p. 108.
34 Taylor, ibid., p. 549.
35 Thomson, ibid., p. 110.
36 Idem, ibid., pp. 110-111.
37 Dispatch of Colonel Hulme. – *Parliamenary Records* 1845.
38 Thomson, ibid., p. 112. – A. Kennedy, *New Zealand*, ch. IV, p. 113.
39 Idem, ibid., p. 113.
40 Thomson, ibid., pp. 114-115.
41 Idem, ibid., pp. 114-115-116.
42 Thomson, ibid., p. 116.
43 Idem, ibid., p. 116.
44 Idem, ibid., p. 117.
45 Taylor, ibid. p. 549.
46 Thomson, ibid., pp. 117-118.
47 *British Parliamentary Records* 1846, No. 337.
48 Thomson, ibid., p. 122.
49 Rusden, ibid., p. 418.
50 Records and official documents of the Colonial Government.
51 Thomson, ibid., pp. 126-127-128. – Rusden, ibid., p. 419 and following.
52 Taylor, ibid., p. 550.
53 Thomson, ibid., p. 132.
54 Rusden, ibid., p. 434.
55 Thomson, ibid., p. 134.
56 Anglican Bishop Selwyn, *Visitation Tour*, 1848.
57 Fox, *Six Colonies in New Zealand*. – Thomson, ibid., p. 182.
58 Dr Thomson, ibid., p. 202.
59 Dr Thomson, ibid., pp. 139-140.
60 Rev. R. Taylor, ibid., p. 155. – Rusden, ibid., p. 441.
61 Rev. Taylor ibid., pp. 555-558. – Thomson, ibid., pp. 142-143.
62 Thomson, ibid., pp. 145-146.
63 Idem, ibid., pp. 147-148-152. – Rusden, ibid., vol. I, p. 495.
64 Rusden, ibid., vol. I, p. 495.
65 Thomson, ibid., p. 166.
66 Cf. *British Parliamentary Records* 1847-1848.

Chapter Eight

1 Thomson, ibid., p. 156.
2 *History and Politics*, etc., by R. Wakelin, ch. II, pp. 8, 9. Wellington, 1877.
3 *History and Politics*, etc., by R. Wakelin, ibid., ch. III, p. 11.
4 Cf. *British Parliamentary Records* 1847 and 1848.
5 Rusden, vol. I, ch. 8., appendix p. 534. London, 1882.
6 Thomson, ibid., p.158. – Rusden, ibid., p. 538.
7 Rusden, ibid., p. 539.

8 Dr J. D. Lang, *New Zealand in 1839*, p. 33.
9 *A Voice from New Zealand,* by Rev. Joseph Fletcher, Wesleyan missionary at Auckland, pp. 2, 3.
10 Rev. W. Yate, *An Account of New Zealand*, ch. IV. p. 168. 2nd edition.
11 E. Shortland, *The Southern Districts of New Zealand*, p. 268. 1851 edition.
12 Rev. R. Ward, *Life Among the Maoris in New Zealand*, ch. V, p. 103. London ed.1872.
13 Terry, *New Zealand,* etc., p. 189.
14 Selwyn, *Lord Bishop of New Zealand,* 1st Letter, p. 51. 1853 edition.
15 Cf. Brown, *New Zealand*, appendix, p. 272.
16 Dr Lang, ibid., p. 30.
17 Idem, ibid.
18 Dr Lang, ibid., p. 30.
19 Idem, ibid.
20 Idem, ibid., p. 33.
21 *Letters from Wanganui,* p. 39. 1851 edition.
22 *Rowings in the Pacific,* by a Merchant, etc., vol. I, ch. IX, p. 223.
23 Rev. R. Taylor, *The Past and Present of New Zealand,* ch. III, p. 72. London, 1868.
24 *United States Exploring Expedition*, by Charles Wilkes, vol. III, ch. XII, p. 401.
25 *Rambles in New Zealand*, by J.C. Bidwell, p. 36.
26 Thomson, ibid., vol. I, p. 317.
27 Rev. Yate, *Account of New Zealand*, ch. V, p. 222.
28 J. Bright, *A History of New Zealand*, ch. VII, p. 127.
29 Dr Selwyn, *Church in the Colonies*, No. VII, p. 44.
30 Rev. Robert Ward, *Life Among the Maoris of New Zealand*, ch. V, p. 101. London, 1872.
31 Dr Thomson, ibid., vol. II, p. 156.
32 Fr. O. Barsanti, ibid., p. 258.
33 Dr Ernest Dieffenbach, *Travels in New Zealand*, vol. I, p. 407.
34 Fr. Barsanti, ibid., p. 259.
35 Dr Thomson, ibid., vol. I, p. 326.
36 Earle, *Nine Months Residence in New Zealand*, pp. 171-173.
37 *Adventures in New Zealand*, by John Rochefort, ch. III, p. 28.
38 Wakefield, *Adventures in New Zealand,* vol.II, p. 360.
39 Terry, *New Zealand*, etc. p. 190.
40 Cf. *Propaganda Fide Records*, vol. XVII, p. 59, January 1845 file.
41 *The Gospel in New Zealand*, by Miss Tucker, ch. X, p. 117 and ch. XX, p. 253. London, 1855.
42 Augustus Earle, *Nine Months Residence in New Zealand*, p. 171
43 Rev. J.D. Lang, *New Zealand*, p. 43.
44 Dr Thomson, ibid., vol. I , p. 316.
45 *Asiatic Sydney Journal*, vol. XXIX, p. 189.
46 Bright, *History of New Zealand*, p. 126.
47 Idem, ibid., p. 121.
48 *Savage Life*, by Mr Angas, vol. III, p. 118.
49 *Savage Life*, by Mr Angas, vol. III, p. 121.
50 *A Summer's Excursion in N.Z.,* p. 157.
51 Idem, ibid., p. 165.
52 Cf. *British Parliamentary Records*, vol. 45, p. 12. London, 1854.

Chapter Nine

1. Rusden, ibid., pp. 489-490. – Thomson, ibid., vol. I, p. 152.
2. Thomson, ibid., p. 192.
3. Cf. *New Zealand Parliamentary Records*, 1854. – Thomson, ibid.
4. Thomson, ibid., p. 193.
5. Rusden, ibid., p. 531.
6. Fr. Ottavio Barsanti, ibid., pp. 38, 39.
7. Thomson, ibid., vol.II, p. 225.
8. *Life Among the Maoris of New Zealand,* by the Rev. R. Ward, ch. XIII, p. 306.
9. Idem, ibid., p. 307.
10. Idem, ibid., p. 306.
11. Report of Mr Cooper, Government Commissioner to the Governor, 1854.
12. Thomson, ibid., pp. 227-228.
13. Rev. Ward, ibid., pp. 308-309.
14. Rusden, ibid., vol.1, p. 578.
15. Thomson, ibid., pp. 227-251.
16. Dispatch of Colonel Browne, 20 September 1859, to the Secretary of State.
17. Thomson, ibid., p. 225. – Rusden, ibid., p. 555.
18. Rusden, ibid., p. 556.
19. Rusden, ibid., vol. 1, p. 597, note.
20. Thomson, ibid., p. 259.
21. Rev. R. Ward, ibid., ch. XIV, pp. 332-333.
22. Rev. R. Taylor, *The Past and Present of N.Z.*, etc., ch. VII, p. 114.
23. Rev. Ward, ibid., p. 334.
24. Rev. R. Ward, ibid., ch. XIV. p. 326.
25. Rusden, ibid., pp. 573-574.
26. Rusden, ibid., vol. I, p. 579.
27. Rev. R. Ward, ibid., p. 338.
28. *First Epistle to the Corinthians*, ch. IV, verse 8.
29. Rusden, ibid., p. 582.
30. Rev. R. Ward, ibid., p. 339.
31. Thomson, ibid., p. 241.
32. Rusden, ibid.,vol. I, p. 569.
33. Thomson, ibid., pp. 269-271.
34. Cf. *Hansard* (Colonial Parliamentary Records), vol. I, pp. 104, 105.
35. Cf. Official Records, *Hansard*, vol. IX.

Chapter Ten

1. Cf. *Parliamentary Records* 1881.
2. B. Wells, *History of Taranaki,* p. 208. 1878.
3. Rev. R. Ward, ibid., p. 392.
4. Cf. *Hansard,* Parliamentary Records 1860.
5. Rusden, *History of New Zealand*, vol. II, p. 76. London, 1883.
6. Rev. Taylor, *The Past and Present of New Zealand*, ch. VII, p. 131.
7. Idem, ibid., p. 132.

8. G.W. Rusden, ibid., vol. II, p. 79.
9. *Bush Fighting*, by Major-General Sir J.E. Alexander, appendix II, p. 311. 1873.
10. Rusden, ibid., p. 93.
11. Rusden, ibid., p. 108.
12. Rusden, p. 108.
13. General Alexander, ibid., ch. III, pp. 41-42. – Rusden, ibid., pp. 134-135.
14. Rusden, *History of New Zealand*, vol. II, p. 136.
15. Idem, ibid., p. 155.
16. Major General Alexander, ibid., ch. IV, p. 65.
17. G.W. Rusden, vol. II, p. 183.
18. Rusden, ibid., p. 199.
19. General Alexander, ibid., ch. X, p. 170. – Rusden, ibid., pp. 204-209.
20. Rev. Ward, ibid., ch. XVIII, pp. 411, 412.
21. General Alexander, ibid., ch. XI, p. 202.
22. General Alexander, ibid., ch. XI, pp. 190 and following.
23. Rev. R. Ward. ibid., ch. XX, p. 427.
24. Major General Alexander, ibid., ch. XIII, p. 229.

Chapter Eleven

1. Fr. O. Barsanti, *I Protestanti tra i selvaggi della Nuova Zelanda*, p. 83.
2. Idem, ibid., pp. 84, 85.
3. Idem, ibid., p. 86 and following.
4. Fr. Barsanti, ibid., p. 186.
5. Ward, *Life,* etc. ch. XXII, p. 443.
6. Rusden, ibid., pp. 274, 275.
7. Idem, ibid., p. 275.
8. Rusden, ibid., pp. 310, 311.
9. Fr. Barsanti, ibid., pp. 120, 121.
10. Ibid.
11. Fr. Barsanti, ibid., pp. 120, 121.
12. E.M. Bourke, *A Little History of New Zealand*, p. 60. Melboourne, 1882.
13. *The Weekly Register,* July 1865 in Fr. Barsanti, p. 126.
14. Influential chief, taken prisoner on 8 February, as already mentioned.
15. Captain Levy's brother, charged by the Hauhau to take the letter to the governor in Auckland and bring back his reply.
16. Fr. Barsanti, ibid., p. 136 and following.
17. Fr. Barsanti, ibid., p. 141.
18. Driven from his diocese like a thief, Williams was angry that Catholic priests did not suffer the same fate and wrote to a London newspaper that, 'the Hauhau superstition was similar to the abominations of Papism'. Such blatant calumny angered many Protestants themselves as well as journalists. The *New Zealand Herald*, among other papers, wrote, 'The Bishop of Waiapu is full of bile.'
19. Rusden, ibid., vol. II, p. 323.
20. Idem, ibid., p. 350.
21. Rusden, ibid., p. 396.
22. Rusden, ibid., p. 398.
23. Idem, ibid., p. 488.

24. Colonial Parliamentary Records, 1869. A. No.10.
25. Rusden, ibid., p. 504.
26. Rusden, ibid., p. 528.
27. Rusden, ibid., p. 476.
28. Idem, ibid., pp. 451, 491.
29. Rusden, ibid., p. 499.
30. Rusden, ibid., p. 512.
31. *Reminiscences of the War in New Zealand*, p. 255. London, 1879.
32. Rusden, ibid., p. 513.
33. Rusden, ibid., p. 528.
34. Rusden, ibid., pp. 136, 137.
35. Rusden, ibid., p. 560.
36. Colonial Parliamentary Records, 1870. Doc. No. 36.
37. Rev. Ward, *Life* etc., ch. XIX, p. 424. – Rusden, ibid., pp. 448-449.
38. Cf. *Hansard* Parliamentary Records, vol. XII, 1872.
39. Ibid. vol. XII, p. 166. 30 July 1872 session.
40. Cf. Parliamentary Records, *Hansard*, vol. IX, p. 185.

Chapter Twelve

1. Barsanti, ibid., p. 121.
2. Cf. *Life of Selwyn*. London, 1879.
3. Rusden, ibid., vol. II, pp. 458, 459.
4. Father Barsanti, ibid., p. 110.
5. Fr. Barsanti, ibid., p. 134.
6. Rusden, ibid., vol. II, p. 450.
7. Mons. Moran's Report to the Sacred Congregation of Propaganda, cf. Propaganda Archives, New Zealand, vol. X.
8. Cf. Propaganda Archives, New Zealand, vol. IX.
9. This information was obtained from the records of the Franciscan headquarters in Rome, and from Father Mahoney, who died in 1888 and provided details personally to the author in 1882.
10. There is only brief information in this *History* about the missions and missionaries in New Zealand, because of the dearth of material in the Propaganda archives. The little we have mentioned was taken partly from the records of Propaganda Fide and from sources in New Zealand. In 1889 we asked the Marist Fathers in Rome for further information on their missions and missionaries in New Zealand. They replied that their extensive records were in their Lyons mother house. We were informed that Marist priests were working on the history of their missions, particularly that of New Zealand, their first mission, and that it would soon be published. Perhaps this explains why Lyons did not send us the information requested, given the extraordinary amount of information the Order possesses. We are certain that their opus will be extremely interesting and of the greatest importance and we hope to see it soon available to the public.
11. Cf. *Annals of Prop.*, etc., July 1876 volume.

Chapter Thirteen

1. Rusden, ibid., vol. II, p. 595.
2. Rusden, ibid., vol. II, p. 156.
3. Cf. *Hansard*, or Official Records, 1869.
4. Rusden, ibid., vol. III, pp. 10, 11.
5. Idem, ibid., p. 24.
6. Rusden, ibid., p. 156.
7. Idem, ibid., pp. 28, 29, 49.
8. Idem, ibid., pp. 149, 150.
9. Idem, ibid., p. 153.
10. Rusden, ibid., p. 352.
11. Cf. *Hansard*, Official Records, vol. XII, pp. 228 ff.
12. Rusden, ibid., vol. III, p. 85.
13. Cf. *Hansard*, ibid.
14. Rusden, ibid., vol. III, pp. 11, 46.
15. Rusden, ibid., p. 354.
16. Rusden, *New Zealand*, vol. III, pp. 121-122.
17. Cf. *Hansard*, Official Records, 1876.
18. Rusden, ibid., vol. III, p. 13.
19. Rusden, ibid.

Chapter Fourteen

1. Cf. Official records, *Hansard*, 9 June 1882.
2. Idem, ibid.,
3. Cf. *Hansard*, ibid.
4. Cf. Report of Governor Gordon to the British Government, 26 Feb. 1881.
5. Gordon's Report. – Rusden, ibid., p. 239 and ff.
6. Cf. Report of 26 Feb. 1881.
7. Cf. Official Records, 1882.
8. Ibid.
9. Cf. Official British Government Records 1882.
10. For more information concerning the amazing phenomenon, the reader is referred to vol. I, pt. I, ch. IV, pp. 60 and ff. of this *History*.
11. While the present volume was going to press, unfortunate news was received of the sudden death of Monsignor W.E. Luck in Auckland on 22 January 1896, through a heart condition which he had suffered for many years. R.I.P.
12. Father Coignet S.M., *Maori Tales*, no. VII, 1894.
13. Thomas Cholomondeley, *Ultima Thule*, ch. XVI, pp. 271, 281. London, 1864.
14. Idem, ibid., p. 71.
15. *The Past and Present of New Zealand,* by Rev. Taylor, ch. III, p. 70.
16. Th. Cholomondeley, *Ultima Thule*, ch. XVI, p. 196.

Index

The Italian edition of this book was not indexed: this index has been created for the English edition. Occasionally Vaggioli's spelling of proper names differs from the modern spellings used here. Where confusion might arise, cross-references between spellings have been provided. In a few cases, Vaggioli's spelling has been used, as the person or place referred to has yet to be positively identified.

Active 30
Ahikereru 227
Akaroa 55, 57, 88, 100-2, 112
Aletag, Fr *see* Alletag
Alexander, Maj. Gen. J.E. 186, 197-8
Alexandra 293
Alletag, Fr Jean Joseph 241-2
Alligator 67-8
Angas, George xix, xx, 145
Anglicans 29-34, 36, 38, 42, 66-7, 69-70, 94-8, 110-12, 116, 137-41, 149-50, 162, 204, 209, 215-16, 235-9, 307; land acquired by missionaries 30, 34, 48-50, 66-7. 69-70, 72, 75, 79, 110-12, 137-41 *see also* London Missionary Society
Aparima 62
Arapawa 13
Arawa tribe 196, 214, 227, 209
Armitage, Judge 188
arms trade 43-5, 48, 51, 54-5
Arney, Sir George 271
Astley, Constance xix
Astrolabe 50
Atkinson, Harry (PM) 286
Aubert, Mother Mary (Suzanne) xx, xxii
Auckland 100, 102, 106, 107, 108, 112, 113, 118, 119, 122-6 *passim*, 134, 146, 160, 179, 206, 207, 218, 244, 262, 293, 293-4; tribes 186 *see also* Catholic Church: Diocese of Auckland
Austen, Col. C.W. 188
Australian settlers 150

Baker, C. 111

Banks Peninsula 55, 60, 88, 100
Banks, Sir Joseph 14
Banks, Sir Robert 20
Barrett, Dicky 91-2
Barsanti, Fr Ottavio xv, 34, 50, 97-8, 111, 204
Bay of Islands 25-30 *passim*, 36-48 *passim*, 51, 58, 59, 65-7, 64-7, 74-9, 86, 98, 99, 110, 112, 113, 119-24, 127, 145, 146, 159, 183
Bay of Plenty 36, 46, 59, 195, 247 *see also* Opotiki, Tauranga, Whakatane
Belich, James xvii, xxiii
Bering, Francis 89
Berry, Mr 26
Biggs, Maj. Reginald Newton 223-4, 225
Boibieux, Fr Francis 206, 246
Bolland, Rev. Bruce vii
Booth, Col. H.G. 196
Booth, Judge 220
Bourke, Sir Richard 67
Bourne, Fox 46, 106
Bowen, Governor George 218-20, 228, 232, 233, 271
Boyd 26-7, 29, 42
Bret, Fr C. 80, 81
Bright, Mr 83, 145
Britannia settlement 99
Broughton (army interpreter) 214
Brown, Capt. 226
Browne, Governor Gore 160, 163, 165, 166, 170, 175-80, 180-2, 236-7
Bryce, John xxi, 286, 289, 290-2, 297
Buckingham, Duke of 219

Bunbury, Maj. 96
Burnett, Commodore 193
Burton, Commander 193
Busby, James (British Resident) 49, 66-7, 72-9, 94, 98, 109
Byrne, J. 49

Calliope 130
Cambridge 230, 293
Cameron, Gen. Sir Duncan Alexander 180, 185, 186-91, 196, 208-9, 213, 229
Canterbury Association 149-52
Capel, Capt. 226
Carey, Brig.-Gen. G.J. 191
Carr, Capt. 224
Catholic Church: *cathedrals*: 254 (Wellington), 301 (Auckland); *churches*: St Benedict's, Newton x, 295-6, 301-2; St Mary's, Wellington 252; *diocese*: Auckland 142, 240-1, 247-8, 250, 251, 252, 294-5, 300-2, 307, 309; Christchurch 304-5, 309; Dunedin 249-50, 309; Wellington 142, 147, 251, 252-5, 305, 306-7, 309; Wellington-Otago 248-9; *missions* 79, 81-9, 142-8, 295, 306-7; *orders*: Benedictines viii, 295, 300-2, 309; Christian Bros 309; Dominicans 250, 309; Franciscans 148, 239-41, 251-2; Good Shepherd nuns 309; Jesuits 294, 296, 309; Josephites 309; Little Sisters of the Poor 309; Mill Hill Fathers 307, 309, 310; Nazarenes 309; Sacred Heart nuns 309; Sisters of Mercy 146, 156, 250-1, 256, 309; Sisters of Our Lady of the Missions 249, 250, 256, 306-7; Society of Mary (Marist) 142, 147-8, 152, 249-50, 253, 305, 306, 309; Tertiaries of Mary 309; *schools*: 146-7, 152, 157, 240, 250-1, 256, 279, 305, 306-7; *statistics*: 88-9, 136, 233, 255-6, 306, 309; *summary* 308-9
Chanel, Fr Pierre 80, 81
Chatham Islands 59, 216, 221, 222, 305, 309
Chevron, Fr J. 80, 81
Chinese 143, 306
Cholomondeley, Thomas 307, 310
Christchurch 149-50, 151, 152, 239, 292 *see also* Catholic Church: Diocese of Christchurch
Chute, Gen. Sir Trevor 217-18, 219
Clarke, Rev. George 111, 137, 138
Clifford, Lord Charles 160
Cloudy Bay 57, 60, 67, 105
coal 174
Coater, Dandeson 89
Cobbett, William 32, 33
Coleridge, Rev. 238
Colomban, Michael 83
colonial army statistics 231-2
Comte de Paris/Conte de Paris 100
Cook Strait 52, 53, 59, 77, 88, 91, 98, 135, 165
Cook, Capt. James 13-15, 18, 21, 99-100
Cooper, Mr 163
Coquille 50
Coromandel x-xi, 156-7, 199, 241
Croke, Rev. Thomas 248, 250-2
Crozet, Capt. Julien 16-17, 18

Danes 265
Darling, Governor Ralph, NSW 47, 57
Darwin, Charles xix, xx, xxi
Davis, R. 111
Davitt, Michael xix, xvi
De Bry, Theodore xxiii
de las Casas, Bartholomew xxiii
de Solages, Mons. Gabriel Henri Jerome 80
De Surville, Jean François-Marie 16
de Thierry, Baron Charles H. 71-5, 81
D'Entrecasteaux, Admiral Antoine Raymond Joseph Bruni 19
defence, foreign 272-3
Delphine 80
Despard, Col. Henry 126, 127
Dieffenbach, Ernst xix, xx, 82, 143
Dilke, Charles xix, xx
Dolphin 121
Domett, Alfred 189
Druid 90, 93
Drury 184, 186
D'Urville, Capt. Dumont 50, 64
Dunedin 134 152, 173-4; native reserve 275 *see also* Catholic Church: Diocese of Dunedin

Duperry, Capt. 50
Durham, Lord 28, 47, 89-90, 139, 140
Dusky Bay 12, 18, 19, 24

Earle, Augustus xix, xx, 144, 145
earthquakes 106, 135, 165, 255, 302
Eclipse 185, 210, 212, 213
education 171, 278-82; New Zealand University College 232, 279-80 *see also* Catholic Church: schools
Egmont, Mt *see* Taranaki, Mt
Elizabeth 55, 57
Emerald 290
England, Capt. 105
Europe 81

Fairburn, W.T. 111
Featherston, Dr Isaac Earl 264
Fencibles 134
Ferguson, Sir James 271
Fines, Rev. Fr *see* Fynes
Firth, Joseph Clifton 229
FitzRoy, Sir Robert 107-8, 111, 113, 115, 118-20, 124, 127-8
flax 44-5, 63, 76, 261
Fletcher, Rev. 139
Ford, S.H. 111
forests, exploitation of xi
Foveaux Strait 62, 77
Fox, Sir William (PM) 185, 232-3, 260
Fraser, Capt. 276, 285
Fraser, Maj. James 216
freemasonry 278-80, 282, 298, 307-9
Fremantle, Commodore 213
French 52, 64-5, 100-2, 265 *see also* Akaroa
Fulloon, James 213-14
Fynes, Fr Henry 251, 252, 296, 302

Galatea fort 228
Garavel, Rev. Joseph Marie 242-5, 247
Garin, Fr Antoine Marie 253
Gascoigne, Lieut. 222
Gate pa 196-7
Gavin, Fr *see* Garin
George III 15
George IV 36
Germans 265
Gillies, Judge Thomas Banntyne 292

Gipps, Sir George 93, 119
Gisborne viii-x, 216, 223-4, 225, 226, 295
Gladstone, W. E. 137
Glandston, W. E. *see* Gladstone, W. E.
Glenelg, Lord 79
gold 155-8, 171-2, 174, 199, 218, 229, 248-9, 259, 260
Gold, Col. Charles Emilius 177-8
Golden Bay 172
Gordon, Sir Arthur 272, 288, 290-2, 297
Gore, Lieutenant 15
Gorst, John Eldon 185
government: 1848 constitution 135-6; 1852 constitution 158-9; 1880s 297-8; provincial government 159, 160, 170-1, 260, 273-4; responsible government 169-70
Grace, Rev. Thomas Samuel 210, 212, 238, 244
Grace, Dr (MP) 279-80
Grange, Fr Jean 204, 206, 247
Grant, Capt. W.E. 127
Greer, Col. H.H. 195-7, 209
Gregory XVI, Pope 80, 81
Grey, Earl 135, 147
Grey, Sir George 127-8, 130, 132, 133-4, 135-6, 137-8, 156, 158-60, 165, 176, 182-6, 195, 197-8, 208, 209, 211, 212, 214, 218-19, 243, 244, 271-2, 275, 286, 293
Grimes, Mons. John 305
Guard, Capt. John 67-9
Guard, Elizabeth 68
Gudgeon, Lieut. T.W. 226

Hadfield, Octavius xix, xx, 244, 245
Hall, Sir John 29, 30, 286, 291, 294, 297
Hamlin, J. 111
Hangaroa River 224
Harriet 67
Hauhau *see* Pai marire
Havelock 199
Hawkes Bay 152, 164, 216
Hawkesworth, Dr 15
Hazard 118, 120-1, 126
Heemerkirk 13
Heke, Hone 98, 115-27, 138
Helswell, Edward 112

Henare (chief) 214
Hepanaia 204
Herald 94
Herd, Capt. 48
Herrick, Col. J.L. 227
Hikioi (newspaper) 185
Hiko 56
Hikurangi 127, 129
Hinaki (chief) 37-40
Hingstone, Mr 119
Hobson, Capt. William 59, 90, 93-6, 98, 99, 101-2, 103, 104, 107, 108, 111, 113
Hokianga 34, 36, 42, 48, 72, 75, 84-8, 97, 111, 112, 140, 240, 241, 307
Hokitika 174, 199
Home, Sir Edward 125
Hongi Hika 25, 35-45, 51-3, 58, 72, 115-16
Hooker, Sir Joseph Dalton 98
Horomora/Solomon, Tiu 213
Hughes, Robert xvii
Huke, Noa *see* Noa, Waikato Tainui
Hulme, Col. William 118, 124-5, 130
Hunahuna pa 42
Hunter, Maj. William Magee 221
Hursthouse, Charles 12, 76-7, 96, 104
Hutchinson (MP) 285
Hutt valley 91, 99, 129-30, 148

Ihaia (chief) 164, 165, 179
Ikorangi *see* Hikurangi 127, 129
Irish 249-50, 256-7, 265
Italians 265

Jackson, Capt. 189
Jervois, Sir William 297

Kai Tahu xix *see also* Ngai Tahu
Kaikohe 115
Kaipara 39, 41, 86, 88, 104
Kaitake 203
Kakatore *see* Katatore
Kanaks 277
Kapiti Island 55-6, 60
Karaka, Arama 164
Katatore (chief) 163-5, 179
Kate 213
Katikora River 185

kauri gum 122-3
Kawau Island 198, 219
Kawhia 52, 53
Kawiti (chief) Te Ruki 58, 95, 120, 124-5, 127, 128, 129
Kemp, James 111
Kendall, Thomas 30, 34, 36, 51, 72, 75
Kennedy, A. 108
Kereopa 204, 209, 211, 214, 215, 231, 238, 243
Kereti 214
Kerikeri 30, 118, 125
Kihikihi 191, 292
Kimberley, Lord 299
King Country 167-8, 180-93, 228, 230, 231, 293-4, 303
King movement 167-9, 180-93, 208, 232, 238
King, Capt. 20, 29, 30
King, J. 51, 111
King, William *see* Te Rangitake
Kingi, Wiremu *see* Te Rangitake
Kohekohe 185
Kohimarama 181
Kororareka 25, 28, 59, 65, 66, 67, 75-8, 85, 87, 94, 98, 111, 112, 115, 116, 118-22, 125, 129, 146, 240, 241
Kororareka Association 78-9
Kotore 128

La Favorite 64
La Perouse 19
Lambert, Capt. 68
Land League 162-5, 166-7, 180
land: acquisition (1820s-30s) 48-9; confiscation 189, 193, 208, 274-5, 286; Crown pre-emption 93-4, 108, 170, 300; government inquiry into 109-11; Maori communal ownership 48, 161, 169, 285-6; Maori petition against sale of 298-300; South Island 133, 149, 154; summary of Maori land acquisition 274-6 *see also* Anglicans: land acquired by missionaries; New Zealand Company; Waitangi, Treaty of
Lang, Rev. Dr J. D. 28, 49, 50, 62, 110, 139, 140, 145
Langlois, Capt. Jean François 100

Lautour, Dr 292
Lawry, Rev. Walter, 139
Lee, Dr Samuel 38, 42
Leo XIII, Pope xiii, 294, 300, 304
Levy, Samuel 210, 211, 112
Lloyd, Capt. 190, 202, 206
Lloyd, Henry D. xix, xxi
London Missionary Society 29-30, 66, 69, 70, 72, 79, 81-2, 90, 110, 137-41, 206, 236
Lord Worsley 193
Lord, Mr 116
Luck, Dom John Edmund x, 300-2, 307
Lyttelton 149

McDonald, Fr James 123, 251, 307
McDonnell, Col. Thomas 217-18, 220-1, 229-30
Mackay, James 288
MacKillop 121
McLean, Donald 164, 175, 216, 229, 230, 260, 275, 286, 288, 293
Mahia Peninsula 225
Mahoney, Fr 295
Mahungamuka *see* Maungamuka
Mair, Maj. William Gilbert 227
Makaretu 226
Maketu 88, 213, 307
Manawapou 162
Manawatu 52, 53
Mangatawhiri 184-5, 186-7
Mangonui 16, 86, 104, 240, 241
Maniapoto, Rewi 192, 215
Manning, Cardinal 255, 300, 305
Manukau 102, 193
Maori forces 231-2; fatalities 232
Maori preserved heads 45-7
Maori seats in Parliament 218, 259
Maori sovereignty 98 *see also* King movement
Marion du Fresne, Marc Joseph 16-17, 65
Marist *see* Catholic Church: Orders
Marlborough 199
Marlow, Capt. 126
Marquis de Castro 16,17
Marsden, Samuel xix, 25, 29-30, 34, 36, 37
Marshall, W. B. 68

Martin, Fr Aime 249
Martin, Sir William 176, 219, 245
Marutuahu 15
Mascarin 16
masonry *see* freemasonry
Matakitaki pa 40-1
Matamata 58, 88
Matara 25
Matata 307
Matekatea 217
Matilde 121
Maungamuka 42
Maungatawhiri *see* Mangatawhiri
Maunsell, Archdeacon Robert 96, 111
measles 159
Mellon, Mr 119
Mercer 293
Mercury Bay 39
Meremere/Meri-meri 188
Methodists *see* Wesleyans
Métin, Albert xix, xx
Michael, Br *see* Colomban, Michael 83
migration policies 171-4, 264-9
Moanui (chief) 164
Mohaka 227
Mohanga 25
Moka 145
Mokau 165
Mokena (chief) 214
Mongonui *see* Mangonui
Moran, Cardinal Patrick Francis 249-50, 304
Moreau, Fr Delphin 248-9
Morgan, Lieut. 122
Morison, Dr 30
Mormons 256
Moturoa 221
Mounsell, *see* Maunsell
Moutoa Gardens xxi
Muaupoko tribe 54
Mundy, Col. 121
Murderers Bay 13
musket wars *see* tribal wars

Nanto-Bordelaise Company 101
Napier 148, 152, 153, 164, 216, 225, 229, 231
Native Land Courts 285

native reserve, Dunedin 275
Nelson 103-9 *passim*, 112, 113, 118, 172, 199, 253
Nene, Tamati Waka (Thomas Walker) 39, 41, 95, 118, 120, 124-6, 129, 133, 183
New Caledonia 142
New Plymouth 102, 112, 176, 179, 217, 221, 288, 291, 292
New Plymouth Company 102
New Zealand Company 89-92, 93, 98-9, 102-10, 112, 113, 118, 134, 149, 154-5, 169
Newcastle, Duke of 159, 182, 184
Nga Puhi 36, 58, 59, 115, 299
Nga Roimata 56
Ngai Tahu xx, 57
Nganui (chief) 16
Ngapora, Tamati 229
Ngaruawahia 168, 189, 190, 293
Ngatapa pa 226-7
Ngatata, Wiremu Tako 285
Ngati Apa 54
Ngati Awa 59, 167, 175, 209
Ngati Hine 13
Ngati Kahungunu ix, 164
Ngati Kaungunu *see* Ngati Kahungunu
Ngati Maniapoto 52
Ngati Maru 39
Ngati Raukawa 52
Ngati Ruanui 162, 178, 208, 209, 286
Ngati Whatua 41, 122
Ngati-rua-nui *see* Ngati Ruanui
Ngatiaua/Ngatiawa/Ngatihawa *see* Ngati Awa
Ngutu-o-te-manu 220
Nias, Capt. Joseph 94
Nicholas, John L. 26, 30
Nikorima 165
Noa, Waikato Tainui x
Nopera, Panakaraeo (chief) 97
Norfolk Island 19-20
Normanby, Lord 94, 271, 272
Norwegians 265

Oakura 209
Ohaeawai 126
Ohau 53
Oheawai *see* Ohaeawai

Ohinemutu 294, 307
Okaihau pa 125, 133
Omaha 198
Omata 185
Oneroa 125, 126
Onslow, Lord 297
Opepe 228
Opotiki 88, 145, 204, 210-15, 220, 227, 228, 231, 238, 241-3, 247, 303
Orakau pa 191-3
Orange, Claudia xvii
Orau-moa 57
Orohihi 229
Orokawa 17
Orpheus 193
Otago 134, 149, 150, 154, 172, 174, 199, 222
Otaki 52, 106, 130, 145, 148
Otaki River 59
Otepawa pa 217

Pacific Islands, slave trade 277-8
Pai marire 152, 202-6, 209-17, 220, 225-6, 230-1, 237-8, 241, 243, 244, 245-7, 250, 256, 287, 303, 306
Paihia 138
Pakeha-Maori 25, 63-4
Pakowai 148
Papahurihia xix
Papakura 188
Paparatu 224
Parakino 300
Parata, Wiremu Te Kakakura 232
Parihaka 286, 287, 290-3, 297
Parliament Buildings *see* Wellington, Government Buildings
Parore, Te Awha (chief) 299
Parris, Robert Reid 217, 288
Patara (prophet) 204, 209, 213, 243-4
Patea 220
Patene (native mediator) 195
Paterangi pa 190-1
Patteson, Bishop John Coleridge 277-8
Peata 123
Pehi *see* Te Pehi
Petre 102
Phillip, Governor Arthur, NSW 20
Phillpotts, Lieut. George 120, 127

Pikiriki 209
Pius IX, Pope 142, 248, 249, 252, 255
Pokaikai 217
Polack, Joel Samuel 120
Pollen, Dr 276
Pomare (chief) 58, 124-5, 130
Pompallier, Jean Baptiste François, Bishop 80-6, 120-4, 142, 176, 219, 239-40, 242, 243, 245, 248, 252
population: European 112, 136, 174, 232, 233, 265, 282; Maori 112, 174, 232, 233, 282, 305, 310, 311
Porirua 130, 131
Port Chalmers 134
Port Cooper 149-50
Port Nicholson 88, 91-2, 98
Port Ohiwa 303
Potatau I *see* Te Whero Whero
Potatau II *see* Tawhiao, King
Poverty Bay 163, 215, 221, 223, 225, 255
Pratt, Maj.-Gen. Thomas Simson 178-80
Prendergast, James 272, 290-1, 297
Presbyterians 134, 149, 235
Pringle, Capt. 213-14
Propaganda Sacred Congregation 80, 85, 249, 250, 255-6, 295, 300
provincial government 159, 160, 170-1, 273-4; abolished 260, 274
Puhoi 210
Pukehinahina 196
Pukekohe 188
Pukere 165
Puketakawere pa 178
Pungarehu 217, 291
Purua pa 53
Putahi pa 217
Putiki pa 53

Queen Charlotte Sound 18, 60, 62, 91

Rangatira 213
Rangiaowhia 168, 190-1, 229
Rangihaeata *see* Te Rangihaeata
Rangihoua 30
Rangihu *see* Rangihoua
Rangiohia *see* Rangiaowhia
Rangiriri 188-9
Rangitake (disciple of Te Ua) 204

Rangitake *see* Te Rangitake, Wiremu Kingi
Rapihana (chief) 228-9
Rattlesnake 59
Rauparaha *see* Te Rauparaha
Rawiri 163, 175, 197
Razorback fort 188
Redwood, Very Rev. Francis M. 253-5, 296, 306, 309
Regiments: 40th 192; 43rd Infantry 196; 58th 159; 99th 118; 96th 106
Reignier, Fr Euloge 144, 152
Reischek, Andreas xix, xxi
religious affiliations 88-9, 136, 255; Maori 256-7, 308-9
Resolution Cove 60
Richardson (New Zealand Company agent) 106
Richardson, Maj. W.A. 224
Richmond, C.W. 169
Richmond, J. C. 226
Richmond, Maj. 106
Rifleman 222
Ring, Charles 156
Riseborough, Hazel xv
Robertson, Capt. David 120, 122
Robinson, Mr 213-14
Robinson, Sir Hercules 272
Rochefort, Mr 144
Rodney 59
Rolland, Fr 249
Ronald, Fr 221
Rongotute 13
Rook, Col. 218
Ropata, Wahawaha (chief) 214, 216, 226-7, 230, 231
Rore (chief) 53
Rosario 223
Ross, Capt. William 98
Rotorua 36, 39-40, 228, 246
Rotorua tribes 58-9
Ruapekapeka 98, 129
Ruatara 25, 36
Ruhe 125
Rusden, G.W. xxi, 57, 96, 97, 119, 190, 191, 216, 218, 245, 259, 261
Russell 76, 124 *see also* Kororareka
Russell, Capt. 276
Russell, Lord 67, 76, 77, 93, 101, 112, 113

Russia 273

St Benedict's, Newton x, 295-6
St Jean Baptiste 15
Saint John, Col. J.H.H. 227, 228, 229
St Louis 121
St Mary's, Wellington 252
St Patrick's College 305
Scots 265
Scott, Dick xvii
Scottish Association 134, 149, 154
sealers 23-5, 26, 35, 59-60
Selwyn, Rev. George Augustus xix, 102, 121, 137, 138, 139, 141, 160, 176, 184, 191, 212, 219, 236-9, 244, 245
Servant, Fr 80, 81, 83, 85, 86
Sheehan, John (MP) 276, 286
Shepherd, J. 51, 110, 111
Shortland, Edward xx
Shortland, Willoughby 60, 104, 106, 108, 111
Siegfried, André xix, xx
Simeoni, Cardinal Giovanni xiii
Simmons, David ix, xv
slave trade, Pacific Islands 276-8
Smith, Mr 195
Solander, Dr Daniel 14
Soulas, Fr Christophe 306
Stafford, Sir Edward William 169-70, 218, 228, 232, 260
Stanley, Lord 106
Starling, Commodore 278
Steins, Mons. Walter viii, 294-7, 300
Stewart Island 62, 133
Stewart, Capt. 55-7
Strachan 83
Sullivan, Fr Adalbert x
Swainson, William 78, 97
Swanson (MP) 176, 275
Sydney 23, 29, 36, 45, 46, 93, 109

Ta Waho *see* Vaggioli, Dom Felice
Tahutai 204
Taiaroa 275
Taikomako 215
Takamoana, Karaitiana 275
Takouri (chief) 17
Tamaiharanui (chief) 55-7

Tamiana, Wirimu *see* Te Waharoa
Tara, chief's son 26, 42
Taranaki 52, 103, 107, 108, 112, 161-5, 185, 189, 190, 218, 286, 294; Pai marire converts 202-3, 243-4; tribes 55, 58-9, 68, 69, 71, 162-5, 177, 186, 187, 288, 292, 300, 303-4; war 98, 175-80, 181, 182, 190, 193-4, 198-9, 208, 222, 227, 286 *see also* Parihaka
Taranaki, Mt (Mt Egmont) 14, 58
Tarawera, Mt 302
Tasman Bay 102-3
Tasman, Abel 12-13
Tataraimaka 185
Taupiri 185
Taupo 163, 166-7, 228, 229, 307; tribes 59, 186, 229, 230, 242
Tauranga 59, 88, 190, 204, 227, 228, 242; hostilities 98, 195-7, 198, 208, 209; Maori Catholics 195, 196
Tawhiao, King (Potatau II) 169, 183, 184, 185, 193, 220, 223, 228-31, 232, 243, 244-5, 245-6, 290, 293-4; visits Auckland 294; visits England 299-300
Taylor, Rev. Richard 36, 41, 46, 49, 56, 111, 127, 137, 141, 310
Te Ahuahu 202
Te Anawa, Hori (chief) 220
Te Araha (chief) 229
Te Arei pa 179
Te Ariki 302
Te Aro 99, 103
Te Awaiti 62
Te Awamutu 185, 191, 294
Te Hapuku (chief) 164, 310
Te Hemara 213
Te Heu Heu 127, 163, 167
Te Kooti xix, 216, 222-6, 225-32, 303
Te Pahi (chief) 25-7
Te Pehi 55-6
Te Puni 133
Te Rangi (Hill) 197
Te Rangihaeata 55, 103, 105, 129-31
Te Rangitake, Wiremu Kingi 162, 164, 175-80, 180, 181, 193
Te Rauparaha 52-9, 103, 105-7, 108, 124, 129-31
Te Rongo/Te Ronga 106

Te Taniwha 15
Te Ua Haumene 202-5, 209, 214-15, 244, 246, 287
Te Waharoa 52
Te Waharoa, Wiremu Tamihana Tarapipipi xx, 143, 167-8, 178, 181, 185, 219, 242-4
Te Wheoro (chief) 294
Te Wherowhero (Potatau I) 58-9, 103, 108, 122, 124, 133, 167-9, 181, 229
Te Whiti O Rongomai xix, xxi, 287-93, 292-3, 297, 300, 303, 304
Terakako 88
Tere (chief) 51
Terry (Protestant) 97
Terry, Mr 139, 144
Thames 37-8, 199, 241; tribes 58, 186
Thompson, Henry 105-6, 108
Thomson, A. S. xxii, 15, 28, 36-7, 41, 45, 46, 48-9, 51, 57, 61, 62, 63, 65, 68, 76, 77, 78, 82, 89, 94, 96-7, 102, 104, 109, 111, 116, 118, 127, 131, 133, 141, 143, 144, 145, 155, 163
Tierry, Mons. viii
Titokowaru (chief) 220-2, 227, 229, 286, 287, 291
Tohu Kakahi xix, 291-2
Tory 90, 91
Totara 83
Totara pa 39
Travers, Mr 276
Treaty of Waitangi *see* Waitangi
tribal wars 38-45, 51-9, 103, 163-5
Trollope, Anthony xix, xxi
Tuapeka 172
Tucker, Miss 144
Tui (chief) 51
Tuke, Maj. 291
Tupaea, Hori 212
Tupaia 14
Turanga *see* Gisborne
Turner, Miss 89
Turton, Rev 139-40
Tuwhakaharo, Te Ua *see* Te Ua Haumene
Tuwhare (chief) 52
Twain, Mark xix, xxi

United Tribes of New Zealand 74-5, 79

Urewera 227-30, 231, 303
Uriwera *see* Urewera

Vaggioli, Dom Felice vii-xii; *History of New Zealand* xii-xiv, xv-xviii
Vancouver, Capt. 19
Viard, Mons. Philippe 142, 152, 248, 249, 252-3, 255
Victoria, Queen 230, 239, 262, 277, 299
Vogel, Julius 232-3, 260-2, 264, 269, 274, 278-9; emigration schemes 264-5; public works 262-3, 269-71, 272-3
Volkner, Carl Sylvius 210-13, 214, 215, 231, 238, 243, 244
Von Tempsky, Gustavus Ferdinand 220

Waharoa (chief) *see* Te Waharoa
Waiapu 215
Waikanae 108
Waikanai *see* Waikanae
Waikato 88, 303; tribes 58-9, 178, 179, 181-6, 230; war 98, 183-99, 208, 229, 238, 242-3
Waikato (chief) 36, 38
Waikauri 198
Waikouaiti 62
Waimate 286, 288, 290, 288, 291
Waingongoro River 286, 288
Waipa River 53, 58
Wairarapa, Lake 53
Wairau 98, 104-8, 154, 165
Wairoa (near Gisborne) 216, 226
Wairoa (near Mt Tarawera) 302
Waitangi 94-5; Treaty of 94, 98, 99, 108, 118-19, 128, 136, 175, 181, 184, 186, 189, 232, 272, 294, 299
Waitara 162, 164, 169-70, 175-80, 185, 190, 194-5, 208, 222, 286
Waitemata 88
Waitotara 208-9, 288
Waka (newspaper) 238
Wakatane *see* Whakatane
Wakefield, Capt. Arthur 103, 105-6
Wakefield, Col. William 90-2, 99, 102-3, 106, 107, 129
Wakefield, E. G. (Gibbon) 36, 42, 82, 89-92, 93, 144, 154, 155, 160
Wallis and Futuna 81

Wanganui 28, 52-3, 102, 103, 106, 107, 110, 112, 148, 214; hostilities 98, 190, 208-9, 215, 217-18, 220-2, 230; tribes 54, 55, 59, 131-3, 186-93, 300
Wangarei *see* Whangarei
Wangaroa *see* Whangaroa
Ward, Rev. 27, 77, 78, 97, 139, 143, 162, 167, 180, 194, 196, 206
Warea pa 178
Wareaitu (Martin Luther) 131
Warre, Col. H.J. 190
Weare, Col. 217
Webb, Beatrice xix, xxi
Webb, Sidney xix, xxi
Weld, Frederick 181, 206, 244
Wellington 88, 99, 102, 103, 106-7, 109, 112, 113, 129, 130, 131, 132, 135, 165, 186, 206, 207, 215, 217, 218, 288, 291, 305; Government Buildings 269-70 *see also* Catholic church: Diocese of Wellington
Wellington, Duke of 89
Wells, Mr 178
Wentworth (lawyer) 109
Wentworth, Mr 49
Weraroa pa 209
Wesleyans 42, 140, 162, 222, 235, 238
Westrup, Maj. Charles 223-4, 225
Whakatane 204, 213, 214, 227, 228, 247
whalers 23-5, 26, 27, 35, 54, 59, 60-2, 99, 115, 116
whaling 76, 77, 112
Whangarei 104
Whangaroa 26-7, 36, 42, 88, 240, 241
Whareherehere, Hemi Waikato x
Whareongaonga 223
wheat 150-1
Whitaker, Frederick 189, 206
White Cliffs fort 222
White, Mr 140
White, trader 213-14
Whiteley, John 222
Whiteley, Rev. 178
Whitmore, Col. G.S. 216, 221-2, 223-4, 226-7, 229
Wi Parana 204
Wilkes, Commodore 47, 141
William IV 65, 66, 82
Williams, Bishop William 96, 111, 138, 206, 210, 212, 215-16, 238
Williams, E. 127
Williams, Rev. Henry xix, 69-70, 94-7, 110-111, 138
Wilson, Capt. J. 225
Wisniowski, Sygurd xxii
Wohlers, Johannes xix
wool 150
Wynyard, Col. Robert Henry 159-61, 164

Yate, Rev. William 49-50, 139, 141